RELIGION AND COMMUNITY

RELIGION AND COMMUNITY

KEITH WARD

CLARENDON PRESS · OXFORD
2000

OXFORD

UNIVERSITY PRESS

Great Clarendon Street, Oxford OX2 6DP
Oxford University Press is a department of the University of Oxford.
It furthers the University's objective of excellence in research, scholarship,
and education by publishing worldwide in

Oxford New York

Athens Auckland Bangkok Bogotá Buenos Aires Calcutta
Cape Town Chennai Dar es Salaam Delhi Florence Hong Kong Istanbul
Karachi Kuala Lumpur Madrid Melbourne Mexico City Mumbai
Nairobi Paris São Paulo Singapore Taipei Tokyo Toronto Warsaw

and associated companies in Berlin Ibadan

Oxford is a registered trade mark of Oxford University Press
in the UK and in certain other countries

Published in the United States
by Oxford University Press Inc., New York

British Library Cataloguing in Publication Data

Data available

Library of Congress Cataloging in Publication Data
Ward, Keith, 1938–
Religion and community / Keith Ward.
p. cm.
Includes bibliographical references and indexes.
1. Religion and sociology.   I. Title.
BL60.W36   2000
291.1'71—dc21   99–40921

ISBN 0–19–875258–X (hardcover)
ISBN 0–19–875259–8 (pbk.)

1 3 5 7 9 10 8 6 4 2

Typeset in Plantin
by Jayvee, Trivandrum, India
Printed in Great Britain
on acid-free paper by
www.Biddles.co.uk

For Marian

CONTENTS

Introduction

Religions take shape in particular human cultures and they come to have distinctive social forms. Indeed, it is part of the belief-structure of most religions that there should be a particular society which protects and sustains their basic values and beliefs, within which one may pursue the ideal human goal, as defined within the society.

As religions become embodied in social forms of life, a number of tensions, polarities, and ambiguities arise which are important and perhaps ineliminable features of the phenomenon of religion. One polarity is the very fundamental one between the religious belief-system and the culture in which it is embodied. There are a number of possible relations between religion and culture, all of which have probably been exemplified in every fairly long-lasting religion, but each of which can be primarily associated with a specific religious tradition.[1]

(1) It is possible for a belief-system and a culture to be identified, so that an entire community will base its life and social structure around the pursuit of a religiously defined goal. In such a society, the religious leaders will also be the social leaders, and there will be no distinction between religious and secular law, or at least secular laws will have to be consistent with religious law, which the society will enforce. Some Orthodox forms of Judaism aim at such an identity,[2] and Christianity in medieval Europe, for example in the decrees of Pope Boniface VIII, sometimes made claims of this sort. This view may expand to embrace the aim that the whole world should form such a community, so that there will be a final unity of religion and human social life. Islam contains ambitions of that sort, sometimes aiming at the rule of religious law over the whole world, though there is almost always a separation between religious and secular law in Muslim countries. More often, Islam aims at a global spiritual

---

[1] Richard Niebuhr, *Christ and Culture* (New York: Harper & Row, 1951), sketches a set of relations between the Christian churches and culture. I have broadened and extended his analysis to consider other religious traditions.

[2] Rav Kook, the first Chief Rabbi of the Ashkenazi communities of Palestine, held this as an ideal, at least for the Messianic age, but it has never been achieved in practice.

community which would allow many different expressions of religious belief and social practice within its universal embrace, though all of them must be consonant with the revealed law of God. Some writers, such as T. S. Eliot, who have called for a Christian state or for a revival of Christendom, seem sympathetic to a close association between religious and secular law.

(2) At the other extreme, one could have a religious belief-system which has no interest at all in forms of general social life, which refuses political involvement and social responsibility, and regards most of the culture in which it exists as either irrelevant or positively harmful. Forms of ascetic renunciation and some forms of Theravada Buddhism seem to separate themselves off from the culture of 'the householder' in such a way. Within Christianity, there have been monastic and separatist communities, such as the Amish, which have adopted such policies.

(3) There is a range of intermediate possibilities. A belief-system may exist independently of and in critical tension with a cultural system, sometimes opposing, sometimes validating, sometimes seeking to transform and yet often resisting change. The religious community may refuse to identify itself with any particular social or cultural form, yet be committed to positive social change in many diverse contexts. Many forms of Christianity stand in such a relation to the cultures in which they exist, and perhaps this is the typical form of modern Christian relations with the states in which the churches exist. While the religion and the state remain distinct, historical circumstances may encourage a variety of relations between them. The state may tend to control the religious system, perhaps appointing religious leaders and controlling official forms of worship. This has often happened in the Orthodox Christian world, and where religions are established by law, as in England and Sweden, this has tended to happen. It is also possible for one religious institution to control a relatively autonomous state, appointing rulers, confirming morally relevant legislation, and validating major social celebrations. This is rare in the modern world, though one historical example would be the claim of the popes to appoint and control the Holy Roman Emperor, or to exert a certain moral control on state legislation. It is more usual in the modern world for a religious community to claim autonomy from the state, thereby being enabled to exist in many different states, while seeking to influence states noncoercively, by discussion and persuasion.

(4) Finally, one may have a belief-system that does not seek to embody itself in a social system at all, either a monastic or a political community, but encourages individuals to follow teachers or gods who appeal to them. Religious belief becomes more a matter of individual or family choice. Such an individualistic view is uncommon in the Christian world, though in the United States membership of various Protestant churches is often regarded as a matter of individual choice. Hinduism, with its many gods and paths of devotion, perhaps comes closest to this possibility. The Indian situation is complicated by the fact that a very strong religiously validated cultural system exists, though it is not controlled by one authoritative religious hierarchy. Perhaps no fully individualistic religion could exist, yet it is true that Indian spirituality favours individual or personally adopted approaches more than the Christian and Muslim faiths, which emphasize the necessity of community in religion.

I am by no means wishing to argue that each religious tradition does or must fall into one of these four 'ideal types'. On the contrary, I am quite clear that traditions are very complex, changing, and fluid in various ways, so that there is no one essence of each tradition that constitutes its central core. The types should be considered as importantly different logically possible forms of relationship between a religious tradition and the social forms in which it is embodied, and the relationship between those forms and the wider community within which they exist.

My aim in this volume is to consider particular examples of these various forms of the religious life, and I have usually chosen to accept the sometimes rather idealized view of them that has been presented by apologists for those forms. I have also, however, pointed to some of the ambiguities and tensions which result when such idealized forms are actually embodied in particular societies. This is necessary if one is to consider the ways in which the many religions of the world might develop in future, as their diverse views of the proper relation of religion to culture interact.

A main concern has been to investigate various religious views of the foundation and nature of ethical thinking, and the way in which they impinge on social and political life. I try to bring out the internal diversity and complexity of each tradition, while also seeking to identify the distinctive relationship between religious faith and morality which is characteristic of them, the way in which principles of human action are related to a distinctive view of a supreme spiritual reality and goal. My aim has thus not been to write an impossibly short and over-general social history of each tradition, but to focus on the ethical vision which lies at the heart of a tradition, and the ways in which it has affected, and in turn been affected by, the various social conditions in which it has existed.

I do not write from some Olympian height of detached objectivity, but from one particular perspective, a specific sort of Christian belief. From that perspective, it is part of my aim to develop a view of the Christian community, the church, which can be enriched by some of the positive insights of other traditions, and also be more aware of the negative possibilities in the church's traditional understanding of itself.

Christianity contains examples of all the various attitudes mentioned, yet the fundamental social reality which is important for Christian faith is the church, and in that respect Christianity has a distinctive form of social embodiment. It claims to be a community which mediates the power of the divine love, the Spirit, to the world. In other religious traditions a similar variety of attitudes to the religious community also exist, yet each has a distinctive normative form which gives a dominant tone to each religious community.

Judaism and Islam are both concerned with the observance of religious law, though they both embrace very different ways of interpreting such observance. Hinduism and Buddhism both give a special importance to ascetic and renunciatory practice, though they both embrace many different assessments of the reality and goodness of secular life. Christianity contains strong strains of both an obedience ethic and a renunciation ethic, and in some periods and cultures Christian faith has seemed to be almost wholly a matter of obedience to rules or an austere ascetic discipline. Yet there is little doubt that the predominant emphasis of Christianity is on a transformative community living by the power of the Spirit of Christ, which is believed to liberate both from the necessity of obedience to law and from the need to achieve merit by good works or ascetic practices.

Christianity has been beset by internal disputes and conflicts of many sorts, and its sometimes violent history has led some to reject any form of organized or institutional religion. Part of the argument of this volume is that Christian faith is essentially a communal faith, but it needs to learn from its own history and from the history of other religious traditions the sorts of limits on power and authority that are needed to counterbalance the repressive tendencies which seem inherent in all human institutions.

It is inevitable in any discussion of the church that decisions need to be taken between diverse conceptions of its structure and authority. One cannot avoid a certain degree of apologetic defence of such decisions, so that in a sense there is here an apologia for a Protestant interpretation of Christianity that is found in, but not restricted to, the Anglican Episcopal church. I hope, however, that the discussion is more eirenic than that may suggest, and that there is a broad ecumenical dimension to the analysis. I have tried to describe the varying conceptions fairly, to give some idea of their historical origins and development, and to suggest ways in which the many forms of the Christian church in the modern world might develop in unity of fellowship and understanding.

The realities of human history are more complex and ambiguous than the dogmatic formulae which sometimes seem to float in the crystalline air of the intellect, but religious life must be anchored in historical reality. It is a salutary exercise to survey the diversity and development of that reality, to realize that evil and egoism seem ineliminable from all things human, and to perceive none the less that through fragile human institutions humans have felt themselves called into a community of love, which might endure when all historical ambiguities have passed away.

In developing a view of the distinctive characteristics of the church as a teaching, charismatic, sacramental, and moral community, and in bringing out some of the major traditions of communal self-understanding which have emerged in its history, my aim has been to see how the church, as a religious form of life, claims to offer a transformative clue to the meaning of history, while never escaping the ambiguities of history. By placing this conception of a religious community within the global context of human religious life, it may be possible to discern both the distinctiveness of the Christian community, and its basis in a general human concern to establish and sustain appropriate ways of being human, and of attaining the highest human goal, in relation to one or more superior spiritual beings or states. That is perhaps the primary function of religion in the eyes of believers, and it is largely by their success in fulfilling that function that the religious communities of the world need to be assessed by their own adherents.

In a full comparative study, the adherents of many faiths would

need to co-operate in an interactive analysis of their diverse communities. In this volume, I can speak only from one historically located
viewpoint. From that viewpoint, the intention is to place the idea of
a Christian community within a wider spectrum of ideas of religious
community, and to suggest ways in which it can work with and learn
from other communities. If there is a more universal underlying
theme, it is that religions in the modern world must unreservedly
accept religious diversity, and learn positively to respect difference.
They must defend freedom of conscience and the principle of
personal consent to faith. They must endorse a real concern with
human welfare, both individually and socially. They must admit the
ambiguity of all religious institutions, as of all human institutions.
And they must seek ways in which they can be positive and creative
forces in the contemporary project of constructing a consciously
global society whose members can live in mutual understanding and
co-operative action.

PART I

RELIGIOUS COMMUNITIES
IN THE WORLD

I

Judaism and the Nation of Israel

ORTHODOXY AND ORTHOPRAXIS

In the tribal societies in which all religions arose it would be difficult to separate out a religious belief component from the social practices of the tribe. Rituals centred on annual events of hunting, planting, and major seasonal changes, and would have involved attempted communication with the spirit powers which controlled such things, and rites to ensure fertility and success in the hunt. Rites often continue after such beliefs die out: many people bring trees into their homes at Christmas and decorate them, without believing that they are dressing and feeding the tree god and invoking his power to bring Winter to an end.

Stories of the great heroes of the tribe, and of the gods who constituted the world order, can similarly lose their function of describing spirits who are to be worshipped and become simply well-loved stories about human folly and heroism. And social rules which may once have embodied the decrees of the gods become the peculiar customs of the tribe, which give them a sense of history and identity, but no longer speak the words of a god.

Judaism is a particularly interesting case of a religion that was originally tribal and continues to be valued by many Jews simply as a system of rituals, customs, and stories; whereas others—especially, though not only, the Orthodox—insist that the belief dimension, belief in the existence of a God who ordained the rites and rules and who acted salvifically and inspirationally in the history of the Jews, is central and must be retained.

The sacrificial system which defined the relation of the tribes to their God ceased with the destruction of the second Temple, but many rituals remain, most obviously the celebration of the great annual festivals, and of the weekly Sabbath. There can be no doubt that these celebrations are concerned, quite explicitly, with the worship of God and the commemoration of God's mighty acts of liberating Israel from Egypt, and leading them to the Promised

Land. Nevertheless, Jews can take quite a relaxed attitude to theoretical beliefs about what 'God' might be. There is no history of
intense theological debate about the nature of God such as is found
in Christian tradition.

It is possible to commemorate the escape from Egypt and the
period in the wilderness as momentous events in Jewish history,
without enquiring too closely into what is meant by attributing them
to God's actions. So it is often said that to be a 'religious' Jew is to
observe the rites and customs, rather than to have any specific theological beliefs. It is sometimes even claimed that 'Jewish religion is
distinct from Christianity in that it has neither a dogma nor is it
organized on ecclesiastical lines'.[1] This, however, seems to be an
exaggeration. In saying that Jewish religion has no dogma the author
wishes to draw attention to the emphasis in Jewish religious discussion on the interpretation of Torah, on practice rather than on
speculation. Nevertheless, the scriptural accounts clearly state that
there is a creator of the universe, who acted to liberate, protect, and
sometimes to judge, Israel. There are definite theological beliefs in
Judaism, and they make definite claims to truth. It must be said,
moreover, that some Jews would want the application of Halakhah to
be determined by the authority of the *Beth-din*, a court of rabbinical
sages, and applied as law in the state of Israel. This is asking for more
religious control over the life of a sovereign state than Christian
churches now usually claim, so it is not quite fair to suggest that in
matters of dogma or of religious authority there is a crucial difference between Jewish and Christian religion. There are differences,
but they lie mainly in the fact that Jewish religion is more overtly concerned with a divinely revealed law for one particular nation than is
Christianity.

It is probably true, however, that as long as the law is maintained,
there is not a great concern to ensure that Jews have 'correct' theoretical beliefs about the nature of God. Few heresies have been formally identified in Judaism (though Spinoza apparently managed to
hold one of them, and the belief that Jesus is Messiah may well be
another). If not publicly flaunted, diverse speculative beliefs may
flourish alongside the practice of Torah. And the keeping of Torah
need not even be associated with any theoretical beliefs. What

---

[1] Eliezer Schweid, *Democracy and Halakhah* (New York: University Press of
America, 1994), 7.

happens in practice is typical of most religions. A large number of people keep the festivals without probing their theological basis, largely as expressions of identification with a particular social history. More than that, they often prefer the traditions to be upheld by the Orthodox, who can be trusted to conserve the more strict and ancient forms, even though they themselves could not share the beliefs of the Orthodox. There is often even some pressure not to indulge in theological speculation, or attempt to revise archaic practices, as that would only upset the social cohesion which conformity to established tradition is thought to maintain.

This should not be seen as mere hypocrisy, since what is happening is that the rites are treated as regulative rather than constitutive. For instance, the Passover meal is an occasion when the value of family life is affirmed, when one thinks of the conditions of slavery and oppression under which many people live, and when one undertakes to help to liberate all the oppressed. One also celebrates one's membership of the Jewish people, and recalls its attempts to establish a society of justice, mercy, and peace in an often hostile world.

Nor need this be a purely humanistic occasion, as though one is simply recalling some of one's past history and making certain moral commitments. That history and those commitments are placed in the wider context of a cosmic and morally demanding reality, so that human life is related to some supra-human dimension of existence, which somehow validates one's striving for meaning and motivates one's moral aspirations. Whatever is said about that reality should be said in hieratic and symbolic language, always preserving a sense of mystery and reticence, but striving to see life *sub specie aeteritatis*.

In this way, any attempt to enforce Orthodox theological beliefs as opposed to practices may be seen as an often over-rationalizing or 'scholastic' response to the basic attitudes and reactions which religious ritual expresses in its own distinctive way. But the rationalizing can be ignored, or left to the experts, so that it is not really for most people a serious matter for discussion. This attitude is helped by the fact that most expert disputation in Judaism is about the interpretation of Torah, not about whether God exists or how God acts. There are theological beliefs in Judaism, but there is not much stress on—even a certain antipathy to—theological discussion. Such beliefs are apt to be taken for granted, or left without a detailed interpretation.

THE COVENANT PEOPLE

The rites and customs of Judaism define a certain community and separate it off from the rest of the world. When Jews see themselves as a 'holy people', they are emphasizing precisely the fact that they are 'set apart'. Marriage with non-Jews is frowned upon or forbidden. One may eat with others only under the restriction of the kosher food laws. Sometimes, all unnecessary social relations with non-Jews are discouraged. Separatism is central to Jewish tradition, the preservation of a distinctive culture and society from which, at least in its fullness, others are excluded.

Moreover, this separatism is largely defined in hereditary terms. A Jew is anyone born of a Jewish mother. There can be converts to Judaism, though conversion has not usually been encouraged, except in cases of marriage with Jews. And after such conversion, all children of a Jewish mother will automatically be Jews. In this sense, Judaism is not a faith that is chosen. One is a Jew by birth, whether one likes it or not. If one becomes a Jew, one enters a distinctive community and culture—it is not just a matter of meeting together from time to time with like-minded people. In either case, it is hardly a matter of deciding to adopt a set of religious beliefs, which may leave most of your social life unchanged.

Of course, it is by no means the case that all Jews today form a distinct ethnic or genetic group, descended from some common ancestor, whether Israel or anyone else. Many groups have attached themselves to Judaism for many diverse reasons. Elazar and Cohen have suggested the Hebrew word *'edah* as a term which suggests a social community based on consent.[2] The notion of 'consent' being used here is, however, rather idiosyncratic. How one becomes a Jew is a matter of dispute. Some groups claim that one must be received into the community by Orthodox rabbis (this is necessary for citizenship of Israel, but it clearly requires much more of converts than is required of ethnic Jews), whereas others find this too restrictive. In any case, males would need to accept circumcision and undertake some religious obligations, so that it would not be a purely social matter. Yet that step having being taken, the children of a Jewish mother would automatically be fully Jewish, whatever they believed.

---

[2] Daniel J. Elazar and Stuart A. Cohen, *The Jewish Polity* (Bloomington, Ind.: Indiana University Press, 1985), 11.

Perhaps one can only say that Judaism is a particular social community, membership of which is normally hereditary, with an underlying religious dimension which has to be formally accepted by non-Jews who wish to join the community.

With the idea of such a distinctive culture there naturally arises the idea of a territory within which it can be sustained. The Hebrew Bible makes it unmistakably clear that God promised to the Jewish people a homeland, in which they were to worship God according to Torah, and live by the laws of justice and social life laid down therein. In that land, the children of Abraham, Isaac, and Jacob, together with those who had freely joined them, were to live under the laws of God revealed to Moses.[3]

The idea of a piece of territory possessed by divine right is politically explosive. The ancient Israelites, on the biblical account, escaped from an oppressed existence in Egypt, and after many years of nomadic existence, took the land of Canaan by military conquest. Indeed, God told them to wipe out all inhabitants who opposed them, and to subjugate the rest pretty thoroughly. Each of the twelve tribes was given a specific territory, to possess for all time. In partial justification, it is said that the inhabitants to be displaced were an evil lot, and had been warned many times in vain, so that they deserved what was coming to them. It is hard to see, however, how children and non-combatants could be justifiably regarded as victims of wholesale slaughter—even if such 'justifications' were given long after the event, and grossly inflated the military success of the Israelites.

One can hardly refrain from asking whether God really commanded the conquest of Canaan, and the wholesale slaughter of many of its inhabitants. It may well be said that the Israelites were only doing what most nations were doing at that time in world history. In a world of constantly moving populations, one had to fight to survive, and perhaps the alternative to the conquest of Canaan was death in the desert. So one might plausibly argue that the conquest was a necessity of survival.

Furthermore, it is not uncommon for tribal war-gods to enjoin the slaughter or enslavement of hostile native populations. The biblical record gives a fair picture of the social and religious beliefs of many peoples at that time. But can it be seen as a higher moral view than

[3] Cf. Numbers 34.

that of the Canaanites, who were probably sceptical about God's wish for their extermination? My own view is that, in a harshly competitive environment in which there was a constant clash of peoples and empires, the Israelites were quite justified in establishing a homeland by military action, where the laws of God could be followed. But the laws of God are laws of justice and mercy, and therefore any conquest would have to cause minimum harm, and would have to consider the welfare of the residents of the conquered territories.

By this standard, fully exemplified in the teachings of the major prophets, some of the early teachings (e.g. of *herem*, or the total destruction of the conquered[4]) must be seen as morally superseded. Most Jews would accept that there are morally primitive elements in Scripture, which later prophetic teachings and rabbinic interpretation have wholly superseded. The Orthodox seem committed to the view that these really were divine commands. But the sort of Orthodox interpretation which insists that God did command such things usually stresses that the destroyed people were consciously opposed to the divine will, and thus deserved destruction. Furthermore, there is no precedent in such ancient and particular divine commands for the present destruction of populations. Such divine commands are inappropriate in the modern world, even if circumstances made them appropriate in the ancient Near East.

The Israelites believed that God wished them to have a homeland, and that armed opposition was obstruction of the divine will. The harsher passages concerning these events must be balanced by the many more positive statements about the fair treatment of 'resident aliens' in Torah.[5] Whereas the Canaanites of that time were seen as corrupt and sinful, it is obvious that present-day Palestinians are not, as such, more corrupt than other people. Nor is it clear that what was apparently the divine will to expel the Israelites from the Holy Land has yet been wholly changed. When the Jews were expelled from the Holy Land, the conditions within which the divine covenant operated were changed, and it is not at all clear in what sense God's promise to the children of Abraham is to be fulfilled in the world. The present situation is quite different from that of early biblical times, and the ancient biblical commands to occupy a particular geographical area cannot be carried over into the modern world, as though the Diaspora had never happened.

---

[4] Deuteronomy 20: 16–17.   [5] Leviticus 19: 34.

The danger, none the less, is obvious, that one may without too much strain maintain that warfare and conquest is sometimes enjoined by God, that *eretz Israel*, the land 'from Dan to Beer-Sheba', is rightfully and by divine decree part of the state of Israel, and thus that Palestinians must be ejected from their homes by force. The medieval Jewish thinker Nahmanides maintained that it was a religious duty to wage war to conquer the biblical land of Israel, though he would have considered such a war unjust if it had little chance of lasting success, or involved innocent or disproportionate suffering.

The world is very different now than it was two to three thousand years ago. Then the colonization of Canaan would have been an unremarkable local conflict, of little interest to the major world empires. Now the global interests of the Arab world and their allies, and of the United States and its allies, are all closely bound up with what happens in Israel and the adjacent Arabic countries. Instability in this geographical area could threaten the existence of world peace, and poses very different political issues. For that reason alone, the extreme belief that *eretz Israel* must be taken or settled by force is, to say the least, not very clearly willed by God.

In this connection, a published statement in 1980 by Shilo Refael, a judge of the Jerusalem rabbinical court, and Ovadiah Yosef, the Sefardic Chief Rabbi of Israel, states that 'it is permitted to return territories of [biblical] Israel in order to remove the possibility of war, for nothing stands in the way of *piquach nefesh* (the saving of life)'.[6] There is a strong element of realism in this statement, but its theological point is that Israel has no divine right to take land by force when it is stupid and perhaps futile to try to do so. God may work miracles, the statement goes on to say, 'in a generation where all are righteous', but one cannot count on it in the present world situation. In fact, one might well hold that the possession of the whole Promised Land may only be consummated with the coming of the Messiah, and to try to accomplish it prematurely by force may actually be in conflict with the will of God. Certainly, Orthodox groups such as the Hasidim of Sotmar hold such a view.

More deeply, one must ask what God's purpose is in making a covenant with the children of Israel. A minimalist view would be that

---

[6] Quoted in Norman Solomon, *Judaism and World Religion* (London: Macmillan, 1991), 125.

this people is to worship God in a divinely appointed way, and create a nation-state in which justice and mercy shall flourish. Other nations can go their own way, and Jews would be happy to co-exist, without attempting to expand or proselytize in any way. On this view, there is no reason for a covenant with Israel, except that God chooses them to be related to the divine in a particular way. God may choose to be related to other nations in other ways. Genuine religious pluralism, on a global scale (other people can believe what they like), coexists with absolute exclusivism at the national level (this nation must live according to Torah).

As has been pointed out, however, even this view is committed to the belief that there is a creator God, who has revealed a purpose for Israel, and who has acted providentially in history to establish Israel as a nation. Presumably, therefore, whatever other religions or nations there are ought to believe that much, simply because it is true. While early Scriptures might suggest that each nation has its own god, the later prophets are clear that there is only one God, the God of Israel. This God would presumably not act quite differently in regard to other nations, and it would be odd to think that God had a purpose for Israel, but not for any other creatures at all, or that God did not act providentially in general human history. So even minimalists usually hold that Gentiles are bound by the Noachide covenant,[7] which enjoins at least some form of monotheistic worship and moral conduct.

A maximalist view of the role of Israel in world history is that God elects this people to be the priests and spiritual and moral teachers of the human race. When Israel attains its true destiny, all the nations of the world will come to worship at the Temple in Jerusalem, and the Torah, at least in its universal aspects, will be the model for codes of law and justice throughout the world. The strongest maximal view is that the whole world will ultimately be converted to Judaism, and keep Torah. But the more usual view is that Israel will always remain a separate nation, bound to God by special laws, and having a particular covenant with God. But its role in world history is to proclaim the true worship of God to all nations, and teach the ways of justice and truth. Haim Hirschensohn holds that 'the Jewish religion is entirely national', but it has a global dimension. 'Jewish national identity calls for filling the world with a love of humanity

---

[7] Genesis 9: 1–17.

that is as the love of God.'[8] On this view, Israel is a missionary nation. It does not try to turn all people into Jews, but it does try to teach them the fear and love of God, and obedience to laws of justice and mercy. That is its true calling and vocation.

An intermediate view would be that Israel has its own distinctive contribution to make to the world's understanding of the nature and will of God. It has its own covenant-tradition, to which it must remain loyal. Other peoples and groups may have their own contributions to make to a global religious view. They, too, will remain distinct in their particular relationship to God, but they may contribute something to Jewish understanding, just as Jews contribute to theirs. Thus the world will contain many different traditions of faith, forming distinct communities, but each will have its understanding of human life enlarged by what it learns from many others.[9]

None of these views of the calling of Israel is compatible with expropriating all Arabs from *eretz Israel* by force, since that would hardly be a beacon of justice and peace in the modern world. Ezekiel 47: 22 provides explicit directions for the treatment of non-Jews in a Jewish state: 'The aliens who reside among you . . . shall be to you as native-born sons of Israel; with you they shall be allotted an inheritance among the tribes of Israel. In whatever tribe the alien resides, there you shall assign him his inheritance, says the Lord God.' That is sufficient to rule out expropriation. Jews may have political control over Israel, but they do not have the right to exclude or mistreat non-Jews.

Israel is called to set the standard of universal justice, to exercise mercy and to 'seek peace and ensue it'.[10] Whatever God is thought to have said to Joshua, through the later prophets God taught that the foreigner is to be treated with justice, and that retribution is to be visited only on those responsible for grievous sin. So what God enjoins today for Israel is not to be read from the early pages of the Hebrew Bible. Indeed, the Talmud continues the tradition of legal interpretation, seeking to apply Torah in new circumstances, which allows great flexibility in interpreting the laws concerning the land of Israel, and their application to contemporary situations.

---

[8] Eliezer Schweid, *Democracy and Halakhah*, 14.
[9] This is basically the view taken by Rabbi Dan Cohn-Sherbok, in *Judaism and Other Faiths* (London: Macmillan, 1994), esp. ch. 9.
[10] 1 Peter 3: 11.

The whole situation is complicated enormously by the facts of the Diaspora, the *shoah*,[11] and the founding of the secular state of Israel in the modern world. While the land of Israel was given to the descendants of Israel 'for ever', the people were taken into exile by the Babylonians, and the state finally dismembered under the Romans. The usual Jewish explanation for these catastrophic events is that the failure to observe Torah had led to a divine judgement on Israel. For almost two thousand years the Jews lived as a people without a country. When Israel came to be re-established, it was on very different terms from the first conquest of the land, and it would be wholly anachronistic to see it as a second conquest with a similar divine mandate.

Jewish attitudes to the refounding of the state of Israel vary enormously. Hermann Cohen regarded Zionism as a return to a primitive nationalistic form of Judaism, which should be superseded by a purely universalistic prophetic religion.[12] Leo Pinsker, while looking for a Jewish homeland, was opposed to any idea of restoring the ancient boundaries of Israel, which he took to have been destroyed for ever. It was Theodore Herzl, one of the great founders of Zionism, who promoted the idea of a settlement in sparsely populated Palestine, insisting on full co-operation with the non-Jewish elements of the population who were already there.

In the event, the Balfour declaration set up Israel as a secular state. For some Orthodox Jews, this secularity is sufficient to dissociate the country entirely from any idea of the fulfilment of God's ancient promises. But others, such as Emil Fackenheim, saw the establishment of the state of Israel as the enactment of what he called the '614th. commandment', the command that those who perished in the *shoah* should never be forgotten, and that the people of Israel must always survive, as a symbol of the triumph of human hope in the most extreme adversity.[13]

Some would go much further than this, and see the state of Israel as a reinstatement of God's ancient promise to Abraham, or at least as the beginning of it. Rav Kook, the first Chief Rabbi of the Ashkenazi communities of Palestine, saw the establishment of Israel as the 'commencement of redemption', a foreshadowing of the Messianic

---

[11] Hebr. for 'destruction', i.e. the Holocaust.

[12] Hermann Cohen, 'Religion und Zionismus' (1916), in F. Rosenzwerg (ed.), *Jüdische Schriften* (Berlin: C. A. Schwetschke, 1924), ii. 319.

[13] Emil Fackenheim, *To Mend the World* (New York: Schocken Books, 1982).

kingdom that is yet to come in its fullness. Jews, he thought could live in a secular state and wait for God to effect its final transformation, when the sacrifices and the monarchy would both be restored.[14] Rav Kook stressed the importance of holiness and of working for peace in bringing in the final consummation. Some who claim to be his followers, however, are among those who now seek the settlement of the whole land by force if necessary.

INTERPRETATIONS OF TORAH

It is clear that Israel is a secular state, not strictly speaking a theocratic one. Even in ancient Israel the monarchy was distinct from the priesthood, and a religious Jewish state would not be ruled by priests or rabbis. It would, however, exist in conformity to the dictates of the Halakhah, as interpreted by the *Beth-din*, a supreme religious court. Possibly, in its fullness, the monarchy would be reinstituted, the Temple would be rebuilt, and the sacrifices restored—though, again, many rabbis, such as Haim Hirschensohn, look for an undefined 'spiritual' form of sacrifice, and do not expect a literal monarchy.

There is room for a wide range of viewpoints on such matters in Israel. There are those who wish to keep Halakah in its full traditional form, with no concessions made to secular values. This will involve traditional forms of religiously based education, separate treatment of men and women, strict observance of food rules and of *shabbat*, and adherence to traditional rules of marriage, divorce, and inheritance. There seems little possibility that these groups will achieve a majority in Israel, and so they seem destined to be permanent minorities, even in a Jewish homeland. They sometimes find it hard to refrain from attempting to convert the whole Jewish culture to their point of view as the 'truly Jewish' one. But unless their view is somehow imposed by force, it is highly unlikely that they will become the only form of Judaism. There will always be small groups which regard themselves as the only righteous remnant in Israel. But most of the Orthodox will accept plurality of views in practice, allowing perhaps that God wants there to be revisers of tradition as well as those who remain true to the ancient laws.

Many groups, however, seek to retain a respect for the traditions

---

[14] See Ben Zion Bokser, *Abraham Isaac Kook* (New York: Paulist Press, 1978).

of Halakic teaching, but look for underlying principles which may be applied in new situations. They do not insist on the retention of customs which may have developed in very different circumstances, but look for new ways of showing obedience to God's laws in a new world. They may retain a great respect for traditional interpretations, and seek to embody the principles of the Talmud in fairly specific, though revised, ways. Or they may sit much more loosely to past history, and simply try to embody the main religious and moral principles of Judaism in new forms of worship and social activity. The problem for these (Conservative, Liberal, and Reform) groups is that of agreeing on what the underlying principles are, and what the limits of permissible change are. Interestingly, they are not very strong in Israel, and flourish mostly in the Diaspora, where they attempt to maintain a form of Judaism which is open and responsive to new influences. At one time it seemed as though Jews might become totally assimilated to the European culture of *Haskalah*, the Enlightenment, at least in so far as that movement was still allied with a general ethical monotheism. But as the Enlightenment became more fully secular, the distinctive religious roots of Judaism reasserted themselves.

There are, nevertheless, avowedly secular groups in Israel which seek to implement a secular democracy in which individual liberty and freedom of thought have full sway, in which women will participate fully in political life, religious practice will be an option, and no appeal will be made to religious authority in political life. Their main problem is in deciding what constitutes Jewishness, if it is not adherence to a religious tradition, and how, if at all, it is to be distinguished from nationalism.

It is in Israel that the extremes of ultra-orthodoxy and secularism meet, leading to a battle between varied forms of allegedly 'true Judaism' and the secular democratic nation-state. Conflict seems to be inescapable, even (or, one might say, especially) when one seeks to define correct beliefs or practices as precisely as possible. Every attempted definition arouses opposition, so that even the most scrupulously Orthodox divide into diverse groups which scarcely communicate with one another. Internal diversity is an inescapable feature of religious practice.

What unites the most diverse groups within Judaism is first, an acceptance of largely hereditary membership of a specific social community, and secondly, an acceptance that this community originated because of belief in a divine vocation: 'You are a people holy to the Lord your God; the Lord your God has chosen you to be a people for his own possession, out of all the peoples that are on the face of the earth.'[15] Through exile, occupation, diaspora, and attempted genocide, the Jews have continued to exist as a distinct people, and the inner and undisputed core of that continuance is the belief, even if it is not actually held by all, that they are bound to God in a unique way. The sign of that bond is the living out of the Torah, the teaching of God, so that their whole social life expresses obedient worship of God and the pursuit of the justice and mercy which God requires.

It might be said that the idea of vocation or calling is the central idea of Judaism which holds it together. This people are set apart for divine service: 'You shall be to me a kingdom of priests and a holy nation.'[16] Priests are those who sacrifice on behalf of the people, who offer praise and thanksgiving to God, and who mediate forgiveness and reconciliation to the world. If this is Israel's vocation, it exists not so much for the sake of Israel, as for the sake of the world within which Israel is to play its special role. Israel exists for the sake of the nations, that they might find their relation to God through this people, in whom praise is to be perfected and through whom reconciliation is to be mediated.

This may lead to major modification of the traditionally non-missionary understanding of their faith which many Jews have had. Indeed, Michael Goldberg has written that the mission of Jews is to expand throughout the world, successively including all others within the community, until the whole world comes under the rule of Torah. So, he says, 'The Jewish people is indispensable to the redemption of the world.'[17] It is through them that the world's redemption will come.

The trouble is that priests also tend to be patriarchal, authoritarian, status-conscious, censorious, and reactionary. They easily become censors of public morals, opposed to all change and insisting on the strict observance of rules, with little regard to the welfare of individuals. It is no accident that these are precisely the criticisms of Orthodox Judaism which are made by the liberal-minded.

---

[15] Deuteronomy 7: 16.   [16] Exodus 19: 6.
[17] Michael Goldberg, *Why Should Jews Survive?* (Oxford: Oxford University Press, 1995), 168.

The reason why priests become like that is easy to discern. They believe that they are the guardians of the revealed law of God. That law permits no change; all who oppose it are opponents of God. Such opponents readily become demonized as rejecters of God, to be opposed and perhaps suppressed. The priests themselves, however, are deserving of the utmost respect, since they stand as the guardians of God's rule, the very mouthpiece of the divine oracles. They will humbly accept tribute and salutation, since it is really God, they will say, who is thereby being honoured. There are, of course, no priests in Judaism. But there is a danger that if the whole people is regarded as a priesthood, they may come to exhibit these negative religious characteristics.

One can see these dangers even in Michael Goldberg's moving book, *Why Should Jews Survive?* Rabbi Goldberg's case is that Jews should survive mainly because 'God's lot in the world is inextricably bound up with Israel's.'[18] Only if the Jews survive as a people devoted to living out the *mitzvot* will God 'keep his reputation intact'. They must survive as a witness to God. Such witnessing has a global meaning: Israel 'is to serve the Lord by enabling others to serve him also'.[19] 'By performing the *mitzvot*, God's commandments, Israel makes manifest God's holy character to the world.'[20] In particular, Jews are commanded to refrain from oppressing strangers, and to establish a rule of strict justice if they are to have God's favour.[21]

This sounds highly appealing. But there are darker possibilities present in the account. First, inevitable conflict is built into any view which insists on keeping to a traditional law-code in a changing world. Rabbi Goldberg is in favour of counting women in the *minyan*, the congregation of ten needed for public worship. But he admits, 'I know of no synagogue where the inclusion of women in the *minyan* has been accomplished without causing considerable pain and anger.'[22] There is a saying that where there are two Jews, there are three views. Changing views of the status of women, and that of animals, will lead to conflicts about the interpretation of the *mitzvot* which may well be bitter and divisive (can women be rabbis? Should the sacrifices be restored, or the rules of ritual animal-killing adapted?). Torah does not in practice unite more than a small minority of Jews. It rather divides them into more or less hostile

18 Michael Goldberg, 69.   19 Ibid. 15.   20 Ibid. 95.
21 Jeremiah 7: 3–7.   22 Ibid. 115 n. 13.

factions, often quarrelling over things which seem wholly unimportant to the rest of the world. Because the whole Torah is given by
God, even the most minute details take on a cosmic significance. So
families can be divided over matters which would be of no intrinsic
importance if God was not believed to have ordained them.

One cannot deny the presence of such factors in Judaism, but conflict is inevitable if there are to be any advances in human understanding. The rabbinic tradition is much more tolerant of conflict
and argument than many Christian traditions are, and debate over
Talmudic texts is deeply enshrined in Jewish education.

Second, the possibility of intolerance is never far away. Goldberg
refers to a view he attributes to Maimonides, that 'the Noachide
commandments are the minimal requirements needed for a non-Jew
to be treated as a *ger-toshav*, i.e. as a resident alien whose presence is
to be tolerated by the larger, normative culture'.[23] Jews have, of
course, got used to being minorities, so they have rarely had the
chance to work out what is implied in 'tolerating' resident aliens. But
it might well imply exclusion from political power, or limitation of
access to the best educational or economic opportunities. Jewish
and non-Jewish slaves were given different treatment in Torah, and
while Jewish judges could not be bribed, non-Jewish judges could be
bribed with impunity. In a Jewish state, would non-Jews (say, Arabs
and Muslims) be given equal freedom of activity and expression?

The aim of Judaism—God's own aim—is, according to Michael
Goldberg, 'non-Jews universally coming to accept the whole of
Torah as binding on them'.[24] Of course, what one has in mind is the
free acceptance of Torah by individuals, but there is an almost universal tendency for dominant religions to impose their laws on others
for their own good. God says 'I will bless those who bless you and
curse him who curses you.'[25] How easy it is to see the rejection of
God's law as a curse. And how easy it is to see God's curse as requiring punitive action, once one has the power. Of course it is ironic to
accuse Judaism of intolerance, when Jews have been persecuted
throughout history by others. There may seem little danger of Jews
becoming aggressive expansionists, at least beyond the boundaries of
eretz Israel. But it would be naïve to overlook the potential for aggression in the biblical tradition. At the same time, there is no doubt at all
that peace, *shalom*, is an absolutely basic goal of Jewish life, and peace

[23] Ibid. 119.   [24] Idem.   [25] Genesis 12: 3.

cannot ultimately flourish without justice between peoples. When a distinction is made between a truly evil, egoistic, or malicious rejection of divine law, and a conscientious dispute about what God's law is, one will be able to define the bounds of toleration more precisely.

More realistic is the possibility of intolerance within the state of Israel. Rabbi Goldberg writes that 'any Jewish state that fails to recognize the central role of the covenant for its politics is illegitimate as a Jewish state'.[26] Israel must be ruled by Torah, and 'the politics of a Jewish state ultimately must be the politics of God'.[27] Whereas a secular Jew will think that laws must be hammered out by human discussion and compromise, the religious Jew may regard his view as God's view, and thus as immune from compromise, and not subject to democratic vote. When God enters politics, everything becomes more intractable, and the emotional weight becomes immensely magnified. It is essential to democracy to accept defeat after a fair vote. The guardians of God's law are unlikely to do so.

Individual choice may also be restricted, as rejection of social custom may be equated with rejection of God and of the whole society. There is, it seems, an inevitable conflict with liberal democracy built into observant Judaism, and in a Jewish state in which the religious are in a minority, this is a recipe for permanent social unrest and for a degree of personal unhappiness produced by intractable situations within the main area of such conflicts: family, marriage, and inheritance law.

Again, however, it is possible to distinguish between one's own interpretation of God's law and that law itself. The Jewish view is that Torah will only be properly understood when the Messiah comes, so it is impossible, theologically, for anyone to equate his understanding of Torah with that of God. The antidotes to the dangers of repressive priestcraft are a lively sense of the diverse and changing interpretations of law which prevents one from seeing it as wholly changeless and perfectly understood, a keen sense of human inadequacy in understanding the ways of God, and an acceptance that God has many ways of dealing with creatures, which prevents one from regarding all others simply as infidels. It has to be said that Jewish rabbinic tradition possesses all these antidotes in good measure. It is important, then, to try to ensure that they are clearly understood and duly emphasized.

---

[26] Goldberg, *Why Should Jews Survive?*, 142.   [27] Ibid. 148.

Nevertheless, there is a conflict between liberal democracy and the ideal of a theocratic state, except under two conditions. One is that everyone freely consents to a theocratic state, while always retaining the possibility of rejecting it. That outcome is unlikely in the extreme. The other is that communities of strict observance can be permitted, and even encouraged, within a wider community living under more flexible laws. The first possibility will probably be realized only in the Messianic age. The second can be accepted by Orthodox and liberal alike, precisely because the Messiah has not yet come, so the Orthodox cannot equate their rule with the rule of God, and the liberals can value the Orthodox as the guardians of tradition, whose role under the providence of God is not yet clear. Both Orthodox and liberals can see that religion is inseparable from conflict and repression (the Orthodox see that, at least, in the case of Christianity!). It is not hard to see why people oppose it. Religion is often harmful, and both Orthodox and liberals have an interest in seeing that there are mechanisms in place to lessen or counteract that harm. The drive for power in religion, as elsewhere in human life, will lead to attempts to negate such mechanisms. It is in the interests of faith itself to strengthen them.

It has to be recognized that there are genuine conflicts of value here, within Judaism as much as without it. The beginning of wisdom in religion is to recognize that such conflicts are inevitable, in a world of rapid social change and cultural interaction. Whatever the values of Orthodoxy, the fact is that the strictly observant are usually going to be a minority even within the faith, and a much smaller minority within the Jewish people worldwide. It is not a matter of the vast majority of good men enforcing obedience on a minority of weak-minded or weak-willed apostates. Those who disagree are as intelligent, morally committed, and spiritually sincere as the Orthodox. One needs to establish that, as a matter of fact, there are value-disputes among people of knowledge and goodwill. Therefore conflict is inevitable, and it is not always between the pious on one side and the self-willed on the other.

LIVING WITH PLURALITY

For a religious person, to *accept* disagreement is to see it as within the providence of God. The difficulty for the religious is to see how this can be so, if one thinks that one's own beliefs are God-given and

God-validated. Jews, however, have no problem with the idea that God does not reveal the divine will to all people in the same way. Nor do they have any difficulty with the belief that God wills different things at different times—the destruction of the monarchy and the Temple clearly entail that God's commands to the people of Israel are not changeless. God apparently wills both change and difference—'Diversity is obviously the plan and goal of Providence.'[28] Why this should be so is not always clear. But it is a natural supposition that different cultures may be able to see God in different ways, and that these ways may complement each other in a generally beneficial manner. If that is so, one may, while remaining true to one's own tradition, move beyond tolerance to a positive respect for those aspects of the beliefs of others which might complement one's own. Of course, one will not know what those are until one has a fairly good understanding of others. So there is a positive requirement to seek understanding of the religious traditions of others.

There are clearly limits to the existence of such positive respect. One cannot respect a view that is based on self-interest, cynicism, or hatred. One cannot respect a view that causes what seems to be a grievous harm. The first requirement is a requirement of character, that the adherent must be sincere and disinterested, not hypocritical or culpably ignorant. Culpable ignorance shows itself in the misdescription of the views of others, when adequate knowledge is readily available. Hatred shows itself in the use of highly emotive terminology, or in the tendency to make others sound contemptible or ludicrous. Hypocrisy shows itself in making professions of compassion and peace, whilst one ignores the poor and stirs up conflict. It shows itself more subtly in the failure to apply to others the same principles one applies to oneself, thereby making a special exception in one's own case, but not allowing such a move to others.

The second requirement naturally depends upon what one takes to be harm. It is fairly clear, however, that the deprivation of life, food, or home, and the avoidable causing of pain, injury, and poverty are harms. Disputed cases are such things as the exclusion of women from certain roles and the killing of animals in a ritual way, since not all would agree that they are cases of harming. Similarly, it is not clear whether the acceptance of homosexual relations harms

---

[28] Moses Mendelssohn, *Judaism and Other Writings* (New York: Cambridge University Press, 1969), 105.

family life, or whether their prohibition harms individual liberty. There are many border-line or disputed cases. Some people believe that even genocide, which clearly causes harm, is justified if it leads to establishing a certain sort of society. Ancient Hebrews thought it about the Canaanites, and Nazis thought it about modern Jews. Even then, however, the Canaanites and Jews, respectively, had to be seen as positively corrupting influences before genocide could be recommended.

The *shoah* was not initiated because of any religious revelation or doctrine, and this fact should raise a sceptical doubt about whether it is belief in divine commands which is responsible for great human evils. It rather seems that it is hatred of 'aliens' as such which is endemic to human nature. Yet religions are not good at reducing such hatred, and often contain elements which are useful in increasing hatred (e.g. my belief that your group might corrupt the superior values of my group).

Despite this fact, religions are concerned with human good; Torah is given 'for your good',[29] and God protects and liberates Israel, and wills it's ultimate welfare. But religions can be slow to see that God's concern extends to all humans, male and female, Jewish and Gentile, and beyond that to all living creatures and to all creation. They can be very slow indeed in seeing what such universal divine concern implies. Judaism, with its doctrine of a special covenant with Israel, defined in laws belonging to a patriarchal and militaristic social era, is certainly prone to such myopia. It may seem better if these views would wither away. The phenomenon of Jewish atheism is at any rate easy to understand. And that suggests one reason for diversity in religion, even within the Jewish faith and people—without diversity, traditions will never develop to encompass new forms of understanding and recognize the restrictiveness of comfortably accepted practices. Perhaps God wills Jewish secularism as a reminder of the radical deficiencies of Jewish religious observance.

The picture of Judaism as a monolithic and repressive system is a caricature, since an infinite capacity for self-criticism is one of the most apparent features of Jewish religious life. There is a law, but there is no central agreed authority for implementing it. Instead, there is a set of shifting authorities, interacting in various ways, none

---

[29] Deuteronomy 10: 13.

of them wholly definitive of Judaism. Conflict is not, after all, wholly negative. It provides the necessary constraint on autocracy. Conflict and disunity may be good if they prevent ossification into one repressive authoritarian structure, and as long as they do not degenerate into hatred and violence.

No system is absolutely immune from the destructive effects of human hatred and greed, but the Prophetic writings unequivocally condemn injustice and oppression, and enjoin benevolence and mercy. There will always be disagreement between those who want to defend traditional marriage, education, and economic customs and those who want greater freedom of individual choice and equal opportunity. A liberal society is one which allows both groups to co-exist, as long as they do not try to eliminate each other. What is disallowed is the attempt by one group to compel others to conform to its own values. Consent becomes a key value in membership of a social order. Neither Orthodox nor liberals should compel even their own children to conform to their own values, once they have reached maturity.

There is no way of getting all believers to agree to tolerate and respect one another, and religion will always be used to repress alternative views and to declare them degenerate. Religion will, however, always also contain strands which call for liberty of conscience, toleration of human diversity, and respect for the conscientious beliefs and practices of others. These strands are strong in forms of Judaism that call for a personal commitment to relationship with God, accept that different cultures will have different ways of relating to God, and stress individual responsibility and the diversity of human interpretations of Torah.

It seems clear that religion is not in itself ennobling of human character. It deepens and intensifies the motivations and feelings humans have, both for good and ill. It is itself part of the struggle for human goodness in face of human egoism, and in its structures the battle for good and evil is played out, often in peculiarly intense forms. The establishment of religion cannot give any guarantee that cynicism, corruption, and manipulation will not triumph over honesty, sensitivity, and compassion. Religion does not provide a haven of peace and light in a world of darkness. It shares in the moral ambiguity of the world at large.

Nevertheless, the *ideal* of total devotion to truth, reverence for all creation and its Creator, justice and mercy, is a light to humanity.

The Hebrew Bible never gives the impression that Jews are morally better than anyone else. The history of ancient Israel is largely a story of faithless priests, false prophets, and failed kings. What is important is the Torah that is held in trust until the Messiah comes and makes its true interpretation plain, its full observance possible. The community preserves the ideal, and the hope for its future fulfilment. But, though it is bound in unbreakable covenant with God, it is largely a broken, divided, and penitent people.

Thus the religious idea of the state of Israel can motivate Jews to hate, banish, and destroy the Arab population of Palestine, or it can motivate Jews to nourish the land and include all its people, of whatever faith or race, within its benevolent justice. The religious idea of a vocation to be a 'holy people' can motivate Jews to cut off relations with Gentiles and live in cultural isolation, or it can motivate them to seek to be channels of reconciliation and fulfilment for all the peoples of the earth. The religious idea of a revealed law for society can motivate Jews to compel everyone to conform to an inflexible set of repressive regulations, or it can motivate them to seek for fuller expressions of justice and mercy in society.

It would no doubt be nice if only the good attributes of religion could be preserved, but that would be to ask that human nature itself be changed. That will happen when the Messiah comes. In the meantime, what Judaism represents, religiously, are the values of community, of loyalty to a distinctive disclosure of the divine, and of universal hope for a just society. This leads to both negative and positive consequences. But one may certainly hope for the flourishing of a secular Jewish state, within which Judaism, in diverse forms, has a privileged position in relating the community to God. Israel will always form an obstacle to any attempt to establish one monolithic global faith. It will always be a source of active hope for a just human society. It will always be a witness to the demand of God for that fidelity in relationships which is the core of human goodness.

Judaism expresses one clear form of the identity of religion and culture. The language, rites, stories, and customs which bind Jewish culture together in one historical continuity have a religious basis, in response to an alleged distinctive revelation from God. Yet there are two important qualifications to be made. The culture is open, in the sense that it is not wholly ethnic. New members, of many ethnic groups, can join it, so it is not straightforwardly racial in character. Also, the religious component, though central to Judaism, is by no means universally shared among Jews. A number of diverse religious groups constitute a sort of religious core of Jewish society, to some of which the majority loosely ally themselves. Judaism is not simply a religious culture; it is a culture with a rather diverse religious core, the importance of which varies at different times.

Since Judaism is a culture, it may, like any other culture, breed a sense of its own superiority, and seek to exclude all 'aliens' as undesirable influences. On the other hand, Judaism is not just like any other culture. Its religious core describes it as a culture with a special vocation, which is to be a moral standard for the world, showing true justice, mercy, community, and compassion. The Israelites were slaves in Egypt, and therefore they are called to have a special concern for the liberation of the oppressed and care for resident aliens and those without a homeland. Jews are called to show true worship of the Creator of all, which entails honouring the whole of creation, and working with God for the fulfilment which He desires. Finally, Jews are called to be a priestly people, suffering and working for the redemption of the whole earth. They are not to impose their law on others, but to help others to see where their own proper fulfilment of the divine purpose lies.

Judaism will continue to exist, in secular, liberal, and orthodox forms. It will resist all attempts to achieve conformity to some new global religion. But at its best it will stand for the search for universal justice and acceptance of a plurality of religious communities. As such, it will call for tolerance and a full acceptance of religious diversity by others. Judaism can take its place in the modern world as the faith of a people called to prefigure the Messianic age of true justice, and to serve the other peoples of the earth in finding their own appropriate form of relationship to the universal Creator God. Yet they can never think unduly highly of their success in this regard. The Jewish community is a very imperfect sign of a future age of peace and justice. This suggests that Jews are not the guardians of a perfectly understood Torah, implementing it with all the wisdom and compassion that God requires. They are called to be the faltering vanguard of an ideal future when Torah will be fully and appropriately embodied throughout the whole of human society.

2
Islam and the Universal *Umma*

ISLAMIC STATES AND THE GLOBAL COMMUNITY

Islam is like Judaism in seeing the appropriate way to human fulfilment in obedience to a divinely revealed law, the Shari'a. It is unlike Judaism in positing this law as given to be followed by all humanity, and not just by one special community. The Qur'an accepts that the Hebrew Bible was the result of genuine prophetic revelation, but maintains that it contains misunderstandings and errors, due to *tahrif*, or corruption of the Scriptures, which the revelation given to Muhammad sets out to correct. One of these misunderstandings is the unique role given to the descendants of Abraham, Isaac, and Jacob by the Hebrew Bible. The Qur'an maintains that the prophetic revelation is universal, and the laws of God are meant to apply to all people without exception. Consequently, Islam aims to set out a law which can be the basis of all human social life. The way to true relationship with God is a way of living righteously in the divinely guided, just society. If one lives thus, one may be assured that God will raise one from death and welcome one into Paradise—the ultimate reward for the servants of God who freely and gladly submit to the divine will. It has often been claimed that Islam is more a religion of law than of theology. The way to fulfilment is the way of obedience to divine law, which is the way of obedience to God's will.

From the very first, therefore, Islam set out to be an integral social and political community, not a separate institution within a religiously neutral political state. Thus it is often said—though, as I will show, the practice is often very different and much qualification is needed to such a blunt statement—that Islam makes no distinction between politics and religion, between state and religious institutions. The state is to be a religiously guided state, and religion is simply sincere obedience to the laws of the *umma*, the Muslim community. God's will is not for some spiritual élite or minority set against or in tension with the political structures of society. It is for the whole human community, organized to express the purposes of a merciful, just, and compassionate Creator.

Such a programme, though perfectly coherent, is also somewhat paradoxical, for Islam must start out as one particular minority community in a larger, unconcerned, or even hostile world. So it started in Mecca, and even after the removal to Medina it existed for some time as one community among others, though quickly becoming the majority, in a religiously plural society. In the modern world Muslim states form a distinctive group which is by no means a majority of the world's population. The paradox is that a faith which sees itself as meant to govern the whole world seems destined in fact always to be just one distinctive social group among others. It even emphasizes this distinctiveness over against others by often insisting on distinctive modes of dress, language of worship, and social customs. One can describe Muslim states in ethnic terms without too much difficulty, and the contrast sometimes made between 'Islam and the West' makes the point that Islam is in practice one geographically definable faith among others, and in the conditions of the modern world seems likely to remain so.

All revelations are given in particular social contexts, and the revelation given to Muhammad was given in the Arabian peninsula. The first Muslims were Arabs, and the Arabic of the Qur'an remains the language of worship. Many other ethnic groups are now Muslim, from North Africans to Pakistanis and Malaysians. In fact the largest Muslim population in the world is in Indonesia, and there are many Muslims in China and Eastern Asia. Nevertheless, most Muslims explicitly define their identities over against the liberal democracy of the West, or of Europe. This is hardly surprising, when one realizes that most Muslim countries were colonized by European powers, and have only recently achieved independence. The economic and technological superiority of the West, and the virtual domination of the Muslim world by Europeans in the recent past, has allied Islam with rising forces of nationalism and desire for independence first from the political and then from the economic hegemony of the West.

This is ironic, since the *umma* is to be a universal community of believers, and many of the traditional scholars of Islam, the *ulama*, oppose nationalism as antipathetic to the universal spirit of Islam. Abul Ala Mawdudi (though far from being a traditionalist) writes: 'Those who accept the principles of Islam are not divided by any distinction of nationality, class or country.'[1] If Islam is indeed meant to be a global community, then it is self-defeating for Islam to oppose 'the West', when Westerners should be Muslims too, and when many are. One of the major tensions within Islam is between the drive for a global community, inclusive of every race and nation, and its alliance in fact with many countries of the developing world, finding in Islam a political tool for rejecting the colonial and economic domination of the white Western nations.

The global vision of Islam is of the whole world united under one world government that is concerned to fulfil the divine demand for social justice and compassion, especially for the poor, and to honour the name of the Creator of all. The salvation of humanity lies in the freeing of all peoples from oppression and from nationalistic hatred, and in the construction of a society in which a wide range of human possibilities for good, implanted by the Creator, can be actualized. It is integral to this vision that human fulfilment should be achieved in a communal life of fellowship, loyalty, and trust, and that all human life should be related to God, who is its final goal, so that this life is a training and preparation for an endless journey into the joy of the divine being. It is God alone who can make such salvation possible, and God will do so in so far as humans are obedient to the revelation of the divine will in Shari'a.

The symbol of universal government should be the Caliph, a sort of world president, the vicegerent (*khalifah*) of God, who will be no autocratic ruler, but one who is responsible to all the people, who practices consultation (*shura*) as widely as possible, and aims at a consensus (*ijma*) of the relevant experts. The world government will permit and encourage many different forms of cultural custom and law, in accordance with the distinctive histories and languages of different nations. The only condition is that all must conform to Shari'a, the divinely revealed principles that show the way to justice and goodness. Thus one must work for 'neither nationalism nor imperialism but a league of nations',[2] guided by the fundamental principles of personal integrity in relationships and respect for all life as created by God.

---

[1] Abul Ala Mawdudi, *Nationalism and Islam* (Lahore: Islamic Publications, 1947), 10.
[2] Muhammed Iqbal, *The Reconstruction of Religious Thought in Islam* (Lahore: Muhammed Ashraf, 1948), 139.

For all people, obedience to the divine law will order their lives towards God, even though they have no deep inclination to pursue a spiritual path. Yet the esoteric heart of Islam is Sufism, the cultivation of the knowledge of God in the inmost self. So Islam offers an outer way that keeps humans true to the divine will, and an inner way for those who are ready to progress further on the spiritual path that will eventually await everyone, and experience *fana*, the cultivation of that fading of self which enables the reality of God to be inwardly manifest and known.

Whereas Judaism is content, or even proud, to stress its difference from other creeds and nations, Islam has an intrinsic missionary drive to include the whole planet in the household of faith, the *umma*. The fact is, however, that this ambitious project seems doomed to failure, since many—not least Jews, Christians, Buddhists, and humanists—will not assent to the finality and inerrancy of Muhammad's prophethood. The crucial question is what happens in face of that failure. Muhammad himself perhaps did not believe that the whole world would become Muslim. At least there are passages in the Qur'an which seem to speak of diversity of faiths as God-willed.[3] The 'people of the Book' are expected to continue to exist, and at least some of them are said to be certainly 'in the ranks of the righteous'.[4] Moreover, there is to be no compulsion in religion,[5] so that the *umma* is to be a community which one may freely join and (though apostasy is in fact a grave sin), one would think that one should be able freely to leave.

One might then think of Islam as a world-wide faith without national boundaries, an international community of those bound to obedience to God's law, as revealed in the Qur'an. As such, it would live together peaceably with all those who in good conscience seek truth and justice, and unite in common action especially with those who seek to obey God in different *din*s, or ways of life. It would oppose all narrow national or ethnic interests, and strive, in co-operation with all who share its ideals of justice and compassion, to realize an ideal fellowship of all humans under God. As for the correctness of the claim that the Qur'an is God's final and definitive

[3] 'If God had so willed, He would have made you a single people, but [His plan is] to test you in what He hath given you,' Qur'an 5. 51.
[4] 'Those who follow the Jewish scriptures, and the Christians and the Sabians . . . shall have their reward,' Qur'an 2. 62. Cf. Also Qur'an 3. 114.
[5] 'Let there be no compulsion in religion,' Qur'an 2. 256.

revelation, and its universal acceptance, that is a matter that God will decide. Perhaps the universal rule of Islam is to be postponed to the coming of the Mahdi, inaugurating a Messianic future in which injustice and wrongdoing will be things of the past. In the present world order, Islam must seek to persuade and invite those who will respond to its global message, and leave what actually happens to the will of God. If a global league of nations under God is not possible, still Islam can aim to be a global, tolerant, and just community, striving to promote peace and integrity in all human relationships.

That is an idealized picture. The historical reality of Islam is rather different. It originated in Arabia, retained Arabic as the language of worship, and was a motivating force in the conquest of much of the world to form an Arabic Empire. Having been resisted by Christian Europe, it was most successful in the collapsed Byzantine Empire, and in a crescent of countries from North Africa to Malaysia. Virtually all those countries have since been colonized by European powers, and have only recently asserted their independence, though they are still seeking to define their own identities in face of vast European and American economic superiority. In this process, Islam has been used as a rhetorical tool, both by authoritarian regimes and by radical populist movements, for defining a new sense of national pride and identity, against the colonialist infiltrators and the national élites which allied with the colonists. Consequently, Islam has been a strong nationalist and ethnic force. Pakistan was founded on the slogan, 'Islam in Danger', and in Malaysian it is said that to become Muslim is to become Malay (*masuk Melayu*).[6]

Furthermore, since the law of God is a law for human social life together, and is meant to guide all human relationships, it naturally seeks to become the social law of the political community. The Egyptian theorist Rashid Rida (d. 1935) has written: 'The Muslims consider in fact that their religion does not really exist unless an independent and strong Islamic State is established which could apply the laws of Islam and defend it against any foreign opposition and domination.'[7] Rida touches here on two important points in contemporary Muslim self-understanding. First, one should seek to establish an Islamic state, not simply to be one group among others

---

[6] John I. Esposito, *Islam and Democracy* (New York: Oxford University Press, 1996), 125.
[7] Id., *Islam and Politics* (Syracuse, NY: Syracuse University Press, 1984), 63.

in a secular or religiously non-committed state. Second, any such state will always be in danger of opposition, and must be armed against forces which may seek to overthrow it. This is well rooted in tradition, for when some of the followers of the Prophet wished to sell their arms, he forbade it, and said, 'A body of my people will not cease to fight for the truth until the coming forth of the Antichrist.'[8] The community of God may often need to take up arms to fight for its existence.

Islam has, for better or worse, entered into the nationalism of the twentieth century, and Islam is often used as a putatively cohesive force for holding together new nation-states, in opposition to colonialism and, in general, to the economic hegemony of 'the West'. Consequently, rather than being seen as an international and peacable community, Islam is widely perceived by non-Muslims as an Arab-led association of countries which are mostly beset by economic poverty and illiteracy, often as opposed to each other as they are to any outsiders, and often involved in violent terrorist or warlike acts, largely against each other. From the Muslim viewpoint, these are indeed major problems of the social reality of Islam, but they are outweighed by the success of Islam in overcoming the domination of the West, with its drug culture, breakdown of family life, and addiction to gambling and sex. Between the ills of capitalism, with its creation of an underclass without hope, liberal individualism, with its seeming capitulation to sensual and corrupt desires, and socialism, with its ultimately repressive and atheistic ideology, Islam offers a divine law of social justice and a recovery of personal and national self-respect.

At the same time, one must ask if it really is the Muslim ideal to have a distinctive group of Islamic states, forming an identifiable power-bloc in the world, in competition with other blocs such as the European Union, the United States of America, and the countries of the Pacific Rim. For if such a scenario is accepted by non-Muslims, the presence of growing numbers of Muslims within other countries will almost inevitably be seen by them as a threat, a fifth column from an alien power. Islam will also always be a divisive force, in overt, if not violent, competition with other ideologies, whether Christian, Confucian, or secular.

Not only is Islam potentially divisive internationally, as it forms a

---

[8]   al-Bukhari 81, 27.

distinct power-bloc, but surprisingly, perhaps, it turns out to be very divisive internally, within the household of faith itself. The divisiveness of Islam is partly the result of the diverse ethnic groups of which it is composed, but it is also the result of factors more central to the faith. Islam has been a very effective force in supporting nationalistic movements. At the same time it has been an influence making for internal conflict and dissension rather than harmony and fraternity. Thus there have been movements of Sunni Islam (the *sipah-i-sahaba*) in Pakistan calling for the physical elimination of Shiah Muslims as *kafir*s, unbelievers.[9] There are continuing disputes over the extent to which traditional Islamic laws should be imposed. And religious riots and acts of terrorist violence in the name of Islam are unfortunately regular occurrences in the life of Pakistan. It seems that Islam flourishes when it can rally support against an identifiable external enemy, such as Western colonialism. But it very easily breeds dissension and violent conflict within its own community, as differing interpretations of Islam clash.

TRADITION AND MODERNITY

It may seem inimical to Islam that it should identify itself as being in opposition to most of the world, and that it should breed conflict and violence within its own community. But the factors which lead to these effects are deeply rooted in the faith. Muslim writers are profoundly divided over the way in which Shari'a should be applied to society. For some, the ideal would be the uniting of political and religious leadership in one person—as it was in the case of Muhammad and perhaps in the case of the four 'rightly guided' caliphs, the immediate successors of the Prophet. However, the caliph became separate from the religious authorities thereafter, and religious experts tended to advise the political rulers rather than become rulers themselves. In 'Twelver' Shiah Islam, the twelfth Imam should hold together both political and religious rule, but he has been taken from the world, and will only return at a time in history chosen by God, so that again there is in the meanwhile a division between political and religious rule. Shiites have usually eschewed direct interference in politics, though extraordinarily they have indulged in a form of direct rule in revolutionary Iran. There,

---

[9] Reported in Ahmed Rashid, *Far Eastern Economic Review*, 24 (9 March 1995).

Khomeini's doctrine of *vilayat-e Faqih*, government by the jurist, introduced quite a new element into Shiite thought. It is clear that it is not in fact the case that religion and politics are indivisible in Islam, though political decisions are certainly meant to conform to the requirements of Shari'a.

The caliphate was ended in 1258 by the Mongols, but there is in many quarters desire to see it restored in some form (a conference in 1925 at al-Azhar University agreed that the caliphate is necessary to Islam). Such a caliphate would give *dar al-Islam*, the community of Muslim nations, a titular head, though he would not necessarily directly exercise religious power. What has happened since the tenth century is that the religious scholars, the *ulama*, have sought to be involved as advisers in various ways, to ensure that state laws are in conformity with Shari'a, especially in the realms of family and religious laws. Traditional schools of interpretation have grown up, and what might be called 'traditional Islam' seeks to follow such laws. Traditional Muslims often see themselves as being in opposition to modern thought, which they associate with colonial European or American influences.

It is not hard to see what such opposition is based on, given the definition of 'modernity' they have. Seyyed Hossein Nasr, for instance, says, 'For us, "modern" means that which is cut off from the Transcendent.'[10] The rejection of revelation, of intuitive knowledge of the divine, and of appeals to authority in matters of truth, is certainly part of the heritage of the European Enlightenment, and no religious believer would be happy to accept such rejection entirely. Various other things are included in what is seen as the enlightenment package, however, including the denial of any immutable moral principles, espousal of the theory of evolution, the use of reason as an independent and reliable source of knowledge, practical materialism, and a utopian stress on the possibility of human perfection through purely human means.

These various factors may need to be carefully disentangled. It is not at all easy to discern which moral principles are really immutable, and which relate only to particular historical situations. There is nothing anti-religious about evolutionary theory, as long as it does not insist on blind chance alone, and such Muslim thinkers as

[10] Seyyed Hossein Nasr, *Traditional Islam in the Modern World* (London: Kegan Paul, 1987), 98.

Mohammed Iqbal have made good use of it in a Muslim perspective. The critical use of reason may itself be an expression of the vicegerency of humanity, upon which the Qur'an insists. Materialistic attitudes spring from human greed, a vice common to religious and non-religious alike. And utopianism is not either confined to or an important part of modernity, which does insist on the importance of education and the encouragement of independent thought, but is not by any means committed to the belief that there can ever be a perfect society.

Self-styled traditional Islam, as seen from other Muslim perspectives, is thus in danger of conflating traditional culture and respect for a rather narrowly educated group of *ulama* with immutable divine law and obedience to God. This emerges clearly in the traditionalist response to democracy, which again tends to be seen as a Western and alien concept, incompatible with Muslim social ideals. King Fahd of Saudi Arabia has said, 'The democratic system prevalent in the world is not appropriate in this region . . . the election system has no place in the Islamic creed, which calls for a government of advice and consultation.'[11] On this view, the ruler is certainly responsible to the people, and could be deposed in extreme cases by the *ulama*, but there are no political parties or elections of the ruler or government.

What is primarily being rejected is the view that the people are sovereign, whatever they decide. Islam aims to live, not by the will of the people, but by the will of God. This, for traditionalists, must be determined largely by those expert in interpretation and learned in tradition. In practice this establishes hierarchical and conservative forms of government, whose responsiveness to popular feeling very much depends on the personal character of the ruling élite.

For Sunni Muslims, all are equal under the law of God, so there is no hierarchical religious organization, there are no specially devout groups of monks and nuns, and there are no priests. It is obvious, however, that some will be more able and judicious than others, will have more time for research and reflection, and will accumulate more experience of directing practical affairs. Thus there arose the class of *ulama*, the experts in Shari'a, who could refer to a whole body of traditional opinions, and form considered judgements on

---

[11] Reported in John I. Esposito, *The Islamic Threat, Myth or Reality?* (New York: Oxford University Press, 1992), 217.

matters referred to them. The *ulama* rarely claim to rule directly, but more often seek to function as a council of legal experts, to whose judgements, however, the political authorities are subject in all matters pertaining to revealed law.

In recent years, however, radical movements have arisen that reject the authority of the *ulama* because it is seen as compromising with autocratic, 'Western'-influenced, élites. These movements aim to go back directly to the Qur'an and the Sunna for their inspiration, and claim the right of *ijtihad*, or private judgement by all the faithful, in interpreting the law. They see the traditionalists as 'medieval' and reactionary, whereas in return the traditionalists see them as in fact propagating ideas taken from the French Revolution and disguised in Islamic form.[12]

In the face of the perceived tendency of traditionalists to favour autocratic regimes, which have failed to resolve some of the greatest social problems in Muslim countries, some Muslims have propounded a different view of Islam as a democratic, egalitarian, and just global community. Abul Ala Mawdudi opposes what he calls 'Western democracy': 'Islam, speaking from the viewpoint of political philosophy, is the very antithesis of secular Western democracy.'[13] That is because God, and not the will of the people, is sovereign. Nevertheless, in interpreting the revealed law, which is in itself infallible, Mawdudi rejects the claims to privilege made by the *ulama*, who attempted to 'close the door of interpretation' in the tenth century, and reasserts the traditional right of *ijtihad*, private interpretation: 'Every Muslim who is capable and qualified to give a sound opinion on matters of Islamic law, is entitled to interpret that law of God.'[14] So there is a proper form of Islamic democracy: 'Every person in an Islamic society enjoys the rights and powers of the caliphate of God and in this respect all individuals are equal.'[15]

On such a view, Islam is essentially democratic, because the doctrine of *Tawhid*, the unity of God, lays down that there is no sovereign but God. Monarchy is therefore at best a compromise in

---

[12] Cf. Seyyed Hossein Nasr, 'Islam in the Present-Day Islamic World', in *Traditional Islam*, ch. 5.

[13] Abul Ala Mawdudi, 'The Political Theory of Islam', in Khurshid Ahmad (ed.), *Islam, Its Meaning and Message* (London: Islamic Council of Europe, 1976), 159.

[14] Ibid. 161.

[15] Id., *The Islamic Way of Life*, trans. Khurshid Ahmad (Delhi: Markazi Maktaba Islami, 1967), 42.

Islam, even though there are at the time of writing six monarchies in the Middle East. God is the only ruler, and the law has been definitively laid down for all time, and can be consulted by each believer.

This is still a theocratic democracy, very different from ideas of democracy which makes the will of the majority sovereign. For Islam, it is a potentially disastrous policy to let a society be controlled by whatever the majority (or even, in a parliamentary democracy, a dominant minority) wants. Human desires, left to themselves, may lead to licentious sensuality and injustice. They must be controlled by the law of God, which can lay down the proper limits for living together in a just society.

The law of God, it is sometimes said, is not human law, and it does not require any human legislator. It is given in the Qur'an and the Sunna (the life of the Prophet). Under that law, however, societies are free to order their lives in many ways that may be consistent with it, and in many societies what becomes important is *shura*, consultation with the whole body of believers, who have the right and duty to interpret the law in accordance with reason and local custom. The very diverse ways in which Islamic law may develop are highly complex, and permit many forms of interpretation. In some of those forms, consultation aims at *ijma*, or the consensus of the faithful, so that Muslim democracy is not seen as adversarial, as expressed in opposing political parties. It is rather seen as seeking a common mind by the discussion of differing possibilities for action. In other communities, *ijma* is not accepted in the same way, but again whatever political structures exist must always show themselves to be compatible with Shari'a, which can never be overthrown by 'democratic' vote.

There are clearly deep potential tensions in this system. The most obvious arises from the attempt to determine what exactly the law of God is. It may seem obvious that it is what is written in the Qur'an and Hadith. There are indeed Muslims who take that view, and who seek to have the Quranic laws, especially with regard to education, the relations of men and women, marriage and inheritance, and criminal penalties (the *hudud*), implemented in society. But any lawyer knows that attempts to apply laws literally in rapidly changing social contexts are likely to undermine the inner spirit of the law itself. A law permitting a man to have four wives as long as he cares properly for each may be a radical reform in a society where women are considered as no more than property. But it may prove quite unacceptable to a society in which women have acquired freedom from incessant child-bearing and also have equal economic freedom and social and geographical mobility. If things go well in society, such permissive laws may be quietly ignored, and complemented by laws strengthening the rights of women, as well as enhancing their status, so that polygamy becomes practically non-existent. That is what happened in Judaism, and in predominantly Muslim countries such as Turkey. But if things go badly, traditionalists may blame the ills of society on new more permissive attitudes, and call for the confinement of women to the home, and the complete separation of sexes, so that equal education and work opportunities are non-existent. Reformers on the other hand will point to the egalitarian aspects of the law in general, and argue that new circumstances call for new legislation, in accordance with the spirit, not the letter, of Shari'a. Khurshid Ahmad writes: 'God has revealed only broad principles and has endowed man with the freedom to apply them in every age in the way suited to the spirit and conditions of that age.'[16] It is clear that these are very different attitudes to the interpretation and application of Shari'a, even though both claim to represent the true spirit of Islam.

Disputes founded on such different attitudes have been prominent in Ahmad's own country, Pakistan, and have led to violence on many occasions. But there are further reasons for dispute also. Early in Muslim history, four main schools of law arose within Sunni Islam, and Shiah Islam has its own quite different schools of interpretation. They differed on such things as divorce, inheritance, and taxation law, and it was generally accepted that such differences were legitimate. Indeed, difference has been seen as a positive virtue in Islam, so that Shari'a has never been seen as a monolithic set of agreed and unchanging laws. *Ijtihad*, or personal interpretation, has been acceptable in Islam, though the *ulama* have traditionally held that such a right of interpretation closed after the tenth century CE, when the main lines of legal interpretation were held to have been finalized—though in fact the gate of *ijtihad* never closed.

There is thus not only dispute between traditionalists and reformers, but each of these broad groups splits into two. Among the traditionalists, there is dispute between the conservative *ulama*, who seek to close the tradition of private interpretation, upholding trad-

---

[16] Khurshid Ahmad (ed.), *Islam: Its Meaning and Message*, 43.

itional precedents, and neo-traditional 'fundamentalists', who claim the right of *ijtihad*, and want to go directly to the Qur'an and Sunnah themselves as the sources of their judgements.

These two groups further divide into those who support national-ist forms of Islam, and those who look for a pan-Islamic grouping of nations, and into those who take what might be called a literalist view of Quranic injunctions and those who take a 'precedent' view. The literalists seek to institute a 'pure Muslim society', often with penalties of amputation for theft, and stoning for fornication or adultery, the complete separation of the sexes and the seclusion of women from public life, the death penalty for apostasy and the ban-ning of alcohol and the public serving of food during Ramadan, and prohibition of dancing, theatre, and music. Most traditionalists, however, take more of a case-law approach, building on past cases and adapting to new situations, as they seek to achieve a consensus of legal opinions. Thus, for instance, amputations and death by stoning have not been implemented in Pakistan, and few Muslim societies think it right, in a very different social and economic world, to continue to have a society exactly as it was in the time of the Prophet.

Among the reformers there are those who simply seek to interpret Shari'a sensitively to developing social conditions while supporting the idea of an Islamic society, and there are more radical modernists who would virtually confine the Shari'a to matters of religious obser-vance, or who would give Islam a privileged position, with perhaps its own laws, education, and charitable services, but within a largely secular government. The former group adopt what might be called a 'principle' interpretation of Shari'a. They seek underlying principles of which specific Quranic injunctions are context-dependent ex-amples, and then seek to apply these principles in different situ-ations. Behind the rules of *hudud* one can discern immutable principles for upholding personal responsibility and punishing injustice. Behind injunctions concerning family life and the relation of the sexes one can find principles calling for respect for person-hood in men and women alike, and the building up of stable family and community life. Behind particular religious and social prohib-itions lie immutable principles enjoining the integrity of the person and the honouring of the name and reality of God. All these prin-ciples are opposed to the wholly secularist view that criminals are not responsible for their actions, that there should be no binding rules for family life and sexual relationships, and that everyone should be free to act entirely as they wish. But it is important to refer both to *ijtihad* and to *ijma*, to informed interpretation and consensus in the community, in deciding how these principles are to be formulated and implemented at particular times. Disputes will be inevitable, and the temper and violence of such disputes will probably be a function of the stability and perceived fairness of the society in question. Islam will never be a panacea for social ills, but in the reformist view it contains principles which motivate and support a concern for social justice and personal integrity, once that concern exists.

The fully secularist view goes even further, in seeing the Muslim *umma* as one voluntary association among others, though it may have the status of an established faith in a majority Muslim state. The particular laws of Islam could be operative in the community of those who voluntarily join the community, while the larger society permits the free expression of other religious and non-religious views. To some extent, many so-called 'Muslim states' are secular in this sense, at least in so far as they permit different Muslim legal systems to operate in different branches of Islam. It is not a great extension of this tolerance to embrace other faiths—even a morally committed atheism—within a truly tolerant state. Thus Anwar Ibrahim of the Islamic Youth Movement of Malaysia has written: 'Islam regards discrimination as a criminal act because it is contradictory to the call to unite different communities and to encourage tolerance, friendship, and mutual respect among all human beings.'[17]

There is perhaps little difference between a tolerant 'principle' view and a sensitive secular view. But one might suspect, given the evidence of history, that when religions gain power, they are very prone to autocracy, intolerance, and the preservation of privilege. To that extent, secularism might better preserve a truly disinterested pursuit of social justice, universal compassion, and the guarding of responsible human freedom. However, human societies are extremely volatile, and secularism can easily turn to promoting anti-religious policies that repress some of the very freedoms they are supposed to be protecting. It is impossible to dissociate the variety of interpretations of Islam from the social histories and cultures in

---

[17] Anwar Ibrahim, quoted by Chandra Muzzafar, *Islamic Resurgence in Malaysia* (Kuala Lumpur: Government Press, 1962), 50.

which they are embedded, and which they largely express. It should be obvious that Islam is flexible enough to adapt to new situations in creative ways, though it will always be prone to express the human vices that are inseparable from social and political life.

ISLAM AND POLITICAL LIFE

Appeal to divinely revealed law is not a uniting factor in society, unless everyone agrees that the revelation has occurred, what the law is, and how it should be implemented. The history of Islam gives little hope that such agreement will ever be achieved. Again it seems that conflict is an essential part of religion. One chief argument for liberal democracy is that the necessity of conflict is accepted, and built into the system in such a way that it does not lead to violence and the breakdown of the system. Islam contains the materials for such an acceptance of internal diversity, but that does entail that no one interpretation of Shari'a can be imposed as mandatory on everyone. A liberal Islam can exist, meaning an Islam that permits differences of interpretation within a generally permissive national law. Such an Islam does exist, for example, in countries where Shiah and Sunni live together, though admittedly they do not always do so in harmony.

That will necessitate a distinction of political and religious structures, in that the political ruler will not be identical with the leaders of particular schools of legal interpretation. There will be a number of Muslim schools, all accepting the same general structures of communal prayer in the mosque, and accepting the Qur'an as their foundational text, but differing as to how to implement the law of God. This means that there will exist an important distinction between the basic defining laws of Islam and its more particular, changing enactments. There are disputes within the Muslim nations as to how far particular legal enactments should be imposed on all members of society, and how far they allow modification in new circumstances. There is no monolithic understanding of what an Islamic state should be, but an acceptance of a wide degree of diversity, from the secular constitution of Turkey to the Islamic constitution of Saudi Arabia. Such acceptance, however, is continually threatened by conflicts which can become violent where one group feels itself excluded from the political process. There is thus a strong argument from within Islam itself for the institution of a democratic constitution, in which the rights of minorities are safeguarded, and there is room for the expression of competing views on particular topics.

Anyone who looks at the very different interpretations of Islam in countries that call themselves Muslim must allow that there is toleration of great diversity in Islam. How far will such an acceptance of diversity extend? A crucial question is whether it extends to non-Muslims, or whether it assumes that all right-thinking people will be believers. Under the Umayyad caliphs, non-Muslim lands were known as *dar al-harb*, the land of warfare. Europe and America are still often described under this heading, though there is a possibility that they could rather be *dar al-sulh*, the abode of peace, where Muslims live in a minority but can practise their faith freely. It may also rightly be said that *jihad* does not necessarily mean physical violence, but an earnest striving to maintain the way of God. The 'people of the book' especially, have the status of *dhimmi*, protected people, in Muslim countries, and can in theory practise their faiths freely, though they do not have equal rights with Muslim citizens. Nevertheless, the punishment for apostasy (changing one's religion from Islam) is death, Muslim women cannot marry non-Muslims, and other religions are usually forbidden to proselytize in Muslim countries, even though Islam continues to proselytize actively throughout the world. In Pakistan the Ahmadiyya and in Iran the Bahai have been ruthlessly persecuted. Moreover, such groups as the Kharijites have regarded *jihad* as a duty to revolt against non-Muslim rulers. All religions are by no means equal for Islam, as it actually exists.

Can one envisage a liberal Islam that accepts a truly global coexistence of religious and humanist traditions? Much depends on the socio-economic conditions of Muslim countries, and on whether they will yet have to face the critical questioning of scriptural authority that has forced changes on most forms of Judaism and Christianity. At present most Muslim thinkers are sanguine that they can rebut all such challenges, that a just and self-confident Muslim social order can be established, and that the Qur'an will stand justified before every critical onslaught.

My view is that Islam will continue to be a resource for many different and competing political movements, and as such it will continue to be involved in the general animosities and often violent struggles between ethnic and economically unequal groups. Islam proclaims itself to be a 'politically realistic' faith that does not make its moral requirements unrealistically high and does not shrink from justifying the use of violence when necessary.

I think that the Qur'an justifies violence only in defence of human or religious rights which are being threatened, and even then it insists on a balanced consideration of the probability of a just and succesful outcome of any conflict. The Qur'an teaches that 'God does not love the aggressor'.[18] But it also says, 'Kill them whenever you meet them, and expel them from any place from which they have expelled you,'[19] and there will always be groups who believe that violence can be used to protect Muslim values when they are being attacked even by other Muslims, or by people with non-Muslim views. This will continue to be a problem in the Muslim world, though it can be mitigated by seeking to ensure that there are no underprivileged groups excluded from that real consultation the Qur'an requires, and by overcoming the sense that simple disagreement constitutes an attack on Islam.

There will continue to be conflicts over such issues as the role of women in society and the banning of alcohol, concerts, dances, and cinemas. Conflicts on these or similar issues are common to all religions, and indeed to all human societies. Traditional societies of all sorts delineate the role of women as one of subordination and homekeeping, and attempts to control social and cultural behaviour by various forms of censorship were as common in the avowedly atheistic societies of Russia and China as in any religious culture. Authoritarian policies of social control are not particularly religious. In so far as a religion has been around for a long time, it tends to be identified with traditional culture, and it is natural that any religion based on a historical revelation will be conservative, in the sense of looking back to that past revelation for the source of its principles and values. To that extent, religion can be used by traditionalists in support of their own social attitudes.

It becomes clear on reflection, however, that religion can also be used in radical ways, to overthrow traditional authorities. The Qur'an itself is often seen as in some ways engaged in a radical critique of the traditional society of Muhammad's day. For example, it opposed many traditional religious and social practices in the name of the God of justice and compassion. The Prophet applied the immutable principles of the Qur'an in creative ways to the

---

[18] Qur'an 2. 189.   [19] Ibid.

various changing situations in which he found himself. There is ample scope for taking the Qur'an and the example of the Prophet as validating a creative approach to social problems, which allows new solutions to particular problems, within the general principle of total commitment to God and to the egalitarian community (without a central religious authority) which must pursue justice in the light of its own historical perspective.

Thus revolutionary movements within Islam can also appeal to the Qur'an, as they call for an overthrow of traditional structures, whether peaceful or violent. As Seyyed Hossein Nasr says, 'The central reality in the Islamic world will most likely become the battle . . . between traditional Islam and various counter-traditional and leftist ideologies parading as Islam.'[20] Nasr sees in these movements Islam being used for extraneous political ends, whereas their supporters would think of themselves as recovering 'true Islam' against its traditional corrupters.

This may suggest that a religion which sets out to control political life is in practice likely to be controlled by the ambitions and interests of politicians. It may also suggest, contrary to what has often been claimed, that Islam as such contains no unambiguous pattern of social life that can be applied fairly straightforwardly in all circumstances. Yet that is not to say that Islam is not after all politically relevant. It contains checks and fundamental principles which sooner or later challenge all purely sectarian and divisive political ambitions and interests, and measure them against the command to honour God and God's creation, and accomplish the universal human fulfilment which is the will of the compassionate and merciful Lord. Such continually renewed challenges from rereadings of the Qur'an lead to new stages in the dialectic of opposition and reconciliation which marks the life of Islam, as of all religions, set as they are in the complexity, imperfection, and ambiguity of human society.

VARIETIES OF ISLAM

It is hard to imagine that the whole Muslim world will be unaffected by the sorts of secularism and critical readings of sacred texts and traditions that is so marked in Europe and America. There will be

---

[20] Nasr, *Traditional Islam*, 314.

those who conscientiously deny the existence of God, and who regard the Qur'an as a limited and fallible document. At present there are parallel systems of religious and secular education in most Muslim countries, and one would expect conflicts to grow between secularists and the orthodox. Although one can speak of a 'modernist' Islam, there is not at present an established tradition of Muslim thought that is critical of its own revealed foundations. Looking back in Muslim history, however, the classical philosophers were able to voice such criticisms, and it is more a comment on the culture of Muslim countries in the recent past than on the religion itself that such independent philosophical traditions are rarely to be seen within Islam today.

All these factors lead one to see the 'house of Islam' as much more varied and flexible than Western commentators sometimes suppose. Islam is not an inflexible, universally agreed, political system that offers a complete and unchanging blueprint for society. It is a sharer in the vicissitudes of the societies in which it exists, and is by no means the only determining factor in giving shape to the politics of Muslim countries. On the contrary, it is itself largely shaped by wider social and economic factors. A liberal Islamic modernism exists, in such writers as Fazlur Rahman, al-Afghani, and Muhammed Iqbal, which accepts new scientific modes of thought and education, and seeks to present Islam as a creative force for a socially committed ethical monotheism.

One might accordingly hold that the ritual laws of religion are changeless, but that with regard to social laws, what is basically revealed is the necessity for consultation (*shura*), the elements of social virtue, and some permissive penalties. Other modernists, however, reject the liberal agenda, and are influenced by Marxist thought, as they see Islam as the champion of the Third World and of underdeveloped countries. A third approach is that of Mahdism, which looks for the destruction of the existing social order and a divine end to this age of world history. Such movements are strengthened in so far as Muslim societies feel themselves to be threatened or oppressed by stronger forces from more developed parts of the world, and come to feel that Islam itself is in danger. Fourth, again as a defensive reaction to Western cultural invasion, there are what may be called puritanical calls for a return to a strictly enforced keeping of law, which embody a retreat from too much contact with wider social forces at play in the world as a whole. The

Wahhabis of Saudi Arabia often embody such a view. Fifth, there are the much more revolutionary and violent fundamentalist movements, which become vehicles for voicing the frustration and anger of those permanently oppressed by and excluded from their own political processes, and which seek to overthrow the traditional authorities of Islam. Both these types of movement may be either pan-Islamic, calling for a united Muslim world, or nationalistic, calling for Islam in one nation. Sixth, in contrast there are revolutionary regimes which try to give the *ulama* direct political control, as in modern Iran. And seventh, there is a traditionalist Islam, which tries to retain the classical traditions of education and legal interpretation, seeing that as the best defence against the atheism and radicalism of much Western culture.

The array of possible Islamic forms is bewildering. What is common, under these vast differences, is a commitment to the Qur'an as a revelation of God to Muhammad, the seal of the prophets, and as a source of law or social principles for a universal and just human society acknowledging the sole sovereignty of God, and leading eventually, beyond this life, to the reward of Paradise. What is clear is that the interpretation of Shari'a is heavily qualified by social and cultural conditions. One cannot therefore simply speak of a contamination of Muslim principles by secular or alien cultural forces. One must rather speak of a global community which itself embraces many differing approaches to worship and justice, but which insists on the sovereignty of God and the continuing search for principles of full human equality and fulfilment.

Once one sees Islam as a set of diverse and historically changing schools of interpretation, it may well appear that the *umma* is not so different from other forms of religion as is sometimes said. Many Muslim writers have seen Christianity as having a restricted vision because it regards religion as a private matter for the individual. But such a view ignores the extent to which there have been, and still are, Christian states, and the number of Muslim states where the government is largely secular, even though Islam is the state religion.

The reality is that day-to-day political rule is in fact largely concerned with matters not covered by the requirements of religious law, and where it is directly relevant that law is not necessarily vastly different from the universal human ideal of a democratic, egalitarian, and just society. The call for an 'Islamic state' largely arises out of the rejection of Western colonialism, and the perceived failure of 'modernizing' or secularizing governments to establish just and prosperous societies. The crucial areas of disagreement with secular states—legal processes and penalties, family law, different treatment of men and women, educational programmes, and the privileged position of Muslim faith and practice—are all disputed within Islam itself. If a secular state is viewed, not as one that rejects the authority of God, but as one which declines to favour one religious tradition over others, and preserves strict impartiality between religious institutions, Muslims can live in such a state, as the community of the Book of God, a community with its own communal laws on specific matters. If the Muslim community becomes the majority, then one can have a Muslim state, though the full freedom of other faiths should be assured, together with the acceptance that either individuals or the state may change allegiance, freely and conscientiously.

The critical choice for Islam in the modern world is whether it will opt for a set of Islamic states, armed to defend themselves against 'non-Islamic influences', or whether it will aim to be a universal or international community of divine law, striving for justice and fellowship under many different forms of government. The former choice would probably bring it into conflict with those forces which make for freedom of religion and democratic government. The latter choice is the only one compatible with the existence of Islam as a truly world religion, which can coexist with other faiths on an equal basis. One might expect, then, that those strong economic and social pressures making for greater global interaction and interdependence will lead to the latter path, which is arguably in any case most true to the spirit of Islam as a religion of justice and peace.

It may be very important to stress that the perfect state will only exist with the coming of the Mahdi, so that no actual Muslim state can be equated with a perfectly just society. Where both the diversity and imperfection of Muslim communities are recognized, and where it is clearly seen that the non-existence of a truly global *umma* requires an accommodation and, where possible, co-operation with differing world-views, one can no longer speak of a 'true Islamic society', in conflict with a world of *kafir*s, unbelievers (which may include most Muslims who disagree with one's own view). However, one must be aware that the faith will always present a temptation to such ways of thinking, and to the extent that it is misused to try to produce a 'true Islamic state' here and now, Islam will always contain the potential for violence and divisiveness, even though its declared aim and central message is one of peace and unity.

It is hard to see, however, how any religion which is seriously concerned with issues of social justice and with ways of developing integrity and harmony in personal relationships, could avoid being involved in all those disputes and corruptions which mark human social relationships. Religions do not offer perfect alternatives to actually existing social structures, and do not magically transform human ambitions and motives. The goal of the believer should thus be to strengthen those aspects of religious faith which make for human reconciliation and fulfilment, and to build social structures which make a sensitive, informed, and intelligent grasp of religious truth possible. Islam may contain the potential for violence and division, just because human beings do. But it is fundamentally founded upon the goal of a universal society of peace, compassion, and unity that will reflect the nature of God in the human world. That is part of its enduring greatness and surely also, any believer in God may rightly say, a divine revelation for the whole world, Muslim and non-Muslim alike.

3
Buddhism and the *Sangha*

SUFFERING AND DESIRE

What is so striking about Judaism and Islam is their undaunted optimism about human society in the face of almost overwhelming contrary evidence. Human societies throughout history are filled with violence, conflict, destruction, and debauchery, but Jews and Muslims on the whole continue to believe that a society of justice and peace is possible, even that they will be instrumental in bringing it about, and that with a little effort all people could obey the laws of God.

Buddhism has no such optimistic hopes. For most Buddhists, the whole structure of human society is doomed to failure, to endless suffering and frustrated desire. Buddhists do not seek to bring the world under the rule of the laws of God. There is no Creator God, and if there were, a God who could create such a world of suffering as this would not be entitled to obedience as an ultimate moral authority. Social laws are human constructs, and they can do no more than mitigate to some extent the conflicts engendered by that greed, hatred, and ignorance which are the universal marks of human nature.

It might be said that Buddhists are so pessimistic about human society that they see no point in trying to construct a perfect social system. There is every point in trying to decrease the suffering of all sentient beings, but no social rules or policies are going to accomplish that. So Buddhism stands at the opposite pole of religious attitudes to human society from Judaism and Islam, the religions of obedience to divine law. In that sense, Buddhism is a religion of withdrawal from, and opposition to, the world of human culture and political organization.

There is a Buddhist social organization, the *sangha*, the community of monks or nuns. But it is a community that renounces the world and its concerns entirely, and has as its ultimate goal the transcendence of the world and of personal individuality in the attainment of nirvana, the ultimate bliss beyond action and self-interested desire.

Almost by definition, the *sangha* is for the few, although it is intended to influence all, and to spread compassion throughout society. Its requirements are severe, and not intended to apply to all people. Indeed, it is essential to the survival of the *sangha* that there should be householders, who marry, have children, and produce food and clothing. Householders will provide the necessities of life for the *bikkhu*s, the monks, who must survive by being given their food, without possessions or the attachments of family life.

The *sangha* (which I shall hereafter call the Community) originated with the Buddha, who gathered a group of disciples around him, and such Communities have been in existence ever since. There are two main traditions, the Theravada (now mainly existing in Sri Lanka, Thailand, and Burma), and the Mahayana (which is strongest in Japan). There are Communities in Tibet, China, Vietnam, North Korea, Laos, and Cambodia, which have suffered varying degrees of persecution in the twentieth century, and there are many Communities in the Western world, partly as a result of that persecution.

Lay followers of the Buddhist way often undertake five precepts—vowing not to kill, steal, have improper sexual relations, lie, or become intoxicated.[1] Monks intensify these precepts, vowing to abstain from harming any sentient life so far as is possible, not to take what is not freely given, and not to have sexual relations at all. They take a further five vows—not to eat after noon, not to dance, sing, or attend unseemly shows, not to use things which adorn the body, not to use 'high' (luxurious) beds or seats, and not to handle money.

The rationale behind these precepts is that one should renounce all activity that causes harm to any sentient being, and that one should renounce all activity which binds one to the world through desire and attachment, or which threatens that constant mindfulness and full attention which should characterize the life of one on the way to liberation. In renouncing the causing of harm, one is counteracting that hatred that characterizes so much of human life, and that arises from seeing the desires of others as in competition with one's own desires. In renouncing attachment, one is counter-

---

[1] An excellent exposition of the precepts is in Peter Harvey, *An Introduction to Buddhism* (Cambridge: Cambridge University Press, 1990), 199–208.

acting the greed that tends to inflame human desires beyond what is rationally controllable. In insisting on mindfulness, one is counteracting that ignorance or delusion that arises from failing to see reality as it is, and taking transitory pleasures to be satisfactory goals of human endeavour. So the five precepts are intended to counteract the three fires that bind human life—greed, hatred, and ignorance— and that inevitably bring suffering into the human world.[2]

Buddhism sees itself as a middle way between a life of sensuality and a life of total asceticism such as is found in the Jain ideal of the naked ascetic. Buddhist monks wear simple robes, eat what is given to them, and live in a Community of mutual support and friendship. They do not seek to torture the body by flagellation or starvation, or to perform extraordinary penances. Living a life of great simplicity, they seek that sense of selflessness and non-attachment that is conducive to liberation from the bondage of suffering.

The idea of 'conduciveness' or 'skilfulness' is central to a Buddhist view of social life. Given the basic insight that human life is filled with suffering, and that suffering is caused by grasping desire, it follows that the ending of suffering is to be brought about by the rooting out of grasping desire. What is to be sought is the most skilful way to extinguish desire. That may depend upon the personality and situation of the individual, and various means, from the hope of a reward in a heavenly world or the fear of a miserable rebirth, to devotion to a great spiritual teacher or the correct performance of ritual acts, may be appropriate in different cases. The life of the monk is for those who are ready to move on to that more complete renunciation that will break all ties with the world of the desires, and liberate one from the realm of suffering, never to return.

Belief in rebirth and in karma has been an important part of Buddhist belief. It is often taught that each person has had innumerable births in this world, and has inhabited virtually every form of sentient life. One form of Buddhist meditation is to think that every sentient being has in some life been one's own mother.[3] There is a real kinship between all sentient beings, since every insect and animal either has been or will be a human being, and one will be wise to treat them as one would treat oneself.

---

[2] Cf. the 'fire sermon', in *Vinaya Pitaka* (*The Book of the Discipline*), trans. I. B. Horner (London: Pali Text Society, 1938), i. 34–5.

[3] Cf. *Samyutta Nikaya* (*The Book of Kindred Sayings*), trans. Rhys Davids and F. L. Woodward (London: Pali Text Society, 1917), ii. 189–90.

Every being has the birth and life-pattern it does because of its accumulated karma, but this is not to be understood as an explicit reward or punishment for some fully conscious exercise of moral responsibility. It is rather a natural working-out of the consequences of desires, and the various forms which those desires take. There is no god who requires one to act in a specific way and devises punishments for failure to comply. It is rather that if one allows desires of a certain type to dominate one's life, one will be involved in future existences in which those desires continue to work themselves out in ways which, sooner or later, engender the specific forms of suffering which they cause by their inner nature. On the other hand, if one becomes free of desires, then the suffering which is part of the natural pattern of causality is cut off and ended. Free from suffering, one can live calm and at ease in a state of selfless bliss. The wheel of causality has been stopped, at least in part, and one will be born no more. That is the ultimate goal of the life of the monk, and it gives the rationale for the existence of the Buddhist Community.

Would that rationale continue to exist if there were no rebirth? Although it has been an important part of Buddhist belief, the idea of rebirth is in some ways in tension with the central Buddhist belief in *anatta*, selflessness. After all, to hope for a better birth in the next life is a form of prudence, and is that not a subtle form of attachment to a particular self and concern for its future? A common Buddhist way of dealing with this paradox is to say that householders require the thought of a better rebirth as an incentive to seek release from sorrow. But those on the path to enlightenment have passed beyond all sense of self, and seek only to end one chain of sufferings by resolute action.

Believing that there is no enduring self, Buddhists see the nature of the chains of causality which bind together the five elements of which our transient selves are constituted, and how passions have psychic consequences that have the nature of unease or suffering. This is true, in general, for all sentient beings, so the Buddhist sees all sentient beings as conglomerates of psychic forces—thoughts, desires, and sensations—which are interconnected throughout the natural world. The monk does not seek personal pleasure, but the decrease of suffering in the world, in the most effective way possible.

The starting-point of Buddhist morality is thus an insight into the interrelations of all things, and the causal link between specific desires and specific sorts of suffering. There is no idea of a commanding moral will, or some sort of absolute categorical obligation, calling for action simply for the sake of duty. One needs to begin with a close attention to the psychological forces within human life, to what makes for sorrow and what makes for happiness. Buddhist insights into the nature of these forces, and the causal chains which link them, form the basis for adopting a way of life that will break the causal links and liberate sentient beings from sorrow.

Does desire inevitably cause suffering? And does renunciation of desire offer freedom from suffering? Common sense might well accept that there is a link between the passions of greed and hatred and the existence of suffering, and that a calm and mindful life is apt to bring happiness. Yet it does not seem to be universally true that attachment as such inevitably brings suffering. If I love another person deeply, I may be sad at the thought that our friendship may one day end. But it would be odd to let my happiness be clouded by the constant thought of such an ending. I may be wise to determine not to let my life be totally devastated by the loss of a friend. Yet it might not be wise to eschew friendship because of the possibility of its loss.

In any case, it might be said that in such cases it is not the desire which causes the suffering. Suffering is caused by death, for instance, which is a perfectly natural process, not affected by my desires or lack of them. It may well be true that I would not suffer grief if I had not loved. Yet my love does not cause the grief. Furthermore, my love may be valued more, just because it is known that its loss would cause grief—how could we truly love someone for whom we did not mourn?

So love often is followed by grief, but many people would not say that love should therefore be given up. To this extent, a common-sense view may say that there are good desires, even attachments, that do not cause sorrow, though they will often bring sorrow in their train. It is even possible to have a love that is not thwarted by tragic loss. Such lives may be fortunate and rare, but they may also be thought desirable—in which case it would not be true that desire is universally a cause of inescapable sorrow.

Moreover, the renunciation of desire does not always bring happiness. Perhaps only a certain sort of personality can find happiness in renunciation. Not everyone would enjoy being a monk, and there are plenty of miserable, bored monks, as well as many contented householders, who may live simply but do not wholly renounce attachments.

It seems that if one dispenses with belief in rebirth, the basis of Buddhist morality is weakened, and though it would not be destroyed, it might be restricted in scope. It might just say that excessive attachments are unlikely to bring happiness, and that a certain degree of renunciation or simplicity of living is conducive to calm and contentment, if such states seem desirable. The Buddhist ethic would be reduced to a set of prescriptions for people of modest ambition and a desire for a comfortable life, a sort of utilitarian ethic for the middle classes.

It is obvious that Buddhism is not that. The Buddhist ethic seems to most householders to be rather a heroic degree of renunciation (even if it is supposed not to be extreme), aiming at a goal that is hardly even conceivable for the average person. So there does seem to be in Buddhist ethics a necessary element of belief in rebirth, or at the very least in an afterlife in which self-regarding desires are causally linked to suffering, and in which it is possible to overcome such desires and achieve nirvana, a state of supreme happiness. The doctrines of rebirth and karmic law are the ways in which Buddhist thought typically construes these preconditions of Buddhist morality.

The doctrine of rebirth also explains the very different levels of spiritual aspiration and attainment that characterize human beings. Buddhism naturally suggests a hierarchical view of human society, for which beings of great passion are spiritually inferior to beings who find renunciation easy. A sort of caste system is a plausible corollary of belief in rebirth and karma—and yet one of the distinctive features of Buddhism is its rejection of the brahminical priesthood. What is rejected is that externalization of hierarchy which decrees that a person belongs to the highest, priestly, caste by birth, not by inherent spiritual attainment. Thus the Buddha taught, not that there are no brahmins, but that the true brahmin is the one whose desires are pure and calm, whose inner nature is that of a spiritual teacher.[4] The spiritual hierarchy of Buddhism is not ascribed because of birth. Anyone may become a monk. Yet if they do, it is because they have spent many lives preparing for the great good fortune of being born into a society where the life of a monk will be possible for them.

---

[4] *Sutta-Nipata*, iii. 621 trans. H. Saddhatissa (Richmond, Va.: Curzon, 1994), 72.

It is natural to think, then, that Buddhist morality is founded on a subtle form of prudence. Given the fact of rebirth, of the inevitable generation of suffering by desire, and of the possibility of release from suffering by renunciation, it is simply good sense either to seek a better future birth by accumulating merit, or, if one is able, to seek total release by entering the Community. Most Buddhists would not reject the simple desire to avoid personal suffering as a motivation to follow the path of renunciation, but they would place it very low on the scale of human insight. Prudence is not the main motivation for a Buddhist ethic.

In meditation one quickly comes to realize that it is not one's own future suffering that is important, but the fact that the whole world, with all its sentient beings, is bound to the wheel of suffering. Rebirth is not really a way in which one continues to exist, as just the individual one is, with a particular concern for the sufferings and happiness of that individual—that would be, for a Buddhist, the error of 'eternalism'.[5] Rebirth is rather a way in which the causal connections between desire and suffering can be worked out. It is the fact that one's present desires cause future suffering for some sentient being that is important. It is not important that the future suffering being is oneself. Indeed, such a sense of continuing selfhood is strongly discouraged in almost all Buddhist schools.

In this way, belief in personal rebirth to some extent recedes in importance. My hatred and greed and ignorance may not produce more suffering to me than would naturally accrue in any case. But they will certainly produce suffering for sentient beings, and if I do not see that, I fail to see things as they truly are. Similarly, renunciation of hatred, greed, and ignorance may not bring great happiness to me personally, but it will certainly lessen the suffering of sentient beings.

It can also be said that there are desires, like some forms of love for another, which do not generate suffering, and such desires are not to be renounced, but rather to be cultivated, once their proper form has been found. The sorts of desires which bind to the wheel of suffering are classified under the heading of 'craving' (*tanha*), which has the sense of thirst. So one might properly refer to these as 'selfish

[5] *Milindapanha* (*Milinda's Questions*), trans. I. B. Horner (London: Pali Text Society, 1963), 40.

desires', which seek gratification for the agent, not as desires for things of objective value.

It is not prudence that leads one to renounce greed, hatred and ignorance, but the realization that they produce suffering for many sentient beings. It is out of compassion for sentient beings that one should seek to renounce the sorts of desires that cause them to suffer. Compassion is aroused by a clear and impartial knowledge of what suffering is, of where it exists, and of how it can be eliminated. Such a moral outlook is founded neither on prudence nor on obedience to some objective moral law, but on clear realization of the nature of suffering and its causes.

IS BUDDHISM WORLD-DENYING?

Buddhism is often seen by its critics as having a negative approach to life, concerned with renouncing rather than with positive action and enjoyment. Such a judgement would, however, miss the ultimate goal of Buddhism, which is the liberation from sorrow into boundless bliss, the bliss of nirvana. While one can refrain from harming other beings, one cannot attain for them boundless bliss. That lies in the cultivation of mental states which must be engendered by long practice. Even though one seeks nirvana for oneself, however, this cannot be considered a self-interested practice.

One aim of meditation is the cultivation of the four mental states known as the 'immeasurables' (*brahma-viharas*).[6] These are equanimity (*upekkha*) arising from the realization that suffering and joy are both inescapable parts of existence; compassion (*karuna*), the desire that beings should be free from suffering; sympathetic joy (*mudita*), happiness in the joy of others; and lovingkindness (*metta*), desire for the happiness of all beings. The meditator seeks to extend these feelings to all sentient beings without exception. There could hardly be a more unselfish practice than this, and it is concerned with the happiness of others as well as with their liberation from suffering. The *Sutta-Nipata* says: 'let his thoughts of boundless love pervade the whole world'.[7]

At this point one might almost say that Buddhist ethics is utilitarian: it considers what will make for the greatest happiness of the greatest number. At least it makes the reasonable assumption that

---

[6] Harvey, *Buddhism*, 209.   [7] *Sutta-Nipata*, i. 150 (p. 16).

beings wish to escape from suffering and be happy. Classical utilitarians often suppose that happiness lies in whatever people think makes them happy. As Jeremy Bentham said, 'Pushpin is as good as poetry,' if it makes you just as happy. Thus utilitarians try to weigh the intensity and duration of various types of pleasure against one another, to discover what the 'greatest happiness' is. Buddhists, however, would regard most people as in the grip of ignorance about the sources of true happiness. What is required is insight into the nature of happiness and the causes of suffering.

It follows that it is virtually impossible for a Buddhist to devise a social policy based on procuring the greatest happiness of the greatest number. For the greatest happiness lies only in the renunciation of attachment, whereas the greatest number are bound to attachments of many kinds. It is true that the greatest true happiness of the greatest number would lie in their renunciation of greed, hatred, and sensuality, but that is never going to happen.

The best one can do is to aim at forms of social convention and constraint which are most conducive to renunciation, given the prevailing circumstances, to aim at a society which will not inflame greed, hatred, and acquisitiveness. The way to true happiness, cutting off the chains of desire, must lie in the Community, which will be a society within a society, wherein alone ultimate happiness can be found.

Again, this may sound paradoxically selfish, as though the monk was devoted to the pursuit of happiness for himself alone. But what the monk, like the utilitarian, aims at is not simply personal happiness, but the greatest possible happiness of all—the welfare of all sentient beings. If happiness can be gained only by renunciation of selfish desire, no one can finally accomplish that on behalf of someone else. One can aim not to harm other beings, to teach them the way of release, and to offer them the support of the Community that will encourage renunciation, but they must take that way themselves. So monks have always gone out to preach and to show by example the way to the ending of sorrow. They do not realistically expect that many people will join the Community, but people in general may nevertheless be influenced by its common life.

In Theravada Buddhism, there is a sincere wish that all beings should be delivered from suffering, but in the end each being must accomplish deliverance for themselves, by their 'own' power. Nevertheless, the Buddha teaches that monks should 'take to the road: travel for the good of the many; travel for the happiness of the many, out of compassion for the world'.[8]

In Mahayana Buddhism, there is a much greater emphasis on the way in which liberated beings can positively help others. The *boddhisattva* vow is that one will aim for the release of all suffering beings, and the compassionate *boddhisattva*s positively help their devotees by surrounding them with compassionate lovingkindness, and even by delivering them from concrete perils such as poverty and storms.[9]

Perhaps the most crucial Mahayana doctrine is that of *sunyata*, emptiness. This can be interpreted in many ways, but it has the minimal meaning that nothing possesses inherent or substantial self-supporting existence. The whole world is a flux of ever-changing and interdependent phenomena. When one sees that this is the case, one no longer distinguishes between 'self' and 'other', since both are conceptual constructs on a common stream of experienced phenomena.

This leads to a doctrine of the unreality or dreamlike quality of the world. There is no underlying substantial reality. Or if there is, it cannot be spoken of in any conceptual terms, and so one cannot even distinguish conceptually between nirvana and samsara, between liberated existence and illusory existence. 'There is not the slightest bit of difference between the two.'[10] To make such a distinction would be to erect a conceptual duality, and therefore to misunderstand the non-duality of things. This world of hatred and greed is at the same time a world of compassion and unlimited freedom. One does not seek to pass beyond the world to some higher realm. One seeks to live in the world as part of the pure shining flow that expresses the nature of the real.

This is a deeply paradoxical view of the world, but it is not negative in any obvious sense. Ethical action flows naturally from insight into the true nature of things. For once one sees that 'self' is a construct, and transcends it, there is nothing to which one can be attached, and nothing to attach it to. Seen thus, morality is basically a matter of a change of attitude, a new vision of the world. It is not at

---

[8] *Vinaya-Pitaka*, ed. H. Oldenberg (London: Pali Text Society, 1964–82), 20–1.
[9] *Astasahasrikaprajnaparamita* (*The Perfection of Wisdom*), trans. E. Conze (Bolinas: Four Seasons Foundation, 1973), 163.
[10] Nagarjuna, 'Madhyamakakarikah', 25. 20, in J. W. de Jong (ed.), *Mulamadhyamakarikah* (Madras: Adyar Library, 1977).

all a matter of effort and struggle. One simply has to uncover one's inherent Buddha-nature, and by drawing aside the illusions of self, to merge with the flow of reality in its inherent shining purity. This is not prudence, it is not a concern to maximize whatever people happen to call pleasure, and it is not a determination of the will to do what is right, whatever the cost. It is an entrance into a state of consciousness where the self and its concerns fade away and are replaced by the spontaneity of the liberated life of compassion and joy, 'by nature brightly shining and pure'.[11]

Because, in these forms of Buddhism, there is no ultimate distinction between samsara and nirvana, the world-denying renunciation of Theravada, seeking to escape this world of greed, hatred, and delusion, can be transformed into a world-affirming vision of a fully liberated, happy, and successful life in human society. This has happened in Japan and to some extent in China, where original Buddhism has been mixed with large doses of Taoism, Confucianism, or Shinto. Organizations such as Soka Gakkai in Japan seek to wield political influence and encourage positive value-creation in society. They tend to blur the distinction between monks and laity, allowing marriage to priest-monks and preaching liberation for all by devotion to various holy beings.

The real basis for Buddhist ethics, therefore, is insight into the nature of reality, from which moral action will naturally flow. However, the precepts of morality also outline parts of the path, the eightfold way, practice of which is needed to lead to that rather rare insight. There is thus a twofold approach to ethical matters. At one level, moral rules are means by which the self is trained in the way of liberation from sorrow. At a higher level, rules are transcended, and joyful, compassionate, mindful, and loving action flows naturally from the attainment of transcendental insight into the true nature of things.

For this reason, the Buddhas are sometimes said to be able even to do evil acts out of compassion. It would, however, be fatal to pretend that people at a lower level of attainment could do similar things. This two-level (or many-level) view is central to Buddhist practice. One can begin moral practice out of personal desire for happiness (for a better rebirth), or out of respect for a Buddha or teacher, who tells one how to act, or out of compassion for the suffering of others.

---

[11] *Lankavatara Sutra*, trans. D. T. Suzuki (London: Routledge, 1973), 77.

That practice, together with meditation and training of the mind, can lead to a state in which one will act selflessly and with compassionate wisdom, because one has seen that there is no self and there are no others, that the ultimate emptiness of all things is identical with the Pure Mind which is free from all taints and defilements.

At no level is moral practice an end in itself, a duty that stands opposed to desire. The central motivation lies in what one might call an existential knowledge of human existence, in one's grasp of the values and disvalues which are involved in human life, in one's grasp of the conditions of human life and one's affective response to them. For the Buddhist, most people will understand their lives as opportunities for various sorts of sensory pleasure, the satisfaction of being praised by others, or the exercise of power over others. They will be in the grip of selfish desires, and they will reap the consequences of their understanding. Just as scientific insight can give a deeper view of the sensory world and lead one to see its underlying structure, so existential insight can give a deeper view of human desires and their fruits. Pleasure, praise, and power can be seen to be empty, to bring no lasting satisfaction, and even to distract one from what gives real significance to life.

THE CENTRAL VALUES OF BUDDHIST ETHICS

The Buddhist way is a way of reflecting on what gives value to existence, and on what is ultimately shallow and insignificant. A Buddhist would not be surprised to be told that people might disagree about what gives value to existence. Buddhists expect people to disagree on these things, since most people are in the grip of illusion, lacking insight. An enlightened person, a Buddha, is one who can present the highest values of existence in an attractive way, who calls disciples to seek to embody those values, and who teaches the way to the ending of sorrow.

Those values are freedom from the compulsions of selfish desire and passion, wisdom to see things as they truly are, in their interdependence and transitoriness, knowledge of the sufferings of beings and the way to end them, happiness in the knowledge that suffering is overcome, and compassion for all sentient beings who are still in the bondage of greed, hatred, and ignorance. 'One who has overcome all, who knows all, who is intelligent, who does not cling to any object, who has abandoned everything, who has freed himself by destroying desire, is called a sage by the wise.'[12] The Community of monks is the society of those who have undertaken to pursue these states of mind, and so to seek a life of supreme and imperishable value.[13]

A consideration of these central values of Buddhism will illustrate some of the main similarities and differences between the Buddhist view of ethics and that of the Abrahamic traditions of Judaism and Islam. All people, it may reasonably be claimed, have the desire for freedom. Such a desire may begin as a simple desire for power, for freedom from the constraints other people place upon one. Deeper insight will disclose that true freedom is freedom from selfish desire, including the desire for such power. Freedom will be found in the equanimity of one who is no longer dominated by anxiety for the future or regret for the past, who is self-possessed and liberated from sorrow. Especially in Mahayana literature, such freedom is not merely a freedom from desires. It includes the power to intuit the thoughts of others, to help them in compassionate ways, and even to create a Buddha-realm in which many beings can be set on the path to Buddha-realization. If Buddhism has no Creator God, it has sometimes developed the idea, especially in the Yogacara schools,[14] of worlds created by compassionate Buddhas, overlaid by defilements of selfish desire, and yet offering and promising ultimate liberation to all sentient beings in those worlds.

The power to dominate others has become the power to help all sentient beings in ways which respect their own life-choices. It is developing insight into the true nature of power that brings about this transformation, and such insight is learned through many lifetimes of experience. The ultimate power of the enlightened sage is the power that has no needs to fulfil, no reason to seek to dominate or oppress others, no objects which have to be possessed before one can be satisfied. Thus it is a power that is realized solely in aiding others to come to the same liberation in which one participates, the power of unlimited compassion. It is a combination of experience and insight that transforms this universal human desire for some degree of power over one's own life into compassion for all sentient beings, and the creation of worlds in which they can achieve the

---

[12] *Sutta-Nipata*, i. 211 (p. 22).

[13] A good exposition of Buddhist ethics is: W. Saddhatissa, *Buddhist Ethics* (London: Allen & Unwin, 1970).

[14] For a brief explanation of the Yogacara teaching, cf. Harvey, *Buddhism*, 104–13.

highest possible bliss and knowledge. So Amithaba creates the Pure Land of the West, for the sake of those bound to sorrow, who may be born there because his power is sufficient even to obliterate the causal chains of karma.[15]

Wisdom, too, is a universally desired quality, in the sense that no one, on reflection, wishes to act in ways that will entail suffering. The lowest level of desired wisdom is the prudential knowledge that will enable one to avoid extreme suffering in the near future. Increasing insight brings one to see the subtle links between attachment and suffering, and so leads one to a higher wisdom, which discerns that it is the root desires themselves which must be transcended, if suffering is to be avoided. Everyone desires the wisdom to avoid suffering; only the enlightened see what such wisdom entails, the cessation of grasping desire.

The basic Buddhist perception is that there are universally desired values, and indeed that ultimate values are nothing more than what is universally desired. But such universal desires take many forms, and exist at many levels of insight and understanding. The tragedy of human existence is that universally acknowledged values are understood at a naïve and short-sighted level, so that the desire for power and for prudential efficiency are pursued, instead of the desire to show universal compassion, in the knowledge of the consequences of passionate and uncontrolled desire.

No one would deny that knowledge is a value, a thing to be desired, if it is pointed out that lack of knowledge will usually lead to disaster. But humans may shrink from the full implications of having a knowledge of existence that is fully open to all the suffering and pain that exists in the world. Ignorance is bliss, if it insulates one from the pain of sentient beings bound to the wheel of sorrow. So humans desire enough knowledge to save themselves from pain, but suppress knowledge of the suffering that their actions cause throughout the world. Once again, it is insight into the deep interconnections of things that discloses that even a knowledge of what will save an individual from pain needs to take into account the ultimate causes of pain for all sentient creation, and thereby overturns the thought that my happiness can be accomplished without consideration for the pain of others. The key is, once again, insight,

---

[15] Cf. *Sukhavativyuha Sutra*, in *Buddhist Mahayana Texts*, trans. E. B. Cowell (New York: Dover, 1969).

as one is led from consideration of what will benefit me to the consideration of what could end the suffering of every sentient being. Such insight is rare, but what is central to the Buddhist view of morality is that it is insight and its absence which is at stake, not some incomprehensible choosing of evil for its own sake over a clearly perceived good.

How is it possible not to desire insight, true knowledge of the nature of things? Because gratification is stronger than understanding, the thirst for pleasure is stronger than the perception of truth. All people desire knowledge, but only enough to make pleasure possible. Nevertheless, the desire for knowledge, once aroused, will ultimately disclose that truth, and not pleasure, is the final and proper object of the human mind.

Happiness, too, is something that everyone desires, but conceptions of happiness are as diverse as human life itself. Aristotle said that true happiness, for humans, lies in the exercise of those excellences which are proper to human existence.[16] Buddhists would not quite put it like that. Yet the underlying thought is the same, that true happiness lies in the discovery of the true nature of what it is to exist as a human being. At first people may seek happiness in sensual pleasure of various sorts, but they will come to see that such pleasure suffers the defects of transitoriness, loss, and eventual disillusionment. Insight discloses that only the cessation of grasping brings secure and abiding contentment of mind, and the enlightened person will desire such happiness for all sentient beings, regarding them with loving kindness, and desiring their release from the bondage of selfish desire. 'Whoever is allowed the pleasures of the five senses does not . . . lead an ascetic life.'[17]

Finally, humans are social animals. We depend in many ways upon others, and find much satisfaction and pain in the way they regard us. We spend much time trying to get the good opinion of others, or at least of those others we admire. Or we may be consumed by the thirst for revenge for some real or imagined slight. Envy of the good fortune of others, pride in one's own superior position, maliciousness, and fear are the marks of much human social life, so that, as Jean-Paul Sartre wrote, 'Hell is other people.' Social

---

[16] Aristotle, *Nicomachean Ethics*, 1098ᵃ8–27, trans. J. A. K. Thomson (London: Penguin, 1976), 76.
[17] *Vinaya-Pitaka*, II. 297.

life is often a continual competition either to dominate others or to be wholly dominated by them, either dehumanizing the lives of others, or losing one's own responsibility and self-respect altogether.

There are various ways of coping with the unsatisfactoriness of social life. The Buddhist way is to renounce involvement in society at large, and become as self-sufficient as possible, not relying for happiness upon others, and not being upset by what others think. Yet no human being can exist solely alone, and in the Community, with its ordered discipline and companionship of those devoted to the same life of renunciation, to study, chanting, and meditation, one can be sustained in a life devoted to attaining freedom from attachment to the opinions of others.

Within the Community, monks do care about the good opinion of others. Before the half-monthly *uposatha* ceremony, at which monks recite the rules of the *patimokkha*, the code of monastic discipline, they ask the community whether they have committed any faults of discipline, and they confess such faults either before the gathering or, more usually, before some senior monk. 'Whoever has committed an offence must declare it.'[18] The Community is both a supportive and a disciplinary body, though the punishments for offences, at their most severe, only involve such things as refusing to talk to or advise offenders, or expulsion from the Community, not anything physical or retributive.

Monks are also closely bound to the wider human society, since they depend upon householders for food and shelter, and in return they teach the way to release, and often exercise a pastoral role, especially at funerals and occasions of importance in village life. Monks are commanded to live not too far from towns and not too near them. Their very presence gives occasion for merit-making activities by householders, and it reminds householders of the higher way that leads to final release. 'The Community of disciples . . . is worthy of offerings, worthy of hospitality, worthy of gifts, worthy of respect, the greatest field of merit for the world.'[19] Renunciation is not just leaving society completely behind; it points the way to true happiness and wisdom for all beings, and in this sense the Community exhibits compassion for wider society.

---

[18] *Vinaya-Pitaka*, III. 175.
[19] *Diga Nikaya* (*Dialogues of the Buddha*), trans. T. W. and C. A. F. Rhys Davids (London: Pali Text Society, 1921), iii. 227.

Monks practise extending the mental attitudes of compassion and sympathetic joy to the whole world. It is not usual for them to undertake work of any sort, since that is not seen as fitting for one who has renounced all attachment. Yet in Mahayana traditions, monks vow to defer liberation until they have helped to lead all beings to release, and the laity are often encouraged to undertake works of practical compassion, in hospitals, education, and social work. In considering what work they should do, Buddhist laymen and women are not to accept any employment which involves pain or harm to sentient life. They should not, for instance, be butchers or arms manufacturers. There is thus a pressure on them to be involved in society in ways that bring practical benefit to others. Since the Community cannot exist without wider society, it is not true that Buddhism has no ethic of practical social reform, though it is true that such work must be undertaken by the laity, and the higher way, explicitly for the few, is the way of renunciation.

All humans have an interest in creating a stable society which can enable them to pursue their plans in relative freedom and achieve a reasonable degree of security and happiness. So everyone has a good reason to require minimal rules of justice, and to create sanctions for breaking the rules. The Buddhist will realize that all such rules can be no more than external constraints upon human desires, and that lasting freedom and happiness can be attained only by moving to a higher level of understanding. The Community of universal compassion must remove itself from the social world of competing and disordered desires, yet remain near enough to that world to keep the way of liberation open to all who may wish to pursue it. Moreover, since not all can be monks, many laity will pursue the practice of compassion and lovingkindness in their daily lives. It is said to be possible for a householder to become an *arahant*, a liberated being, though it is hard and rare.

There are lay Buddhist organizations, such as Soka Gakkai in Japan, that encourage welfare programmes, exercise political influence, and give advice on family life and social values. The Western Buddhist Order is another example of the way in which the strict discipline of the Community can be modified for married people, and Buddhism can become a way of meditation and mental discipline for those, both men and women, who are not members of the traditional Community. Such an extension of Buddhist values to the laity sometimes goes along with a fairly radical change in how liberation is conceived. In both Pure Land and Nichiren schools of Buddhism, nirvana is no longer seen as a supreme achievement after many life-times of disciplined renunciation. By the grace of a compassionate *boddhisattva*, one can achieve liberation into a Pure Land of bliss and knowledge, just by the sincere repetition of the name of a Buddha, or of a mantra of devotion to the Lotus Sutra.[20] In this way, the basic values of Buddhism can be reoriented so that even Samurai warriors can benefit from the practice of *zazen* meditation, and success in business and in love can be assured by the practice of chanting. Just as, for some Mahayana schools, nirvana becomes identical with sam-sara, so the life of the enlightened sage may be seen as identical with the life of the householder. Of course, householders will in some sense still have to live a 'renounced' life, a life of non-attachment, wisdom, and compassion for all beings, and their ultimate happiness will lie, not in success or pleasure as such, but in the enlightened per-ception of the pure, empty flow of existence. In this sense, the Com-munity may be extended to include all those who pursue the insight into the nature of human values which Gautama taught.

This sort of movement has also taken place in the Theravadin tradition of Sri Lanka. It has been called 'Protestant Buddhism',[21] and though that term is strongly denied by many, one can see why it is not a wholly inappropriate term to point to the increased empha-sis on lay participation in a wider Buddhist community. It might be said that the Community has always contained such a possibility, for the Pali texts refer to 'the fourfold assembly' of monks, nuns, male, and female lay followers who exist in due dependence on one another. None the less, there can be no doubt that Gautama estab-lished the original Community as one of monks (and later of nuns) who renounce all family, work, and ownership, and it is a large revi-sion of Buddhism to hold that the normal way of liberation is not to be found with such a monastic Community.

BUDDHISM AND THE ABRAHAMIC TRADITIONS

The Abrahamic traditions of Judaism and Islam can be sharply con-trasted with the renouncing tradition of Buddhism. The former seek to obey the laws of God, which are not questioned in detail, but must

---

[20] Cf. Lotus Sutra, trans. K. Tsugunari and Y. Akira (Berkeley: Numata Center for Buddhist Translation, 1993), ch. 24.

[21] Cf. Richard Gombrich, *Theravada Buddhism* (Routledge, 1988), ch. 7.

simply be accepted on the authority of the Creator of the universe. The latter rejects any idea of divine moral law, and appeals instead to natural human desires, and developing personal insight into the way of realizing them in a fully satisfying way. The former stress the importance of living in society, of marriage and family, of social justice and mercy, and of working actively to realize the potential goodness of the created order. The latter calls for a renunciation of family, of possessions, and of work, a turning away from a world of suffering to the realm of the deathless, which cannot be described in conceptual terms at all. The former see religious obedience as the key to establishing a just and peaceful society, which will eventually come into being, if only by the intervention of God. The latter sees human society as endlessly immersed in selfish desire, greed and hatred, and privileges a Community in which discipline and the cultivation of higher mental states is a goal which can only be attained by few, seeking to 'work out their own salvation with diligence'.

The contrast seems total, and indeed in China Buddhism was opposed by the Confucian philosophy of hard work and involvement in a highly regulated social life in which the individual was largely subordinated to the requirements of the state. Confucianism is hardly Abrahamic, but it stresses in an analogous way the importance of social life and obedience to law, as opposed to the way of the renouncer who seeks individual insight, and who is largely indifferent to the pressures of technological and economic planning and research. Confucianism has in turn been overtaken in China by a Marxist ethic which is, in theory, much less hierarchical and tradition-bound, but which shares the ideal of a harmonious society in which individuals must contribute materially to the common good and participate fully in social and political life. In the face of such an ideology, the Buddhist Community is seen as socially backward, economically unproductive, and ensnared in primitive superstition and useless introspection.

Buddhism has fared particularly badly at the hands both of Muslim invaders in India and, in this century, of Marxist forces from the Chinese People's Republic. In the Theravadin countries of Thailand, Sri Lanka, and Burma, Buddhism exists in societies in which there is rapid industrialization or severe political unrest. Because the ordination line died out, there is no obvious way in which Theravada nuns can now be formally ordained, and so in Thailand women are unable to be full members of the Community, or even to spend some months or years in the Community, as many men do. Both the rise of feminism and the possibility of economic development pose new problems to traditional values of a male religious élite which is indifferent to economic progress. In Sri Lanka Buddhism is closely tied to Sinhalese nationalism, in the face of what is often, however unfairly, seen as invasion by Hindu Tamils from the mainland of India. This has led to its becoming, paradoxically, a state religion, with close links to the Sinhalese ruling élite and large holdings of land donated by pious laypeople.

However unworldly the Community is supposed to be, it is not immune to the same sorts of alliances with power and privilege that beset the more politically focused Abrahamic religions. Sri Lanka is filled with grandiose temples covered in gold and jewels, and in seeing Sri Lanka and its political rulers as defenders of Buddhism, it is closely involved in the ethnic violence between Tamils and Sinhalese. In 1959 the prime minister, Mr Bandaranaike, was assassinated by a Buddhist monk, and there is a popular tradition in Sri Lanka that there has been no enlightened monk for over a thousand years.

In Burma there is constant tension between the government and the Community, and Buddhism finds itself again involved in political conflict in a very unstable society. Clearly the defence of traditional Buddhist values and a Buddhist way of life can be highly volatile factors in rapidly changing societies. Once a world-renouncing Community has become a valued part of society, it seemingly inevitably becomes affected by the power and prestige of the ruling élite, and the promotion and defence of the Community and its values by laity become potent political factors, closely associated with the defence of cultural and ethnic groups against what are perceived as alien incursions.

The influence of Buddhism is still strong in Theravadin countries, but monks are often seen as comparatively uneducated, and as opposed to the sorts of economic and social change that are able to bring prosperity and health to these countries. As defenders of a basically rural traditional order, as propagaters of such things as astrology, fortune-telling, and folk medicine, and as exponents of a sort of education which largely consists in learning ancient scriptures by heart, monks are increasingly seen to be out of touch with the needs of the modern world. All this is in accordance with Gautama's prediction that the Community would die out altogether 5,000 years after his death.[22] Surprisingly, however, the Theravadin tradition has recently established itself in the Western world in a number of locations, where perhaps its minority status enables it to return to its roots in poverty and the disciplined practice of meditation.

In Mahayana countries the story is different, but again it illustrates the strong and morally ambiguous relation between culture and religious practice that marks even a religion whose Community renounces worldly values. In the first place, a religion can only begin to flourish in a culture which has an intelligible place for it. The original Community began in a society in which religious mendicants and renouncers were accepted social figures. The Community was one of the ways of spiritual practice which was accepted in India, along with many others, more or less extreme. But Indian renouncers live in a society which has its own complex structures of Brahminical priesthood, ritual, and social norms. The Community became non-orthodox by rejecting those structures, and as such it began to differentiate itself from orthodox (*astika*) Indian traditions. But it could not ignore the desires of its lay supporters for objects of devotion and less exalted religious practices. Lay supporters naturally desire something more than the opportunity to support a Community of religious virtuosi. So the many gods and demons of popular religion were simply incorporated into the Buddhist worldview, and placed in heaven or hell worlds which were open to laity but were all below the level of supreme enlightenment attained by a Buddha. As far as most lay followers were concerned, Buddhism was an intellectual faith for the renouncing Community, surrounded by a mass of devotional and ritual practices for assuring good fortune in this life and in lives to come.

Since these practices were virtually indistinguishable from those of general Hindu culture, Buddhism became virtually extinct in India, the country of its birth. Indian polytheism simply took over the central Buddhist insights and subsumed them into the unitive philosophy of Vedanta. Between the abstract ideas of Vedanta and the equally abstract ideas of scholastic Buddhism there was no doubt little to choose, as far as most laypeople were concerned.

Moving outside India, Buddhism later found fruitful ground in Tibet, where the folk religion of Bon formed the background for a further development of Buddhist ideas. A number of influential

---

[22] Cf. Gombrich, *Theravada Buddhism*, 153.

monasteries grew up, but a crucial turning-point came when the Mongol rulers appointed the fifth Dalai Lama, abbot of one of the greatest monasteries, as political ruler of the country. Until the Chinese invasion of 1950, Tibet was a country ruled by the head of a Community which had renounced the world.

One would not expect a Community which is uninterested in scientific discovery or in economic productivity to motivate a dynamic and creative society. Tibet was for centuries virtually a closed society of a very traditional sort, living under a form of benevolent despotism, with the whole laity in practice serving the needs of the Community, which naturally included a great number of the most able men. Tragically, Tibetan Buddhism has been devastated by Chinese Marxist subjugation, and now exists in exile, where it is ironically most influential in popularizing meditation for the laity, who by tradition did not meditate at all. That may suggest that where a renouncing religion such as the Community gains social power, it will promote a benevolent but essentially static society, but that as a minority but international Community in the global society it functions as a resource for raising the aspirations of many laypeople, including non-Buddhists, for cultivating more reflective, self-aware, and insightful mental states.

In China and Japan Buddhism entered very different worlds, where social harmony and happiness within a strongly sanctioned social and family life were dominant cultural values. There was no strong mendicant tradition, and a religion of complete renunciation was a novelty. Mahayana thought, rather surprisingly, contained the resources to make the transition into such a culture. The doctrine of selflessness resonated with the idea of harmony within a greater whole, and the doctrine that nirvana and samsara are identical made it possible to think of achieving liberating insight without leaving the social realm. Moreover the cult of ancestors and of lineal pride and loyalty could be combined with belief in the many *boddhisattva*s, each with their own 'Buddha-land', where the dead might be reborn. In the Pure Land sects, such as Jodo Shin Shu, devotion to Amida— a being of universal compassion, identified with the Pure Mind, of which all flowing appearances are the direct expression—becomes a major feature of the faith. And in Ch'an or Zen schools, the emphasis is on doing whatever one is doing—and that includes, almost uniquely in Buddhism, hard manual work for monks—with full mindfulness.

These views are very non-traditional, and they have led to many monks in Japan, for instance, being married hereditary temple-priests, rather than celibate forest-dwellers. They have a much more this-worldly emphasis, and tend to teach that, by one means or another, enlightenment is available now, not after hundreds of rebirths, for laity as well as monks, women as well as men. They are also sometimes quite activist, in the sense of sponsoring social welfare and educational and even political campaigns.

As one might expect, this has led to conflicts of a sometimes serious nature. In Japan, Nichiren called for the banning of all other religious organizations but his own. The warrior-monk tradition became quite widespread. And the connection with nationalism, when the nation was seen as the true defender of the true faith, has sometimes been quite overt. Most Japanese schools of Buddhism originated in China, but in China first a revival of nationalist Confucianism and then the Communist revolution decimated the Community. It has made some recovery in recent years, and a blend of Taoist, Confucian, and Buddhist ideas is quite common. This allows a central monastic discipline, popular ritual practices for gaining good fortune, and a general lay ethic of balance and compassion in an ordered social life to exist alongside one another.

When monks engage in teaching and social work, and when lay people meditate, the traditional distinction between Community and laity is blurred. It may then be questioned whether the Community is a world-renouncing community any longer, but has not rather adapted to being a helpful aid to success in living. It is not that nirvana has been renounced in favour of merit-producing rituals, as in much traditional lay Buddhism, but that nirvana has been reinterpreted as enlightened living in the world—in which case the idea of complete literal renunciation becomes irrelevant. It seems likely that there will be an increase in Buddhist lay organizations, for which commitment to a simple lifestyle, the practice of meditation, and compassionate social action will be central. Other forms of Buddhism will probably continue to exist, especially Communities under a traditional monastic discipline, and some forms of devotional Buddhism such as the Pure Land school.

Buddhism has found it impossible to renounce the world entirely. Indeed, it would betray the central value of compassion to be wholly unconcerned with society in general. The history of Buddhism suggests that when even such an unworldly faith becomes linked with state power, it is not immune to corruption, laxity, and national chauvinism. That is, of course, just what its central belief—that human life is ensnared in greed, hatred, and ignorance—would lead one to expect. Repeated movements of reform arise, as the Scriptures continually remind monks of the eightfold path of wisdom (right views and right thought), moral practice (right speech, action, and livelihood), and mental discipline (right effort, mindfulness, and concentration) which they are supposed to be following. The problem for Buddhism in the modern world is what form of Community is most conducive to following that path in very different social circumstances. Many forms, from a traditional obedience to the 227 rules of the Theravada monastic discipline, to membership of a mixed Community of socially committed practitioners, are possible. But the path itself will remain, as one which brings insight and discipline to bear on human desires, and leads to the goal of liberation from sorrow.

In the light of these facts, the gulf between Abrahamic and Buddhist ethical attitudes is not as great as it may at first seem. Buddhists are pessimistic about the possibility of a just society made up of unjust human beings. But those who believe in Buddha-realms and Pure Lands do conceive of some form of communal existence which is blissful and removed from evil, in which compassion and sympathetic joy are universal and unbounded. Even the most severe Theravadins, having compassion for all beings, would support actions by the laity to sustain social justice—in Burma, they have supported movements for democratic government. There are differences about the nature of ultimate freedom—whether it lies in transcendence of individuality or in a fuller social life. These differences exist within Buddhism itself, and what is common is that the social goals for the vast majority, the laity, are those of peace, justice, and mercy.

Buddhists have no divinely revealed law that they feel obliged to obey. Yet traditional monks have hundreds of rules—the Code of Discipline—which they obey simply because the Buddha is believed to have laid them down. These rules are taken to be aids to liberation, not arbitrary commands. The Buddha formulated them because of his superior insight, and those of lesser insight do well to obey them out of respect for the wisdom of the Enlightened One. In a similar way, no Jew or Muslim would hold that the laws of God are arbitrary commands. They are taken to lay down a way of living which is conducive to ultimate happiness, and are given on the authority of God, who embodies supreme wisdom. Moreover, since God implanted desires in human lives, informed insight will disclose that human desires are to be fulfilled best by obeying the laws of God. This may not seem to be true in ordinary life, but Muslims and Buddhists agree that when life after death is taken into account, all will see that present obedience to law is for the sake of future fulfilment of truly ordered desire.

There are, then, both similarities and differences between Abrahamic and Buddhist views of ethics, as there are between diverse interpretations of those traditions. Jews and Muslims accept, with Buddhists, that freedom, wisdom, knowledge, happiness, justice, and compassion are universal values. They express the proper fulfilment of the basic human faculties of will, understanding, and feeling, possessed by beings which exist in codependence upon one another. Theists tend to locate the supreme realization of these values in God as Creator, while Buddhists see them as supremely exemplified in enlightened Buddhas.

Differing views of the nature of existence lead to differing interpretations of these values. Theists tend to see freedom in terms of positive creativity, whereas Buddhists tend to see it in terms of freedom from attachment to selfish desires. Theists see wisdom and knowledge as expressed in the intelligibility and beauty of the universe, while Buddhists see them in the perception of the insubstantiality of all phenomena, and the universality of suffering. Theists see happiness as to be found in a social world of friendship and relationship, whereas Buddhists see happiness as lying in a wordless nonduality beyond pleasure and pain.

It is not surprising that these differing insights into the same basic values lead to differing forms of social action and organization. There can be little doubt that Buddhism has been a less violent and aggressive religion than Islam, and a less ethnically oriented, and thus potentially nationalistic, one than Judaism. Its vices, where they have been realized, are those of indolence and indifference. Its virtues are those of universal compassion and non-attachment. Lay Buddhism can readily combine creativity with non-attachment, scientific understanding with discernment of the insubstantiality of sensory existence, and compassionate social action with meditative insight into ultimate non-duality. The monastic Community may remain as a society of renunciation, and there will doubtless be many who continue to think of it as the only sure way to ultimate liberation. There is perhaps a growing tendency, however, to see it as a community of those who teach all who will hear the way of non-attachment to self and union with nirvana, an indescribable state which nevertheless has the characteristics of supreme compassion and bliss.

The religion of withdrawal becomes a religion of exemplary practice, committed to the compassionate teaching of insight into the way of liberation from sorrow. In such a form, Buddhism can exist as an international, non-aggressive set of diverse communities, united in the quest for selflessness and the pursuit of that wisdom, compassion, and bliss for all sentient beings which is the central Buddhist path.

4

Hinduism and the *Sampradaya*

Judaism theoretically tries to construct a society which lives under the revealed law of a merciful Creator God, and can thereby be an exemplary pattern to the rest of the world. Islam theoretically attempts to create a global society living under the law of God, which will make it easier for people to achieve that fellowship with God that Muslims see as the Creator's purpose. Buddhists theoretically form a Community of monks and nuns who renounce the world and its concerns, and pursue the path of final liberation from sorrow.

In practice, things are not quite like that. Israel is a secular state, and religious (rabbinic) Judaism is a set of very diverse groups scattered throughout the world, almost the only common feature of which is a strong commitment to ethical monotheism, and some sort of commitment to simply being Jewish. The *umma* of Islam is in fact identifiable with a particular group of national states, and with many minority groups of Muslims throughout the world. Attitudes within that *umma* vary considerably, and again the only common commitment is obedience to a God who commands social justice, mercy, and potentially universal fellowship among human beings. The Buddhist *sangha* is involved in a number of different ways with the governments of South-East Asian countries, and interrelates with lay organizations which are committed to varying programmes of social action and with encouraging greater compassion and sensitivity in the wider human society.

The more rigid and abstract ideals of all these faiths run up against the hard fact of human cultural diversity, and produce many varying cultural forms of religion. Yet in all three cases there is a primary focus on a social organization, a community under a law or discipline, which is to play a specific role in the world, however differently that role may be conceived from one place and time to another. There is another possibility for religious life, and that is an insistence that religion is the business of individuals, not a group activity, or

that at least there may be many different religious communities
which coexist within a wider society. This is the possibility one finds
in the group of religious traditions usually classified under the name
'Hinduism'. It embodies a pluralist ideal of many religious paths,
none claiming exclusive efficacy, and adopted by individuals by
personal choice or inclination.

It must be said at once that the ideal does not find very clear
embodiment in India. Like other abstract ideals, there are important
cultural factors which blur it considerably. Nevertheless, there is
little doubt that Hinduism quite often sees and presents itself as
encouraging many paths to the religious goal, and many ways of conceiving that goal.[1] There is not just one religious community, but
many diverse communities existing side by side. That may be called
the pluralist ideal of Hindu faith.

The unit of religious allegiance in India may be called a *sampradaya*, a school which follows a particular teacher or *guru*, who normally claims to stand in a lineage from an ancient revered teacher.
Some lineages are hereditary, but most are teacher–pupil lineages,
and in principle one is free to choose a guru for oneself and to change
gurus. A guru is ideally an enlightened person who has learned the
discipline leading to enlightenment from his teacher, and who is able
to pass it on by personal training.

Hindu religion is not individualistic in the sense that anyone can
make up whatever they like. It makes a strong appeal to authority, in
the person of the guru, who will indeed be treated with great reverence, even as a divine manifestation. Moreover, such teachers almost
always claim the authority of the revealed scriptures, the Vedas and
Upanishads, as sources of supreme insight. It may be doubted, therefore, if Hinduism is quite as pluralist as it may seem at first.

The texts most often quoted to support a pluralist view are the
sentence from the Rig-Veda, 'Truth is one: the sages call it by many
names.'[2] And similarly from the *Bhagavad Gita*, where Krishna says,
'Whatever form a devotee with faith desires to honour, that very faith
do I confirm in him.'[3] In the Indian context, it is possible to worship

---

[1] So Radhakrishnan says, 'The claim to the possession of a unique revealed truth,
which declines to be classified as one among many, is ruinous for men,' in *The Philosophy of Sarvapalli Radhakrishnan*, ed. P. Schilpp (New York: Tudor, 1952), 810.

[2] Rig-Veda, 10. 164, in *Hindu Scriptures*, ed. and trans. R. C. Zaehner (London:
Dent, 1984), 46.

[3] Bhagavad Gita, 7. 21, in Zaehner (ed.), *Hindu Scriptures*, 281.

many gods, from Indra or Hanuman to Vishnu or Shiva. It is not too difficult to see these gods as different faces of one supreme reality. Yet even in saying so little, one is saying that there is a supreme reality which can appear in many different ways. The *Bhagavad Gita* unmistakably teaches that Krishna is the true form of that supreme reality, and that the final secret disclosed by Krishna is: 'I love thee well.'[4]

There is a final truth about the way things are, and it can be truly apprehended by human beings. Since humans are so different psychologically and culturally, they may see different aspects of that complex truth. Yet in the end they will see truth as it really is, and in the meanwhile it is possible to be quite mistaken about it—if, for instance, one says that there is no supreme spiritual reality at all.

There are Hindu materialists, and in this respect Hindu orthodoxy shows itself to be more like Judaism than like a universal religion. Proponents of *Hindutva* (Hinduness) in contemporary India proclaim that 'It is the Hinduness of a man that makes him a national of India,'[5] and they take acceptance of the *Sruti*, the revealed scriptures of Vedas and Upanishads, as the test of Hindu orthodoxy. Also important is acceptance of the general brahmin-oriented customs and rituals, and of the fund of myths and stories in the great Indian epics. As in Judaism, following the customs of the ethnic community is valued more highly than particular theoretical interpretations of religious doctrines. What is taken to be important by Hindu nationalists is general acceptance of a culture in which the gods of the Vedas are ritually worshipped in traditional ways, in which the brahmins are honoured and traditional rituals for marriage and death are accepted, and in which the great epics, particularly the story of Rama, form a basis for moral and spiritual teaching. Traditional rituals, customs, forms of social order, and stories are much more important than adherence to specific doctrines. *Hindutva* has arisen partly as a reaction against 'foreign' influences, such as Islam, Christianity, and the economic hegemony of the Western powers, and as an assertion of Indian self-confidence and distinctiveness.

Within this overall concern, however, there is an almost universal acceptance of what might be called denominationalism in Indian religious life. By a denomination I mean a voluntary association,

---

[4] Bhagavad Gita, 18. 64, ibid. 324.

[5] Balraj Madhok, *Indian Nationalism* (Delhi: Bharati Sahitya Sadan, 1969), 95.

grouped around a guru or particular form of temple worship, which does not overtly claim to be the only true form of Hindu faith, but accepts that it is one of many Hindu paths. None the less, 'Hinduness' is usually important, and it is a common core of rituals, customs, and stories that ensures some form of unity, however complex.

One feature of late nineteenth-century and subsequent Indian religious traditions is the way in which attempts have been made to export non-ethnic forms of Indian religion, usually by establishing small groups which follow a particular guru, whether Sai Baba, Maharishi Mahesh Yoga, or some other Indian 'enlightened teacher'. In such groups, Indian social customs are often almost entirely dropped or radically amended, but the stories and rituals are often preserved, since they provide focal points of religious practice.

Although Hinduism is like Judaism in many ways, being centred on social practice more than on theoretical belief, it differs from Judaism in being much less unified. At least in ancient Israel, the sacrificial cult was centralized on the Temple in Jerusalem, and great stress was placed on the worship of only one God. In India, there are still thousands, if not millions, of local gods and goddesses, who are ritually worshipped at their own shrines. These local cults are more or less integrated into greater devotional cults, mostly to Vishnu or Shiva, but even they have many groups with differing particular interpretations of belief and cultic practices.

It is easier to say what is not Hindu than to define what is. If sacrificial rites to the gods are eschewed, if the gods themselves are regarded as irrelevant, if the brahminical priesthood is rejected, if the Vedas are said to have no authority, then one is certainly not an orthodox Hindu. Like a secular Jew, a secular Hindu may still be claimed as Hindu by association of birth, but that becomes a purely ethnic matter, and Indian Muslims, Jains, Buddhists, and Christians find such claims unacceptable.

Any attempt to achieve a universal pluralism is doomed to failure, simply because it is conceptually impossible. If one person says that there is a supreme God who can be fully known after death, and another person denies both God and life after death, there is no way in which both views can be equally acceptable. At least one view must be false. Indian pluralism does not, however, assert the impossible thesis that all religious and non-religious views are equally acceptable. It builds on a basic assertion that the deities of the Hindu pantheon represent aspects of a spiritual reality, which may be approached in many ways, largely depending upon temperament, history, and culture.

These ways have become generally divided into three types of spiritual practice.[6] The way of ritual sacrifice (karma yoga), of dressing, feeding, and reverencing the images of the gods, is the priestly way. For most Hindus a visit to a temple where such rituals are practised to make an offering to a consecrated image, and the reverencing of such images in the home, is a central religious practice. The way of renunciation (*jnyana* yoga) is that of the *sanyassin*, renouncing family and possessions to practise austerities and attain higher states of consciousness. This is the way of the guru, the spiritual master, perhaps taken as a manifestation of a god, who will lead one to an inner spiritual awareness of the Supreme Self, beyond description. The way of devotion (*bhakti* yoga) is that of ecstatic devotion to a god—often Krishna or Shiva—expressed in dancing, singing, and chanting. This is the way of the devotee, best expressed in small groups or in huge public processions, where highly emotional states of love and loyalty are encouraged.

It is perfectly intelligible that there may be many different images of a spiritual reality, which appeal to different people, and that people of different temperaments may be attracted to formalized ritual, solitary contemplation or communal devotion. In Hinduism this diversity is recognized by the existence of temples to many different gods, gurus who are free to set up their own *sampradayas* or ashrams where disciples can be trained and taught, and devotional associations each following their own succession of teachers.

The underlying belief that makes this form of pluralism possible is that the infinity of the divine being can be manifested under many different names and forms. Whereas Judaism and Islam prohibit all images of God, Hindus accept a great number of images, in which divine powers are said to dwell, at least temporarily. While Judaism and Islam have both been intolerant of 'deviant' religious practices, Hinduism has typically absorbed them into its pantheon, as additional forms of representing the divine.

Are there any limits to what can be thus absorbed? It may seem not, for even such dark powers as Durga and Kali become objects of worship, and in Tantric practices sexual taboos are broken and

⁶ Cf. Bhagavad Gita, 3. 3, 6. 47, in Zaehner, *Hindu Scriptures*, 262, 279.

drugs are used to break through the barriers of conventional thought. At a popular level in Indian religion the most extraordinary practices can be found—people placing metal hooks through their flesh and being suspended from poles, or hammering metal spikes through their cheeks—and astrology and magic spells for success and fertility are tools of the trade for many local holy men and women.

If one is concerned for rationality and moral enlightenment in religion, one will find plenty of it in Hindu thought. But one will also find much concern with ritual and ascetic practices that assume a magical world-view and seem only remotely connected with morality, though one can see their alleged association with averting evil influences and gaining some relief from the grinding poverty of much Indian life. These were the facts that led some Christian missionaries to see Hinduism as a mass of primitive superstition. It must have seemed to them, with little knowledge of the intellectual traditions of India, that here there still thrived the idolatrous practices condemned in the Old Testament, which encouraged sexual licence and magic, and had virtually no moral content.

THE QUESTION OF IDOLATRY

The issue of idolatry is of major importance in the meeting of Abrahamic and Indian religious traditions. Why does the Judaeo-Islamic tradition so strongly condemn the making of 'carved images', which form the mainstay of most popular Indian religion? The prophetic viewpoint seemed to be that idols were constructions of the human mind, projections of a people's desire for power, and so idols magnified the desires and hatreds of their makers and legitimated the power-structure of their society. Moreover, they were foci of the sexual powers of fertility, and of a savage thirst for blood and for human sacrifice which would persuade the gods to give children, fruitful rain, and success in battle.

Jews held that, through the prophets, God made a covenant of faithfulness with Israel, and revealed the divine as a liberating and personal Creator God, Lord of all time and space, with no rivals who might ultimately frustrate the divine will. God demanded justice and mercy, and promised an abundant life in which he would be known and loved faithfully. Idolatry had the flavour of adultery, of disloyalty to the covenant, of lack of trust in God's promises, and of an attempt to control the future by making pacts with the powers of nature and fate. So when the ancient Israelites made the golden bull at Sinai[7] this was seen as a lack of trust in Jahweh, and an attempt to harness the natural powers of nature (symbolized by the bull), to bribe or flatter those powers into giving the people what they wanted, immediate gratification of their desires.

In Islam idolatry was associated with polytheism, the acceptance of many non-rational, limited, and often competing spiritual powers, who were to be feared, and who might be persuaded into giving humans what they wanted. It is not surprising that such powers could be seen as demonic, as limited spiritual forces which made no moral demands, which were pleased with offerings of human blood and death, and which promised sensory gratification in return. Such gods were barely personified supernatural forces, controllable by magical rituals, binding humans and their societies ever more closely to the greed and hatred which corrupted their vision.

Into such an atmosphere of amoral and arational magic, of religion as an attempt to control the ultimately arbitrary powers of fate, the idea of one infinite God, demanding justice and mercy, revealing one invincible purpose for the world, offering a personal relationship of love which was not manipulable for the ends of individual or social power, broke like a refreshing gale. Intoxicated with belief in the sole sovereignty of the one Creator God, all images and sacred pillars were broken down and destroyed, and replaced by loyalty to the divine, imageless word, unconcerned with flattery and beyond manipulation, a God of command and promise.

There was no such prophetic revolution in India. Yet it would be a great mistake to think either that the Abrahamic tradition successfully escaped from idolatry, or that the Indian tradition remained immersed in it, just because Judaism and Islam have no carved images and Hinduism has many. It is necessary to identify those elements of idolatry that were condemned by the prophets, to penetrate beneath the outward forms of religious practice, and to identify where those elements are to be found in modern religious practice.

If idolatrous religion makes national gods who are projections of the aspirations and values of a particular society or ruling élite, it must be said that the God of Israel was often treated as just such a

---

[7] Exodus 32.

projection of the national will to power.[8] The major prophets
protested against seeing the God of Israel as just one tribal deity
whose job it was to give success in war, but the lack of a carved image
did not prevent the idea of God being continually misused in that
way. Similarly, Jahweh is often seen as a god of fertility, promising
many children and fruitful fields, in return for obedience to Torah.
One should not fall into the trap of thinking that the Abrahamic God
is beyond the danger of idolatry, when the basis of idolatry is seen as
the use of supernatural powers for bringing success, fertility, and the
gratification of desire.

Nor are the images of the gods in Hinduism necessarily idolatrous, in that sense. Many of the local deities may be little more
than amoral powers which will gratify desires in a quasi-magical
way, but most sophisticated Hindus regard the images of Vishnu
and Shiva, or the carved symbols which represent them, like the
lingam, as finite and disposable channels of the grace of one supreme
God, conceived in a particular way. It is not the artefact that is worshipped, but the one divine reality which the artefact is believed to
manifest, in a temporary and limited way.

If idols are seen as symbols of an infinite divine creator, with
whom a personal relationship can be established, and who cannot be
manipulated by ritual actions in a quasi-magical way, then they do
not show the presence of idolatry. For idolatry would be the worship
of a finite power, by amoral means, for the sake of the gratification of
selfish desires. This point, while it clears most Hindu practice of
idolatry, does reiterate the fact that the many paths of acceptable
religious practice must be morally enhancing paths to the one infinite God. The amoral propitiation of finite powers is not an acceptable path. Even if such paths are in fact permitted in Hindu local
cults, they cannot be seen as profound and acceptable paths for
reflective, spiritually minded people.

DIVERSITY AND DISPUTE

Hindu pluralism is thus heavily stratified. There are indeed many
religious paths, but many of them are for the simple-minded or
selfish. The person of spiritual insight will take one of the higher

---

[8] The classic case is 1 Samuel 4: 3, where the Ark is led out to assure victory in
battle, but is then captured.

paths, in which there is a discipline of the mind and an attempt to gain knowledge of the one infinite divine reality. The doctrine of rebirth plays an important role here, for people are born into a particular social position, a caste, as a result of their past acts and thoughts in previous lives. There are different levels of spiritual attainment, and that is why there can be different levels of religious practice.

The highest caste, that of the brahmin, has a privileged religious role. Traditionally, only brahmins could read the sacred texts, learn the religious rituals, and perform the sacrifices on which the good fortune of society depends. At the bottom of the social hierarchy, the untouchables were excluded from brahminical religious rituals, and had to devise their own forms of religious practice. So part of the variety of religion is due to social stratification, itself theoretically based on levels of spiritual attainment built up over many previous lives.

Brahminical religion was partly devoted to the legitimation of the ruling élite, and the gods of the classical Indian pantheon functioned to embody the social aspirations of the many Indian states. Another part of the variety of religion is due to the simple agglomeration of local socio-political cults, as the country of India was formed. The *Hindutva* movement, in affirming that pantheon, and in stressing the role of Rama, warrior god who defeated his foreign enemies, is seeking to revive religion as a badge of national identity. Even though the caste system has been illegal since 1947 in the secular state of India, the attempt to re-establish traditional social roles is a response to the pressures of rapid change and the eroding of local cultures by international influence through television, computerization, and trade.

If pluralism is seen as a result of social stratification and the legitimation of traditional social values it may look less attractive, less like an idealistic tolerance than like social and cultural expediency. *Hindutva* is certainly intolerant of Islam and Christianity, requiring that Indian Muslims and Christians 'become properly Hindu', though it is not clear just what this would imply. In fact Indian spirituality has not been confined to brahminical cults. Ascetic renouncers, charismatic gurus, and leaders of devotional cults have managed to establish ways of religious practice outside the traditional caste system. Unlike Muslims and Christians, they do not directly challenge the traditional pantheon, and so are not seen as 'non-Hindu'. What they do is to select parts of the Vedic tradition and develop them to express rather different spiritual concerns.

The great teacher Sankara, revered by virtually all Hindus, promoted the worship of Shiva, to whom he wrote hymns. But in his hands, Shiva becomes a symbol or personal form of Brahman, the supreme reality who is beyond all names and forms, and even beyond worship.[9] Followers of Sankara today will practise traditional rites of the worship of Shiva, but all such rites belong to the realm of maya, and the enlightened sage will regard them as empty. Here again, then, a sharp distinction is drawn between popular, unenlightened attitudes to religion, and the enlightened stance of the spiritually advanced. Not all understandings of what is going on in religion are on a level, as if many different understandings were equally good. Different sorts of religion may be right for different sorts of people, but that is because people are at different levels of spiritual attainment. It looks as though many diverse rites and gods can be accepted precisely because all of them are illusion, and the reality lies beyond them all. This sort of pluralism depends on a relativization and a downgrading of all particular divine or holy beings.

There is little problem with seeing Vishnu and Shiva as different representations of Brahman, as long as one can hold that Brahman really does manifest in different ways to different people as suits their temperaments or attainments. But are all these manifestations of equal worth and validity? Suppose that Brahman manifests as a god who demands conformity to the *varnasrama-dharma*, the code of caste ethics set forth in the *Manu-samhita*, and threatens rebirth in a hell world for all who refuse so to conform. But that same Brahman manifests to Sri Caitanya in the form of Krishna, teaching that conformity to the rules of caste must be abandoned, since every individual is equally a part of the divine, and that loving devotion and service is the proper response to the divine.[10]

These beliefs will appeal to different personality types, no doubt. However, they cannot both be accepted by the same person at the same time. How does a particular individual know which way to follow? Is it just a matter of temperament, so that one first analyses

---

[9] 'His omniscience, omnipotence and so on all depend on ignorance; in reality, none of these qualities belong to the Self,' *Vedanta Sutras*, trans. George Thibaut, Sacred Books of the East, 34, ed. Max Muller (Delhi: Motilal Banarsidass, 1962), 329.

[10] Cf. *Srimad Bhagavatam*, A. C. Prabhupada (Los Angeles: Bhaktivedanta Book Trust, 1987), i. 107, where the four *varna*s are classified by 'work' and not by 'birth'.

one's own personality, and then decides which teaching suits one best? That seems strangely upside-down, and relativizes revelation completely to personal taste. It makes religion a form of social custom. Some people may like eating with chopsticks, others with a knife and fork. That is a matter of taste, since it does not really matter in what particular way one eats, as long as others do not find it offensive.

There are many customs in religion, and many forms of ritual, degrees of ceremony, ways of dressing, and so on probably are just matters of taste. But it is unlikely that a follower of Sri Caitanya is simply saying, 'If Brahmanic customs do not appeal to you, we can offer you an alternative.' He is more likely to say that considerations of human equality require the abandoning of some birth-caste regulations. 'The *dharma* of loving devotion (*prema-bhakti*), supersedes in excellence and relativises (though it may not invalidate altogether) other forms of *dharma*, including certain kinds of Vedic and other Brahmanic *dharma*.'[11] The claim to higher truth, together with the qualification that other ways may not be wholly invalid, is very typical of Hindu *sampradaya*.

The caste rules, Vaishnavas say, were not wholly misleading, and may have been right for a past age. Even now, there are ways of interpreting them (in terms of general spiritual types of people, for example) which are illuminating. Nevertheless, they have been superseded by a higher way, which is right for our age, and for all who have the discernment to accept it. There are many ways of approaching the divine, but one is higher than the others.

Thus Sankara can allow that devotion is suitable for simple, uneducated people. But the enlightened sage will see that devotion belongs to the realm of the unreal, and beyond it lies the unitive vision of truth, that the all-inclusive non-duality of Brahman supersedes and relativizes both god and devotee (though it may not invalidate them altogether, for the vast majority who are snared by illusion). At this point, Ramanuja would regard such unqualified non-dualism as an incorrect interpretation of the sacred texts, and as philosophically flawed.[12] In other words, he would hold that

---

[11] Joseph T. O'Connell, 'Does the Caitanya Vaisnava Movement Reinforce or Resist Hindu Communal Politics?', in *Journal for Vaishnava Studies*, 5: 1 (1997).

[12] So Ramanuja says of Sankara, 'His view rests on a fictitious foundation of hollow and vicious arguments,' *Vedanta Sutras*, trans. G. Thibaut, Sacred Books of the East, 48.

Sankara's view is not just an alternative, it is actually mistaken. Not all paths to the divine are equally reasonable and morally enlightening. On inspection, it turns out that virtually every Hindu group that espouses the pluralism of religion also holds that its own interpretation of the Real and the way to it supersedes the others, for those advanced enough (or favoured by God) to see the truth.

Hindu pluralism in fact expresses a combination of two very distinctive, widely held Hindu beliefs. One is that Brahman, the supreme spiritual reality, manifests in the whole world, so that everything is in some sense part of Brahman.[13] The other is that most human beings are lost in selfish partiality and illusion, bound to the wheel of rebirth until they obtain release, when they will be reborn in this world no more.[14] The first belief leads one to say that Brahman can be worshipped in every finite form, since every finite form is part of Brahman. The second belief leads one to think that most religious beliefs and practices will be infected by partiality and ignorance, though they will be appropriate to humans at a certain stage of spiritual development, and may help to lead them to a higher stage, if only in a subsequent life. The combination of both beliefs leads one to think that only the few, those about to be liberated from rebirth, will ascend to knowledge of Brahman as it really is, and such knowledge will probably be incommunicable to the majority of people— another reason for having a plurality of religions, suited to different human needs. There will be an esoteric core of religious teaching, but many more or less inadequate ways of representing it in more material forms for the masses. Pluralism of this sort, ironically, turns out to be a form of spiritual élitism. It belongs naturally to a system in which a small spiritual élite adapt their teachings in various ways for the sake of those who cannot understand them properly.

In fact, of course, there is no authoritatively established spiritual élite. The brahmin caste, when regarded by reasonably impartial observers, is fairly obviously not a group of spiritually advanced humans. The self-designated gurus and avatars, often called the 'god-men' by the Indian press, disagree with each other, while accepting the authority of the Vedic scriptures in a very wide sense.

---

[13] 'Thou art this whole universe,' Kaushitaki Upanishad, in Zaehner, *Hindu Scriptures*, 151.
[14] 'He who roams abroad in dream, glorying in himself—this is the Self'; 'Once it is freed from the body, pleasure and pain cannot touch it', Chandogya Upanishad, 8. 10. 1, 8. 11. 1, ibid. 129.

So spiritual élitism does not in India lead to the establishment of one authoritative institution. Authority is diffused in many ways, which makes the task of nationalist 'Hinduizers' extremely frustrating. Indeed, it has been pointed out that 'the strongest and most meaningful resistance to Hindu essentialism will have to come from Hindus themselves'.[15]

The dispersed authority of Hinduism makes it virtually impossible to say that is has an essential nature. However, one could point to the Vedic scriptures as the common source of the many *sampradaya* of Hinduism. At a sophisticated level, there is a widespread belief in rebirth and in a supreme spiritual reality of bliss and wisdom, the Brahman of the Upanishads, whose nature is expressed in the material universe. Within that general structure, there exist many particular systems of belief and practice, mostly based on the claims of various gurus to have achieved privileged knowledge of or even union with Brahman. Members of one such system do not regard the others as equally acceptable. They do, however, often accept the general fallibility and partiality of most human beliefs, the variety of human temperaments and attainments, and the fact that Brahman transcends every human attempt to describe its nature.[16]

Intolerance does exist in India, and religious riots involving members of differing schools are not uncommon. Sikhs and Muslims in the Indian subcontinent have felt driven, whether justifiably or not, to seek a separate 'homeland' because of what they have experienced as Hindu oppressiveness. Traditional Hindu society can apply quite rigorously the laws of *Manu* and the other customs of brahmin religious life. The four *varna*s, or classes, each with their own proper rights and duties, subdivide into thousands of castes, or *jati*s, which are hierarchically ordered, largely along lines of birth. The *Gita* teaches that it is better to do the duty of one's own caste badly than to do the duty of another's caste well.[17] The customary rules of caste can govern the details of a villager's life in India in such a way as to allow very little personal freedom, and seem oppressive to those who are underprivileged or excluded by the system.

From a religious point of view, the stages of a man's life are

---

[15] C. Ram-Prasad, 'Hindutva Ideology: Extracting the Fundamentals', in *Contemporary South Asia*, 2: 306 (1993).

[16] 'It is beyond speech, nothing can be likened to it, one cannot tell of it,' Maitri Upanishad, 6. 7, in Zaehner, *Hindu Scriptures*, 229.

[17] Gita 3. 35, ibid. 265.

divided into the four *ashrama*s, that of the student, householder, religious seeker, and renouncer, and each of these have specific duties prescribed. Not everyone needs to pursue these stages, and traditional Hindu thought allows four different goals of human action—duty, material gain, pleasure, and desire for liberation. The last of these is the highest, but they are all acceptable. Renunciation is seen as the highest spiritual vocation, but it is for the few. For everyone, however, traditional Hindu customs and practices are highly regulated, and the pressure to conform, especially in rural areas, is strong. It is not really true that one is free to choose one's beliefs and way of life in traditional India. On the contrary, one's life will be finely regulated by the rules governing one's station in life. The highest way is the way of the renouncer who seeks liberation from rebirth, but for the majority the worship of either local or the pan-Indian deities (mainly Vishnu and Shiva), especially at times of festival and in the home, is the way of religion.

Such traditional ways tend to break down under the pressures of modern life, increased social mobility, and political measures such as the declared illegality of caste. *Hindutva* may be seen precisely as a conservative reaction against such breakdown. As such, it is more concerned with tradition and established social hierarchies than with matters of religious doctrine. Because the major social rituals and the best-known stories are drawn from Vedic religion, such traditionalism has been associated with 'being Hindu'. But it does seem that the major motivation at work is clinging to tradition, with religion being used, in what of course must be a traditional way, to support what is perceived to be a threatened status quo.

The paradox of this situation is that, whereas of course rural religion tends to be traditional, the Vedic tradition itself allows for many sorts of reinterpretation and revision. The dispersed and unformalized nature of religious authority in Hinduism means that new authorities can spring up at any time. They will be wise to claim a basis in the Vedic scriptures, but those scriptures are so complex and many-sided that there is little difficulty in interpreting them in very diverse ways.

Most schools have always accepted that there is a variety of legitimate interpretations of the Vedic tradition, so that even if they hold their system to be the most adequate, they allow the right of others conscientiously to disagree and follow a different path. One might say that in Hinduism there is a common basic scripture which contains a common core of beliefs and also sets out some normative rituals and social practices, but there is no common interpretative authority, and there is no prohibition on religious teachers adding further scriptures or texts (*smirti*) which may provide a very distinctive gloss on the Vedic tradition.

DIASPORA HINDUISM

Hinduism has for much of its history been content to remain an ethnic or national faith, without much concern for carrying its teachings to the rest of the world. The many *sampradaya* all continued to exist within a generally Vedic framework, and without contesting the basic outlines of the laws of *Manu*. Where that framework of brahminical practice and belief was challenged, as by Buddhists, the new faith was regarded as non-Hindu. Where it was not contested, even if it was relativized, as with Vaishnava devotional cults, and where a plausible claim to interpret the Vedic scripture could be made, new schools of Hinduism were simply added to the list.

There is much more latitude for an orthodox Hindu to adopt a revisionist attitude to social conventions based upon the laws of *Manu* than for an orthodox Jew, say, to reject some of the provisions of Torah. It is also not difficult to offer a new doctrinal system, as long as it can plausibly claim to be a commentary on one of the many Upanishads or classically established systems. In the last hundred years or so a whole succession of teachers has appeared who have done precisely this, forging what is often called 'neo-Hinduism' out of a combination of classical Vedic thought and various European philosophies, especially that of Hegel. Radhakrishnan, Vivekananda, and Aurobindo are just three major figures out of hundreds of gurus and teachers who have reinterpreted Vedic tradition to construct a form of Hinduism with a global mission.

Diaspora Judaism took Torah wherever Jews lived, and regarded adherence to it as a sacred duty. But where ethnic Indians live outside India, they have not had such a strong loyalty to the laws of *Manu*, which are closely linked to the land of India and the conditions of life there. More emphasis comes to be placed on the teachings of Hindu faith, and such teachings have had to be systematized by various gurus, who have often been staking a claim to represent 'true Hinduism' and take it to the whole world. To take just one example, in England, where there are many ethnic Indians, some of the major Hindu movements are the International Society for Krishna Consciousness, the Sri Narayan temple, and the disciples of Sai Baba.

There are many other Hindu movements, most of them promoting the practice of meditation and offering realization of 'the God within' as the goal of spiritual practice. Many of them universalize the Vedically based pluralism of India, and teach that all religions, or at least all great religious teachers in every religious tradition, offer paths to God and to spiritual realization. Naturally enough, these paths to God turn out to be, in their inner core, identical with the path they themselves teach.

Thus Sai Baba teaches that all religions are true, but that he himself is the avatar, or manifestation of God, and as such is identical with, for example, both Jesus and Allah. He stands in the Saivite tradition, in which supreme reality is envisaged in the form of Siva. Yet this is not an exclusive allegiance to one form of the supreme. All religions are true in that they all teach that there is a supreme Self of bliss and knowledge, and all great religious teachers are 'realized souls', who have overcome the sense of individuality and experienced unity with the supreme Self. Such realized souls should be regarded as manifestations of the supreme Self, and they inaugurate a *parampara*, a succession of gurus, who can initiate others into such realization. Most Hindu movements throughout the world follow a guru who stands in such a lineage, and they accept the guru's interpretation of the scriptures and method of attaining god-realization.

In what sense are such movements pluralistic? The core belief which they share is that there exist many perfectly realized souls, who have achieved an overcoming of individual personality by realizing the non-duality of all things. Paradoxically, this often leads to a cult of personality, in which the guru becomes the object of devotion, even of worship. It also leads to a specific idea of what human perfection consists in. The realized souls may take virtually no notice of their surroundings, may live naked on rubbish heaps (like Zipruanna of Nasirabad in northern Maharasthra), and may be absorbed in silent meditation. Theirs is often a sort of madness, though it would be said to be the apparent madness of the enlightened man in an insane world devoted to the pursuit of selfish desires. Their importance lies in their inner mental states, which are said to be states of perfect bliss, omniscience, and paranormal power. They have passed beyond the human, so that their bodies seem to be merely trappings which they carry about until they are finally freed from the realm of suffering altogether.

The aim of the disciples of such perfectly realized souls is to follow their teachers in realizing the divinity within. Since most people are, in various degrees, in bondage to the illusory self, they can only hope to begin this quest in this life by devotion to the guru and by obedience to his teachings. Again paradoxically, the teaching that everyone is part of the divine often leads in practice to the most extreme authoritarianism, in which the disciple renounces all individual capacity of thought and action in favour of complete obedience to the guru. Except for a very few realized souls, the mark of religious faith will be obedience to and worship of the guru.

Disciples who follow such a guru will be very conscious that they are a small group among many others. In that way, they will rarely show any desire to impose the rules of their group upon others, or upon society as a whole. Moreover, they usually regard the body and the world as relatively unimportant, so that religion does not engage directly in political issues. They will spend time in meditation, in seeking to cultivate states of inner peace and joy. So one would expect them to be peaceful, rather introspective types, of a generally kindly disposition.

More disconcertingly, they may renounce their powers of private judgement and follow the guru blindly down some idiosyncratic pathway. Belief that the guru is divine and omniscient, together with the fact that madness is hard to distinguish from religious ecstasy, has sometimes led devotees into irrational and disturbing patterns of action (as with the followers of Bhagwan Rajneesh). Inner peace and joy are, unfortunately, quite compatible psychologically with hostility to the 'world', which is the realm of hatred and desire. Especially if they are ridiculed or rejected, such sects can develop an almost paranoic relation to society as a whole. After all, they form a spiritual élite in a world of fallen souls. The potential is there for a suspicious and inward-looking community in which the members love each other but hate and distrust everyone else.

There remains a fundamental ambiguity in all this, since the world is at the same time the expression of Siva and the illusory realm of ignorance and desire. Different schools, at different times, may therefore stress different aspects of this ambiguity. One danger is that moral sensibility may be seriously compromised. Bliss and knowledge are the ultimate goals. But since everything manifests

Siva, evil and conflict may be necessary intermediate goals, by which unenlightenment can be destroyed. After all, no one can really kill or be killed, according to the *Gita*.[18] Where non-dual reality can so easily be split from the world of dualities, juxtaposed as reality to illusion, violence may belong to the world of illusion, and the perpetrator can remain apart and untouched, just as the saint can live in perfect bliss on a rubbish heap. Moral indifference is one of the dangers of Hinduism, which qualifies any thought that it is intrinsically a tolerant and peacable faith.

HINDU PLURALISM

Diaspora neo-Hinduism is pluralist in the sense that it exists as a large number of different *sampradaya*, each following a particular guru, and none claiming to be the only 'true' Hindu school. Yet each school claims that its own guru is a truly realized soul, and thus (in so far as other schools are accepted) that the divinity is manifested in many human lives, human persons who are omniscient and omnipotent. That is clearly a contentious claim, as is the allied claim that every human person is divine, or is a part of God, though this fact is concealed by *avidya*, ignorance.

Many Hindu teachers extend the hand of tolerance to other faiths by simply accepting their founders as realized souls. But it is fairly obvious that such tolerance is often thinly disguised imperialism. It is saying that other teachers can be accepted if they are reinterpreted in terms of Hinduism. Orthodox Jews would be highly affronted to be told that Moses was not a fallible human prophet who always remained no more than a reverent servant of God, but an omniscient and omnipotent manifestation of God. Orthodox Muslims would react in the same way to any claim that Muhammad was actually the God whose laws he recited. Even orthodox Christians, who believe that God was incarnate in the human person of Jesus, would cavil at the thought that there are a great many incarnations, all of them omniscient, but most of them, oddly enough, in India.

One form of Hindu pluralism extends only as far as those who are prepared to see the whole cosmos as the self-expression of the supreme Self, and who believe that many humans can fully realize godhood in the course of their earthly lives, probably after many

---

[18] Gita 2. 19, ibid. 256.

previous lifetimes of spiritual discipline and renunciation. In such a system, there will be many realizations of the divine, all of them properly worthy of worship, and the supreme spiritual goal will be such god-realization, which will also be the ending of the chain of individual existence. This is a pluralism of divine manifestations within a generally non-dualist world-view.

Of course there are also dualistic or qualified non-dualist schools, such as the *bhakti* schools of Vaishnavism. They too may interpret the religious teachers of all traditions as perfected devotees. But the very fact that they disagree so fundamentally with the non-dualist schools shows that the attempt to bring all religious teachings under some one head of agreement is doomed to failure. The stubborn fact is that the *siddhi* of Saivism, who are claimed to be one with undifferentiated absolute consciousness, do teach a different spiritual goal from such teachers as Chaitanya, who see the goal as that of a community of liberated souls related to a personal God, and who do not accept the possibility or even the desirability of union with non-dual consciousness.[19] So there is a wider pluralism of differing interpretations of the Vedic tradition, which are regarded as acceptable or possible interpretations, though they cannot all be regarded as true or correct.

It is further possible to have forms of Hinduism which are devoted to a personal creator who is distinct in existence from the cosmos. There are modern forms of Hinduism (for instance, that of Aurobindo) which adopt evolutionary theory, and so can speak of a moral purpose in the world, a purpose of evolving a community of justice and mercy. There are many schools (like that of Madhva) which refuse to speak of non-duality at all, and see the relation of the soul to God as one of loving service. In many respects they are very close to the Abrahamic traditions. Such schools remain Hindu because they take as their scriptural basis the Upanishads, together with additional scriptures of their own tradition. They worship the divine under the form of one of the traditional Indian gods—usually Shiva or Vishnu. And they usually accept a basic Upanishadic world-view of the wheel of rebirth, the law of karma, and acceptance of *moksa*, release from rebirth, as the final spiritual goal.

[19] So Swami Prabhupada, in his commentary on the *Gita*, says: 'The last illusion, the last snare of *maya*, to trap the living entity is the proposition that he is God,' *Bhagavad Gita As It Is* (Los Angeles: Bhaktivedanta Books, 1991), 858.

The field of differing interpretations now becomes wider, though it is still generally qualified by acceptance of the customs, rites, and core beliefs of traditional brahmanic religion. This widening of the Hindu tradition raises the possibility of an even more extensive pluralism which fully accepts the existence of many ways of spiritual belief and practice, seeing them as virtually inevitable consequences of the limitations of human understanding and the infinity of the divine being.

Such a pluralism would not require any acceptance that the world-views of the different paths were somehow equally true, or compatible at an unknown higher level. But it might well suggest that any attempt to construct a coherent total world-view would be a partial success at best. It would be subject to revision, probably incomplete in many ways, and almost certainly mistaken in some respects. It might also suggest that, though incompatibilities cannot just be said to be resolved in some higher synthesis, yet our world-views are likely to exaggerate some features and neglect others, and the final truth is likely to be one that none of us have discovered yet, which will show all our present views to be inadequate in some ways.[20]

There is still a conceptual limitation on such a form of pluralism, as there must logically be if pluralism is to assert anything at all. Religious practice will be an attempt to gain knowledge of a spiritual reality that embodies the highest values that can possibly coexist. So materialism, and a crude polytheism which has many conflicting and flawed spiritual forces, are ruled out. The goal of religious practice will be to relate to that spiritual reality in such a way that the ideal values which it embodies will be encouraged in the practitioners. So quasi-magical attempts to use spiritual powers to achieve material success, and religious practices that encourage hatred and greed are ruled out.

On that general basis, one may proceed to ask what can be said about the supreme spiritual reality—probably on the basis of the claims of spiritual teachers or allegedly inspired prophets—and how

---

[20] John Hick's 'pluralistic hypothesis' is that 'the great post-axial faiths constitute different ways of experiencing, conceiving and living in relation to an ultimate divine Reality which transcends all our varied visions of it,' *An Interpretation of Religion* (London: Macmillan, 1989), 235–6. That is a formulation which almost any theist could accept. It does not entail that all these ways are of equal validity or value, though Hick argues for that stronger thesis.

one can most effectively relate to it in an appropriate way. It is at that point that different spiritual paths open up, not just on the basis of different temperaments and cultural histories—though they are important factors—but also on the basis of differing claims about the facts of history and science, and about the interpretation of basic moral values. Because many of the facts are difficult to decide conclusively, and many of the value-interpretations are disputed, these paths will often conflict at various points.

One might then say, not that they are all more or less equally true, but that it is very hard to decide on the truth in these areas, so that those who conscientiously disagree are not to be condemned. If so one might be called an epistemic pluralist, to signify that while all views cannot be equally true, many conflicting views seem to be roughly equally justifiable. Such a pluralist is also likely to say that the really important thing about religious practice is the difference it makes for good, both in individual and in social life. Religious claims will be judged very largely on whether they make for fulfilment in personal and social life. Though there is disagreement about exactly what 'fulfilment' is—between a non-dualist and a personalist, for example—both will agree that it involves the overcoming of selfish desire. Both will agree that the supreme reality has great power or freedom, being the source of all things, great knowledge and intelligence, and bliss. These are the qualities that a perfected consciousness would have, and they are the qualities which realized human beings experience as they pursue the disciplines of devotional worship and meditation.

THE EXPERIENTIAL BASIS OF MODERN HINDUISM

The way of life of the disciple is based ultimately upon experience—the experience of the guru but also the more limited experience of the disciple—of a reality of freedom, wisdom, and bliss. It is not perhaps surprising that some will experience that freedom primarily in terms of a freedom from attachment, anxiety, and selfish desire (being absorbed in the non-dual), while others will experience it in terms of freedom to create new forms of beauty and self-expressive creativity (sharing in the *lila* of self-expressive Spirit). Some will experience wisdom as an intuitive insight which transcends all concepts (objectless intelligence), and others will experience it as a compassionate and empathetic knowledge of the inner nature of all beings. Some will experience bliss as a pure state free from all sorrow, and others will experience it as the happiness of deeply felt loving relationship.

Some forms of spiritual practice will accordingly interpret 'realization' in terms of self-contained equanimity and joy, while others will interpret it in terms of membership of a joyful community of devotion. Though these ways differ in many of their practical consequences, both are wholly opposed to materialism, selfish greed, deceitfulness, and violent emotion or action.

The main stress in Hindu religious tradition has been on the former types of interpretation, aiming at a spiritual goal of equanimity and bliss through personal discipline. There has not often in Hindu religious thought been a primary concern with issues of social organization or social justice as such. This is partly because belief in rebirth has led to a certain acceptance of the social order as being all right as it is. The caste system is a good expression of this attitude. The impetus of moral thinking is on the development of qualities in the individual soul, and since most people are at fairly low stages of spiritual progress, they can be left to the natural outworking of karma. Karmic fatalism, and a certain degree of self-absorption in one's own spiritual state, are negative possibilities within Hindu belief.

Nevertheless, if the realized individual does express the qualities of freedom, wisdom, and bliss, one would expect that there would naturally arise a recognition that these are the ultimate goals of all humans. If all sentient beings are in some sense parts of Brahman, the supreme spirit, then one should do what one can to enable them to realize their inner nature. One should make society such that people can pursue freedom, wisdom, and bliss. It is the thought that one cannot do much about that, since karma must be worked out, together with the thought that such qualities are qualities of mind which may flourish in adverse material conditions (on rubbish heaps, for example), that have to some extent impeded any strong religious impulses for social reform.

The Judaeo-Muslim tradition sees liberation as only truly existing within a just society, which therefore must be created as a condition of human fulfilment. The Indian tradition tends to the view that the vast mass of people will always be lost in greed and ignorance, so that a just society can never exist. Fulfilment is properly found within, in a turning away from the concerns of society. As it becomes clear that

it is possible to aim at material prosperity and to achieve real technological advances, many movements have arisen within Hinduism
that seek to take a much more positive view of social action. It still
remains broadly true that the Hindu tradition is concerned with disciplines that encourage specific mental states, rather than with programmes of social organization. The important spiritual teaching is
not that there is a law of God for a just society, but that there is a
way—or there are a number of ways—to experience the divine
Spirit, and realize inner freedom, wisdom, and bliss.[21]

Such a stress on mental discipline and on inner experience is
clearly seen in diaspora Hinduism, in the way the meditational and
yogic practices of Hindu tradition have been adopted by many, especially in the Western world, who have no particular religious beliefs.
Such practices become means to achieve mental serenity and vigour,
and though they have a basis in varying conceptions of a divine
reality, that basis can be ignored by practitioners who are more inter-
ested in benefits in terms of mental and physical discipline.

At this point the authority of Hindu tradition tends to dissipate
altogether. Anyone can set up as a teacher of yoga, and there are literally hundreds of schools which have virtually no contact with
teaching lineages. The teaching of such schools is often very eclectic,
and so open to an undiscriminating pluralist view that almost anything, from Tarot reading, nature-worship, the 'wisdom of the Pyra-
mids', and an assortment of diverse scriptures can be mixed together
in quite new combinations. Whereas in India such diverse practices
usually originate in local traditions, in the West they may be drawn
together in new ways by self-appointed gurus, who claim direct
paths to enlightenment, and demand absolute obedience—and
large sums of money—from their disciples.

The chief problem for Hinduism in the modern world is perhaps
to discern where the lines of proper spiritual authority lie, and
how one can sort out genuine spiritual teachers from charlatans.
Hinduism will probably remain a primarily ethnic faith, centred on
the cultic worship of Indian deities, based on the Vedic scriptures,
the Upanishads, and the *Gita*, and respecting those ascetic renouncers who give up family and possessions to seek to realize a sense of

---

[21] So, typically, Radhakrishnan says, 'Religion is in essence, experience, or living
contact with, ultimate reality,' 'The Spirit in Man', in *Contemporary Indian Philosophy*
(London: Allen & Unwin, 1952), 492.

God. In its international form, it has no centralized authority, but has given rise to many schools of spiritual discipline, aiming in various ways to train the mind in non-possessiveness and inner joy, and to produce an experience of the divine Spirit. The price of such diversity is that, faced with such a bewildering degree of choice, it may be difficult to distinguish the serious from the shoddy, the profound from the simply confused. There is evidence that some people have been caught up in psychologically damaging sects that have separated them from their families and undermined their powers of judgement and responsibility. But such dangers are perhaps no greater than the danger of large-scale oppression which the Semitic faiths contain.

Some 'Hindu' schools may be on the edge of rationality, but diaspora Hinduism has brought some benefits to the modern religious scene. Apart from the *frisson* of letting European Christians know what it is like to be missionized by a 'foreign religion', there are, I think, three main positive features of the international Hindu revival. These are: acceptance of religious pluralism in some form, emphasis on the possibility of personal experience of the divine, and the promotion of practical disciplines for encouraging non-attachment, wisdom, and compassion. It is possible, of course, to see these things much more negatively. Pluralism can be seen as uncontrolled confusion. Claims to God-realization can be seen as fantasizing wish-fulfilment. Meditation and yoga can be seen as encouraging morbid introspection. It is probably true that every human activity is to some extent ambiguous, and none is immune from corruption. Yet it seems to me more likely overall that a stress on pluralism, on personal experience, and on spiritual discipline will promote tolerance, happiness, and compassion. Such, at the very least, is their ideal aim.

In respect of each of these factors, the influence of Hinduism is perhaps greatest in the way it has affected the perceptions and practice of non-Hindu faiths, than in the way it has gained converts for itself. Perhaps, in a way analogous to the situation in Judaism, the destiny of Hinduism is to be 'a light to the world', one which is complementary to that found in the Semitic traditions, and much to be desired to mitigate the intolerance, emphasis on external conformity, and spiritual ineffectiveness in transforming personal lives of the Semitic faiths.

5
The Secular State

In 1789 the American Revolution introduced to the world in a formal way the idea of a secular state. The first amendment to the constitution of the United States of America, drafted two years later, laid down that there would be 'no law respecting an establishment of religion, or prohibiting the free exercise thereof'. The idea of a secular state was born.

In primal societies 'religion' is hard to distinguish from the general rituals and festivals of the tribe. Ancient Hebrew religion was a primal religion, in which the lives of the people were governed by laws that were inextricably religious, social, and political. Inevitably, however, religious and political leadership became separated. The 'judges' of Israel might have been religio-political leaders, but in a later age the kings and the prophets were different and often at odds with each other. The religious became partly supportive of, and partly critical of, the state. But there remained a close connection between political rule and religious practice. Rulers would no more claim to be neutral with regard to religious matters than they would with regard to moral and social matters. It is natural for there to be a generally agreed, state-supported religion, just as there is a general social agreement on modes of conduct and moral practices. This practice entered into the constitution of the states of modern Europe, and a principle almost universally accepted among the European nations after the Reformation was 'Cujus regio, ejus religio'—let the religion of the people be that of the ruler.

Such a view in fact espouses localized intolerance. Rejection of the tribal cult is disloyalty, and religious belief is closely associated with what would later become 'nationalistic' attitudes. We have seen this attitude breaking down, in the case of Islam, by missionary expansion which seeks to bring the whole world under the law of God, and actively opposes the 'polytheistic' practices of various national groups. Religion is now seen, not as a matter of the expression of a tribal or national tradition, but as an arena in which beliefs conflict and compete for superiority. The criticism which Islam makes of other religions, that they are inferior in morality or rationality, cannot fail eventually to be applied to Islam itself, which must then justify itself as a superior religion in terms of the greater morality and rationality that Islam has claimed for itself. Considerations of natural justice also suggest that if religions such as Islam wish to have the right to convert others, they must allow the right of others to convert their followers if they can.

We have noted how hard it is for Islam to separate itself from ethnicity, but at least it poses the ideal of a global, non-ethnic household of faith. That ideal, however, in practice produces conflict, as Muslim states find themselves ranged against non-Muslim states that refuse to accept the Qur'anic revelation as final and normative. The nature of the debate changes from one of group loyalty to one of agreement with or acceptance of alleged truths of revelation. At that stage it starts to become odd for different belief-systems to find themselves correlated with different nation-states. For how is it possible that facts of geography and social kinship could be so closely correlated with logically distinct questions of religious belief?

The reason for the correlation is, of course, that children are trained by their parents and teachers, and so they will properly tend to believe the views of their immediate social group. It is only when those views produce unmistakable internal tensions, or when they come into conflict with the views of other groups, that critical thought comes into play. At such points the demand for a justification of belief arises—not some sort of absolute, history-free justification, but a resolution of perceived problems in the tradition in the light of specific internal or external challenges.[1] Such a resolution will, however, raise questions of truth and justification which, once raised, cannot be quenched by mere insistence on tradition.

There arises a conflict between a sort of religion which expresses the peculiar identity of a particular social group, and a sort of religion which raises wider questions of truth and justifiability. Émile Durkheim viewed the maintenance of social unity as the main function of religious practice and belief,[2] but he notoriously set aside

---

[1] Alisdair MacIntyre, *Whose Justice, Which Rationality?* (London: Duckworth, 1988).

[2] 'The idea of society is the soul of religion,' É. Durkheim, *The Elementary Forms of the Religious Life*, trans. J. W. Swain (London: Macmillan, 1915), 419.

considerations of the truth of religious claims about the divine being and human destiny. When such claims are considered seriously, there is bound to be a division between factors which make for social unity and identity, and factors that are concerned with the objective truth of religious claims.

Religions very rarely claim to be based entirely upon reason, in the sense that any reasonable human beings could see them to be true. They are usually based on some claim to revelation, to a particular disclosure of truth to some outstanding founding figure, to which the religious community is called to be loyal. When, in the course of history, communities meet and interact, diverse revelatory traditions clash. When that happens, one tradition may simply take the other over, as happened with Islam and the tribal religions it encountered. They may continue as separate socially defined traditions, as has largely happened in India. Hinduism can be seen as a huge collection of primal traditions yoked together by acceptance of certain common texts and rituals. It embraces many differing truth-claims, but each tradition is fairly content to accept that it is one approach among many to knowledge of spiritual reality. On the whole, there is coexistence of differing local traditions with varieties of more personal, guru-centred, spiritual teaching. However, when the brahminical norms of ritual and social practice are themselves rejected, as they are by Muslims and Christians in India, social relations can become strained, and such activities can be seen as 'un-Indian'. Like Israel, India is, and has been since 1947, a secular state, partly in order to allow many such traditions to coexist without expressing an official preference between them.

Judaism very ambiguously maintains a close link between group membership and religious practice. The link is ambiguous because Israel is a secular state, and religious Jews are uneasy to be thought of as just an ethnic group. Most rabbis think, after all, that the God of Abraham is the one and only true God, whatever that God requires of Jews and Gentiles respectively. The Jewish response to the historical clash of traditions has on the whole been one of retreat into a non-aggressive defence of tradition within one social group.

However, simple takeover or non-interference policies become unstable when there is a balance of international powers, together with increased economic and social interaction between the powers. Cultural and religious pluralism occur when different social groups begin to mix. The boundaries become confused, and various forms of syncretism arise. In this process, issues of truth become separated from issues of social identity, and to that extent religious belief becomes 'privatized'.

Such a process is not primarily the consequence of secularism, as an anti-religious movement. It is a consequence of the simple historical fact of increased socio-economic interdependence and interaction. Of course, that historical process does give an impetus to secularization, as people increasingly realize that there are many different alleged revelations, and since they conflict at many points, they cannot all be true. The recognition of truth in a contested area, it comes to be felt, must be left to individuals, who must decide for themselves what is true.

Most individuals have neither the time nor the interest to decide such arcane and difficult issues as the relative truth of different revelations. Most people will follow traditions that they trust, as shaped by wise and learned predecessors. But it becomes increasingly clear that people must be permitted the freedom to adopt a religious view which seems to them most illuminating, in cases where they feel dissatisfaction with their received tradition. It is the interaction of societies in a global economy which makes freedom of religious belief, including the freedom to move from one tradition to another, desirable.

Islam struggles uneasily with its traditional ambition to be embodied in Islamic states, while Muslims form minorities in many countries, and while many different forms of Islamic state can be found even in what may be called the Muslim world. It seems obvious that the more competing truth-claims are made in religion, the less happily can a national state be committed to just one religious system. The more the area of religion is seen to be an area of competing claims about facts and values, however hard such claims are to adjudicate, the less reasonable it is to have particular religions established in particular geographical areas.

This became particularly clear in the United States, to which many immigrants had come because they were more or less persecuted religious minorities, or at least because they wanted to find greater freedom to practise their beliefs. The institution of the secular state was not an abandonment of religion or a declaration of its unimportance to social life. It was a recognition of the fact that, in a society of many competing beliefs, no one set could reasonably be set up as normative. In practice, American society remained strongly

Christian, though split into hundreds of different sects, seeking to exercise influence in whatever way they could. This form of secularism could be called a secularism of positive tolerance, since it regards religious belief as of such importance that it cannot be left as a matter of unconsidered tradition. It must be a matter of positive assent and commitment, and so it must be left to the conscience of the individual to respond to diverse revelatory traditions as seems right.

In such a view, there is a value-commitment to religious assent, not as obedience to tradition, but as a positive personal commitment. It might seem that this is a peculiarly Protestant stance, calling for 'commitment to the Saviour' rather than for the acceptance on authority of a set of revealed propositions as true. Yet it seems a virtually inevitable consequence of the historical pressure to move from seeing religion as social cement to seeing religion as one truth-claiming tradition of revelation among others.

FROM REFORM TO ENLIGHTENMENT

In fact a serious commitment to truth in religion entails an acceptance of plurality and tolerance. For truth can only be discovered by investigation, by critical testing, and by continual openness to new and possibly more illuminating ideas. That entails that all religious traditions must be open to investigation and criticism, and that the individual right to follow conscience where it leads must be respected. What Ian Markham has called 'the American discovery', the discovery that religious commitment can actually encourage plurality and tolerance,[3] and that indeed tolerance may flourish best with a certain sort of religious commitment, is indeed a transformation of attitude that history virtually imposes upon one. It just happens that America was the place where the secularism of positive tolerance was first enshrined in a state constitution.

In France, Spain, and Italy, secularization, which came much later and in various forms, had a different basis. It was a secularism of protest against privilege. Being part of a general revolution against the monarchy and against what was perceived to be unjust privilege, it was a specific revolt against the power and wealth of the Roman

---

[3] I. Markham, *Plurality and Christian Ethics* (Cambridge: Cambridge University Press, 1994), 25.

Catholic Church, and the hierarchical society it supported. It thus had a more positively anti-religious tone that tended to regard religion as inherently reactionary and a threat to liberty, equality, and true fraternity.

After the French Revolution the attempt was still made to have an established religion, though for a short time the French tried an almost wholly unsuccessful experiment in creating a tailor-made new religion of 'Reason'. Napoleon restored the position of the Catholic Church, though many of the old privileges of the church were withdrawn, and gradually France, in common with most European countries, moved towards a division between education, family law, and religion, and towards full acceptance of many diverse forms of religion, with one—some form of Christianity—retaining more a primacy of honour than anything else. France remains, however, the only country in Europe that has an officially secular constitution.

The great majority of people do not care about the intricacies of religious debate except when they become associated with major ethnic or social conflicts. They can live with whatever rites and ceremonies are provided, and continue the practices of folk-religion in the guise of quite different symbols and stories. This sort of folk-religion is not as simple as is sometimes thought. It takes great sophistication to reinterpret the doctrines of the theologians to fit the needs of lay practitioners. But it can usually be managed, as long as too much fuss is not made about it.

Nevertheless, the history of Europe is littered with religious wars and persecutions of minorities. The same subtlety which can reinterpret doctrines to fit folk-religion can also reinterpret them to fit racial and social prejudice. Christianity, which bids one turn the other cheek and love one's enemies, can be turned into a savage organ of repression against those who can be seen as threatening the integrity of the true faith, and therefore as endangering the possibility of eternal salvation. Thomas Aquinas wrote, 'As for heretics, their sin deserves banishment, not only from the Church by excommunication, but also from this world by death. To corrupt the faith, whereby the soul lives, is much graver than to counterfeit money.'[4] The Bible is replete with talk of avenging angels destroying the

---

[4] Thomas Aquinas, *Summa Theologiae*, II-II q. 11 a. 3, trans. Thomas Gilby (London: Blackfriars, 1964), xxvii. 89.

wicked, and the judgement of God poured out in wrath upon the anti-Christ.[5] When the church is seen as an instrument of God's will, and as the guardian of God's truth, it can readily become the agent of wrath to those—Jansenists, Huguenots, Catholics, or Waldensians, depending on one's point of view—who threaten the integrity and purity of the truth.

Toleration has been a hard lesson for the Christian churches to learn, and they have learned it largely through the growing indifference and sometimes hostility with which they have been viewed by the culture of the European Enlightenment. There are many sources of disenchantment with religion in modern Europe. One important source is internal to the Christian religion itself. The Protestant Reformation aimed to reform what was seen as the corruption of the Catholic Church, and to bring the church under the authority of the Bible as the sole norm of God's revelation. Four of its main effects, however, were to establish the right of private conscience to dissent from ecclesial authority; to undermine the traditional authority of the church, in both social and doctrinal matters; to increase literacy, as the reading of the Bible became more important for Christians; and to encourage the laity to participate in forms of social life in an active and more democratic way.

Such consequences were much more far-reaching than they were intended to be. Once liberated from the censorship of authority, the right of private conscience was to become the right to private interpretation, and possible rejection, of Scripture as well as tradition. It took three hundred years for this consequence to work its way through to Reimarus's rejection of the New Testament as a fraud perpetrated by the apostles.[6] But one cannot consistently claim the right of dissent for onself and deny it to others.

Rejection of authority was to become the watchword of the Enlightenment, apostrophized by Kant in the motto *sapere aude*, dare to be wise, to think for oneself and to free oneself from the tutelage of others.[7] The spread of literacy opened a much wider range of opinions to ordinary people, and encouraged the growth of knowledge about social inequality and injustice, which paved the way for the revolutionary movements of the eighteenth century. Similarly,

---

[5] Cf. Revelation 19: 7–15.

[6] Reimarus, *Wolfenbuttel Fragments*, published by G. Lessing, 1774–8.

[7] Kant, *What is Enlightenment?*, trans. L. W. Back, in *On History* (New York: Bobbs-Merrill, 1963), 3.

movements to widen political participation were a natural extension of lay involvement in church organization, and of the rejection of hierarchical forms of government on the ground that they were not rooted in original New Testament practice.

Thus the Reformation, though it was based for the most part on the absolute authority of the Bible, prepared the way for the Enlightenment, for which liberty and autonomy of thought, the free choice of beliefs, and the equal participation of all competent humans in their own government became of paramount importance.

THE ENLIGHTENMENT PROJECT

The values of the Enlightenment are by no means incontestable. A society which values liberty above all things will have to permit many forms of human behaviour which seem bizarre or irrational to the majority. In the wholly free society, drugs, consenting pornography, homosexuality, and varied forms of sexual relationship will be permitted as long as they cause no harm to others (which, of course, is by no means clear).[8] There may be no general conventions which are normative for training humans in particular conceptions of moral excellence or virtue, and a bewildering variety of options for living may be available. At the extreme, moral norms may be rejected altogether—though at that point the paradox exists that it is precisely the moral norm of individual liberty which leads one not to penalize people who reject one's own moral norms. No doubt there will always be a minimal morality which enables people to live together at all. But there will be no absolute or overriding moral norms—except that of individualism.

To attain consistency, it may be said that autonomy is not a moral absolute, but just a preference that one has. Then, however, it may well be rejected by many who prefer to have an authoritative moral teaching based on a securer access to truth than is available to everyone, or simply based on a Hobbesian belief that it is better to have absolute power than moral anarchy. The belief that everyone has a right to express their own opinion may degenerate into the belief that everyone has a right to *make up* their own opinions, to think whatever they like, especially in matters of morality. In this way an assertion of radical individualism may lead, by way of an acceptance that moral-

---

[8] J. S. Mill, *On Liberty* (Harmondsworth: Penguin, 1974).

ity is based upon individual preference or choice, to the recognition of morality simply as a tool for seeking or resisting power. Then it is easy for totalitarian regimes, both right and left wing, to seize power, while the intellectual leaders of culture will be paralysed by their inability to provide any principled opposition to such an exercise of preference, which may well be supported by the masses. In this way radical individualism can be transformed into radical totalitarianism overnight. The state becomes the arbiter of right and wrong, and morality itself fades away as an outmoded outgrowth of a superseded social system.

This is what Marx hoped for, though he also hoped that the dictatorship of the proletariat would in turn fade away as a society without hierarchy or compulsion came into existence, once all reactionary classes had been cleared out of the way.[9] Unfortunately, dictatorship does not seem a very effective means to a wholly egalitarian and just society, and most communist societies never progressed beyond the totalitarian form of dictatorship by the Party. At the other end of the political spectrum, fascism proposes a strict form of social control in the name of a perverse rewriting of Rousseau's 'general will', which only the governing elite can discern. Again, morality has no independent reality which can be a basis of social dissent and criticism. What is right is what the state declares to be right. The Durkheimian dream of the beginning of religion becomes the Leninist nightmare of the ending of religion in the rule of the state over the conscience of the individual.

Such a consequence signals what Alisdair MacIntyre has called the failure of 'the Enlightenment project', the search to find a universal secular basis of morality and reason.[10] It is certainly true that one of the aims of the philosophers of the Enlightenment was to free morality from its entanglement with institutional religion. Immanuel Kant opposed heteronomy, the reception of moral beliefs on the authority of others, even of God, to autonomy, the reflective construction of one's own moral beliefs. He called on his readers to throw off the chains of passive obedience, and take responsibility for their own moral decisions.

Kant would have been appalled at the thought that people could

---

[9] Cf. Marx and Engels, *Manifesto of the Communist Party* (Moscow: Foreign Languages Publishing House, 1959), ch. 2, p. 74.

[10] Alisdair MacIntyre, *After Virtue* (London: Duckworth, 1985), 117.

differ widely in their moral choices. He proposed one crucial rule for moral thinking, the Categorical Imperative, the rule that all putative moral prescriptions must pass the test of being applicable equally to everyone and prescribable equally by everyone.[11] He assumed that everyone, by applying that rule, would come to agreement on basic moral principles. What Kant was insisting upon was that all moral rules must be justified, and the justification must ultimately rest upon principles that every rational person would accept. It is not enough, he argued, to say that some rule is to be found in a Holy Text, and so must be unquestioningly obeyed.

Are there principles that every rational person will accept? There should be no difficulty in admitting that there are such principles in logic and mathematics. The Enlightenment project was to apply this model to morality, to find virtually self-evident principles from which moral beliefs could be deduced. Kant himself suggested two—happiness and perfection.[12] Everyone wants to be happy, and everyone wants to realize their distinctive excellences, to 'express their natural dispositions and inclinations'. Such natural inclinations range from desiring to eat, be warm, and have sexual relations, to satisfying one's curiosity, listening to beautiful music, and telling or hearing stories. Tying the two together, Aristotle had said that happiness lies in the unimpeded exercise of one's characteristic virtues, or excellences.[13]

The key principle is that one looks to human nature, to natural human dispositions and behaviour, to discern what sorts of activities injure or frustrate such dispositions, and what activities aid or facilitate them. Such a procedure was by no means new with the Enlightenment. It has its roots in Aristotle and the Stoics, and entered into Christianity in the form of an appeal to 'natural law', the basic moral code which is accessible to universal human reason and is not dependent on revelation.[14]

In its Christian interpretation, natural law is founded upon the will of God to create beings with a particular nature, which suggests

---

[11] Kant, *Fundamental Principles of the Metaphysics of Ethics (Grundlegung)*, trans. T. K. Abbott (London: Longmans, 1959), 46.

[12] Kant, *The Doctrine of Virtue (Pt. 2 of Metaphysic of Morals)*, trans. Mary Gregor (New York: Harper, 1964), 33.

[13] Aristotle, *Nicomachean Ethics*, 1098^{a}8–27, trans. J. A. K. Thomso (Harmondsworth: Penguin, 1976), 76.

[14] Cf. Aquinas, *Summa Theologiae*, I-II q. 91, a. 2.

that God intends the fulfilment of that nature, the realization of the potentialities God has implanted.

The complication in the Christian story is that human nature has been impaired by egoism and the rejection of fellowship with God. The fulfilment of human nature properly lies in the employment of the powers of the mind and will to know and love God. Such fulfilment will therefore be dependent upon a reciprocal relation between God and humanity, in which natural human powers are drawn out and directed by divine inspiration.

In this perspective, freedom does not lie in the fact of humans deciding to do whatever they want, without reference to the needs of others and the will of God. It lies primarily in the uniquely creative response which each person makes to the loving invitation and empowerment offered by God. It is a freedom of creative response to the call of love. True freedom lies in creative co-operation, by which the self is empowered to create and contemplate new values, in a continuing realization of new forms of understanding, beauty, and friendship.

This creative responsiveness is impaired by the fall into hatred, greed, and ignorance which now characterizes human life. In the fallen state, freedom is seen as essentially self-centred, as the ability to seek pleasure and power in whatever ways one wants. It becomes clear that the potentialities of human nature include potentialities for conflict and corruption. To speak of self-fulfilment in a fallen world is to be heard as speaking of the pursuit of pleasure and power.

Aristotle, the Stoics, and Christian theologians all believed the world to be teleologically structured. That is, they thought there were distinctive human excellences that it was the purpose of human life to realize. For Christians, who believe life would continue beyond death, those excellences will be fully realized in a new creation, so that any inability to realize them in this life does not throw doubt on the obligation to pursue them as far as one can.

Kant was really not very far from this tradition of thought. In asking each person to consider what principles they could positively legislate for all humans, he was of course supposing that they would take human desires and dispositions into account. He was in effect asking each person to put themselves in the place of God, a God who was equally concerned for all human creatures, and who wanted them to be as happy and fulfilled as was compatible with the happiness and fulfilment of all other persons. The application of the

Categorical Imperative is a way of getting persons to adopt a view-point of disinterested or egalitarian benevolence. But for him there is now no active co-operation with or creative response to a God who really exists and can be experienced, and who might actually command the adoption of universal benevolence.

The first thing that happens to natural law after its Kantian revision is that it is no longer based on a human nature that has been created by God precisely in order that its positive potentialities might be realized by co-operative and creative effort. As Sartre was later to put it, 'Existence precedes essence'—there is no divine pattern to which human nature or human action has to conform. One can select which inclinations to follow by personal choice, and it is not reasonable to conform to any pre-existing pattern.

The second thing that happens is that there is no law of karma or warning of divine judgement that might ensure that good and evil acts might issue in morally balanced good or evil outcomes for the agent. There is no guarantee that justice will reign in the universe, or that the course of events will, even in the long run, somehow prove favourable to moral conduct. One should, says Kant, let justice rule, though the heavens fall. But there is, after all, no strong reason why one should, if one does not choose to do so.

The project of seeking an understanding of basic human needs and inclinations that will ground a universal morality seems to fall foul of the fact that human needs and inclinations may be almost indefinitely various, and may even conflict with each other so violently that there is no possibility of universal coexistence. Moreover, there is no overwhelming reason why one should view all persons with disinterested benevolence anyway. That might lead, absurdly, to giving the desires of the majority preference over one's own. It could be much more realistic, in a world of constant warfare and violence of all sorts, to cultivate friendship with one's kin and close community, and regard all others with decided suspicion.

If God regards all people with equal benevolence, and commands that we do so as well, it would make good sense to do so, both out of love for God and out of respect for the Creator's power. But if it is only a philosopher from Königsberg who tells us to be universally benevolent, and if he also insists that we should make our own minds up, and not regard the authority of other people (even philosophers from Königsberg), we might well make up our minds not to take any notice of him.

If he proceeds to tell us that our own reason will convince us that like cases should be treated alike, so we know it is rational not to make exceptions in our own case, we may well reply that it is wholly rational to treat ourselves and our loved ones preferentially. Why should I act on principles that I wish everyone would act on, when I know that they will not do so? This is surely a philosophy for dreamers, who pretend the world is filled with purely disinterested rational agents, when in fact it is filled with power-hungry, confused, and self-interested predatory animals.

In a world of ruthless predators, where some can flourish only by oppressing others, it is no use saying that the strong should only act on principles that the weak could also act on. It might be more rational to let the strong prevail by natural processes of competition. The competitive option is arguably more rational, in that it is likely to select over generations for strength and skill, and so will optimize social development. In that case, the rational morality is not one of completely disinterested benevolence, but one of restricted benevolence, focused on one's own family or tribal group.

A Christian might point to a divine command to care for the weak, but it is not clear that such care is more rational than selecting for strength and intelligence by eliminative competition. There are canons of reason, and one of them is that like cases must be treated similarly. But it is quite rational to will that everyone, strong and weak, should be free to compete for survival. Different moralities may spring up for the weak, who may band together in altruistic and egalitarian groups for security, and for the strong, who may prefer a more individualistic ethic, and support a hierarchical social structure.

That is what Nietzsche and Marx believed human society to be like—an essentially competitive structure in which there could be no universally shared norms. Different social groups would have differing norms, depending on their economic and social circumstances, and reason alone would not be able to adjudicate between them. The liberal dream of universal rational norms ignores the facts of human conflict and self-interest, and the deep-seated natural human inclinations to fight for family and tribe against all outsiders.

The complete rejection of the Enlightenment project is found in the claim, made by some sociobiologists, that reason itself is an adaptive evolutionary tool, selected because it has been useful to survival.[15] Far from being some absolute standard free from the blind conflicts of passion and power, it is part of the conflict. In its application to human conduct, it expresses the rising power of the bourgeoisie. The demand for universal justification at the bar of reason is an effective weapon against aristocratic privilege and tradition. Thus utilitarianism, demanding that all moral rules must be shown to be for the greatest happiness of the greatest number, was explicitly seen as an instrument of social reform in Britain. But its optimistic assumption of a universal agreement in opinions, to be brought about by increased education, was unable to cope with the idea of conflicting, class-based moralities that threw doubt on the ideal of one harmonious community of self-legislating moral agents.

For Marx, rational argument is the froth on the surface of the deep socio-economic changes which are the real driving force of moral change.[16] Moralities of individual freedom and universal co-legislation are expressions of emerging global free-market economies. They rest upon the exploitation of the working masses, an exploitation that is hidden because all have access in principle to the means of government, while in fact the mechanisms of the free market concentrate real power in the hands of a few manipulators of popular opinion. Talk of individualistic human rights is used by the affluent, who can afford to protect such rights, as a weapon to criticize developing societies and manipulate them into doing what the rich nations wish. Different social arrangements will result in different sorts of morality.

Paradoxically, Marx propounds a deeply 'moral' idea of a perfect society, when the state apparatus of government has withered away, and when all live in personal freedom and abundance. He clearly thinks such a society is preferable to one in which most people are enslaved by capitalism. But the idea that morality is primarily the expression of social relationships clearly permits many other preferences and forecasts, including that of a completely authoritarian state based on the dominance of a small élite. Most Communist states, aiming to follow the Marxist creed, have in practice been such authoritarian states, expressing the dictatorship of the proletariat, or rather of the small élite Communist Party which claims to represent

---

[15] Cf. Michael Ruse, *Evolutionary Naturalism* (London: Routledge, 1995), ch. 6.
[16] 'Your very ideas are but the outgrowth of the conditions of your bourgeois production,' Marx and Engels, *Communist Manifesto*, 67.

their interests. The classless society of Marx's dreams has been postponed to an indefinite future.

SECULAR AND RELIGIOUS MORALITY

Has the Enlightenment project then wholly collapsed? I do not think that it has, though the attempt to base morality on purely rational principles drawn from a neutral analysis of human nature has been shown to be unstable and contested. Human beings may be viewed as bundles of diverse and often conflicting inclinations. So they are, but that does not entail that nothing morally useful can be said about natural human inclinations.

It may not be possible to find anything that literally everyone wants, but one can certainly say that, if anyone has an interest in anything, it is in surviving, in eating and in being secure, in not being tortured or forced to do things he or she really dislikes. So it is quite easy to make a list of evils, of things people have a good reason to avoid. Death, starvation, insecurity, torture, pain, slavery, and oppression are things everyone has good reason to avoid. So the positive correlatives of these things—life, the means of sustenance, security, happiness, and freedom from oppression—are things everyone has a good reason to pursue. There may be many ways of being happy or many different ideas about what oppression is, but there can be little doubt that it is eminently reasonable to seek happiness, security, and freedom of action.

Everyone has a good reason to avoid death, injury, pain, and slavery, and a good reason to pursue life, security, happiness, and freedom. Thomas Aquinas thought that it was a self-evident first principle of action that one should seek good and avoid evil.[17] This principle is not as vacuous as it may sound. We know what basic goods and evils are—they are given by those rational desires and aversions which are natural to human beings as such. We know that if it is reasonable for me to seek certain goods for myself just on the basis that I am human, then it is reasonable for all humans to do so. We also know that if I should avoid an evil which accrues to me just on the basis that I am human, then I should, if I can, avoid an evil which accrues to any human. That is the basis of belief in universal human rights—one should refrain from doing to any human what

---

[17] Aquinas, *Summa Theologiae* I-II q. 94, a. 2.

one would refrain from doing to oneself on the basis of desires which one has simply because one is human.

Humanism is correct in saying that we can know what is basically good and evil for human beings without any appeal to authority or religious revelation. The difficulty comes with the move from acknowledging that there are what may be called objective human goods to the assertion that one ought to pursue those goods not only for oneself, but for all humans. It sounds like John Stuart Mill's infamous move from the assertion that each person aims at their own happiness to the assertion that each person ought to aim at the happiness of all.[18] Indeed there is a double leap involved here, from 'it is reasonable' to 'one ought', and from 'one ought to seek X for oneself' to 'one ought to seek X for everyone'.

A theist can say that God's purpose that humans should flourish turns a rational, but in the end optional choice, into a matter of obligation. God desires the flourishing of all humans, and so makes the obligation universal. But if there is no God, we might rationally choose to ignore the goods of others, especially where they conflict with our own. Reason tells us what things are good, but has no motivating power to urge us to choose good as such and for its own sake. Not even all Kant's *Critiques* could manage to turn a principle of pure practical reason into a categorical obligation.

Thus there is a sort of dialectical relationship between advocating a fully secular basis for morality and insisting on the need for a religious element in its foundation. The secular humanist will say that truth is best found by free critical enquiry—by observation and experiment, or by open debate and exposure to as wide a range of opinions as possible. Religious teachers, thinking they have the truth, often try to prevent free critical enquiry. They burn books, discourage debate, decry the study of differing beliefs, and see their task as the inculcation of traditional and well-tried opinions, which can form a bedrock of certainty in a changing world.

On the other hand, the very idea of objective truth is under attack in much modern secular thought. Everything becomes a matter of persuasion, and everyone can believe whatever most appeals to them. When everything is open to criticism, one may become cynical about every view, and beliefs can be manufactured to order. At such a time, religion tends to uphold the idea that there is an

---

[18] J. S. Mill, *Utilitarianism* (London: Dent, 1960), ch. 4, p. 33.

objective truth which must be sought honestly and rigorously. There is a morality of honesty, which in turn involves trust, co-operation, and fidelity, and religious commitment can prevent the erosion of such ideals by cynicism and mockery.

In a similar way, a secular humanist may say that art should be a matter of free personal expression. Religious teachers, seeing themselves as the guardians of true beauty, often attempt to censor artistic works. They forbid paintings or literature of certain sorts, and try to make all works conform to their own ideas of what is fitting.

On the other hand, the very idea of beauty is under attack in much modern art. Pornography and violence can be seen as acceptable forms of art, and expressions of egoism and destruction replace Romantic dreams of elegance and sublimity. At such a time, religion tends to uphold the idea of an objective beauty which humans can be taught to recognize and create, and religious commitment can harness creative activity to the pursuit of moral goodness in life-enhancing ways.

For secular thinkers of the Enlightenment, the political structures of a society should express the will of the people, and all should be equal before the law, with full access to the political process. Religious teachers often advance a hierarchical or patriarchal view of social structures, defending long-established traditions against all attempts to reform them.

On the other hand, democracy readily degenerates into mob rule, as unbridled freedom leads to the collapse of communal concern, and the majority use their power to silence permanent minorities. At such a time, religion retains a stress on ideals of justice and mercy, and teaches people to be concerned for the common good, for forgiveness and reconciliation, which is a palliative to cynical attempts to gain power by populist bribery.

Humanism does provide basic moral norms, but fails to turn them into universal obligations. In that sense the project of grounding a universal rational morality fails. Nevertheless, the attempt to divorce morality from religion began to undermine the claims of religious authorities to impose moral rules just because they were written in a scriptural text, or were ratified by ecclesiastical tradition. It was seen not to be sufficient to say, 'Do this, because God said so.' All claims to knowledge of what God said were subject to critical scrutiny, and even alleged divine commands had to be brought before the bar of rational morality. If a good person is one who aims at the good of all sentient beings, then even the alleged commands of a good God must be seen to be aimed at the good of all sentient beings.

The biblical God certainly condemns killing, and wishes to bring Israel to happiness and freedom. But it often seems that God is very partial, not caring much for the happiness and freedom of Israel's enemies. The biblical God can seem intolerant, commanding the destruction of foreign shrines. And that God is extremely severe and retributive in the punishments that are meted out to various people and nations. It must be said, in fairness, that love of neighbour and of resident aliens is commanded in the Hebrew Bible, in the book of Leviticus,[19] and that Jesus teaches that such love must be unrestricted and wholehearted. But it must also be said that the very last book of the Bible, the book of Revelation, seems to regard with equanimity, or even satisfaction, the torture and destruction of thousands of human beings. The Bible is an ambiguous guide to moral conduct, containing both injunctions to unrestricted love and warnings of punitive vengeance. Its acceptance of slavery, concubinage, polygamy, child marriage, capital punishment, and female subordination render it suspect as a literal guide to moral conduct for every human society.

Of course the Christian natural-law tradition interpreted the biblical texts in accordance with a generally humane morality, as far as possible. But perhaps it took the shock of a complete break with what Kant called 'heteronomous', revealed morality, to break the hold of the undigested primitive moral conceptions that can be found in the Bible.

With what right can one identify and classify these conceptions as 'primitive'? From a humanist viewpoint this is a simple question to answer. Morality aims at greater life, security, happiness, and freedom for every human life, as far as possible. Such practices as slavery and capital punishment fail to reflect a maximal concern for the welfare of individuals. The former reflects a social institution which sustains a hierarchical order in which some individuals are systematically considered to be of less importance than others. The latter fails to see that all punishment should leave open and even encourage the possibility of reform, whereas killing or solely retributive punishment adds the damaging of one more life to the one that has already been damaged by the criminal.

---

[19] Leviticus 19: 18, 34.

The situation is paradoxical. On the one hand, it is humanism that exposes the vindictive and oppressive nature of much 'revealed' morality. On the other hand, humanism is a very precarious foundation for commitment to a maximally compassionate morality. For it cannot give a convincing reason why one should be committed to what may well seem to be a rather unrealistic or impractical ethic. Theism can do that, since it does not limit its hopes to this world, and does not restrict its demands to what seems reasonable to a specific agent at a specific time. Perhaps the lasting contribution of secular humanism is to spur theistic believers into rejecting unhelpful traditions from an ambiguous past, and drive them to see the true basis of their own moral outlook in the existence of a supremely loving God, who constantly urges people on to new and wider moral insights into what this implies for human conduct in the image of God.

A humanist viewpoint, one that starts from a consideration of what makes for the flourishing of human nature in every person, gives a good standard for considering what a perfectly just and merciful God would lay down as morally obligatory. But that viewpoint can provide no very satisfactory incentive to live by such moral rules. They are, in a world without God, merely abstract ideals of what a disinterestedly benevolent being might will universally. It is therefore not surprising that the rational morality of Immanuel Kant, the utopian utilitarianism of Bentham and Mill, and the bold assertions of the Declaration of Human Rights, have come to be viewed with scepticism by the very autonomous rational agents who were supposed to be their ultimate source and strength.

It is not true, as some religious believers claim, that secular humanism undermines moral standards and leads to an anarchy of individualistic self-will. On the contrary, it is the insistence by secular humanists that moral rules need to be justified in terms of human welfare, not accepted as sheer divine commands, that has led to many social reforms and the widespread rejection of the patriarchal attitudes of medieval Europe. Nevertheless, the record of secular states in the modern world is not a morally impressive one.

The French Revolution led almost immediately to the Terror, and revolutionary movements in general often accept violence as a necessary means on the way to a just society. Horrifying massacres in Russia, Vietnam, and China demonstrate that intolerance and vindictiveness are not the preserve of religious believers only. Of course, these are cases of the secularism of protest and anger. But even in relatively humane secular societies such as the United States, where one finds a secularism of positive tolerance, a culture of violence, of individual licence, and of general indifference to socially structured poverty in society and in the world at large, ensures that the humanist ideal of a free, egalitarian, and participatory society is compromised in practice by human hatred and greed.

Some sort of morality is essential in any functioning human society, but it can often be a tribal, restricted morality based on social convention and economic dominance and dependence rather than on some pure set of humanist ideals. There is very good reason why societies should inculcate a moral sense in their inhabitants. The security and harmony of the social order requires it. But it looks as though the hatreds and prejudices of human beings are expressed as often in anti-religious societies as in religious ones. That is faint praise indeed for religion, but it makes the point that societies will need to inculcate their own tribal values in some way, and religion may well come to hand as an instrumental means. If it does not, other myths of ethnic superiority and manifest destiny, like those of Nazi Germany, can be constructed, so that individuals can have the satisfaction of commitment to a 'higher' cause, while working out their hostilities in a socially approved way on the rest of the world.

Natural human morality is socially conservative, tribal, hostile to outsiders, and vindictive. The repressive use of religion is a symptom of this condition, not its cause. Yet this symptomatic use is enough to ensure that a recovery of religious practice does not automatically lead to a restoration of a purer moral order, or deliver religion from the hatreds of human life generally. It is almost always mistaken to think that religious revival will produce moral renewal. It is as likely to lead to different forms of supine conformism, attempts to enforce rationally unjustifiable but allegedly ancient or revealed traditions, and repressive hostility to those who differ.

Nevertheless, it is not true, as some secularists claim, that the practice of religion is bound to lead to obscurantism, reaction, and hatred. If the practice of religion needs to be humanized by consideration of what makes for the welfare of human beings, secular morality needs to be motivated by belief in a more than human power which can make moral principles objectively obligatory and ensure that in some way moral commitment will not be ultimately in vain. Unfortunately, the conscious invention of the idea of such a power will not be motivating at all. The French 'religion of Reason' was a dismal failure because everyone knew that it had been invented by intellectuals, and was no more than their projection of human ideals onto the cosmic order. Immanuel Kant's postulates of God and immortality proved to be similarly ineffective. If they are props to an independently established morality, then morality can survive without them. If they are really necessary to moral commitment, then Kant's universal and rational morality is a defective analysis of the nature and basis of autonomous, secular, morality. Pure Reason proves to be little more, in the end, than a fading echo of the voice of a dying God.

THE SECULARISM OF POSITIVE TOLERANCE

What is needed is some personal experience of a power which seems to carry moral authority with it, and which offers hope for the vindication of a moral order in the universe. Such an experience cannot be manufactured, and it cannot be affirmed simply on the basis that it is needed to bolster some independent system of moral truths. Religion is neither a prop to sound morality, nor a guarantee of moral probity. Religion has its own proper validity as the realm of the relationship between humans and an alleged spiritual order which bounds human existence. In many religions that spiritual order is construed in terms of a reality of supreme value and power. In so far as a supreme value exists, it will naturally set the goal of human striving and the demand which is placed upon humans to seek it. In so far as it has supreme power, it will ensure that the universe is morally ordered to the realization of goodness.

This idea may be worked out, as it has been in the Indian traditions, in terms of a self-existent reality which is the supreme goal for all sentient beings, and of a karmic law which gives the universe an inescapable moral order. Or it may be worked out, as it has been in the Semitic traditions, in terms of a supreme moral will that demands justice and mercy, and of a cosmic Judgement that will ensure that good and evil deeds reap their appropriate reward. In both traditions, particular moral prescriptions which have become embodied in sacred scriptures reflect the limitations of viewpoint and social custom of their times. But in both, there is an awareness that humans do not understand the Supreme Reality very well, even when it is revealed to them. There is thus a deeper impetus towards seeking to know more fully the nature of the ultimate moral ideal and demand in new social situations, and to achieve a more reflective grasp of what makes for universal human fulfilment.

A wholly secular morality is bound to lack such ideas of an objective moral demand or ideal goal, and of an ultimate moral order in human life. It is likely to see morality as a socially constructed set of principles which, if it is to be generally followed, needs to be enforced by social sanctions. In a world which, like the modern world, is strongly interconnected in many economic and technological ways, it becomes essential to have enforced codes of behaviour that will form the basis for reliable and relatively stable relationships. If social life is not to be a state of incipient total warfare of each against all, there is need of agreements on how various goods are to be produced, shared, and consumed. On such a view, morality is a set of agreed compromises between competing interests and desires. It will not consist of absolutely authoritative commands, but it will be vitally important that the moral rules are followed none the less. It will therefore be sensible to teach people to feel the internal sanctions of conscience as well as to institute the external sanctions of criminal law. A secular morality will not usually call forth a total personal commitment to strenuous moral endeavour, but it will otherwise look very like the basic moral codes shared by all religions. 'Love your neighbour as yourself' may be too extreme for a secularist, but 'Do as you would be done by' will remain a rational and important principle.

Written codes such as the Universal Declaration of Human Rights of 1948 formulate principles of justice which it is generally desirable that all societies should follow. The basic principle is that of establishing a rough sense of equality between persons, so that grievances should not build up and cause social anarchy. These human rights include the right to the basic conditions of physical and mental development, the right to work, to be free to associate and form one's own beliefs, and the right to participation in political institutions. These are things that all rational persons would desire for themselves, which entails that they are desirable (good) for humans as such. If law is to be seen to be just, it must treat all persons with equal consideration, these basic goods must be distributed impartially between persons, or at least inequalities must be justified in some generally acceptable way. So agreement to basic human rights is based on the desirability of certain basic goods, and on a concern that generally agreed laws must be seen to be just or fair.

If a society simply ignores such principles, for instance by failing to consider the needs and interests of specific groups (gypsies or Jews or women), they will be seen to be acting on the basis of power, not of justice. They will thus to some extent at least forfeit any claim to be treated justly by other societies. In the end, global morality has to be enforced by the self-interest of all concerned in agreeing a set of rules that will enable the most profitable sorts of international relationships to develop. These are by definition rules of justice, of equal and universal consideration. Marx was right in thinking that it is relationships of material production and exchange that will give rise to universal principles of justice, and cause them to be enforced, at least to some extent. Human rights are destined to remain only partially realized ideals for the most part, since many people and states will seek to avoid their implementation wherever possible. They will nevertheless provide a universally agreed basis for morality, since no one can explicitly reject them without rejecting their own claim to be treated justly by others.

Human beings will strive to exercise dominance by the use of power wherever it can feasibly be done, but they will have a fairly clear idea of what principles need to be followed if truly lasting security and peace is to prevail in the world. In that limited sense, humans are not naturally good, but they naturally know what goodness is. In matters of religion one is likely to extend toleration to others only when one has reason to ask for toleration of members of one's own faith. One is likely to allow diversity of opinion only to the extent that one wishes to be allowed to disagree with others. One will extend the hand of friendship to people of other faiths only when one needs friendship and support from some of them. It is in that sense that toleration, freedom of expression and inter-faith dialogue have become more widespread in the modern world. As different social groups become more dependent on one another, more mobile and more widely spread throughout the world, each group needs to establish just relationships with others, and that entails toleration, freedom of association, and equality of respect.

A good historical case in recent times is the move of the Roman Catholic Church from repression of religious liberty to positive tolerance. Pope Pius XII, who prepared the way to the Second Vatican Council, although he was not an especially conservative pope could not agree that views incompatible with those of the Catholic Church had the right to public expression. In 1953, in his *Allocution on*

Tolerance, he decreed that error had no rights. By contrast, the declaration on religious liberty of the Second Vatican Council, issued in 1965, states that 'the human person has a right to religious freedom'.[20] Reasons are produced why this doctrine is rooted in Christian revelation. In addition to reasons drawn specifically from revelation, which I will not mention here, there is an appeal to general considerations of human nature as created by God.

It declares that human beings are created with reason and free will, and are obligated to seek the truth. Everybody has the duty, and therefore the right, to seek truth in religious matters. This requires free enquiry, communication, and dialogue. Moreover, humans must adhere to the truth through personal assent. Therefore no one must be compelled to believe against conscience (ch. 1). This clear and elegant argument moves from a rationally perceived purpose of creation (to use reason in seeking truth), to the maximal conditions for seeking truth, and finally to an insistence on free personal assent, in religious as well as in scientific matters. One could hardly have a clearer illustration of the way in which the Enlightenment insistence on 'thinking for oneself' has been incorporated into a theistic framework, with a mutually beneficial effect for both Enlightenment and religious thought.

It is clear that, on such reasoning, secular states can be committed to a universal morality of justice, while protecting the rights of religious groups to exist within the limits of that morality, and while permitting the pursuit of many differing cultural values and interests within their boundaries. Thus bounded by the principles of justice, various religious groups may pursue their own ideals of life in ways that will provide strong internal sanctions for moral conduct. In the words of the Vatican declaration, 'That highest of man's rights and duties—to lead a religious life with freedom in society—must be respected.'[21]

Once religion has been moralized by a secular insistence on principles of justice, it can in turn contribute significantly to the maintenance of moral commitment in society. It will never be free of the compromises and ambiguities which limit all human perceptions of morality, but it can motivate commitment to basic rules of justice,

---

[20] *Vatican Council 2: Conciliar and Post-Conciliar Documents*, ed. Austin Flannery (Dublin: Dominican Publications, 1992), 800.
[21] Ibid. 812.

and in addition it can encourage the pursuit of more rigorous moral ideals of life which will encourage compassionate human acts over and above the strict demands of basic justice.

Perhaps, then, we are now in a position to move to a new approach to religious belief. It may not be true, as Comte held, that humanity moves from religion through metaphysics to positive science. But it may be true that there is a historical movement from religion as social tradition through humanism to religion as an interactive plurality of traditions. In that third stage, diversity itself comes to be seen as a natural and enriching part of the human condition, a condition of exploration into truth by response to the originative disclosures of the divine that we so dimly comprehend. A secular society that encourages forms of freely chosen religious commitment, and that disallows only those religious forms which conflict with or endanger basic human rights, seems the appropriate social structure for such a historical situation.

PART II

THE CHURCH AS A
SPIRITUAL COMMUNITY

6

The Church as a Teaching Community

THE CHURCH AS THE BODY OF CHRIST

Whereas Judaism and Islam seek, generally speaking, to bring the world under the law of God, and Buddhism and Hinduism seek, on the whole, to renounce the world, it is typical of Christian faith to set up a tension between the religious community and the world which is both critical and putatively transformative. There have, it is true, been many attempts to set up a Christian state, but a key part of the tradition is that 'the world' is fallen, that 'you cannot serve both God and Mammon',[1] and that the kingdom of Christ is not of this world.[2] There have been Christian attempts to renounce the world, but the central doctrine of incarnation gives a value to earthly life that is hard to gainsay, and the hope for a renewal of the world by the Spirit of God is at the heart of Jesus' teaching.

So, on the one hand, the world is corrupt, and the faithful are called out of the world to live in Christ, whom the world crucified.[3] On the other hand, the world is created, indwelt, and redeemed by God, and the faithful are called to a ministry of reconciling the world to God.[4] This ambiguity enters into the heart of the Christian community itself. The faithful remain as part of the world, so that their community is one of sinners who stand before God to plead forgiveness. Yet the community of faith is called to be a community of saints, of those who are sanctified by the Spirit, and commanded to be a light to those in darkness.

Do Christians seek to rule or to renounce the world? Is the church the communion of saints or the home of penitent sinners? In the church humans are called to offer the many imperfections of their

---

[1] Luke 16: 13.   [2] John 18: 36.
[3] 'You have died, and your life is hid with Christ in God': Colossians 3: 3.
[4] 'In Christ God was reconciling the world to himself . . . and entrusting to us the message of reconciliation': 2 Corinthians 5: 19.

lives to God, so that God can act in and through them to begin to reconcile the world to the divine life. One might expect, therefore, that the church will be a community vividly aware of its imperfections and yet trying to be a channel of divine grace to the world.

The reason the church should not aspire to govern the world is that it participates in sin, and so in the corruption of all human institutions. It is arguable that the Catholic (Constantinian) tradition has not always been keenly aware of its own corruptibility, and for that reason has sometimes capitulated to the temptation to rule the world. The reason the church should not withdraw from the world is that it is the community through which God wills to make the redemptive activity of the Spirit manifest. There have been repeated attempts from the beginning of Christian history to see the church as a 'community of the pure', rigorously and ascetically separated from the world. Some Protestant churches have tended to retreat into a world-ignoring separateness by not seeing a divine purpose in the development of artistic, scientific, and social culture. This suggests that the structure of the church should be such as to minimize its continual tendency to corruption, and to enable it to be an effective vehicle of the action of the Spirit.

But why should there be a church at all? In the Indian religious traditions there are devotional groups, societies which follow the teachings of a particular guru, and which exist for mutual encouragement in the spiritual life. For Hindus, the religious quest is in the end an individual matter of the progress of the soul, but the support of like-minded people in renunciation and meditation practice is invaluable. The Buddhist *sangha* is a vital resource for living the renounced life, but it is basically a voluntary association of men or women joining together in pursuing the way of non-attachment.

The religion of the Hebrew Bible is quite different. God is held to liberate the twelve tribes as a nation from Egypt and promise them a homeland in Canaan. A covenant is made between the nation and God, so that if they keep Torah they will be blessed with fulfilment and peace in God. A socio-political community is held to be brought into being by the call of God. Individuals do not choose to enter a special community of renouncing practice. They are born into a society, held to be already set apart (made holy, *quadosh*) by God, and they do not choose its fundamental structure or laws.[5]

---

[5] The fundamental Abrahamic covenant is given at Genesis 12: 1–3.

Islam abandons the idea of a covenant people, but retains belief in a revelation of God which calls its hearers into a community of obedience. The *umma* is a socio-political community of response to the declared law of God, and the call to submit to that law is divinely initiated and imperative. Islam is not easily thought of as a voluntary society for worshipping God. It is the community of those who agree to obey the revealed laws of God.

The Christian community, the church, stands between these two distinct sorts of religious community. God calls people into the community of the church by a special divine act. The church is generally taken to have been ordained by God, not to be simply the result of human devising. In these respects, the church is understood to be a divinely constituted community. On the other hand, the church stands in tension with wider human society. It is called out of the world, and advised not to 'love the world'.[6] Moreover, the church has no divinely revealed law, Torah having been abandoned in its earliest years. So in some ways the Christian community looks more like a sectarian community of disciples than a 'Christian state'.

It seems clear that the church must be regarded by Christians as more than a voluntary association of those who follow the teachings of Jesus. In fact the Christian community has a form of relationship with its founder that is virtually unique in religious history. In the New Testament it is repeatedly said to be 'the body of Christ',[7] which implies that its members have an inward and organic relationship to Christ. It would be nonsensical to speak of Jews as the body of Moses, of Muslims as the body of Muhammad, and of Buddhists as the body of Gautama. The nearest parallel perhaps comes in Vaishnava schools which speak of all souls as parts of the body of the supreme Lord. But even there, the particular community of devotees is not picked out especially as forming the body of the Lord, or as in any sense the continuation of his earthly manifestation.

Jesus was, according to Christian belief, the human body and mind of the eternal Christ, and Christ is the one designated to be the deliverer and ruler of the cosmos. Jesus' body was the means by which the Christ was locally present in history, and by which Christ acted in history for the deliverance of humans from sin and death. By analogy, the community of the disciples is designated to be the means by which Christ, the same Christ who was fully manifest in

---

[6] 1 John 2: 15.   [7] One key passage focuses on 1 Corinthians 12: 27.

Jesus, continues to be locally present in history, and by which Christ continues to act to liberate humans from sin and death.

Immediately strong reservations spring to mind. Christians are, and always will be, sinful and ignorant. One can think of Jesus as, by grace, preserved from sin and from ignorance of those things essential to human salvation. It is obvious that members of the church are not so preserved. They are quarrelsome, greedy, ambitious, and divided. They always have been, from the days of the New Testament Corinthian church, and they always will be, so far as one can foresee. How, then, can they be the means by which Christ is present and acts to liberate in history?

Once the question is posed in this stark form, the answer is fairly clear. It is only in so far as the church presents Christ, through preaching and sacrament, and in so far as it expresses Christ, through healing and reconciling acts, that it is the body of Christ. Christ is really and truly present in the preaching of the gospel and in the eucharistic sacrament. In these forms, Christ forgives, liberates, and unites to God. Christ is also truly present when acts of healing and forgiveness are performed in his name, for it is the Spirit who then acts in and through individuals to enable them to be channels of the divine love.

To say, 'You are the body of Christ,' is to say, 'You are to be the place where Christ is to be made present in word, sacrament, and service.' It is absolutely not to say, 'You are the continuing incarnation of Christ, in the sense that when you speak and act, it is God speaking and acting in person. So you are the Lord and designated ruler of the world.' In other words, the church is not the body of Christ regardless of what it says and however it acts. It is a community called to manifest the body, the presence and power, of Christ, in so far as it worthily proclaims gospel and sacrament, and truly serves others in his name.[8] The latter might be called the *institutional view* of the mystical body of Christ. The former is, by contrast, a *vocational view*. The body of Christ is what the church is called to be. But the church may often fail to meet its vocation, and may always fail to meet it fully. The expression 'You are the body of Christ' is best interpreted in the optative mood, as expressing a hope

---

[8] Karl Rahner for this reason discouraged any attempt to speak of the church as 'Christ living on': 'Diaspora Community', *Theological Investigations*, x. 93, trans. David Bourke, as *Writings of 1965–67* (New York: Crossroad, 1977), ii.

or desire. The correct parallel is with statements like, 'You are the light of the world,'[9] which hardly applies to the apostles when they deny their Lord. It means, 'You are called to be the light of the world. If and in so far as you respond to this calling, you will be a light.' So to be the body of Christ is a calling, and not a state in which one finds oneself, whatever one's individual response.

The idea that the church is called to a particular vocation, to make Christ present in word, sacrament, and service, helps to resolve a problem that has been felt about why so few are called into membership of the church. This would be a severe problem indeed if membership of the church was felt to be necessary for salvation. Such a view has been held in Christian history. The Council of Florence propounded the view that 'outside the church there is no salvation'.[10] However subtle one's interpretation of this decree, it seems that it was meant to assert the necessity of communion with the See of Rome for salvation. Since the vast majority of the human race is not in communion with Rome, the decree seems unacceptably harsh. Subsequent Roman Catholic thought has perceived that it is not only harsh, but in conflict with the declared desire of God that all should be saved. So Karl Rahner writes that 'the church is the leaven . . . always and for each and every age',[11] and it conveys God's promise that salvation is offered to the whole of humanity. What has led many Christians to the harsh doctrine that one must belong to a particular church to be saved is their fear that the point of belonging to the church may be obscured, if one can be saved without belonging to it at all.

A helpful light is shed on this problem by a reconsideration of the election of the people of Israel by God. Such an election has not usually been taken to imply that only Jews can be saved. Indeed, it has rarely been thought to have anything to do with personal salvation at all. There have been arguments within Judaism about what the purpose of Israel's election is, but one widely held view is that the

---

[9] Matthew 5: 14.

[10] 'There is no doubt that not only all heathens, but also all Jews and all heretics and schismatics who die outside the church will go into that everlasting fire . . .' Denzinger-Schonmetzer, *Enchiridion Symbolorum Definitionum et Declarationum*, 31st edn. (Frieburg: Herder, 1957), 1351.

[11] Rahner, 'Ecclesiological Piety', *Theological Investigations*, v. 361, trans. K.-H. Kruger, as *Later Writings* (New York: Crossroad, 1983). A helpful study of Rahner's thought on the church is found in Richard Lennan, *The Ecclesiology of Karl Rahner* (Oxford: Clarendon, 1995).

Jews are called to a specific vocation, of being a nation of priests[12] who could lead the whole world to the true knowledge and worship of God. Though God makes a covenant with the children of Abraham, that they will be his people and he will be their God, God is not thereby excluding other people from the divine lovingkindness. The purpose of the covenant is precisely that the whole world will be blessed, brought to its true fulfilment, through the children of Abraham,[13] for they are called to be the people through whom God will be made known and will act to fulfil the divine purpose for the earth.

If the Christian church is a new covenant people, one might expect that they will similarly not be a group selected for salvation from a world otherwise left to judgement. They will rather be a people who are called to make God known and to realize God's will, to be priests of the earth and bearers of good news to the whole world. Calling into the community of the church is not primarily a calling into a select group of the saved. It is a calling into a community with a special vocation to be mediators of the message of God to humankind.

THE CHANGING CHURCH

The early church almost certainly came to see itself in this way quite early in its history. But one can trace within the New Testament a series of very rapid changes in self-understanding on the part of Christians in the first years after the death of Jesus. At first the church was made up of disciples who followed Jesus during his ministry in Galilee and Jerusalem. Jesus was seen by his disciples as the epitome of the calling of Israel, the one who truly makes God known and acts to inaugurate the rule of God within the hearts of men and women. As the gospels present the matter, Jesus' mission was to call the Jews of his day back to their true vocation. His mission was only to 'the lost sheep of the house of Israel'.[14] He appointed twelve men to be the leaders of the twelve tribes, which would be reunited in Jerusalem when the nation turned back in penitence and faith to God. He commissioned the twelve (and later, according to Luke,

---

[12] 'You shall be called the priests of the Lord; men shall speak of you as the ministers of our God': Isaiah 61: 6.
[13] Genesis 12: 3.   [14] Matthew 15: 24.

seventy) to join with him in proclaiming the rule of God, as an imminent, dynamic, and liberating reality which was already mysteriously present in his person. At this stage, the incipient church was a sort of revivalist mission to Israel. If it was successful, Israel could enter into its true vocation of leading the whole world to fulfilment in God.

Jesus' mission failed, in the sense that the Jewish people as a whole did not respond to his preaching, and indeed he was put to death as a troublemaker, having apparently annoyed the religious authorities beyond their endurance. In a deeper sense, however, his mission did not fail, for, in an extraordinary series of events which gave the church a dynamic and vibrant life which was to change the world, he appeared to his disciples after he had been killed. Thereby God vindicated his claim to be truly commissioned by God to announce the kingdom of God. The disciples were empowered by the Holy Spirit to proclaim that Jesus had been designated as Messiah and Lord of the kingdom, and had ascended to the presence of God, until the ending of history, when he would be manifested in the glory of God to bring in the kingdom in its realized fullness. The disciples' first preaching after the resurrection was to Jews in Jerusalem and throughout the Mediterranean region, to call them to accept the Lordship of Jesus.

Many responded to this call. They received the Holy Spirit as a charismatic power of new life and joy, they worshipped Jesus as Lord, and they looked for his return in the glory of God. The church was now a charismatic, Messianic and millennial sect of Judaism, whose members probably saw themselves as the remnant of Israel, saved from the judgement of God about to come on the Jewish people. As the letters to the Thessalonians show, there was an expectation that Jesus would return in glory very soon, to bring in a new world order.[15] The second phase of the existence of the church was as a community which looked for salvation from imminent judgement on the world, by the coming of the Christ.

But what of the rest of the world? If Israel was no longer to be a political kingdom, a spiritual interpretation of Jesus' Messianic function had to be given. The liberation he offered was not from the domination of the Roman empire, but from the bondage of sin. The kingdom in which he ruled was not the state of Israel, but a community of those who were inwardly ruled by the Spirit of God. The

[15] 1 Thessalonians 4: 15–17.

covenant he offered was not one of keeping a divinely given law in return for peace and security, but an inward union with God which would be completed beyond historical time. As the early disciples reflected on these things, it no doubt began to seem clear that the rest of the world, the Gentiles, could not simply be ignored, as though the world could end while the vast majority of humans were still in ignorance of God's offer of salvation.

They began to see that the remnant of Israel, the people of the new covenant, were to take on the vocation of the children of Abraham to proclaim to the whole world Jesus' victory over sin and death, the coming of the Spirit with power, and the promise of eternal life. The letter to the Romans writes of a delay until the 'full number of the Gentiles has come in', after which all Israel will return to the Lord.[16] There is here a development of understanding, even a change of mind, about when the Lord is expected to come in glory. This might be seen as the third stage of the early church, when a universal mission to proclaim eternal life to all people began to seize the infant community. Even then, however, the apostles were at first unclear about how to go about this, and what it might imply.

What is quite remarkable about the earliest years of the church, as recorded in the New Testament, is the obtuseness and incomprehension of the apostles about the nature and role of the church. It has sometimes been supposed that Jesus taught the apostles quite clearly what the church would be like—that it would be ruled by bishops, perhaps with the successor of Peter at its head, and that it was to guard his teachings carefully and without change. With the death of the last apostle, everything necessary to salvation was known and understood, and henceforth the church had only to protect the teaching from dilution or distortion.

That is not the picture presented by the New Testament. During Jesus' lifetime the apostles were obtuse. When, according to the gospels, he taught them that the Son of Man must suffer and rise from the dead, it is recorded that they did not know what he meant.[17] After his resurrection, two apostles confess that they 'had thought' that Jesus would have brought in the kingdom.[18] Perhaps it may be thought that at least during his resurrection appearances, Jesus would have taught them to understand. But apparently not. On two major, and connected, issues the apostles were totally unclear.

---

[16] Romans 11: 25.   [17] Mark 9: 32.   [18] Luke 24: 21.

First, they did not know whether to preach to the Gentiles or not. Second, they did not know whether they should keep Torah or not.

It took Peter a threefold vision to bring him to accept that he could even speak to Gentiles, let alone preach to them.[19] The mission to the Gentiles was obviously not clearly commanded by Jesus himself, or Peter would have needed no persuasion. These visions, and a similar vision experienced by Paul on the road to Damascus, not the words of Jesus, brought about the Gentile mission of the church. Similarly, Acts 15 records a meeting of the church at Jerusalem, at which the question of whether circumcision should be required of new converts came up. If Jesus had taught that Torah was no longer binding on his disciples, there would have been no need for debate. But in fact it was those who had known Jesus personally who supported circumcision, and the parvenu Paul, who had never met Jesus, who successfully argued for its abandonment. Thus, in admitting Gentiles to the new community, and in giving up Torah (though at first only giving up part of it, and retaining the *kosher* food laws), the early church changed dramatically, in ways which had apparently not been explicitly commanded by Jesus.

This entails that the early church had not received all its instructions clearly from Jesus. Under the inspiration of visions and new directions of the Spirit, they felt able to make decisions of fundamental importance to the structure of the church. Far from the church simply preserving and passing on the teaching of Jesus, it seems that in its earliest years the church passed through at least three major revolutions in perspective, from being a revivalist mission to Jews, to being a millennial saviour-cult, at last emerging as a universal mission to proclaim eternal life through Jesus as the Christ. By that stage it had given up the practice of Torah, and taught an inward liberation from sin and union with the eternal God, through participation in the risen life of Christ.

These revolutions are not simply unpredictable changes of direction. They are natural, in that the failure of Jesus' mission to the Jews which led to his death necessitated a reinterpretation of his Messianic role. Reflection on the vocation of the church to proclaim the Lordship of Jesus necessitated embarking upon a global mission. That in turn naturally led to an abandonment of Torah, as a

---

[19] Acts 10: 9–16.

specifically Jewish mark of separateness. Thus one can see these changes as developments rather than revolutionary decisions. Nevertheless, they are developments that were not initiated as such by Jesus, and were even resisted for a while by some of the apostles. This suggests a view of the church as a doctrinally creative community, developing insights derived from faith in Jesus as the Christ which are responses to new situations in imaginative ways. The church described in the New Testament is not a guardian of unchanging and received formulae. It is a community in which, by discussion and argument as well as by prayerful reflection, new insights into the purposes of God revealed in Jesus are prompted by the Holy Spirit.

Jesus had apparently not set up an institutional form destined to last for centuries, for the first believers thought the present age would end in a matter of decades at most. It is thus almost unthinkable that Jesus had, for instance, instructed the apostles to appoint bishops as their successors, and to accept the successor of Peter as their head. One might say that Jesus 'founded the church', in that he called an inner group of twelve men to proclaim the kingdom, to heal and to prepare themselves to be leaders of the twelve tribes. After his resurrection, they became a group, still of twelve, who had been companions of Jesus and were witnesses to the resurrection. That group of twelve died out, and leadership of local churches was dispersed. James, Jesus' brother, became leader of the church in Jerusalem after Peter had left,[20] and Paul founded many churches, with various forms of leadership. It was natural for the apostles to appoint leaders of local churches, and these became the bishops, who, where possible, proudly traced their succession back to one of the apostles. It was equally natural for presiding bishops, or Patriarchs, to be elected in the major cities of the Empire. By the fourth century three main Patriarchates (later to become five), at Rome, Alexandria, and Antioch, became established, sharing leadership of the churches between them. Rome, claiming to be the see of the successors of Peter and Paul, made claims to supreme jurisdiction from an early date, but such claims were never fully accepted by the other Patriarchs—which again suggests the lack of a clear, early dominical teaching on the matter.

---

[20] Acts 21: 18.

THE DEVELOPMENT OF DOCTRINE

It might be held that at least all these developments took place before the death of the last apostle, and so form part of the 'original deposit of faith' handed on to the church to remain unchanged for ever thereafter. That, I think, would be a most implausible belief, in view of the fact that major developments continued to occur, and are well documented, in the first generations of the church. One example is the allegedly Petrine supremacy of Rome, which was never accepted by the Eastern churches, and for which arguments grew more elaborate over the years. The doctrine that the Roman Pontiff is, in virtue of his office, the infallible source of all teaching in faith and morals is a development which seemed to be quite unknown to the church of the first centuries. It could be argued that it is as natural and divinely willed a development as the giving up of Torah, though it took longer. It could not plausibly be argued that it was explicitly taught by Jesus to the twelve apostles, or that the apostles themselves clearly formulated such a view. In fact it is a development that was strongly resisted by the Orthodox Churches, and even by many in the Catholic tradition, before Papal Infallibility was finally defined in 1870, and it still remains a bone of contention even between Christians who would like to be as true to the original apostolic faith as possible.

But the most obvious and important development in the church of the first centuries was the adoption by the church of terms taken from Hellenistic philosophy to help to interpret the role of Jesus in the redemption of humanity. Again, the development may reasonably be seen as entirely natural, since the conceptuality of Messianic Judaism needed to be given a more global, indeed cosmic, framework if Jesus were to be recognized as central to the realisation of the divine purpose for the whole planet. What is indisputable, however, is that such formulae as that of the Council of Nicaea, in 325, that Christ was 'of one substance' with God the Father—a formula which was resisted by many traditionalist bishops for many years because it seemed to make God divisible, like a material substance— were wholly unknown to the apostles, and had not been taught by Jesus himself.

Among the many disputing groups prior to Nicaea, the Arians held that the Christ was a created being, perhaps a senior member of the angelic hierarchies, but not identical with God. Others, following Origen, thought that Christ was subordinate to the Father, but somehow part of the divine Being, even though distinct in some real way. Yet others (Monarchians) saw Christ as a 'phase' of a unitary divine being, without distinct existence. All these conflicting opinions were within that mainstream spectrum which stood between saying that Jesus was just a Spirit-filled man or a non-human 'appearance' of a man. The Nicaean formula, ironically imposed by the Emperor Constantine in order to unite the new religion of the Roman Empire, was eventually accepted by all the Patriarchates, and came to define orthodoxy from that point on.

One can hardly forbear to raise the question of why so many disputes existed in the early centuries of the church, when they might easily have been prevented by a clear statement from Jesus of his own relation to the Father. Biblical scholarship proffers an answer to that question, by pointing to the probability that Jesus never thought of himself in that way. He was not omniscient, with a full knowledge of the subsequent development of Greek technical terminology to cope with the intricacies of incarnational theology, which would have enabled him to solve its problems in advance.

The New Testament asserts that those who had known Jesus personally found in him a person free of hatred, greed, and selfish desire, with an intense sense of God, and of his own vocation and authority to proclaim the kingdom. He assumed the authority to forgive sins and to promise the gift of eternal life. He was, the disciples believed, raised from death, and he had sent the Spirit in power among them. So his authority as the vindicated Messiah of God and ruler of the coming kingdom was testified to by the apostles. That was their chief role as apostles, to testify to major elements of the life and teaching, and to the death, resurrection, and divine vindication of the man with whom they had lived for two or three years.

These basic facts of the apostolic witness are the unchangeable data of Christian faith. But a vast amount remains to be understood—the nature of the God revealed in these events, the way in which God would liberate humans from sin through them, the character of human destiny, and the ultimate goal of the creation. Neither Jesus nor the apostles wrote a systematic exposition of doctrine, or even gave clear accounts of such matters. That was left for the church to work out, by debate and creative reflection. A vast field was left open for speculation. Some of these speculations are more plausible than others, and some seem to be very unbalanced interpretations of the apostolic witness.

It may often seem as though the debates reach into areas so abstruse, and engender conflicts so minute, that they positively detract from the simplicity of the gospel of eternal life. Certainly a huge variety of interpretations existed in early Christianity, or on its fringes, ranging from the view that Jesus was a man designated by God as renewer of Israel to the view that Jesus was a divine being, having only the appearance of a man. Gradually, certain positions came to be thought of as 'orthodox', in that the positions they excluded were thought to be incompatible with a reflective working-out of the apostolic witness. Jesus must have been more than a Spirit-filled man, if Christ lived as the head of the church, which was his body. Jesus must have been truly a man, if he had suffered and died for human salvation. When, at Nicaea, Jesus was said to be 'one in being' with the Father, this clause was probably inserted to counter the Arian claim that Christ was a created being, inferior to God. For in that case, it was thought, it would not have been God who entered the world to unite humanity to the Divine being.

The 'orthodox' definitions of the ecumenical councils were not thought of as new discoveries or new revelations. At their best, they aimed to leave the mystery of the divine revelation in Christ intact, but to exclude views that were thought to imperil the proclamation of God's saving act in the person of Jesus of Nazareth. Out of the rich variety of imaginative interpretations of the apostolic witness, the ecumenical council of bishops at Nicaea determined that some compromised the good news of eternal life in Jesus the Christ. Of course, those who disagreed continued to organize their own churches, often with their own bishops, often for hundreds of years. They had every right to do that, but it has been the judgement of the mainstream church that they thereby lost something of the richness implicit in the apostolic gospel.

What is the status of such judgements? They express the decision of a council of bishops (in the case of Nicaea, strongly prompted by the Emperor Constantine) that certain teachings are incompatible with the apostolic witness. The definition that Christ is 'one in substance with the Father' was not simply handed on from the apostles (who had not thought of it) as a truth to be defended against clearly deviant opinions. It was a formula newly devised to exclude the view that Christ was a created being, which seemed incompatible with the worship that had been given to Christ from apostolic times. It was not so much the discovery of a new truth, as the formulation of new concepts which might enable the apostolic witness to be more deeply understood. Such decisions do not provide new data for belief. They are meant to deepen the understanding of data which are given in the apostolic witness, the *depositum fidei*.

It seems clear therefore that Christian belief searches for new and deeper understandings in new circumstances, as it reflects upon its own tradition and practice. The church does not just hand on truths explicitly formulated by Jesus or the apostles. It seeks to come to a correct understanding of the nature of God and of human destiny, as expressed in the life of Jesus, even though not fully understood then. The definition that Jesus was of one substance with God the Father was not a new belief, so much as a decision as to what the most adequate view was, in view of a widespread dispute about it that had arisen within the church. The church's decision was that the original revelation in Jesus presupposed that Jesus was divine. In a similar way, the church, in decisions made at its first great ecumenical councils, came to declare that Jesus was fully human and fully divine (human and divine nature united in one person), that there are three 'persons' or *hypostases* in the Trinity, and that they are all co-equally divine. These decisions were about what is presupposed in the original revelation, even if the question had not previously been decided.

INFALLIBILITY

Does the church have the authority to make such decisions? This remains a disputed question within the Christian world. Broadly speaking, Roman Catholics and the Orthodox believe that either the Roman Pontiff or ecumenical (world-wide) councils of bishops possess the gift of being protected from error by the Holy Spirit, when they make solemn pronouncements on matters of faith or morals. Protestants think that even general councils of the church can err and have erred, so that there is no infallibility in the institutional church. Nevertheless, all agree that there is a sense in which the church as such cannot finally fall into grievous error, the sort of error that would imperil a true understanding of God and of the divinely appointed means to salvation. The Roman Catholic theologian Karl Rahner puts this in a way that most Protestants would be happy to accept: 'When the church . . . really confronts man in its teaching with an *ultimate* demand in the name of Christ, God's grace and power prevent this teaching authority from losing the truth of Christ.'[21] All are also committed to the fact that at least some development of understanding has occurred in the church. Rahner writes, 'Realisations of truth always remain open to further modification . . . every statement of faith . . . can be modified and transformed by factors belonging to a future that is still unknown.'[22] The orthodox definitions themselves could not have been envisaged by the apostles, and neither did the apostles possess the canon of New Testament scripture upon which Protestants place so much reliance. All must also accept that there have been some mistaken views very widely accepted in the church—Arianism, a form of which was accepted in the fourth-century church at the Council of Sirmium (AD 357), being the obvious, but not the only case. The problem is that of deciding in what sense doctrinal development is assured of truth, in what sense it can be authoritatively formulated, and in what sense it may fall into error.

As Christianity developed, it came to place a great stress on 'orthodoxy', on the correct formulation of beliefs about the nature of God and of Jesus Christ. Judaism had never had an authoritative teaching body that could define which beliefs about God and about human salvation were correct. There were rabbinic courts which had the power to decide on particular applications of Torah, especially in new circumstances; but even then, there was not one divinely appointed 'chief rabbi', whose word was law for all Jews. Rulings are laid down by particular courts, and come to be accepted—where they are—by general consensus of the learned. But there have always been disputes within Judaism about such matters, and 'deviant' groups, such as the Liberal and Reform movements, are free to adopt different interpretations. Jews have hardly ever felt it necessary to define correct theoretical beliefs about God, and it is perfectly possible to be an observant Jew without believing in resurrection or in a literally omnipotent God, for example.

Against this background, which was the background of early Christianity, it may seem strange that it was felt necessary to develop the view that there must be one defining authority for matters of

---

[21] Karl Rahner, *Foundations of Christian Faith*, trans. William Dych (New York: Crossroad, 1995), 381.
[22] Rahner, 'The New Image of the Church', *Theological Investigations*, x. 5.

theoretical belief like the full divinity of Jesus. Would it not make more sense simply to ensure that debates on disputed subjects were fully informed, clearly presented, and reasonably argued? To have majority recommendations, often accepted by a consensus of informed opinion in the churches, but to allow divergent views to exist? Perhaps attempts were made to ensure precisely that in the early church. But one can understand that what was felt to be at stake was not just a decision about the application of some obscure point of law, but a decision as to which of two competing views of Jesus, for example, was true.

Since truth is at stake, and since knowledge of at least some truths—that Jesus inaugurates the kingdom, that God is love, that the Spirit is given to the church—is important to one's relationship to God, it might well seem necessary to have some way of authenticating the truth. One can see the attractiveness of the view, which did in fact develop, that the Holy Spirit would protect from error decisions of councils of the whole church (ecumenical councils) on matters of faith and morals. On the other hand, the history of the church up to that point does not naturally suggest such a hypothesis. The apostles themselves frequently misunderstood Jesus, they disagreed among themselves about the Gentile mission and the renunciation of Torah, and they were mistaken about the imminence of the return of Christ in glory.

Perhaps, then, it is only certain formal decisions of the whole church that are guaranteed as true. Yet it is precisely at this point that disputes and conflicts arose within the church. The attempt to define the conditions under which revealed truth is guaranteed led to disagreement about what those conditions are. What came to be the Roman Catholic Church began to insist upon the primacy of the Bishop of Rome, while what came to be the Orthodox Churches would accept only the decisions of fully ecumenical Councils (of which they think there have only been seven). It is an odd situation when the church cannot agree on the conditions under which it can be certain that the truth has been correctly defined. This suggests that such certainty is not available, since one cannot even be certain of the conditions under which a statement would be guaranteed as true.

The alternative view, which Protestants were later to take, is that all churches can and do fall into error from time to time. Yet all Christian churches claim to be responding to the call of God in Jesus that they should make Christ present in the world. The apostles were the original witnesses to Jesus, to what he did and what he taught. That apostolic witness must be the touchstone of Christian truth. Even if the records of their teaching are not inerrant in every particular, what they testify to are the acts of God in and through Jesus for the salvation of the world. Since Jesus is taken to be the revelation of God in his own person, the apostolic witness is of the highest importance. It is probably to this that John's reported utterance of Jesus that 'the Spirit will guide you into all truth' refers.[23] The Spirit was to stir the minds of the companions of Jesus so that they would recollect teachings that they may well have misunderstood at the time, and begin to see the significance of acts that had seemed mysteriously obscure.

All Christian churches agree that the apostolic witness is the final norm of Christian faith. It is a fact of human experience that recollected traditions soon degrade, and passing them on by word of mouth seriously impairs their reliability in a relatively short time. So the apostolic traditions needed to be committed to writing. The function of the Spirit in this respect was to inspire the process of the collection of traditions into the canon of the New Testament. From that point on, apostolic authority was primarily located in the written Scripture. It is generally agreed by Catholic theologians that 'tradition' does not function independently of Scripture. As Rahner puts it, 'scripture is and remains the concrete norm for the post-apostolic church . . . the church does not receive any new revelation over and beyond this scripture'.[24] The Scriptures do need to be interpreted; but it is not obvious to Protestants that there should be just one binding interpretation, or that some uniquely authoritative interpreting body needs to be institutionalized. The nature of the New Testament is such that it seems more likely that many different interpretations and perspectives are included in the texts, which are amenable to spelling out in different ways in different contexts. Once the primary apostolic authority—of having known Jesus personally—had ceased to exist, and the traditions had been committed to writing, it is not obvious that some specially privileged teaching authority would continue to exist.

One might perhaps say that the apostolic testimony, as recorded in the New Testament, is infallible in the sense that it is not liable to

---

[23] John 16: 13.   [24] Rahner, *Foundations*, 363.

error in what is definitive of salvation. It is not that it logically cannot err, but that in so far as it reports the original apostolic testimony it can be taken as truly expressing what God intended to reveal for human salvation in Christ. We can say that the Scriptures 'teach with certainty, with fidelity and without error the truth which God wanted recorded in the sacred writings for the sake of our salvation'.[25] That truth that God wanted recorded for the sake of our salvation is presumably a subclass of those propositions in the Bible which are true, and of that not completely definite subclass many Christians might be prepared to say that it is not liable to error.

The subsequent teaching of the Christian church may also be called infallible in so far as it correctly reports or deepens understanding of the apostolic witness (the *depositum fidei*). It might well be argued that, even on a fairly strict Roman Catholic view, the Pope is infallible only in so far as he defines some doctrine to be part of the original deposit of faith. If that were so, much of the controversy surrounding papal infallibility might be mitigated. But it would mean limiting the scope of definitions of what is essential to orthodox faith in a more restrictive way than has always been realized, and regarding most other pronouncements of church bodies as having a lesser degree of authority.

Hans Kung, while maintaining that the community as a whole cannot fall away from truth, has argued that even defined propositions of the magisterium can contain error.[26] To this Rahner replied that this was in effect a form of 'liberal Protestantism' with which Catholic theology could find no common ground. As a liberal Protestant, I certainly recognize here a difference about the sort of authority which is to be given to official church pronouncements, but I am reluctant to admit there is no common ground or possibility of convergence. Rahner himself wrote that interpretations of dogma depend on their acceptance by the faith consciousness of the whole church, as represented by the teaching office, and that it is no longer possible to make such claims about the consciousness of the whole church in a pluralistic age.[27] He even held that a believer who

[25] Second Vatican Council, art. 11, *Dei Verbum*.
[26] Hans Kung, *Infallible? An Enquiry*, trans. E. Mosbacher (London: SCM, 1971), 145–58.
[27] Rahner, 'Infallibility', *Theological Investigations*, xiv. 77, trans. David Bourke, as *Ecclesiology, Questions in the Church, The Church in the World* (New York: Crossroad, 1976).

privately rejected papal teaching on a specific issue did not need to feel disobedient towards church authority.[28] While the issue of authority remains a thorny one in Christian ecumenical relations, I feel that progress can be made on clarifying the limits and status of official pronouncements of the church, so that one does not need either to accept them uncritically or reject them as mere matters of subjective opinion. But probably such discussions will need both unquenchable hope and inexhaustible patience, and a preparedness to live together with difference, perhaps for many years.

The point that seems to me correct in what Rahner, however unfairly, calls 'liberal Protestantism' is that all comments on and elaborations of the apostolic witness must be subject to the same standards of rational argument and criticism that characterize human thought in general. When a council of bishops declared Arianism heretical, they came to a consensus that Jesus Christ was of the same nature as God, and was not a created aeon or spiritual being. That statement has been generally received as correct, but I do not think that it should be so received primarily because it was uttered by a particular meeting of bishops. It is authoritative because it has seemed to most Christians over the years to elucidate most adequately what is involved in the Christian practice of worshipping Jesus as Lord.

At the present time that statement may need to be rephrased to express the same concern in terms of a rather different philosophical framework. The Christian theological tradition has construed the person of Jesus in terms of two natures united in one substance (hypostasis). This, however, may seem rather static and unhistorical, as if there were a generalized human nature (not a particular human personality) which unites with an unchanging divine nature in one substance, suggesting the odd idea of one substance with two quite different natures, or two different essential definitions. It may also suggest that such a uniting might have happened at any point in human history, and is virtually unaffected by any particular historical context. It may be more helpful to think more dynamically and historically of a human agent, a particular Jewish man, becoming the free instrument of the divine action to liberate and unite humanity to God, an action whose character essentially depends upon the

---

[28] Rahner, 'Humanae Vitae', ibid. xi. 264, trans. Bourke, as *Confrontations: 1* (New York: Crossroad, 1982).

historical context in which it takes place. One does not think of a substance with two different natures, but of two agents, divine and human, united in one historical person.

But do they just coincidentally agree? No, the divine is a real causal agent working through the human, and the human is an agent freely submissive to the divine. In and through the person of Jesus, his disciples felt a liberation from self and a unity with God. Jesus did not primarily teach a set of theoretical truths, though he commented on Torah. What is revealed in him is not, primarily, a new set of teachings, but the saving act of God, as it is received by faithful response. The theoretical truths involved here may need to be gradually spelled out in a way which leaves room for inspiration by the Spirit. God liberates and unites us to the divine through Jesus and in the community of the church. But that leaves much room for creative spelling-out of what is involved in such a process.

This is just one example of the way in which the church constantly needs to rethink its formulation of doctrines. It is a proper function of the church to seek to initiate thought on such matters, when it seems necessary. But the authority the church then has is the authority of expertise in scholarly theological study, of experience in the Christian practice of prayer, and of discernment of what is conducive to human salvation or fulfilment in God. Christians will be wise to listen carefully to the consensus of opinion that the church forms on these occasions. But individual conscience must always be followed, and it may be that churches will make limited or partial decisions, perhaps because of the restricted nature of those who comprise the decision-making body, or a particular political and social situation which dictates a specific response.

In Christian history, the Orthodox and Protestant churches are committed to believing that the Roman church has erred on at least some occasions, and of course Roman Catholics are bound to believe that non-Roman Christians have erred. In this situation, it would seem reasonable for every tradition to admit that it has on occasion fallen into error. Anyone prepared to read the relevant documents can readily find instances in which solemn decisions of church councils have later been overturned. There is, it seems, nothing which meets the Vincentian requirement that an orthodox doctrine must have been believed by all Christians, at all times, everywhere—unless one refuses to accept as 'Christians' those who disagree with one's own opinion. It looks as though one will not be able to identify the church with one institution within which there is a universally agreed set of shared beliefs. But why should all beliefs be agreed anyway?

A PLURAL CHRISTIANITY

It might be argued that Christians, unlike Jews, identify themselves precisely by the having of certain beliefs, so Christians need to ensure agreement on at least their basic beliefs. However, just as Jews are identified as a people with whom God has made a covenant—even though they may differ about the details of how they obey the divine law, and on exactly what the divine promises are—so Christians can be identified as a people with whom God has made a 'new covenant'—and they might be expected to differ about exactly what God requires of them, and on exactly what God promises them.

Such differences have in fact been a prominent feature of church history. Some Christians, including the apostles at first, thought that God required keeping Torah.[29] Some stress that only faith in Jesus is required, while others think that membership of a particular church, and the acceptance of certain beliefs authoritatively defined, is necessary. Virtually all Christians think that God promises eternal life, but they differ as to whether this is temporal or timeless, whether it is open to non-Christians, whether it involves progress and development, and whether it is on some future earth, or in a different realm altogether. Why should there not be a 'plural Christianity', permitting diverse interpretations of the basic apostolic witness?

The basic faith of the church would be that, by a series of acts which in their specific form originated with and are modelled on the life of Jesus, God calls certain individuals out of the world into membership of a community founded on inner union with the divine, gives them the vocation of showing God's healing and reconciling love in the world, empowers them with the Spirit of love and fulfilment, and promises to them and offers through them to all humanity the gift of eternal life.

The church may then be one 'people of God' existing in many traditions of interpretation and practice, united in their love of the God revealed in Jesus and in their acceptance of the basic apostolic

---

[29] Acts 15: 1–5.

testimony of the gospels. What actually exists in the world is precisely such a plural Christianity. The odd thing is that so many parts
of this plural Christianity think of themselves as the only 'true'
church, and deny the right of others to be parts of a truly plural
church. It is quite possible, however, for many differing traditions of
belief and practice to accept in common that God has acted in
Jesus for human salvation, and that the New Testament provides a
basic canon against which all interpretations should be measured.
That basic canon is itself, however, polysemic to a large extent, and
the history of the Christian churches shows how differing traditions
of interpretation can all claim, no doubt with varying degrees of
plausibility, to be in agreement with it.

Most Christians are prepared to accept that at least the first four
ecumenical councils articulated the idea of the incarnation of the
eternal Word in Jesus in terms of Hellenistic philosophy in a way that
brings out helpfully the unity of divine and human nature in him. But
one cannot fail to note the huge difference in tone between the first
apostolic belief that Jesus was the designated Kingly servant ('son')
of God who was soon to usher in the kingdom, and the 'orthodox'
credal assertion that in Jesus human and divine nature are united in
one person, so that Jesus is one 'person' of the Divine Trinity.

The difference is so great that liberal theologians such as Harnack
saw orthodox Christianity as a Hellenistic imposition upon a much
simpler moralistic faith, which radically changed its character.[30]
Such a judgement ignores those elements in the gospels which imply
a supremely authoritative or even divine status for Jesus, from
Matthew's statement that the magi 'worshipped' Jesus,[31] to the
statement in the prologue of John's gospel that 'the Word became
flesh'.[32] The difference is not one of exchanging one sort of belief for
another. It is rather the difference between Jews who knew Jesus in
the flesh and revered him as the Messianic King, and Gentiles who
knew Jesus primarily as a spiritual presence in worship and revered
him as the glorious Lord who made participation in the divine life
possible. Knowledge of a human personality in a context of Jewish
Messianic expectation had been replaced by knowledge of a spiritually encountered person in the context of an Eastern Mediterranean
desire for liberation from self into union with an eternal divine

---

[30] Harnack's monumental *History of Dogma* (1894–9) is in 7 volumes.
[31] Matthew 2: 11.   [32] John 1: 14.

reality. Differing contexts gave rise to differing ways of expressing what is recognisably the same faith in one who lived in reconciling love, was killed, and was raised from death to the presence of God.

That different form of expression also enshrined a wider understanding of the divine action in Jesus. It was nothing to do with a triumphalist Israeli nationalism, with the church as the vanguard of Messianic rule. It was not even just an expectation of divine judgement on the world and resurrection to eternal life for the faithful, so that the church could be the 'ark of salvation' in a doomed world. It expressed the idea of a sanctification of the whole historical realm by its incorporation into the divine life of the eternal Word. Nature itself was divinized by the incarnation, and the church came to be seen as the community in and by means of which the natural order could be transfigured by the divine life which it mediated.

One might see this widening of the circle of understanding as the result of generations of reflective meditation on the mystery of God's redemptive action in Jesus. The basic apostolic testimony remains unchanging, now set in the written canon of the New Testament. But reflection on the nature and purpose of the God disclosed by that testimony develops in ways that have been enriched by Greek thought and Mediterranean 'mystery cult' spirituality. It is no accident, for example, that the symbol of the cross resembles, not the actual shape of the artefact on which Jesus was nailed, but the Egyptian *ankh*, the symbol of life risen from death. The icons of Madonna and Child resemble the Egyptian representations of Isis and Horus, the divine infant. This is not the incursion of pagan religion into an allegedly pure Hebraic faith. It is a representation of Christ as the fulfilment of the religious intuitions and hopes of the Mediterranean world as well as of Hebrew faith. In many ways, both iconographically and conceptually, the basic apostolic faith was set in a framework of spiritual understanding which was, for its day, of cosmic breadth and richness.

Already, however, one can see the seeds of diversity and dissension as well as what one might call a natural growth of understanding in changing contexts of thought and culture. What some see as a natural growth of understanding is regarded by others as a falling away from primitive standards of purity and simplicity, or as a deviation from revealed truth. Once a written scripture existed, the way was open for putative reformers to rise up and recall what they saw as a syncretistic, culture-dominated church back to its pure roots.

Such attempts have been made throughout Christian history, but some elements of the Protestant Reformation clearly show two unfortunate consequences they tend to have. First, people never seem to be able to agree on what the 'pure and original doctrine' is, and so churches keep splitting into smaller and smaller sections, each one pursuing its version of the original truth. And second, a new tyranny of belief tends to be created, as individual creative reflection is subordinated to 'what the Bible says'. Conflicts with new scientific knowledge or moral understanding become greatly exacerbated when there is little acceptance of the need for the church to re-express its faith in different ways in different contexts, and little enthusiasm for encouraging creative developments in doctrine.

All attempts to return to something exactly like the biblical faith founder on the fact that it is impossible to return to the world-view of first-century Christians, with its spirits and demons, its expectation of an early end of the cosmos, its acceptance of the myths of Patriarchal history, its strongly retributive morality, and its limited moral views of slaves, women, and animals. What is needed is a recognition that the biblical documents are limited by their cultural context, and contain many factual and moral assertions which have become unacceptable, largely through the inner development of Christian thought itself. They remain a canonical witness to the remembered life and teachings of Jesus, taken as the paradigm expression in a human life of the saving acts of God in human history. But the elaboration of this witness into a system of doctrine is a culture-limited and therefore provisional imaginative task, which should seek to place the originative paradigm in as comprehensive a context as possible. This will naturally generate diversity of interpretations, but as long as each interpretative tradition does not regard itself as the only true one, there is no reason why diverse traditions should not live together in the same covenant community.

THE CHURCH IN THE MODERN WORLD

The Protestant Reformation was a protest against the perceived corruption of the church in Europe, and many opportunities to prevent a split from communion with the Roman See were lost. The Roman church undertook its own reformation, emphasizing the sacramental nature of the church as the vehicle of divine grace, which could fulfil human nature by enabling it to participate in the love of God. But Protestants still found the claim of the Roman Pontiff to be the supreme authority in faith and morals, and the claim of the Roman hierarchy to control the means of God's grace in what seemed to be an authoritarian and hierarchical way, which in practice had led to the suppression of all other forms of religious practice, impossible to accept. So the church in Europe was split, as the Eastern and Western churches had been since the Great Schism, conventionally if not entirely accurately dated at 1054.

Freed from the authority of the Catholic Church, the way was open for many interpretative traditions to develop. The Catholic Church was able to be creative within the limits of its own tradition, since it always accepted that the role of the church was to interpret Scripture, and so was open in principle to new developments of interpretation. Some of the more 'orthodox' Protestants, however, lacking a tradition of doctrinal development, tended to become fixated in an impossible attempt to interpret the Scriptures literally, or in accordance with some fixed confessional statement. But they tended to do so in different institutional churches, which were committed to different confessions, and without much tolerance for beliefs other than their own. It was perhaps the weariness of Europe with the ensuing wars of religion that led to the rise of secularism, and at last to the acceptance of tolerance by churches which had become too marginal and weak to impose their views on others.

With the growth of a scientific understanding of the cosmos, of critical methods of historical and literary study, and of a humanist focus on human flourishing as the true end of morality, all previous interpretative traditions found themselves in a radically new context. One response of the churches was to condemn 'modernism and liberalism', a response encapsulated in the anti-Modernist oath imposed in 1910 on all Roman Catholic clergy at their ordination, but also expressed in the rise of 'fundamentalist' movements in the Protestant churches of the United States. Many theologians, however, particularly in Protestant Germany, accepted the scientific world-view, critical analysis of the Scriptures, and a generally humanist attitude to morality, and sought new and more or less radical ways of expressing Christian faith.

In the twentieth century, most mainstream churches have come to some accommodation with these challenges to traditional faith.

Given the stimulus provided by new knowledge of the cosmos, it is not too difficult to recast the faith in terms of an evolutionary world-view. Indeed, in the New Testament vision of Christ as archetype and pleroma of creation, and in the patristic vision of the gradual sanctification of nature by Spirit, one has materials ready to hand for a highly plausible recasting. But one should not be in doubt that it is a recasting, and one which the official teaching hierarchies of the churches resisted for some time. A number of academics who were in the forefront of doing the necessary rethinking were deprived of their posts. Only in 1992 did the Pope admit that the Catholic church had been 'subjectively wrong' to condemn Galileo in 1632. Three hundred and sixty years late, the church admitted that it had been wrong.

In a similar fashion, belief in Hell as unending torment for the majority of humanity, in which Thomas Aquinas unhesitatingly believed, has increasingly come to be seen as incompatible with God's universal love, and the second Vatican Council asserted that God makes it possible for all people, not just Christians, to obtain salvation.[33] Belief in the temporary nature of Hell and in the pos-sibility of universal salvation, too, can be found as implications of major themes in the New Testament, once one looks for them. They are not just alien or humanist intrusions into the theological world. Yet if they are now seen by many, perhaps most, orthodox theo-logians as real insights into the nature and purpose of the God revealed in Jesus, these are insights that the official churches have opposed and denounced on many occasions.

The church was able to enter into debate with and use the con-ceptual tools of Neoplatonic philosophy in the early centuries, and could well make a claim to have preserved at least a major part of the classical tradition through the dark times of invasion and collapse of Empire. In the eleventh and twelfth centuries, the church could claim that it was at the forefront of the revival of Aristotelian learn-ing, and again was in the vanguard of intellectual and cultural life in Europe. But after the seventeenth century the Catholic Church was increasingly seen as a reactionary force, intellectually. Its official teaching simply could not cope with the speed of new scientific advances in astronomy, geology, and history, and it adopted a

---

[33] Cf. especially 'Gaudium et Spes', *Documents of Vatican II*, ed. Austin Flannery (Dublin: Dominican Publications, 1992), ch. 1.

defensive and negative approach to the major trends of European cultural life.

Many great scientific and moral advances were made by Christians, who were inspired in part by their faith. It was the magisterium of the church that condemned Galileo, Giardino Bruno, vaccination, and geneticists' criticisms of monogenism, just to take a few examples. In biblical studies, the church disallowed critical study of the Bible for many years, and has often made specific judgements (for instance, that Moses wrote the Pentateuch, or that Matthew was the first gospel to be written) which it has later had to retract.

These things should not matter much, since one would expect elderly clerics to be largely timid, uninformed, and conservative on such matters (I speak as an elderly cleric). What matters is that the institutional church that has made such mistakes has ruined, or tried to ruin, the careers of many creative scholars, and has continued to claim that its members must submit their intellects to the judgements of the hierarchy. The time has come, indeed it is well past, to ignore such claims, which only bring the church into disrepute.

The proper teaching authority of the church is to lead people into a personal understanding of the nature of God as love, of the promise of eternal life, and of the calling to be agents of reconciliation in the world. It is to promote creative thought which takes full account of the best scientific knowledge and of the widest understanding of human life in all its diversity. It is to teach tolerance, compassion, understanding, and awe at the majesty and intricacy of the created world.

The scientific community has shown that these things are best promoted by the spirit of free critical enquiry, sustained within a community committed to fuller and wider understanding of human life. For that reason, the church should not present itself as a defender of unchanging truths which resist new knowledge and critical enquiry. It should present itself as the bearer of a gospel of greater understanding, of freedom of enquiry, and of creative interpretations of its tradition. It has as its fundamental 'revealed data' the apostolic witness to the acts of God in the life of Jesus, recorded in the New Testament. That is the revelatory source of a Christian understanding of God's world and purpose. But such understanding must be won gradually through exploration and often through disagreement. For that reason the church has a responsibility to ensure that judicious and critical enquiry is made of all topics relevant to its faith in a God who acts to unite humanity to the divine through Christ. It has a duty to make judgements as to what a consensus of informed Christian thought at a given time is on such issues. But the pronouncements of such a church must always be provisional and advisory, and care must be taken not to silence the voice of dissent, since it has so often proved in the past to be the voice of truth.

One might summarize the point by saying that the church should not present itself as the guardian of complete and unchanging truth in a changing world, but as a community of the creative Spirit of continuing growth into truth, wisdom, and understanding. It should be the vanguard and motivator of those free spirits who seek fuller understanding of God's purpose. Its search will be directed by the originative, normative, but only partially understood revelation of God's nature and purpose in the life, death, and resurrection of Jesus of Nazareth. It will be motivated by the creative and inspirational power of the Holy Spirit, which seeks to illumine human minds which are open to it. It is thus a responsive search, responding to a discernment given but dimly understood, which it seeks to reinvoke in the lives of new generations of people who can find new creative interpretations of Christian faith in new contexts of human life and knowledge.

7

The Church as a Charismatic Community

THE COMMUNITY OF THE SPIRIT

I have suggested that the church can best exercise its proper teaching role by faithfully proclaiming its normative discernment of the divine nature and purpose, recorded in the Bible witness to the life of Jesus. Jesus sent out the apostles to preach, exorcize, and heal, and the proclamation of the Word is perhaps the primary role of the church. This proclamation, however, is more than the presentation of a set of factual truths. What is proclaimed is the actual presence of the kingdom,[1] the divine Spirit breaking into the world as an image and foreshadowing of the fulfilment of human potentiality in a community of love which God promises to all who respond in trust. The proclamation is the coming of God to a humanity in bondage, in the power of the Holy Spirit, to liberate from egoism and implant a new life of creativity, responsiveness, and love, to forgive, renew, and raise to eternal life in God. Through this proclamation, God gives new birth, as hearers respond in faith—or if they turn away, to that extent they remain in sin.

The brusque Markan statement, 'He who does not believe will be condemned'[2] should not be taken to mean that anyone who finds it impossible to believe in God, or to become a member of the church, will be doomed to Hell. Interpreted in accordance with the normative proclamation that God is a God of unconditional and universal love, it means that those who do not repent and trust in God do not receive the assurance of eternal life with God that baptism expresses. To that extent, they remain in the bondage of egoism, and on the way to the self-destruction in which such a life naturally results. Two important qualifications need to be born in mind, however. First,

---

[1] 'If it is by the finger of God that I cast out demons, then the kingdom of God has come upon you', Luke 11: 20.
[2] Mark 16: 16.

the possibility of penitence always remains open to them. Second, we can never tell how and when the Spirit is working invisibly in human hearts. As the Pastoral Constitution on the church in the modern world elegantly puts it, the Christian hope that one will be 'configured to the death of Christ', and 'go forward, strengthened by hope, to the resurrection', holds 'not for Christians only but also for all men of good will in whose hearts grace is active invisibly'.[3]

If a person lives in debauchery, greed, and hatred, it may seem very clear that the Spirit is not at work in them. Even in such cases, however, things are not clear-cut. A person whose whole training has been in crime, whose whole experience has been of hatred and conflict, may not look or act like a saint. But in their hearts they may turn towards goodness, and Christ may come to them as he did to sinners in Galilee, offering them new life in ways invisible to more conventional souls.

More commonly, there may be many who seek goodness and wisdom, but who cannot accept religious beliefs because they find them superstitious or irrational. It is often through such lives that the church becomes sensitized to its own shortcomings, and it may well be that God's Spirit works in them for good.

The proclamation, then, is not a narrow and excluding thing. It does not say, 'You must believe exactly these things, in this way, or you cannot be saved.' Of course, in the hands of some Christians, it does say that—which is why one can never make the work of the Holy Spirit simply coincident with the preaching of the church. The proclamation is meant to be wide and including. It should offer the Spirit of universal love, as a power to be received in a personal and creative way by each person. It should offer the Spirit as a power to begin to heal and fulfil the whole world. It is only those who reject healing, reconciliation, and wisdom, and who continue to do so to the end, who stand condemned.

The Spirit who comes with power and gives eternal life is the Spirit who found its originative exemplar in Jesus, who 'baptized with the Spirit',[4] and by his resurrection assured the disciples of his power to open for them and through them the way to eternal life. In the gospels, Christians have a normative witness to the character of

---

[3] 'Gaudium et Spes', *Vatican Council II: Conciliar and Post-Conciliar Documents*, ed. Austin Flannery (Dublin: Dominican Publications, 1992), 924.
[4] Mark 1: 8.

Jesus' life, which definitively expresses the character of the Spirit—forgiving, seeking out the lost, putting human need first, healing, and encouraging kind and gentle love.

In the letters of the New Testament, Christians have a witness to the acts of the Spirit in the early churches. When Paul writes to the Corinthian church, he mentions what must have been typical activities of their meetings—'when you come together, each one has a hymn, a lesson, a revelation, a tongue, or an interpretation'.[5] He says that in this context he values prophecy (building up, encouraging, and consoling others) above speaking in tongues. But he also mentions, as gifts of the Spirit, wisdom, knowledge, devotion, healing, and the ability to perform miracles. There are many gifts of the Spirit, and they are distributed in different ways to different people. But the purpose of all of them is to build up a community in love.

In those early days there were no specifically Christian scriptures, though the Hebrew Bible was no doubt used as a basis for words of 'prophecy', or Spirit-inspired insight into the purposes of God, which had been disclosed in a new way through Jesus, and which continued to be understood in new ways in the communities of the church. Once the New Testament canon was formed, the gospels could be taken as a template for the character of the Spirit, and the letters as a template for the life of the Spirit-guided community.

So the proclamation of the word is identical with the inbreaking of the Spirit of God, which was expressed in a new way in Jesus, and released at Pentecost to suffuse the life of the new covenant community. When one reads the New Testament letters, one of the things that is most apparent is the newness of the Christian experience. In prophecy, the Spirit gives new insights, and the risen Lord speaks with a new voice. The disciples believed they were experiencing 'the pouring out of the Spirit on all flesh' which the prophet Joel had predicted.[6] This was a radical and prophetic community that broke the mould of all formal religious institutions and ushered in a new age.

There are dangers in such a charismatic society, and they were amply realized in the early church. There is little check on fantasizing and mentally unbalanced rhetoric. The line between Spirit-possession and mental instability is very thin, and it is no accident

---

[5] 1 Corinthians 14: 26.   [6] Acts 2: 17, quoting Joel 2: 28.

that shamanistic persons often seem to be hard to distinguish from, and often to be identical with, those who are highly neurotic. One can use 'inspired speech' to condemn those one dislikes, while avoiding accusations of personal prejudice. The notebooks of anthropologists are filled with examples which would make any advocate of unchecked charismatic activity think again.

For these reasons, charismatic churches often develop authoritarian structures, based on the personality of a particular leader, and they can almost instantaneously tip over from being hotbeds of diverse and radical thought into being stereotyped and sycophantic reaffirmations of the teachings of the leader. Prophetic movements of this sort have appeared over and over again in Christian history, and they have tended to collapse in internal divisions or because of a lack of institutional structure.

One basic problem for the Christian church is how to be a community of the Spirit without becoming a vehicle for fantasizing excess. What has happened on the whole is that hierarchical structures have been created which have kept control of charismatic movements, sometimes by repressing or persecuting them. The priests have come to exercise their ancient role of attempting to control or suppress the prophets, and the Spirit has been channelled in ritualized forms which allow little room for the individual expression of 'prophesy, speaking in tongues, and interpretation'. In Protestant churches which lack such a formalized ritual, a similar controlling function is performed by an insistence on close conformity to the beliefs asserted in Scripture. In both cases, little room is left for that creative and often radical voice of 'prophecy' that characterized the early church.

THE SPIRIT IN THE WORLD

One counteractive to such a suppression of creativity is to develop a less church-centred view of the activity of the Spirit of God. This was done in 'Gaudium et Spes', but it has yet to be followed through, and there are voices within the church that would like to ensure that it never is. A church-centred view sees the chief work of the Spirit as being to awaken believers to knowledge of Jesus as the Christ, and to give the gift of faith, seen largely as intellectual assent to the doctrines of the church. A global view of the Spirit takes its starting-point in the vision of the Spirit moving or storming over the waters of chaos, 'in the beginning' of this created cosmos.[7] It will find the Spirit at work in the long march of nature towards the genesis of finite persons, and thereafter in every creative and liberating human activity, which gives increasing insight into truth, responsiveness to beauty, and co-operation and compassion in society.

Where the Spirit works universally, it cannot be confined to the Christian church. Yet in the church the Spirit may be expressed and active in a distinctive manner. The Spirit is given a specific form and definition in the life of Jesus, and thereafter it is given in that form to those who are called into the church by God. The form of the Spirit in the life of Jesus becomes the template for discerning the work of the Spirit in the world at large. In proclaiming the Word, the church is giving the means to discern the universal activity of the Spirit, and to mediate part of that activity in a consciously responsive way.

An awareness that participation in the Spirit is participation in a global divine activity, with a vocation to articulate and mediate that activity for the whole world, helps to prevent an inward-looking spirituality which finds the Spirit only in charismatic phenomena within the church. Prophecy can be seen more clearly as a discernment of God's purposes of enlarging creativity, understanding, and friendship in the world, and as a contribution to the development of the cultural and intellectual tasks of society. The Christian churches have often served this function by encouraging creative activity in painting, music, and literature, by founding schools and universities, and by fostering a sense of responsible community. Christian faith has helped to give rise to a culture of artistic expression, intellectual enquiry, and respect for human dignity. In Western Europe, the achievements of Christian culture are among the high peaks of human endeavour.

These words, however, will ring alarm bells in all who remember the capitulation of many churches in Germany to the forces of nationalist triumphalism. In such churches the prophetic voice of criticism of injustice was markedly lacking, and the 'Spirit of the People' was virtually identified with the Spirit of God. In many parts of the world, 'Christian culture' has been seen as synonymous with colonial exploitation, cultural imperialism, and a philosophy of racial supremacy.

It is precisely in these respects that the template of the Spirit, given

---

[7] Genesis 1: 2.

in the life of Jesus, should serve as a constant reminder that the Spirit raises up the poor and casts down the rich,[8] that the established forces of state and religion will always be tempted to marginalize or destroy the proclaimers of God's word, and that concern for the ostracized is a fundamental criterion of the Spirit's presence. In the twentieth century the growth of theologies of liberation, often at odds with church hierarchies, has manifested a recovery of these insights, which a triumphalist Christendom had largely overlooked.

The New Testament letters provide a template for the life of the Spirit-guided community. Yet the very different situation of the first Christians, as marginalized and often persecuted minorities living in a militaristic world Empire, makes it impossible to transfer their reactions directly into the modern world. They tended to see 'the world' as ruled by the Devil and spiritual powers of destruction and decadence—'the whole world is under the power of sin'.[9] The world, with its structures of military power, sensuality, ambition, and pride, is subject to destructive lust, and 'to be the world's friend is to be God's enemy'.[10] The world is subject to destruction, and early Christian documents sometimes speak vindictively of 'age-long torments in lakes of fire and sulphur'[11] for those who reject truth and love.

There is an important insight here. Humans do seem to be in bondage to greed, hatred, and delusion, and the consequence of such dispositions is isolation and torment. The personification of these dispositions as evil spiritual powers is part of the world-view of that time, which mythologizes the insight that the human mind is in captivity to selfish greed and pride. To be a friend to such dispositions is indeed to set oneself against the purposes of God. Yet it must never be forgotten that the world remains God's world, and it is never without grace. God's Spirit has always been active throughout the world, seeking to liberate humans from their captivity to evil, and to lead them towards truth, beauty, and compassion.

The New Testament writings are aware of the fact that 'God wants everyone to be saved',[12] and that 'God was making all mankind his friends through Christ'.[13] God's purpose is 'to bring all creation together . . . with Christ as head',[14] so that in the end 'all will openly proclaim that Jesus Christ is Lord'.[15] These affirmations

---

[8] Luke 1: 52.   [9] Galatians 3: 22.   [10] James 4: 4.
[11] Revelation 20: 10.   [12] 1 Timothy 2: 6.   [13] 2 Corinthians 5: 19.
[14] Ephesians 1: 10.   [15] Philippians 2: 11.

entail that God will never simply abandon the world, but will make it possible for everyone to return to God if they so wish. 'Everyone who calls out to the Lord for help will be saved.'[16] That in turn entails that God is present everywhere and to everyone in some fashion, offering them the gift of eternal life. Indeed, that is precisely the gospel, the good news, that Jesus proclaimed. God is universal and unconditional love, and God's Spirit is everywhere working to liberate souls into this love, 'to escape the destructive lust that is in the world . . . and share the divine nature'.[17]

The 'world', then, cannot be identified with non-Christians or with non-Jews. It is the whole of created being in so far as it turns from the creative and liberating purposes of God. The role of the church is to make clear the self-destructive nature of sin, to announce with authority the liberating purpose of God, and to open a way to participation in that liberating purpose. Though the Spirit is everywhere active in the world, it is not often recognized as what it truly is, the Spirit of self-giving, redemptive, and unitive love, and therefore cannot be participated in with awareness and understanding of its nature and purpose. The church does not monopolize the activity of the Spirit, but it makes the Spirit's nature and purpose clear, and is thereby enabled consciously to share in the Spirit's true action.

The New Testament letters clearly depict the church as the people of the Spirit, those who know, participate in, and mediate the Spirit of God. It is well known that Christians claim to be saved not by works but by faith. But this can be misunderstood as the claim that God simply selects some favoured few for salvation, whether or not they make any attempt to be good. The reason 'good works' are not enough is that moral rectitude is simply not sufficient to achieve participation in the nature of God. Even if it does not make one self-righteously proud, which is always a danger, it is not capable of raising one from the status of an obedient servant of God to that of a mediator of the life of God. For that what is necessary is the active power of the life of God itself, flooding into human lives and empowering them.

Faith, in a Christian context, is the acceptance of the power of the Spirit, the subjective side of the coming of the Spirit with power, and with the promise of complete freedom, life, and glory. Faith is

---

[16] Romans 10: 13.   [17] 2 Peter 1: 4.

believing God's promise that such freedom will be given,[18] and it is as a result of such faith that 'God's Spirit lives in you'.[19] That, indeed, is the ultimate secret of the Christian life: 'Christ in you, the hope of glory',[20] the power of the Spirit of Christ received by the assent of faith. The church is the community of the Spirit, the company of those 'who have the Spirit'.[21] That is the source of its life and joy.

Yet this life-transforming experience raised a serious dilemma for the early churches. The plain fact is that every society, however highly motivated, consists of people who are quirky, awkward, irritable, and argumentative. The template for the life of the Spirit-led community is found in many passages—Romans 12, 1 Corinthians 13, Colossians 3, and Galatians 5: 22 among others. But the actual life of churches is never just like that. It is clear that the early churches were divided by severe arguments and dissensions—about who were genuine apostles, about whether Jesus had come 'in the flesh', about whether they were free from all moral laws, about whether they should live wholly ascetic lives, about whether they should keep Torah, about the possibility of forgiveness after serious sin, and many other things. How could these quarrelsome groups be the people of the Spirit of love?

In one notorious, and rather untypical, passage, Paul says, 'Do not try to work together as equals with unbelievers . . . you must leave them and separate yourselves from them.'[22] Some commentators take this to be an interpolation in the text, perhaps the text of an earlier letter. It certainly shocks by its uncompromising separatism, implying, it may seem, that Christians should have nothing to do with non-Christians, but should be a 'pure remnant', called out of a world doomed to destruction.

It shocks because it is so obviously quite different in tone from the gospels which speak of Jesus dining with social outcasts and the 'impure', and from the injunction to 'clothe yourselves with compassion, kindness, humility, gentleness, and patience'.[23] Compassion and kindness cannot be limited to a small circle of believers, if Christians are to grow into the image of the Son, who 'died for everyone'.[24] One must assume therefore, that by 'unbelievers' Paul has in

---

[18] Romans 4: 20.   [19] Romans 8: 9.   [20] Colossians 1: 27.
[21] Romans 8: 23.   [22] 2 Corinthians 6: 14–18.
[23] Colossians 3: 12.   [24] 2 Corinthians 5: 14.

mind a specific group of people (perhaps, in context, idolaters who practised sacred prostitution and magical rituals and used religion as a means of worldly advancement) whom some Corinthian Christians had introduced into their congregation. 'Unbelievers' cannot just mean non-Christians, or even atheists, since Paul refers to them as living in 'wrong' and 'darkness', and thus as being positively immoral. The teaching of this passage must then be that one must not introduce immoral practices into the Christian community, but must insist on endeavouring to realize the mind of Christ by walking in the way of the Spirit. It is not that Christians should never co-operate with non-Christians, or that Christian churches must admit to fellowship only those who are morally perfect. That would undermine the whole practice of the forgiveness of sins. As the world is never without grace, so the church is never without sin. While it seeks to be a community of the Spirit, it should never claim to be spiritually pure. The church should never compromise its ideals, but it should never claim to have realized them perfectly.

If salvation is by grace, it cannot be reserved for those who realize the Spirit perfectly, any more than it can be reserved for those who keep Torah perfectly. In the light of this fact, one cannot make an absolute distinction between the church and the world, as if it were coincident with the distinction between light and darkness. One must say that the church is part of the world, a world in which the Spirit of God is universally at work, though it is obscured and impeded by greed, hatred, and delusion. In the church, the nature of the Spirit as redemptive and unitive love is discerned (in the life of Jesus), and the power of the Spirit is mediated to give conscious participation in the divine nature to those who accept it in faith.

But that power is never unambiguously or fully realized, so the church remains a community which proclaims and tries to live by an ideal (the inner rule of God), while always relying solely on the continually renewed, and continually required, forgiveness of God. As Rahner writes, 'the church will always obscure God's light again by the shadows cast by her children'.[25] If 'the world' is creation in so far as it turns from God, both without and within the church, then 'the church' is creation in so far as it is reconciled and united to God, both within and without the institutional church. The limits of the

---

[25] Rahner, 'On the Theology of the Council', *Theological Investigations*, v. 266, trans. David Bourke, as *Writings of 1965–67* (New York: Crossroad, 1977).

church, the community of the Spirit, the body of Christ, are wider than the limits of any institution, but the earthly forms of the church, like the life of Jesus itself, are the paradigmatic means by which God makes the divine purpose more clearly known and seeks to implement it in a consciously appropriated way.

THE UNITY OF THE CHURCH

The changing cultural contexts in which the church has existed have made an important difference to the way it understands the gospel. The persecuted minority sect in a hostile Roman Empire existed in a very different context from the established and state-supported religion of that same Empire after Constantine. No longer could one speak of a small, pure remnant, set apart from a hostile world of demonic powers. The ethic of submissive acceptance changed to one of public policy shaping. It became possible to see that the world could be changed by the church's leadership—though the price would be that the church would be changed by the world's approbation. Thus the church must always live between criticism of the culture in which it exists, and attempts to shape that culture by its own influence. If the former view often leaves the church without significant influence for good in the world, the latter tends to open the church to the very structures of pride and ambition that it exists to subvert. The world might indeed be humanized and moulded by the influence of the community of the Spirit, but the church itself will stand in need of continual reformation, to keep recalling it to its Christlike form.

A perception of the ambiguity as well as the divinely authorized vocation of the church suggests that the institutional forms of the church should always be open to the voices of the marginalized and the radical, who may perceive the temptations to authoritarian repression which beset any successful institutional structure. This reinforces the conclusion that a truly comprehensive church should permit or even encourage a plurality of interpretative traditions, and especially traditions of dissent, while continuing to seek, and indeed as a way of seeking, a fuller understanding of the divine nature and purpose. As Rahner argues, a critical attitude towards the church is an essential part of a believer's relationship to it.[26]

The Christian churches have found it very difficult to accept such

---

[26] Rahner, 'Opposition', *Theological Investigations*, xvii. 129.

a pluralistic attitude. One reason for this has been a concern for the unity of the churches, indeed a concern that all local churches be parts of one undivided church. If the church is the body of Christ and the community of one undivided Holy Spirit, it may seem odd that it should be divided into lots of differing groups. It seems natural to aim at an institutional unity, which might be ensured by having one head of the whole church, and a hierarchy under him which would maintain its unity by a common obedience to him. It must at once be said that this has not worked. The first great schism of the church occurred precisely over a dispute about the claim of the Roman See that its bishop had authority to govern the universal church, and so assure its unity. The method of trying to achieve unity by asserting the primacy of one bishop in fact brought about a major division in the church, so it can hardly be seen as effective.

What sort of unity should the church then have? An institutional unity might well require a presidential or quasi-monarchical head. The Roman Catholic view that the Pope is the head of the college of bishops is the paradigm embodiment of this model. But the complication, as Protestants are not slow to point out, is that the head of the church is actually Jesus Christ, who is present wherever two or three believers are gathered in his name. So one may suspect that the church must comprise a much wider set of communities than one particular institutional structure.

There are other sorts of possible unity, especially if the church is thought of in vocational terms, as a community called to make Christ present in word, sacrament, and service. Then there may be millions of local communities, each seeking to make Christ present in its own context, and so seeking to be a local embodiment of the one Lord who was fully present in Jesus, who is made present in the sacrament of bread and wine, and who works through the Spirit to effect love and joy in the faithful. There may be many variant interpretations in belief and ways of expressing it, and all believers may be free to form their own local communities. So one may have many churches, local communities seeking to make the one Christ present, though that Christ is understood and approached in different ways.

Would such a system realize Jesus' prayer that his disciples should be one, as he and the Father are one?[27] Well, when Jesus referred to

---

[27] 'that they may all be one, even as thou, Father, art in me, and I in thee, that they also may be in us', John 17: 20–1.

his unity with the Father, he was obviously not talking about any sort of institutional unity. He was presumably referring primarily to a unity of being, such that his human will and the will of God interpenetrated and were indivisibly one in action. Now human beings cannot be ontologically identical with one another, so the analogy cannot be referring to their unity with one another in that ontological sense. It may properly be taken as referring to the fact that believers should be united in the one reality of God, and that the one God should be present in all of them. This is a unity of love and of interior relationship. It might be embodied in many different sorts of social organization. It is, one might say, primarily a vertical unity, between humans and God, rather than a horizontal unity, between various believers.

Of course one would expect believers who are united in God, and in whom the one God is actively present, to act together in devotion and in works of compassion and kindness. One might, however, expect this co-operation to take place primarily at a local level, not to be organized hierarchically from above. One might even positively argue, as Muslims do, that submission to the will of God should make one suspicious of any system that requires absolute submission to any human person or committee. For that would identify humans and God too closely, and would fail to circumscribe the all-too-human tendencies to pride and authoritarianism which afflict church dignitaries as much as any one else.

In many ways, the second Vatican Council of the Roman Catholic Church revolutionized the traditional Catholic view of the church. Karl Rahner called the council a 'caesura' in Christian history, comparable to the genesis of the mission to Gentiles and to the Hellenization of doctrine in the early church.[28] Yet the council continued to teach that the church is an essentially hierarchical institution. 'Christ willed that the apostles' successors (the bishops) should be the shepherds in his church until the end of the world.'[29] Further, he put Peter at the head, so 'the body of bishops has no authority unless united with the Roman Pontiff,'[30] and their 'duty of teaching and ruling . . . can be exercised only in hierarchical communion with the head'.[31] Even a full council of bishops has no authority without the

---

[28] Karl Rahner, 'Basic Theological Interpretation of the Second Vatican Council', *Theological Investigations*, xx. 84.
[29] 'Lumen Gentium', in *Documents of Vatican II*, 370.   [30] Ibid. 375.
[31] Ibid. 373.

Pontiff: 'Together with their head, and never apart from him, they have supreme and full authority.'[32] But the Pontiff possesses such authority in his own person, to the extent that 'submission of the will and intellect must be given to the Pontiff, even when he does not speak *ex cathedra*'.

This is certainly an effective way of ensuring complete unity of thought and discipline in the church, since there is only one source of all authority. But it is effective only for those who are prepared to accept such a strongly hierarchical view of authority. Pseudo-Dionysius was the first person to use the word 'hierarchy'; Paul Rorem says that 'Dionysius invented a word for a structure or system for "sourcing" or channeling the sacred, and linked it all inextricably to the single leader.'[33]

One must ask very seriously whether Christ in fact willed that the sacred should be channelled through one human person, and thence downwards to others. The a priori argument for an essential hierarchy in the church does not seem to be a very strong one. The apostles naturally had a leading role in the early church. They were those who had been companions of Jesus and were witnesses to his resurrection, so they could speak with firsthand authority of their experience of the Lord. It is natural, then, that they should pass on their knowledge of Jesus' acts and teachings to their successors. After them, and certainly after a few generations, there was no one who had the same firsthand authority to speak of the human Jesus, and the apostolic role becomes a rather different one of maintaining the traditions handed on to them, in the light of very different circumstances. It is natural that there should be a line of authorized pastors and teachers, who in time became bishops, or leaders of local districts. Few biblical scholars would hold that one could say such an apostolic succession was instituted by Jesus himself, since Jesus perhaps envisaged no long historical future for the church. But few would deny that it was a natural development, and maybe even one that was essential to the survival of the church.

There is nothing in the New Testament that licenses the belief that some specific person or persons is given a continuing authority to organize the whole church and declare its official teachings on matters of faith and morality. The teachings are primarily those of

---

[32] Ibid. 379.

[33] Paul Rorem, *Pseudo-Dionysius: A Commentary* (New York: Oxford University Press, 1993), 21.

Jesus, and they, where they are remembered, are recorded in the gospels. The organization of the church is characterized in the New Testament in an extremely sketchy way, so sketchy that one cannot be sure that there was to be any form of organized professional leadership at all once the apostles had died. It is only natural that various forms of leadership should develop, but it is not at all clear that it was from the first intended to take the form of bishops claiming descent from various apostolically founded sees. The diverse organization of apostles, elders, and deacons needed to develop in ways which had not been clearly set out by Jesus in any recorded teachings that have come down to us.

Claims made for a supremacy of the successors of Peter to be intended by Jesus himself, seem particularly weak. When, in Matthew 16, Simon Peter (*Petrus*) confesses that Jesus is the Messiah, Jesus' reply is that he will build his church on that rock (*petra*), almost always interpreted by early theologians as the rock of faith.[34] Peter is clearly very important among the Twelve, and was in many ways their leader. It is possible that when John's Gospel reports the command of Jesus that Peter should feed his lambs and sheep, this was not only a reversal of Peter's threefold denial, but a pastoral commission to Peter.[35] It hardly asserts that Peter was to be the supreme pastor, above all the others, and such an interpretation, now fairly common in Roman Catholic apologetics, has to be read into the text.

When Paul writes about the 'pillars' of the Jerusalem church, he mentions James the brother of Jesus, Peter, and John together.[36] At the first Council of Jerusalem, James seems to play at least as important a part as Peter (he seems to give the summing up of the council in Acts 15: 13). Paul considered himself able to found and advise churches without much reference to Peter. Peter was preeminent in many ways, but it does not sound as if Jesus had given him some sole individual authority to define doctrines or organize churches. Even less is there any implication that Peter was to hand on such leadership to his successors. It rather seems to be the case that the developing claim to primacy of the Bishop of Rome was due to the eminence of the See of Rome, as the place where both Peter and Paul had allegedly died, and as the capital of the Roman Empire.

---

[34] Matthew 16: 18.   [35] John 21: 15–17.   [36] Galatians 2: 9.

The development of such a primacy was quite natural, but could hardly have been envisaged by Jesus.

THE POWER OF THE CHURCH

Matthew reports that Jesus gave Peter 'the keys of the kingdom',[37] a statement of which those who support Petrine primacy make much. But it is more likely to mean that the confession of Jesus' Messiahship opens the door to the kingdom, both for oneself and for others, than that Peter alone is given the power to admit people to the kingdom. The latter supposition is indeed unthinkable in view of Paul's successful preaching to the Gentiles, and the fact that at the very least all the apostles, and the Lukan seventy, were given authority to preach the kingdom in such a way that their preaching would bring salvation or judgement upon their hearers.[38] It is the preaching of Jesus as Messiah that places before men and women the promise of the kingdom, and it is Peter's first open confession of that belief that therefore opens the door of the kingdom to others. There is no implication that he is to keep the keys for himself, much less that he is to hand them on to his successors. This is a case where a vocational interpretation, that the church is called to proclaim Christ and so open the doors of the kingdom to all, is more satisfactory than an institutional interpretation, that one man and his successors are given authority to allow people into the kingdom or not, as they choose.

One might say that a fundamental difference of perception about the role of the church exists at precisely this point. The institutional view is that the church is the one place where salvation can be found, and the hierarchy has the power to admit or exclude people, a power which carries authority even after death. Such a power of eternal life and death is supreme over all other powers, and it readily gives rise to a view of the church as having power even over princes, to raise them up or depose them. This view found its epitome in the reign of Boniface VIII, who claimed the right to elect or depose sovereigns.[39] The vocational view is very different. It is that the church is given the mission of opening the doors of the kingdom of God to the whole

---

[37] Matthew 16: 19.   [38] Luke 9: 1–2; 10: 1–12.
[39] Papal Bull 'Unam Sanctam', in *Documents of the Christian Church*, ed. Henry Bettenson (Oxford: Oxford University Press, 1963), 115.

world. It is not given a power to lock people out, but to show the world the nature and possibility of eternal life. This is a power of opening up the doors of spiritual perception, of opening the hearts of men and women to the saving power of the Spirit of love. It has little to do with questions of who governs the nations of the world.

Matthew also reports that Jesus gives Peter the 'power of binding and loosing'.[40] This is elucidated in ch. 18, when all the disciples are given that power, and where the context makes clear that what is at issue is the treatment of those who have done some grave wrong to others within the church community. The power of loosing is the power to declare forgiveness, on condition of penitence. The power of binding is the power to 'treat as a Gentile or tax gatherer'—that is, to exclude from the friendship of the community—those who are obstinately impenitent. It should not be taken to imply anything like a condemnation to Hell. It is rather a statement that those who are impenitent exclude themselves from the fellowship of the Spirit. In critical cases, where scandal is being caused in a church congregation, such exclusion may be formally imposed. But the offer of forgiveness must always remain open, since Jesus commands his disciples to forgive 'seventy times seven' times[41]—that is, without limit.

There is a sort of ecclesial authority given here, the authority to declare the forgiveness of sins as well as to proclaim the gospel of the kingdom, to heal the sick, and to exorcize demons. Moreover, the apostles are to be received 'as Christ himself', so there is undoubtedly a sense of being commissioned by the Lord, and given his authority to cause the healing, forgiving, and life-giving Christ to be present in the world. In that sense, the church is not just a group of like-minded religious enthusiasts. It is a community of the Spirit of Christ, called and commissioned by the Lord to make his presence known salvifically in the world, a community whose marks are that it is holy, catholic, and apostolic.

The church is 'holy', or set apart by its special relation to God, given the vocation to make Christ present in the world. But it remains a community of forgiven sinners, always liable to corruption. So it needs to be less dominating and exclusive, and more aware of the possible corruptions of hierarchical power, than it has often been. The church is apostolic, since it continues the apostles'

---

[40] Matthew 18: 18.   [41] Ibid. 18: 22.

task of making Christ present through proclamation, healing, and faithful witness. It preserves the witness of the apostles to the life and teachings of Jesus, which define the form of the Spirit, and therefore of the church's life, for as long as it exists. This witness is limited to the original witness of the apostles, now recorded in the New Testament. The church must continually seek to formulate new insights evoked by increasing knowledge and experience, but those insights can never contradict the original apostolic witness, and they will have the status of advisory guidance, not of inerrant truth. It is catholic, since it is called to grow throughout the whole world, not being limited to any ethnic group, but including whomsoever will respond, without distinction of race, sex, or social position. It is to be a servant community of love in the world, not a society of the saved (the separatist vision) nor the sponsor of a cultural elite (the Christendom vision).

There is a clear sense in which such a church should be one, united in confessing one Lord, one baptism, one eucharist, one hope of eternal life. Yet it may subsist in many local communities, and it may be all the members of such local communities who together exercise the power of forgiving and disciplining their own members, as they faithfully seek to rely on Christ, their only head, and live in the power of the Spirit. Such an interpretation is greatly strengthened by Jesus' repeated teaching, whenever he was asked about who would be greatest, that the greatest would be the servant of all.[42] This counts strongly against any hierarchical view which gives the earthly leaders of the church great privilege and dignity. Jesus taught that no man should be called 'father',[43] that those who sought chief seats and wore fine robes were hypocrites,[44] and that those who wanted to lead should in fact serve others. This seems to be a radically non-hierarchical view, which suggests that the leaders of congregations should not be authoritarian teachers so much as dish-washers and cleaners.

Of course Christian communities will need leaders and teachers, and some visible form of their spiritual unity. Bishops, who have maintained their claim to apostolic succession for centuries, may well be best placed to have such a function. But there is every reason why they should not have chief seats or thrones and wear long gowns, or be treated as having special dignity (which is the point of

[42] e.g. Luke 22: 25–7.   [43] Matthew 23: 9.   [44] Luke 20: 45–7.

Jesus' prohibition on calling anyone 'father'). They may rightly have a function of advising, counselling, and offering interpretations of the faith in their own situations. But their authority remains precisely that of their expertise and experience and holiness. Neither individually nor as a group is there reason to think that they have the authority unilaterally to tell all others what to believe or to do, as Christians. Such decisions are to be made by the church community as a whole—and even so it is severely limited by being required to enforce nothing that is not recorded in the apostolic tradition of the New Testament.

On such a view, well supported by the New Testament, the church will primarily subsist in small local communities, each perhaps formulating its own distinctive approach to doctrine and ways of life. There can and should be a unity between the churches. It will be a unity of fellowship between people often of differing particular views, who can unite around a common devotion to Jesus as the one who shows and mediates the liberating love of God, a common hope for eternal life, by the power of the Holy Spirit, and a common commitment to compassionate love for the weak and oppressed of the earth.

This view of the church as a union of autonomous local communities is typical of many Protestant denominations, and it takes episcopal form in the Orthodox and Anglican communions. This is another point, however, at which there might seem to be a direct conflict with Roman Catholic teaching that the hierarchical structure of the church derives from the Pontiff. Is it possible for Protestants to speak of the church as a hierarchical structure? One might do so, I think, if one does not mean that all power comes from one supreme source, but rather that the church is not simply a democratic society which is free to make up its beliefs by majority vote. It is the guardian of a revelation given by God, and it is a community that bases its life of loving service and fellowship upon that basic revelation in Christ. Any such community needs structures of authority and guidance, and persons who are given authority to formulate and express its views on matters of belief and practice. In some sense any church will need a hierarchy or what might be called a 'management structure', and in that broad sense Protestants would be able to agree that the church is a hierarchical society.

The crucial question is that of how such a hierarchy is to operate, and what its relation to the church as a whole should be. Protestants, partly because of their past persecution by the Roman Church, tend to be suspicious of authoritative views imposed on the faithful by some special élite class. More positively, they often have a strong sense that the Spirit will work within the whole fellowship of the church, rather than in central élite committees, and that local church communities should have a large degree of autonomy in their decisions about such things as forms of worship and matters of church order and discipline. While there are hierarchies—central committees on doctrine and on morals, for example—they do not often have the power to make their recommendations binding on all the churches they represent. Moreover their members are often elected for limited periods, so that a quasi-aristocratic oligarchy cannot become established.

One modern example of a form of church unity that can embrace a plurality of differing polities is the World Council of Churches, founded at Amsterdam in 1948. All major Christian churches, except the Roman Catholic and Unitarian Churches, are members of the World Council. This organization seeks to co-ordinate programmes on theological education, social action, and evangelization, and to sponsor ecumenical relationships between the churches and with non-Christian religions. It may suggest an embryonic pattern for the world church of the future, which will embrace a plurality of patterns of worship and witness within an overarching unity of commitment to the saving revelation of God in Jesus.

At the time of writing, the Roman Catholic Church has accepted full membership of the Faith and Order Commission, and appoints accredited observers to Assemblies of the Council. There are also streams of thought within the Roman Catholic Church that favour a rethinking of traditional Catholic attitudes to the centralization of authority. Karl Rahner was a defender of absolute papal authority in matters of faith and morals, and of the necessity of obedience to the magisterium of the church. Yet he proposed interpretations of these beliefs that would have considerably surprised an earlier generation of Tridentine Catholics. Thus he was a proponent of applying the principle of subsidiarity, well established in Catholic social teaching, to church life.[45] This would give more autonomy to local churches,

---

[45] Rahner, 'Peaceful Reflections on the Parochial Principle', *Theological Investigations*, ii. 321, trans. K.-H. Kruger, as *Man in the Church* (New York: Crossroad, 1975).

and would in fact mean that the Curia would only act in cases not capable of resolution at a local level. He also held that even defined dogmas were not in every sense irreformable: 'realizations of truth always remain open to further modifications . . . every statement of faith posited in the here and now . . . can be modified'.[46] He speculated that bishops in the future might not have any earthly honours or power, but would invite voluntary obedience. The right to make binding decisions might simply not be used, and there might be no further need for papal declarations with the strict force of infallibility.[47] Moreover, though there would always have to be orders of bishops and priests in the church, their form might vary considerably in the future. Bishoprics might even be open to groups of people rather than single individuals, and both Pope and bishops might hold office only for a limited period.[48] Priestly ordination might be held temporarily,[49] and local communities might have the right to nominate their own candidates for ordination.[50] Perhaps even those forms of ministry developed in other churches might be accepted as authentic expressions of the one church of Christ.

It seems clear that the present forms of church structure are not absolutely unchangeable, and that many possibilities of convergence between presently separated churches exist. The future of the church is always open to the creative power of the Holy Spirit, so that it is unlikely to be constrained by what may turn out to be the social prejudices of the past. So one must not foreclose discussion of the proper forms of hierarchy and governance in the church, forms which must both build up fellowship in the universal church, and permit the proper freedom into which the Spirit calls the churches.[51]

---

[46] Rahner, 'The New Image of the Church', ibid. x. 5, trans. D. Bourke, as *Writings of 1965–67* (New York: Crossroad, 1977), ii.

[47] Rahner, 'Episcopacy', ibid. vi. 368, trans. K.-H. and B. Kruger, as *Concerning Vatican Council II* (New York: Crossroad, 1982).

[48] Rahner, *Meditations on Freedom and the Spirit*, trans R. Ockenden, D. Smith, and C. Bennett (London: Darton, Longman, Todd, 1977), 68.

[49] Rahner, 'Consecration', *Investigations*, xix. 69, trans. E. Quinn, as *Faith and Ministry* (New York: Crossroad, 1983).

[50] Rahner, 'Official Ministry', ibid. xiv. 215, trans. David Bourke, as *Ecclesiology* (New York: Crossroad, 1976).

[51] Rahner, 'Freedom', ibid. ii. 97, trans. Kruger as *Man in the Church*.

UNITY IN THE SPIRIT

In the past, the drive to institutionalize Christian unity by requiring some form of closely defined agreement in beliefs has proved virtually irresistible. Almost every Christian group has succumbed to the temptation to formulate a distinctive creed or statement of faith, and to require submission to it as a condition of membership. So much is this the case that to many brought up in a Christian culture it seems essential to religious faith to have a defined and detailed creed to which believers do and should submit.

Yet this is actually a minority view of what religious faith requires, in a global perspective. Of course there are some core beliefs, such as the four holy truths of Buddhism, or the *shahada* of Islam, and there are holy texts which are sources of meditation and doctrine. So in Christianity there are the core beliefs that Jesus is the Christ, the son of God, and that through him God offers eternal life to all humanity. There are the texts of the Old and New Testaments. What is unusual about Christianity is the often almost obsessive concern with discovering a 'correct doctrine' on almost every subject, and with having some identifiable authority who can say what this doctrine is. Most religions manage without a supreme teaching authority, and achieve a unity based on acceptance of a core faith and a common set of sacred texts.

In Buddhist monasteries, for example, Theravada and Mahayana monks can live together amicably, accepting a common practice of meditation and daily routine. In Islam and in Judaism there are learned scholars and lawyers, but their authority is very much a matter of being accepted within a large part of the community, and it is not binding on the consciences of the faithful. In Hinduism there are many teachers, who may be given great authority by their disciples, but who have no institutionalized position which enables them to say what is irreformably true in matters of faith or morals. It may be part of the pathology of Christianity that it often requires some institutionalized way of declaring what is true, and is unable to leave the pursuit of truth even in very obscure and disputed matters to criticism, discussion, and reasoned recommendation by experienced and learned judges.

I think it must be said that Christianity often has an over-intellectualized approach to religious truth. Faith itself is sometimes interpreted, not as a way of living in trust and in dynamic relationship to a personally apprehended God, but as the acceptance of propositions on authority. Of course, faith requires the acceptance of some propositions as true—there must be a God revealed in Jesus and known through the Spirit. But faith does not require a correct understanding of such things as the inner nature of God or the exact programme one can expect after death, especially when that understanding has been formulated by a group of mostly elderly, conservative, and quarrelsome male dignitaries.

If the church had a little more humility, it might actually doubt whether all its utterances had the benefit of being countersigned by the Holy Spirit. If it had a little more charity, it might manage to respect the views of conscientious dissenters, while seeking to present its own convictions with reasonable sensitivity.

The church has all too easily slipped from asserting justifiable apostolic authority—about things they had seen and heard, but usually not understood properly—to claiming a very different sort of apostolic authority—the authority exercised by those who are taken to be correctly appointed successors of the apostles, to decide which religious assertions are true and which are false. It is not at all clear that being a duly appointed successor to someone entitles one to the same sort of authority they had, or that such authority ever applied to general assessments of religious truth anyway.

The church is the guardian of the apostolic tradition. But the tradition remains often obscure, ambiguous, polyvalent, and challenging, rather than clear, precise, and directly prescriptive. It is susceptible of many interpretations, as new conditions and contexts arise. From the first, the church was a diverse group which could hold together many sorts of view. What came to be called 'orthodoxy' was a general agreement among bishops on what was an authentic development from the apostolic witness. Such agreements, especially when they are universal, or ecumenical, command a great degree of respect, since they embody the judgement of the great majority of believers. But there is little a priori reason to expect that they will always be protected from error.

It is understandable that some sort of unity between the leaders of Christian communities, the bishops, should be thought desirable. But one must not underestimate the arguments—between Peter and Paul at Antioch, for instance[52]—that took place from the very first.

---

[52] Galatians 2: 11–14.

The church has always been, and always will be, a diverse set of communities with different traditions and interpretations, all seeking to share in the life of God through a response of faith to the revelation of God in the person of Jesus. The church seeks above all to share in the life and creativity of the Spirit, which might actually inspire diversity of thought and practice, rather than ensuring conformity to one speculative world-view.

Nevertheless, it is not an ideal situation when small groups of disciples gather without reference to the existence of one another. The unity of the body of Christ must mean more than that. Christ wills a unity of fellowship and co-operation, and agreement at least on a basic common faith in the Lordship of Jesus Christ. Rahner, from a Catholic viewpoint, envisages a form of unity between different churches, provided only that no church rejects what is dogma for another, and that no dogma which goes beyond the ecumenical creeds is imposed by one church on another.[53] On this model, the church would be an ecumenical communion of independent churches, with many teaching lineages, each adopting a distinctive interpretation of the biblical Scriptures. There could be meetings for common worship, but a guarantee of toleration for diverse interpretations. There is a place for the primacy of the Pope in such a vision of the church, for one who would be a servant of the servants of the Lord, and a focal symbol of the global mission of the church. But if the church is to be truly catholic, or universal, a great deal more insight will be required into that profound saying of Jesus, 'Whoever would be first among you must be slave of all.'[54]

As one looks at the development of orthodoxy, one might be grateful for the deepening of understanding that conciliar definitions have often brought about. But one might also be uncomfortably aware of the tenuousness of claims to certainty that have been made about very abstruse and uncertain matters, of the intolerance that adherence to orthodox views so often seems to bring in its train, and of the constraining effect of ancient Greek philosophical formulations, if they are thought to be eternally valid, in a very different age.

Perhaps the most persisting heresy of orthodoxy is the claim to be the 'one true faith', disallowing others any distinctive grasp of truth,

[53] K. Rahner and H. Fries, *Unity of the Churches: An Actual Possibility*, trans. R. Gritsch and E. Gritsch (New York: Crossroad, 1985), 25.
[54] Mark 10: 44.

or even any freedom to proclaim their beliefs. Even tiny Protestant sects are liable to make such claims, and to associate with them the restriction of the 'saved' to the minority of human beings who hold the true faith. Two things seem to me of the first importance in this regard. It must be firmly asserted that salvation is possible for those who conscientiously and in good faith have false beliefs. And it must be equally firmly asserted that absolute truth in religious matters is extremely difficult to achieve, so that one must not claim more certainty than it is reasonable to grant. Claims by early witnesses to have met people who saw Jesus raised from the dead have quite a good claim to certainty. Even then, however, it is easy to see how they can be rationally disbelieved, in view of the lack of conclusive evidence and the uncertainty of belief in a God who might raise people from death.

So one must be wary of conflating one's own presentation of Christian truth with the word of God—even though one hopes God will speak through one's personal witness to the power of the gospel. In the end, the two essential moments of faith are insight and liberation. One seeks insight into the presence of the Spirit, a spiritual depth of value and power, mediated in specific finite symbols. And one seeks liberation in the power of the Spirit, from hatred, greed, and delusion. When testimony to insight turns into a claim to objective and certain knowledge, and testimony to personal liberation turns into a claim to possess the only way to escape from evil, faith is in danger of becoming pathological.

Believers will testify to insight, an extension of understanding and vision, mediated by the symbols of their faith, grounded in and developed from the revelatory matrix of their tradition. But how can such a revelation be *certainly* true, when many intelligent and informed people not only doubt but positively reject it? Virtually every religious assertion is disputable and disputed. It is inappropriate to claim theoretical certainty in such cases. One can be wholly committed to a disclosure which has transformed one's life—one can be subjectively certain of it—while admitting that it is not clear to everyone, and cannot be claimed as objectively certain, obvious to all informed, intelligent, and unbiased observers. Religious believers need to accept that people genuinely differ, and that the certainty of faith is a wholeheartedness of commitment to a personal discernment of supreme value.

Revelation should be exploratory, expansive of insight, not

restrictive of human enquiry and repressive of critical examination. The church of the future, in so far as it embraces such a view of revelation, will itself, as the vehicle of revelation, be exploratory, evocative, self-critical, and responsive to a God whose Spirit leads humans progressively towards an always incomplete but developing understanding of infinite wisdom. The universal church of the Spirit must be a pluralistic church. Its unity will be the unity of the one source of saving truth, God, disclosed in the events surrounding Jesus, and the unity of all those who seek to respond positively to that disclosure by seeking to sustain a community of love. This will not be a hierarchical, patriarchal, authoritarian church, but a more egalitarian, participatory, pluralistic, disclosive church, whose unity lies not in obedience to some institutionally appointed functionary or committee, but in its faith in the God disclosed in the self-giving life of Jesus, in the new life of forgiveness and reconciliation in the Spirit, and in hope for the fulfilment of all creation. Then the church will be manifold in the forms of its institutional life, but one in the Spirit which seeks continually and in many ways to 'bring all creation together . . . with Christ as head'.[55] It may continually fail to live up to its vocation, but the calling of the church, which will continually renew and reform it, is to be the community in which the Holy Spirit can be made known, and can begin to transform the whole world into the image of Christ.

[55] Ephesians 1: 10.

8

The Church as a Sacramental Community

The Christian church is a distinctive religious society, in that it is a sacramental community. It is not, like Judaism, to be closely associated with a particular socio-political state. Despite the fact of the church's historical ties to the Byzantine and Holy Roman Empires, and the attempt of some popes to assert political supremacy, the church is truly 'catholic', an international community, existing in many different political frameworks and cultures. It is not, like Islam, a society of obedience to divine law. It has no detailed code of divine law, but seeks to pattern its life on that of Jesus, empowered by the Spirit which was fully manifest in him. It seeks to live by an inward and personal union with Christ, as an organic unity (a 'body') which mediates Christ's life to the world. It is not, like Buddhism, centred on a community of renouncers, leaving the world to attain nirvana. Despite the fact that there have always been groups of Christians who have cut themselves off from the secular world, the church as a whole is a community that seeks not to leave but to transform the world, liberating it from all that separates it from God, and shaping it to express the divine beauty. It is not, like some main forms of Hinduism, a society that seeks a way of individual release from the wheel of rebirth; it is a society that delineates the way to eternal life, life in conscious, communal, and continuing personal relationship to a Creator God who wills the fulfilment of creation.

The church is sacramental, in that it expresses in a visible organization the creative and transforming action of God which brings personal lives to their proper fulfilment. It is sacramental, in espousing a 'worldly spirituality', for which the material is to be made the unequivocal expression of spirit. It is sacramental, in seeking to unite the finite world to the infinite reality of God. Its rituals convey divine power for living in the world. Its prayers discipline the mind for realizing the excellences which belong to human nature and appreciating the values of the created order. Its devotions prepare one to see Christ in all created things, and all things in Christ.

Yet if the church is a means of grace, it is an ambiguous one, for it remains part of the world, with all that implies for the prevalence of greed, hatred, and ambition. Thus the church can easily become a repressive and authoritarian institution, all the more so since it can claim to express the very acts of God. Its rituals can become the exclusive and necessary means to salvation, without which no one can be united to God. Its prayers can become quasi-mechanical devices for causing supernatural powers to come to one's aid. Its devotions can become temptations to enter into an inner fantasy world, divorced from the needs and realities of everyday life.

This ambiguity reflects two main views of how human beings relate to the gods or spiritual powers throughout the history of religions. One may be called the transactional view, according to which one gives something to the gods so that they may give something in return. One may give a precious possession to ensure protection or fertility, or to avert defeat or illness. Or one may simply pay money to a priest or holy person to gain some benefit from the gods. The other is a more personalist view, for which one simply returns to God, the giver of all things, the best of what one has, to show that one is not taking such gifts possessively, but as a steward, in gratitude and love. There is no question here of buying a benefit. It is a matter of acknowledging that God gives all things, relying wholly on divine power, and perhaps asking God to help those for whom one has a special concern. The line between the two can be a fine one. Since the sacraments of the church are seen as means of grace, it is fairly easy to see them as channels of divine power, which can be controlled by the church hierarchy, and obtained in return for prayer or payment. Yet the proper way to see them is as means of personal encounter with the active love of God, to which the appropriate human response is one of gratitude and commitment.

The church is the body of Christ, in that it is an international community, with a special vocation to be a servant community patterned on the remembered life of Jesus, empowered by the present Spirit of God, and trusting in the promise of fulfilment in God. This community has the vocation of participating in the creative and liberating acts of God in history, which are aimed at making matter the sacrament (the true expression) of spirit, by freely responsive faith.

The church is not an ethnic community. Although it sprang from Judaism, and is centred on adoration of one who is acclaimed as 'King of the Jews', in the first few years it opened its doors to Gentiles, and saw itself as a new, more inward and universal, covenant community. It follows that membership is not given simply by birth. Some people are called into membership, and some are not ('two men will be in the field; one is taken and one is left'[1]). One cannot tell why this is, though it is surely wrong to view such a calling as a destining for salvation, from which others are excluded. The fact that membership is felt as a 'calling' from God is signified by baptism, as the initiating rite of membership. In baptism people are said to die and be buried with Christ.[2] They 'die to the world', and this seems like a paradigm of a renouncing community, like the Buddhist *sangha*.

Monks renounce all their property, homes, and family. They die to the world in a very clear way. Christians, too, renounce the world, the flesh, and the devil—which one might take to be symbols of ambition, greed, and hatred—and sprinkling with water symbolizes their purifying from all 'worldly' concerns. There is a clear sense in which the church is necessarily divorced from the political order, and in which one therefore cannot hope for a 'Christian society'. Society as such will remain, so far as one can see, dominated by ambition, greed, and hatred, and in the face of that the church will always be called to be a counter-culture, directed against the dominant concerns of the wider society.

At the same time, the church is not simply a society of renouncers, for it is to be the society in which Christ's life is lived in the world. God acts in the world to create and enjoy new values and experiences. The water of baptism is also the 'living water' which Christ gives, source of new life and joy. With forgiveness of past sin goes empowerment for future perfection. Those whom God calls, God forgives and empowers, and to them God gives the promise of future perfection. When baptism is received in faith, through and by means of it God forgives and empowers, incorporates into the body of Christ, and promises fellowship in the coming kingdom.

One may ask, could God not do this without the ritual of baptism?

---

[1] Matthew 24: 40.   [2] Romans 6: 4.

There can be no doubt that God could. God is not limited by the means of grace, the visible rituals by means of which God wills to give the power and love of the Spirit. We cannot tell how far and in what way God befriends, forgives, and empowers people throughout the whole of human history. But that is precisely the point—we cannot tell how God does that, or even that God does it, or what it is that God does, without some insight into the nature of God's action and its mode of operation.

It is Jesus who teaches, in word and act, that God is love, and that God's liberating action is one that forgives sin, unites to the divine being, and empowers for creative and compassionate action in the world. The rite of baptism was practised by others—John the Baptist, for instance—but Jesus commanded his disciples to use it in a new way.[3] It was not only to symbolize true penitence and purification from sin, but to be the means of bringing about membership of the community of the new covenant, in which the Spirit would bring about new life in unity with the life of God. It would be the bearer of the active power of God to bring new spiritual life into being.

There have been times in Christian history when grace has been regarded almost as a quasi-juridical declaration that punishment is remitted, or as a sort of substance which eliminates sin. The church can then claim authority to issue such declarations, or can control the amount of cleansing substance which is given, and the persons to whom it is given. Grace, however, is nothing else but the personal love of God. What God wills is that created persons should co-operate with the divine will, should consciously know and love God, and should become channels of the active power of God. That active power is action for good, which contributes strength to the human will. How can one receive that illumination which gives knowledge of God, and that power which increases joy, love, and compassion?

The obvious answer is, through an attention to God that is open to the divine action. Baptism is the sign that God acts before we respond, to prepare the mind for illumination and the will for virtue. In Jesus, God was present and active to show the divine nature and to move people to follow him in the way of virtue. People did not first have to pray for God's guidance and help. God came close to them in the person of Jesus to guide and help them.

Of course they did not have to accept that guidance, and many

---

[3] Matthew 28: 19.

obviously did not. Jesus did not compel people to follow him. Yet he really did quite objectively offer them the grace—the loving power of God, which would transform their lives if they allowed it to do so. So we might say that, though God is in some way active everywhere in the world, in Jesus God showed the divine nature and gave the power of divine love, in a manifest and wholly authentic way.

The church, because it lives by the constant anamnesis of the person of Jesus, and especially of his loving life, his passion, and his resurrection, continues to be the place where authentic manifestation of the revelation of the divine nature and the vehicle of divine power occurs—but only so long as it does present a true anamnesis of Jesus. Baptism is an act of the church which is intended to incorporate people into this new community. That act declares the divine nature as a love that wills to unite persons to God, and manifests the divine power of love, in reaching out to call the baptized into union with Christ. It does not make people holy whether or not they respond. But if they allow it to do so, it marks the beginning of a communal life that will transform them into the image of Christ.

Because baptism is, by its connection with the person of Jesus and the mediation of his resurrection life, an authentic instrument of the active liberating love of God, its nature does not depend upon the response of the baptized person. As Jesus, by his presence, truly offered the love of God to all who met him, so baptism, by its application, truly offers the love of God to those who are called into the community of Christ. Baptism is the beginning of a conversation of love between God and the soul, and it is a conversation initiated by God, on the pattern and by the command of Jesus. It therefore seems appropriate to most Christians that even babies can be baptized. As Jesus blessed babies, so God blesses them in baptism, assuring them of the life offered to them in the community of the Spirit, and initiating them into that community even before they can consciously respond.

While God can bring new spiritual life into being without baptism or without the church, if God truly declared the divine nature and purpose in Jesus, one can see how baptism can be such an authentic declaration, which lets one see what the real nature of a salvific relation to God is, and what it is that God offers to each human soul. One can also see how baptism is only the beginning of new life in Christ, and so must be closely associated with the life of the Christian community, in which that new life can be nurtured and directed.

God's relation to created persons is and will always remain deeply personal and moral. Baptism is not an impersonal rite that automatically wipes away the punishment due to original sin. It is the entrance into a community of new life, and it must be the beginning of a personal relationship of love with God, in which the true virtues of human life are realized in co-operation with the divine love.

The new life to which baptism gives entrance is not one freed from the material world. It is precisely the life of a society in the material world, which one is to sanctify by obedience to God. Yet that obedience is obedience to the inward leading of the Spirit, not submission to a written code. A sacrament is the capacity of a material substance to be the expression and vehicle of spirit. The role of the church is to make all creation a sacrament, and so to release it from all that prevents clear and authentic expression of value. Since Christ is the liberator and ruler of the cosmos, he is the spiritual reality which all creation is meant finally to manifest, and the one who will bring creation to that capacity. In the sacrament of baptism, Christ calls persons to a role in this task of realizing the kingdom, promises them membership in the society of the rule of the Spirit, and assures them of the help of divine love in overcoming greed, hatred, and delusion.

What has to be avoided is the impression that the application of this rite will of itself assure one of avoidance of just punishment, and that failure to undergo it will leave one without the help of God. What baptism assures one of is the unconquerable power of the love of God, a power that is offered as a personal and co-operative relationship to those who are baptized. God's grace is offered also to the unbaptized, but it is precisely the task of the baptized to make that grace clearly known and to be the instruments of its more effective action in the lives of men and women throughout the world. The sacraments must never be seen as the only means of escaping otherwise certain doom, as limits on the love of God, under the control of some human group. The church is a sacramental community, in that it is called to be an authentic channel of the liberating love of God, with the promise of fulfilment for all. The sacraments are, in a word, lights of love and hope to the whole world and not privileged pathways from the world's destruction to a mystically achieved personal security. It is in this that the sacraments of the church differ most basically from the Mysteries of the ancient Mediterranean world and of the Gnostic cults.

THE SACRAMENTAL MINISTRY

While baptism is the sacrament of entrance into the fellowship of the church, the main sacrament of the church, and the proper means by which its spiritual life is renewed, is the eucharist. It is rightly named a 'thanksgiving', rather than a propitiatory or piacular rite, for its primary purpose is to enable one to cement fellowship with God and with others, give thanks for the gift of life, and offer oneself in the service of human welfare. It is essentially a communal offering, a participation in the divine love, a making-present in time of the cosmic Christ. It is not a ritual that can buy remission of penalty for oneself or others, in an automatic way. Yet it is a prayer which is effective in so far as it expresses a bond of love effected by God in those who participate in faith.

The minister of the eucharistic sacrament is Christ, and Christ acts effectively wherever two or three disciples gather and break bread in his name.[4] He becomes present, so as to act in the lives of his disciples, in healing, forgiving, and serving love. He gave his life as a prayer of self-giving that the kingdom would come in the lives of his disciples. He continues to offer his life for the sake of the world, and he includes the disciples in this self-offering, so that in him they offer their lives to God, dying to self in order to be filled with divine life.

For Catholic and Orthodox traditions, the consecratory words need to be said by a male human being, who must be specially commissioned ('ordained') by someone who believes he can trace his own commissioning from the apostles, for Christ to be really and truly present in the eucharist. On the Roman Catholic understanding, the priest stands in the place of Christ: 'In the person of Christ he effects the eucharistic sacrifice.'[5] 'Bishops take the place of Christ himself.'[6] The implication is that Christ is not only truly present in the eucharistic elements, but has a special presence in the priest, as it were saying the words of consecration personally in the priest.

This seems to give bishops or priests a special place as manifestations of Christ that is not open to all Christians. From a Protestant

---

[4] Matthew 18: 20.
[5] 'Lumen Gentium', in *Vatican Council 2: Conciliar and Post-Conciliar Documents*, ed. Austin Flannery (Dublin: Dominican Publications, 1992), 361.
[6] Ibid. 374.

point of view, it is important not to confuse Christ and individual ministers of the church, for it would be a form of idolatry to do so. The priest does not become Christ, and even if one did, one would not need to look like Jesus or be of the same race or sex as Jesus to do so.

For the Reformed churches, anyone effects a valid sacrament who is a member of the church, who has been commissioned by the laying-on of hands, and who sincerely says the words of commemoration, believing the promises of Christ. It would be difficult for a Catholic to say that nothing happens, that divine grace is not truly bestowed, in a Reformed Eucharist, since it is accepted that divine grace is not limited to particular ordinances. Perhaps it could be said that grace is not bestowed in a regular manner, in the way Christ wills it to be bestowed. This then seems to be a matter of church order rather than of ontology, and it assumes that Christ wills the hierarchical order of the Catholic Church, which is precisely what is in question. For a Reformed Christian, the body and blood of Christ are truly present and received wherever disciples sincerely gather and intend that to be true. Who is authorized to preside at such celebrations is a matter of church order and discipline.

Of course, if the church is a vehicle of divine grace, its sacramental forms must be authorized by God, and must not be matters merely of human invention. The form of the eucharistic sacrament is given by Jesus' institution of the Last Supper, recorded, though not fully, in the New Testament.[7] The apostles were commanded to celebrate the sacrament, and it seems right that they should have the power to authorize others to celebrate it after them. The 'apostolic succession' is a natural way of seeing that the sacraments of the church are celebrated in a duly authorized way. It is not that God will only give grace when a priest has been ordained in the apostolic succession (the 'ontological' view). On a more personalistic view, God wills to give grace in the form Jesus instituted, by duly authorized ministers of the church, and the normal form of authorization is by the laying-on of hands of those themselves authorized in a continuous line of succession from the apostles. That is not the only way in which God gives grace, but it is, one might reasonably argue, the way in which God wishes to give it.

The matter of due authorization is important, not because the

---

[7] Luke 22: 19–20.

effectiveness of the sacrament depends upon it, but because of what God wills for the structure of the church as a sacramental community. There should be properly authorized ministers who celebrate the sacraments in their proper form. On this issue there are, unfortunately, three major differing views in the Christian world. The Roman Catholic view is that 'the body of bishops has no authority unless united with the Roman Pontiff'.[8] This is because Jesus 'put Peter at the head . . . a lasting and visible source and foundation of unity',[9] so that the fullness of the sacrament of Orders can only be conferred by bishops who are 'in hierarchical communion with the head and members of the college'.[10] Because of the importance of the unity of the church, what God wills is that all ministers of the sacrament should be under obedience to the Bishop of Rome.

The view is not, however, that only Roman Catholic priests are properly authorized priests. Roman Catholics accept the priesthood of those in the Orthodox Churches, who deny Petrine claims to primacy in the form in which they have developed in Rome. In the Orthodox Church, there is a concern to maintain succession of authorization from the apostles, but unity is assured through the fraternal association of the Patriarchates, and the collegiality of all the bishops. This is an episcopal view of church order rather than a papal one. Because the Roman Catholic Church accepts the validity of Orthodox priestly orders, there is room for further discussion on the importance of submission to papal authority. One could envisage and hope for a future in which the forms and limits of such submission would make it possible for Orthodox and Protestants alike to make it, but at present it does constitute a distinct difference of understanding on Christian ministry within the family of Christian churches.

Protestant churches in general have a third, different, view. They would maintain that validity is conferred, not so much by authorized appointment as by right faith. It is possible for priests who undoubtedly stand in the apostolic succession to develop views and practices which deviate considerably from that of their colleagues. Most of the great Christian heresies were, after all, propagated by validly ordained priests. So the problem arises of whether a validly consecrated bishop celebrates the sacraments as God wishes if he publicly interprets them in a way that seems to be at variance with Jesus' intentions, and with those of the church in general.

---

[8] 'Lumen Gentium', 375.   [9] Ibid. 373.   [10] Ibid.

The Catholic response would be to say that episcopal ordination is a necessary, but not a sufficient, condition for the validity of the sacraments. It is also necessary that the community in which the priestly ministry is exercised is the church that God wishes it to be. It is precisely on this issue that Protestants—agreeing with the Orthodox—maintain that the Roman Catholic Church is not the church that God wishes it to be, or at least is not the only such church. For God wishes the church to be conformed in its life and basic doctrines to the witness of the New Testament. Thoughtful Protestants will admit that no church is quite what God wishes it to be. But they will insist that a true sacramental community can be found wherever the life of Christ is truly given and received, in authentic remembrance of him, where the gospel of new life in Christ is preached, where the Spirit is known as a transforming power, and humility and love are shared in fellowship. It is such a community, seeking to conform its life to the New Testament witness to Christ, that can properly authorize someone to be a minister of the sacraments.

In the sacraments, on this view, God wills to give the grace that was present in Jesus, through the supper that Jesus commanded to be taken in remembrance of him, to those who gather in faith around the discernment of God they have through and in Jesus. Since Christ is himself the minister of the sacrament, the one through whom grace is truly given, it does not matter what human being speaks the consecrating words, as long as they can properly claim to be acting for and on behalf of the community.

Such a view is acknowledged by virtually all churches with regard to the sacrament of baptism. As long as water is poured or sprinkled and the intention is to do what Jesus commanded, in a community which intends to declare its faith in Jesus as Lord, the sacrament is taken to be valid, and to make the baptized a true member of Christ. 'By the sacrament of baptism . . . man becomes truly incorporated into the crucified and glorified Christ and is reborn to a sharing of the divine life'.[11] A Protestant would find it hard to see why the same should not be said of the eucharist. As long as good order is maintained, any Christian can validly celebrate the supper of the Lord. Nevertheless, many Protestants would agree that it is highly desirable to have some form of authorization of ministry which the

---

[11] 'Decree on Ecumenism', in *Vatican 2*, 469.

whole church could accept, and to that extent the episcopate, claiming historical continuity with the apostles, can claim to be a visible sign of the sort of unity that God desires the church to have.

THE REAL PRESENCE OF CHRIST

When the eucharist was instituted, Jesus is reported to have said that the bread was his body, and the wine was his blood of the 'new covenant'.[12] Tragically, the sacramental act that was meant to assure a unity of love among Christians has become a cause of major divisions in Christendom. Since the ninth century, there has been controversy about what exactly Jesus meant by his words.[13] At the Last Supper, Jesus was, of course, physically present. Attempts have been made to show how Jesus' body could be truly in the bread as well as being in organic flesh, as though Jesus somehow transferred his body, which was still in existence, into bread. This seems unduly counterintuitive, and the most straightforward interpretation of the situation is that the disciples knew themselves to be in the physical presence of Jesus. His body of flesh was that in which his personality acted and was expressed, it was the appropriate vehicle of the action and expression of his living consciousness. In calling bread the body of Christ, one can see an extension of the notion of 'a vehicle of the action and expression of a living consciousness'. Just as the death of Jesus on the cross was the finite image or icon of the eternal self-giving of God, so the broken bread becomes a finite icon of that same divine self-giving, by which sin is forgiven. One can understand how Jesus, perhaps now clearly foreseeing his death, and having decided to offer his life in order that God's kingdom might come, gives to the disciples a symbol of his sacrifice, which is at the same time a symbol of the divine self-giving.

In saying this, it is important not to think of a symbol as merely a reminder or representation. A symbol, in this sense, participates in and conveys the reality which it symbolizes. We cannot, of course, know what was consciously in the mind of Jesus as he instituted the rite of the breaking of bread. But the reported words imply that he intended the breaking of bread and the offering of wine to be

---

[12] Luke 22: 19–20.

[13] In the 11th century, Berengar of Tours was condemned for taking a 'symbolic' view of the eucharist, and the doctrine of transubstantiation was formally defined at the fourth Lateran Council in 1215.

repeated by the disciples 'in memory of him', and thereby to institute a new covenant community. The self-offering he was about to
make on the cross was presented in a way which could make that
offering and its meaning present at many times and in many places.
According to the gospels, he knew that he would die, and believed he
would ascend to the glory of the divine presence.[14]

That first breaking of bread can be seen as a prolepsis of the
passion. Jesus has determined to sacrifice his life, and presents this
determination as if it were an accomplished reality. After his physical death, the disciples are commanded to break bread in memory
of his voluntary self-offering, and it will then become an anamnesis
of the passion, a recollection of the united human and divine
manifestation of sacrifice in the death of Jesus.

In his death, Jesus offered himself wholly to do the will of the
Father, and his offering became, by divine will, an authentic manifestation in time of God's determination to share in human suffering
and embrace that suffering in order to bring human lives back into a
relationship of love with God. That is a moment of historical time at
which the eternal divine nature is truly shown, and at which in addition God acts in history (brings about physical events) to begin to
unite human lives to the divine in a new and distinctive way. That
divine action is effected first of all in the person of Jesus, for his death
is at the same time his transformation into glory. Dying to self—a
permanent feature of Jesus' life, but one brought to a climax and
consummation on the cross—he is transfigured into the divine glory,
a glory largely hidden during his life, but realized in the freeing of his
life from the confines of this physical space–time.

Because of that authentic appearing of the divine nature and purpose, and because of that effective divine action of uniting human
and divine in love, the cross becomes for this planet, and for those
who can discern it, the supreme revelation of God and the paradigm
of God's universal redeeming action. At the Last Supper, Jesus gives
the disciples a foreshadowing symbol of that revealing and redeeming act. The broken bread presents both the sacrifice of the faithful
servant and the divine passion. The wine originates a new covenant,
sealed by the sacrifice of Jesus, already completed in intention, by
which the life of the eternal Word begins to transform the lives of
men and women. Every subsequent celebration of that supper

[14] Matthew 16: 21.

makes present the same reality, whose significance is greatly enriched by knowledge of the resurrection and outpouring of the Spirit.

Such an interpretation of the eucharist takes a more relational and dynamic view of the sacrament than the sort of dehistoricized static substance view which became characteristic of much Latin theology. The Latin tradition focused on the question of substance, the substratum or bearer of qualities, which could possess some essential properties, making the substance the sort of substance it is, and some accidental properties, which substances of that sort may or may not have. The bearer of properties may get separated from the properties it bears, so that the properties of bread and wine are treated as accidental or non-essential, and they can be borne by a substance which is essentially the body and blood of Jesus—though those essential properties never become apparent.

If one accepts a philosophical scheme for which substances— things—are simply collections of instantiated properties, the Latin account fails to make sense. One cannot have a substance without properties, or with essential properties which never get manifested in fact, or with properties that normally belong to a different sort of substance. A collection of breadlike properties simply is a piece of bread. That may seem to put an end to any hope of resolving disputes about transubstantiation. But such disputes are in fact between different philosophical schemes, and other possibilities of interpretation exist, which may express what the doctrine of transubstantiation was intended to preserve, though approached in a different way.

One need not think of a substance as an isolated, self-existent reality. The temptation to do so originates from one classical definition of 'substance' as an independent and enduring existent, not dependent on anything else for its existence, and remaining unchanged through all changes of its properties. A more relational view would see substances as points of confluence of many transient property-instantiations, in constant flow and causal interrelationship. There is no substance which remains unchanged in nature through that flow. But there are, at each point of confluence, a set of dispositional properties, which realize their natures over time, and of relational properties, which are actualized only in relation to other substances, and of occurrent properties, in a continuing process of change. Since the temporal flow is constant, each set of properties is causally produced by the preceding set, or by a confluence of preceding sets. And each generates new sets of properties, in conjunction with many other points of confluence. This picture of reality is dynamic, since it is one of a process in constant causal change, and it is relational, since changes are the product of many sorts of relations to other points of confluence. Moreover, it is emergent, since many of the more complex sorts of causal relations that exist are generated by an organized complexity of events at a simpler level.

When personal consciousness exists, it modifies the sorts of relationships that exist between substances. A piece of bread, when perceived by a human consciousness, is not just a chemical compound. It takes on a complex set of symbolic associations. It is something to be eaten, with a certain taste and texture, perhaps to be shared, a product of sowing, growing, reaping, and baking, and so of a joining of natural forces with human cultivation. The chemical compound takes on the properties of its causal origin, its intended use, its relation to human senses, and its social context.

An objector may say that these are extrinsic properties. They do not belong to the bread as such, but are imputed as merely subjective associations. I think this would be a false and reductive view. Even in the middle of a desert, lost and unperceived, a piece of bread would still possess the property of 'having being prepared in order to be eaten'. This would be an essential part of what Plato would have called its Form or defining nature. We might then properly say that the essence of the bread is something like this: 'something prepared by baking wheat for the purpose of sustaining the life of human beings'. The essence is not simply a list of chemicals, but includes reference to its mode of coming into being, its intended purpose, and its social context.

One might then say that, if bread is used in a ritual context, its essence (its substance in the sense of that which defines what it essentially is) is significantly changed. The mode of preparation remains the same, and yet part of that preparation becomes its setting apart by an act of blessing. By that act, it is consecrated to God, set apart from common use. It is no longer ordinary bread, and its intended purpose becomes quite different. It is no longer for physical nourishment. It is for making present God's revelatory and redemptive act on the cross of Jesus. It does so by being part of a ritual which proclaims the good news of redemption, explicitly commemorates the sacrifice of Jesus, and prepares the minds of participants for receiving the grace of God. The social context is not just that of eating together. It is that of worship, attention to God through the symbolic form of Christ crucified and risen, and unity with God through receiving the divine life of Christ, whose finite form and expression is epitomized by the cross. So the essence of this bread is something like: 'food set apart for the purpose of making present the revelatory and redemptive act of God, epitomized by the cross of Jesus, in a context of communal worship and devotion'.

It is possible to call this transubstantiation, if one means that the essential nature of the bread has been changed, even though all its physical properties remain the same. All one needs for that interpretation is the realization that the essential nature of a thing can depend upon the human consciousnesses that create it and give it a particular purpose and significance. It is important to realize that this does not make the whole process subjective, as though it were just a matter of what anyone cares to make of it. There is an objective significance to the rite. That significance is given by God, and can be misunderstood by humans. The divine life is truly expressed and conveyed by the rite, just as it was truly expressed and conveyed by the death and resurrection of Jesus. It is the presence and the life-giving power of the eternal Word which is truly given in the breaking of bread, and it is given under the form of the death and resurrection of Jesus, who was the true image of the Word in human history.

THE SUPPER OF THE LORD

Of course the body of Christ that is present on the altar is not the same body that walked in Galilee, or numerically identical with the one that now exists in the presence of divine glory. An early Anglican prayer-book said brutally, 'The body of Jesus is in heaven, and not here.' The human person of Jesus had a particular organic form of flesh and blood. It was composed of atoms in particular complex arrangements, which were in continual flow. No one, I think, holds that those atoms, whether some or all of them, now collect wherever the eucharist is celebrated. They certainly do not organize themselves on the altar into the complex form of a human body, in some sort of hidden way.

At his death, or soon after, the physical body of Jesus ceased to exist, as all physical bodies do sooner or later. The person of Jesus continued in a new form of glorified embodiment, which one must assume is proper to human life, but which cannot be envisaged by us. It was, according to the gospels, capable of appearing in physical form to the disciples, and to Paul in a body of blinding light. But it was not itself physical, in the sense of being subject to the laws of this space–time, laws of change, continuous local presence, and inevitable decay.

If the glorified body of Jesus is capable of appearing in this physical cosmos, in various forms, it could appear on an earthly altar. But there are two main difficulties with such a view. First, nothing unusual which looks at all like a body appears on altars, and second, the body would have to appear on thousands of altars, all over the world, at the same time. Moreover, the eternal Christ is presumably present at every point of space and time, as God is, in any case. So how could he be specially present on a particular altar?

There is no difficulty in saying that the eternal Christ appears in a special way in the person of Jesus. There must be a universal presence of Christ, since the eternal Word, which is Christ, shares in the omnipresence of the divine being. But it is almost always hidden and not discerned in its true nature. In Jesus, Christians believe, it became manifest, so that people could discern in the life of Jesus the nature and action of the eternal Christ. Christ's action was not limited to Jesus, but it was authentically manifested, as it really is, in Jesus. Moreover, in the life and words of Jesus the eternal Word acted in a particular way, made possible by its unique historical context, which is not repeated in that exact form anywhere else.

In the eucharist, it is the self-offered life of Jesus that is commemorated. Jesus was the authentic manifestation of the Christ, and the same Christ can be manifested in the breaking of bread, which can thus be seen as a different form of the same 'body', or vehicle of physical manifestation. Even though the particular acts of the Word in Jesus are not exactly repeatable (there will never again be a young man teaching in a remote province of the Roman Empire) there is a sense in which the liberating action of the Word in Jesus can be repeated in different contexts. What is present on the altar is the eternal Christ in the particular form he took in Jesus, acting to convey divine love and power as he did in Jesus. If one thinks of a body as the means by which a personal agent is present and causally active in the world, one can say that the body of Christ is truly present on the altar of the anamnesis, the making present through recollection and prayer of the life of Jesus. The breaking of bread in remembrance of Christ is the making present of the Word as he took form and acted in the life of Jesus.

There is, of course, no physical shape of a body. In scholastic terminology, the accidents of bread and wine remain the same. Yet there is, in the consecrated bread and wine, a distinctive local presence of the omnipresent Word, distinctive because it has the nature and power of liberating action which it took in the life of Jesus, and which is still truly expressed, in one form, in a historically completed way, in the risen body of the glorified Jesus. That presence can appear in a different form, though one essentially related to the manifestation of the historical Jesus, and to the continuing existence of the glorified Jesus, on many altars simultaneously, and it does not need to have the physical shape or organization of a human body.

Just as the Word took particular form and manifestation in Jesus' physical body, so the Word can manifest in the rite Jesus instituted, so that the Word would be present under the description of his person, in some causal connection with his earthly life, and as a sensorily hidden appearing of his glorified life. Perhaps we need only think of the historical person of Jesus as believing that, after his death and resurrection, God would make it possible for him to continue to be present among his disciples, to pray for and with them, and to renew the covenant of love with them. To this end, he could well have taken the elements of the Passover meal, and used them to provide an effectual sign of the liberation from sin that his sacrifice and resurrection would bring.

It does not seem plausible to say, as Luther at one time did, that the glorified body of Jesus is as such omnipresent, since that is not a property even a glorified human person can have. Yet the glorified body of Jesus does in a sense appear in many places at once, because the power of the Spirit causes it to appear, without taking from it its local presence in the divine realm. The 'appearances', however, are not discernible by the senses, which detect only bread and wine. They are discernible only by the mind, which recognizes the life and power of the risen Jesus, which he has because of the indivisible action of the Word in and through him, made present, by divine power, at a point in historical time.

It is not that there is a human person hidden in the bread and wine, or, as some have said, 'imprisoned in the Tabernacle'. It is rather that in the communal context of the remembering of Jesus' passion and resurrection, he himself will be truly present under the forms of bread and wine, to mediate to his disciples the liberating power of his love. Because of that stress on the communal context of the rite, and on the purpose of the rite as the mediation of divine love, in a particular form, many Christians find it misleading to regard the reserved sacrament, divorced from its communal, ritual, and participatory context, as itself a proper object of devotion.

From the earliest times, the church has taken the sacrament to those who are ill or unable to attend the meeting, and to that end the sacrament must be safely reserved. But there is a danger of changing the dynamic and personal action of Jesus Christ, intended to transform the lives of the worshipping community, into a rather more mechanical act of gaining merit by visiting and gazing upon a holy object. Protestants especially are very suspicious of cults of devotion to what appears to be an inert object which is carried about with some pomp and ceremony, but which does not seem to involve communal participation or personal and transforming encounter with a risen and living Lord.[15]

It is indisputable that Jesus' recorded command was concerned with action and with eating and drinking. It therefore seems right that nothing more than that should be made a matter of obligation in the church. Nevertheless, reverence to the consecrated elements is an intelligible way of showing devotion to Christ that is deeply meaningful to many people. As long as such a practice remains subordinate to the public celebration of the eucharist, and an extension of eucharistic praise when it is not practicable to celebrate the eucharist, it seems a proper form of devotion for those who find it helpful. This is certainly a development from the earliest forms of Christian celebration, but one might expect developments in devotional practices as the church is embodied in new social contexts. The vital principle is that the eucharist should preserve its connection with the dynamic and liberating act of God in redeeming humans from the isolation of ambition, hatred, and greed, and forming them into a fellowship of love.

The liturgical reforms which followed the second Vatican Council fully incorporate all these principles,[16] and to that extent many of the old historical disputes between Catholics and Protestants have

---

[15] So the 25th article of the 39 Articles of the Church of England says: 'The Sacraments were not ordained of Christ to be gazed upon or to be carried about, but that we should duly use them.'

[16] Cf. the document 'Eucharistiae Sacramentum', in *Vatican 2*, 244–5.

disappeared. Even though Catholic church law at this time forbids joint communion between Catholics and Protestants, there has grown an increased recognition in this century of deep and important agreement on the fundamental nature of the Eucharistic sacrament. Few would now maintain, on the Catholic side, that only Roman Catholic priests can offer the holy sacrifice in which Christ is really and truly present, or on the Protestant side, that the Lord's Supper does no more than evoke a memory of Jesus' death on the cross. This is one area in which real ecumenical progress has been made, by a mutual creative rethinking of Christian traditions.

The forms of eucharistic practice have varied greatly at different times and in different places, and such diversity seems both natural and inevitable, given the variety of human cultures and temperaments. The earliest account of a eucharistic celebration we have is in 1 Corinthians 11: 20–34. It seems that this was a full-scale communal meal, during which bread was blessed and broken at the beginning of the meal, and wine was blessed and drunk at its end. In this community the power of Jesus' sacrifice was made present, and the new covenant of the heart was renewed in his blood, at a shared table in which all participated.

There could hardly be a greater contrast than between this meal—at which, apparently, some got drunk and others brought their own food and ate too much—and the medieval celebration of the Mass in a private chapel with only a priest, dressed as a Roman aristocrat, and a server present, using a dead and very hieratic, formal language to pray for some dead soul, for a fee. I do not say this to decry the Mass—I do not suppose getting drunk and the conspicuous consumption of food is more to be applauded than making a living by offering private Masses for the dead. Something, I think it is plain, has gone wrong in both cases. In the former case, there is the danger of 'failing to discern the body', of participating in a common meal without due attention to the presence and power of Christ. In the latter case, there is the danger of turning a rite of communal empowerment into a quasi-magical ritual for obtaining spiritual benefits without any participation at all.

It is significant that the main Christian sacrament originally took place in the context of a meal. It was essentially a community action, not a private ritual conducted by a priest for a suppliant. In this respect it continues the Jewish idea of fellowship-offering, when the community was to be renewed in fellowship by its common devotion to God, and by common obedience to the divine command to promote a community of justice and peace.[17] But the eucharist is primarily a rite in which God unites the community to the divine being, 'living in them', and calling them to 'live in Christ'. In this respect it echoes a vision of the whole cosmos being part of the self-expressive being of God, and of devotees realizing their unity with the divine.

THE COSMOS AS THE SACRAMENT OF SPIRIT

The Christian faith distinguishes itself from the other Abrahamic faiths by replacing the idea of divine law with the idea of living by the power of the divine Spirit. It distinguishes itself from many faiths of the Indian tradition by refusing to renounce the world entirely, and insisting on the goodness of created things. The sacramental principle which lies at the heart of Christianity affirms the goodness of creation, and seeks to unite it to the divine by enabling it to become a vehicle of divine liberating and self-expressive action. The eucharist, in which the bread and wine which cements ordinary social life is transfigured to become the vehicle of the self-giving, unitive, and fulfilling action of God in history, both affirms and sanctifies creation. It thus expresses a distinctive way of spiritual understanding and action, in which humans aim at the fulfilment of all creation by their conscious participation in the active power of the divine love.

When the dominant philosophical system of Western Europe regarded the timeless as superior to the temporal, and regarded God as essentially timeless and immutable, this participation in the divine had to be seen, ultimately, as a participation in the timeless. Time becomes, in Platonic fashion, at best an imperfect image of the timeless, which can add nothing to the timeless, and stands poised insecurely between being and nothingness.[18] For a philosophical scheme in which the temporal has intrinsic importance as the field for the realization of infinite possibility, participation in the divine can be seen more as participation in the dynamic flow of the divine self-realization. Events in time add something to God, since they realize events which hitherto existed only as possibilities in the divine being. The flow of time even in one sense adds to, or is at least an important

---

[17] Leviticus 7: 11–21.
[18] Cf. Plato, *Timaeus*, 7, trans. Desmond Lee (Harmondsworth: Penguin, 1965), 50–1.

part of, the expression of the perfection of the divine, since it realizes creative power, which is itself an intrinsic good.

Using the conceptuality of traditional Platonism, the eucharist was construed as the appearing of the timeless in time, and as essentially changeless. In a more temporalist conceptuality, it can be seen as part of the creative realization of divine action, unfolding one set of possibilities which arise from the past, and being directed towards an as yet uncompleted consummation in future. The future kingdom, existing as ideal possibility in the divine mind, meets the present as the touch of the divine reality and will. The kingdom touches the earth ambiguously, entering into history and yet never fully embodied in it. The ideal form of the future shapes the present in a community which must never simply be identified with the kingdom, but which is called to be its imperfect prefiguring, its ambiguous presence, the proclaimer and mediator of its struggling reality. Setting this vision in its widest cosmic perspective, one might say that the church partly embodies the life of the archetypal cosmic Christ, repeats the life of the exemplary historical Christ, and struggles towards the full expression of the life of the pleromal trans-historical Christ. In this conceptuality, the Ideal Form is not one changeless impersonal ideal, but a living responsive personal reality, into which the community grows, in dialectical, creative, and responsive action.

The sacramental principle is that the material cosmos is transfigured by the creative Spirit of God to become a vehicle and instrument of the exemplary Word of God. This is a distinctive approach to spirituality. It is not simply obedience to divine law, though the Christian will aim to obey the will of God in all things. The notion of a written or fixed divine law has been abandoned, however, in favour of participation in the dynamic life of the Spirit.[19] It is not simply renunciation of the world, though the Christian will aim to renounce ambition and greed. The world cannot be wholly renounced, since human life has its natural and proper context as part of the physical cosmos, not as some sort of 'pure spirit' unfortunately trapped in matter. It is not simply devotion to the supreme Lord, though the Christian will aim to worship and adore the God who is truly seen in the person of Jesus. But the Christian will also aim to be part of the

---

[19] 'We serve not under the old written code but in the new life of the Spirit': Romans 7: 6.

body of the Lord, and thereby participate in the creative, self-expressive, and unitive nature of God, being part of God's creative action and compassionate suffering in time. The Christian hope is that the whole material cosmos itself might become, by the co-operation of God and human souls, the 'body' of Christ, the authentic expression of Spirit's action.

In this co-operative work Christians are bound together in the 'communion of saints', the community of all who become channels of the divine love. This is a community both of action and of prayer, as people support, comfort, and encourage one another by their deeds and prayers. It is natural to think that, since the church opens the door to eternal life in God, its community extends beyond the barrier of death. If any person can be helped by the prayers of another—and, if not, intercession seems pointless—then it is natural to think that those in Sheol can be helped by the prayers of the living, and that the living might be helped by the prayers of those in Paradise. Such matters are not clearly part of the earliest recorded traditions, and it is very difficult to be certain of such things at the best of times. Yet if all believers are members of the body of Christ, it is very natural to think, and certainly to hope, that this unity extends beyond death, so that we may properly pray for the dead, and ask for the prayers of the saints. Many Christians may feel a sense of impropriety at seeming to probe into the mysteries of death, so that it may be right to aim at a certain reserve and generality in such prayers. Protestants certainly believe in the communion of saints, in that those who live with God for ever will live in community, and in recognition of and interaction with one another. Those who are more Catholic-minded will add that even at the present time, the dead are in communion with the living within the church, and prayer for one another, living and dead, is part of this communion in Christ. It is true that the saints cannot physically hear any requests made to them by people on earth. But God can make such requests known to them, and make it the case that the compassionate intercessions of the saints will apply in a special way to those who desire the saints to intercede for them.

Sometimes the church has given the impression that it is only concerned for the welfare of dead Christians (not for all the dead), and that heaven is populated only by Christian saints. Much iconography reinforces this impression, by placing Jesus and Mary close to God (often depicted in recognizable human form), and surrounding them with apostles and martyrs. Rarely are animals or alien life-forms depicted—which is not surprising, since we do not know if there are any alien life-forms, or what they might look like. Nevertheless, this has contributed to a certain cosmic myopia which has been characteristic of Christian tradition.

It is part of Christian faith that God wills all created persons to be saved, and that presumably goes for any non-human personal life-forms that may exist in this or any other cosmos. Those who turn from God to self will suffer the destructive fires of frustrated passion and hatred. Those who accept the love of God, in whatever form it comes to them, will be transformed by the divine Spirit to become full members of the community of all who are conscious sharers in the creativity and compassionate love of God. That community will possibly be much wider than a community of human persons—indeed, the idea of angels already expresses in the tradition an intimation of such a wider community, so it is not altogether a novel idea. Yet the Christian claim is that the true form of the love of God, the earthly template of the universal activity of the Spirit, is given in the person of Jesus, who founded the church on earth as a sacramental image of the coming kingdom of God.

It is reasonable to think that the human responsibility to pray for others does not extend infinitely far. Just as we can only directly affect the lives of those fairly near to us in space and time, so our prayers will be directed to those with whom we have some form of fairly close spatio-temporal relationship. It may seem right, then, to pray primarily for the dead who are known to us, or who are members of our community, in society or church. I think it would be wrong, however, only to pray for those who have been explicitly Christian. Charity requires that we pray for all we have known, that they may seek God and accept divine grace, and progress towards the goal of the realized kingdom of God's rule.

Similarly, we might hope that those in Paradise who have some spatio-temporal connection with us might pray for us—and they may include many who have not been Christians, but who have nevertheless been open to divine grace, and have thereby become fitted to be channels of grace to others. Nevertheless from earliest times, those who died for their Christian faith or who have lived lives of heroic Christian virtue have been regarded as intercessors for others, for whose prayers we could ask God. Mary, mother of Jesus, has come to have a very special place in Christian devotion, as the one who bore the Son of God, who nourished him, who witnessed his death and resurrection, and who was among the company of his disciples. She, 'blessed among women', and 'filled with grace',[20] has come to be regarded as the paradigm of the redeemed soul, and thus in a sense a symbol of the church as the redeemed community.

The tradition that Mary was assumed into Heaven and crowned Queen of Heaven expresses the belief that she has entered into the destiny that is prepared for every faithful soul, and is, with all the saints, an efficacious channel of divine grace. Christians need to be careful, however, not to regard Jesus as a severe figure with whom Mary needs to intercede on behalf of others. It is Jesus who is the teacher of the way of the Spirit and the founder of the church, which is his body. He is the central focus of devotion, the image of the invisible God. Mary remains a hidden figure, historically, and is revered as mother, lover, and follower of Jesus, as a type of the unknown disciple who has been made a sharer by grace in the glory of God. She is, like millions of others, a member of the body of Christ, the community originated by and patterned on the life of Jesus and empowered by his Spirit. Her prayers, like theirs, are offered through Christ for the good of all creation, and Christians may justifiably ask God that we may share in that good. She is an object of special reverence, but only by virtue of her close relationship to the incarnate Christ, and always in total dependence upon him. As such, she has a special place in the communion of saints, the human community of the redeemed, which is itself, we may think, part of a wider community, wide beyond our imagining, of creatures who share in the possibly boundless finite expressions of the infinite being of God.

The sacramental community of the church may be only a small part of the created cosmos to which God is related in love, but it is the place on earth where God reveals the heart of the divine nature, and acts self-givingly and unitively for the sake of the world. Mary and the saints stand as symbols of those in whom the divine action is manifested, and they are all united by and manifest the grace of God which is historically patterned on the life of Jesus, and sacramentally given in the church. It is the Christian hope that at some time, or perhaps beyond historical time, the communion of saints and the whole creation will be mutually enfolding, so that 'everything in

---

[20] Luke 1: 28, 42.

Heaven and on earth' will be united in Christ.[21] Until that time, the church is, on this planet, the community that has the vocation of bringing the part of creation in which it exists to its proper fulfilment within the love of God. That is its vocation as a sacramental community, a community to make the material the true image and creative expression of its spiritual source and goal.

---

[21] Ephesians 1: 10.

9
The Church as a Moral Community

The Christian church accepts, with the other Abrahamic faiths, that God has a moral purpose for the created universe, and that human beings have the responsibility of forming a society which will enable that purpose to be realised. The Christian way is not one of individual release from bondage to the material world. It is a way of communal action to bring into actuality many of the potential sorts of value that the material world contains. There is a positive goal for creation, and that goal lies in the co-operative bringing about and enjoyment of many sorts of good things. The duty of a Christian is to co-operate with others and with the Creator in the actualization of goodness. It is to bring into being a community of justice, peace, kindness, and happiness.

Since human beings have largely created a society of injustice, war, cruelty, and misery, there is also a duty to oppose the forces that make for injustice and oppression, both in oneself and in others. Christian faith is not a way simply of inner union with God, which leaves conditions in the social world to go on in any old way. Admittedly some early Christians thought of the political world, the 'world of the nations', as doomed to judgement, and looked for a supernatural salvation from that judgement by the coming of Christ in glory. Even then, their hope was for a new society, a social world in which justice would flourish, even if that could only come about by supernatural intervention.[1] Their concern was with justice and with the ending of injustice, even if they could see little hope of being able to do anything about it, in remote provinces of a militaristic Roman Empire.

When Christians began, after a century or so, to take positions of political power, when the Empire itself became officially Christian, it began to seem possible to transform the political realm into a more

---

[1] 'The trumpet will sound, and the dead will be raised imperishable, and we shall be changed', 1 Corinthians 15: 52.

just society, or at least to eliminate the grossest injustices, such as infanticide and public torture, in the name of Christian compassion. While Christians may be wise to remain sceptical about the possibility of wholly eliminating evil from human society, it soon became fairly clear to them that they have a duty to eliminate evil so far as possible, and that it is a divine requirement to do so.

The Christian church is, however, different from both Judaism and Islam in one important respect. They seek to bring society, whether nationally or globally, under the revealed law of God, which sets out commands and directives with divine authority, and requires submission or obedience to them. The church began as a Jewish community which kept Torah, but within a comparatively short time it renounced obedience to Torah, and with it, obedience to a revealed moral law.

The church has not denied that Torah was in some sense revealed by God to the people of Israel. But in becoming a Gentile community it regarded itself as free from that law, one of whose purposes was precisely to set apart the Jews as a peculiar people, a purpose that did not apply to Gentiles. The Torah contains many laws of a community to which Christians do not belong. Yet Christians regard themselves as a community of a new covenant, which stands in a close historical relation to the first covenant with the descendants of Israel. The new community finds Torah embodied in a new way, not in a written code, but in the person and life of Jesus. 'If you are led by the Spirit you are not under the law',[2] Paul wrote, and the Spirit is the inner activity of God in the human self, which is patterned on the person of Jesus. 'Christ is the end of the law',[3] in the sense that he brings Torah to an end, at least for the new covenant community, and also in the sense that he is the completion or fulfilment of the law. Indeed, Christ is himself living Torah, the wisdom of God incarnate. Whereas Jews have the written commands and ordinances of Torah as the source of their life—and they continue to have that, by the will of God—the disciples of Jesus have the gospel records of the life of Jesus, and the sacraments of the continuing presence of Jesus, as the source of their life in the Spirit.

The immediate danger is that Christians will take the records of the life of Jesus as a new source of law, so that his recorded words become a new Torah for the church. Christians have often been very

---

[2] Galatians 5: 18.   [3] Romans 10: 4.

selective, however, in the parts of Jesus' teaching which they regard as morally binding. Specially favoured has been the prohibition on divorce ('whoever marries a divorced woman commits adultery'[4]). Usually overlooked has been the teaching in the same section of the gospel that 'if anyone would sue you and take your coat, let him have your cloak as well'.[5] Jesus' teaching that one should not swear on oath,[6] and that one should not call any man 'father'[7] have usually been directly contradicted by Christian practice. And such statements as, 'If your right eye offends you pull it out'[8] have simply been regarded as pieces of hyperbole which do no more than stress the seriousness of sin.

The principle of consistency would suggest an interpretation of this range of sayings which did not pick and choose between them in that way. It is characteristic of Jesus' teaching that he exaggerates his aphorisms to the point of impossibility. It is harder for a rich man to enter the kingdom than for a camel to pass through a needle's eye;[9] wherever two or three are gathered together God will grant their requests;[10] whoever speaks against the Holy Spirit will not be forgiven[11]—taken literally, these and many other aphorisms imply a fanatical faith where forgiveness is often impossible, poverty is a necessary condition of salvation, and every prayerful request of the faithful is granted. This literal interpretation seems to be both false and morally unacceptable. There is another consistent way of interpreting them, which is well known in Jewish tradition. It is to take them as highly exaggerated, but for that very reason very memorable ways of stressing the gravity of sin and the intimacy of the disciples' relation to God.

On such an interpretation, 'call no man father' should not be taken literally. It points to the danger of authoritarianism and pride in religion, which are wrong whatever one calls people. 'Never swear on oath' is not a literally applicable rule, but points to the ideal of being so completely truthful and trustworthy that oaths will not be required. 'Give your cloak to anyone who sues you' would be very stupid advice, taken literally. It points to the ideal attitude of benevolence and generosity, which should govern one's relationships even with opponents. If taken literally, 'marrying a divorced

---

[4] Matthew 5: 32.   [5] Ibid. 5: 40.   [6] Ibid. 5: 34.
[7] Ibid. 23: 9.   [8] Ibid. 5: 29.   [9] Ibid. 19: 24.
[10] Ibid. 18: 19, 20.   [11] Ibid. 12: 31.

woman is adultery' would, in the context of Jesus' day, be extremely harmful to a woman who had been perhaps unjustly divorced by a man, and who would have no other means of support than remarriage. If this statement is interpreted in a similar way to the other aphorisms in this section of Matthew's Gospel, it points to an ideal of preserving the marriage bond, and not seeking to destroy someone else's marriage out of desire for their partners. In Jesus' context, where divorce was a simple matter for a man (but impossible for a woman to initiate), such a stress on an ideal of marriage could well have been found almost too hard to bear by the apostles. It is very unlikely that it could have been taken as a rule which annulled the provisions of Torah for divorce and remarriage. Indeed, Matthew is at pains to stress that Jesus taught that for the Jews to whom he was speaking Torah remained intact in every detail.[12] It seems, then, that Jesus was commending the ideal of lifelong marriage, as an expression of loyalty and fidelity, but not doing something as draconian and humanly harmful as completely forbidding remarriage after divorce.

Some of the teachings of Jesus have been interpreted as absolute moral rules, when they were probably meant to be startling aphorisms. The same process of moral absolutization has taken place with some of the advice Paul gave to the churches to which he was writing. Yet that advice is sometimes limited by Paul's own moral myopia. Paul notably refrains from advising slave-owners to free their slaves, thus implicitly accepting the basically unjust practice of slavery. He utters very unguarded comments about state authorities being agents of God[13] (which subsequent Christian experience of Roman Emperors such as Diocletian would drastically modify). And his comments about the place of women have justly evoked derision from anyone even remotely touched by concerns for the equal treatment of and regard for women and men.

Paul quite clearly advises that women 'should be subordinate, even as the law says'.[14] He apparently extends this to cover not only worship in church, where women should not speak, but social life in general, where it is not right for men to be subordinate to women: 'The head of a woman is her husband'.[15] Such statements should, no doubt, be read in the light of such sayings of Jesus as, 'Whoever

---

[12] Matthew 5: 18.   [13] Romans 13: 1, 2.
[14] 1 Corinthians 14: 34.   [15] Ibid. 11: 3.

would be first among you must be slave of all' (Mark 10: 44), and 'I am among you as one who serves' (Luke 22: 27). If men are to be leaders by being servants and slaves of women, there is little to complain about, and I think it would be fair to interpret Paul in this sense. Nevertheless, there is no doubt that his statements about male headship have not very often been taken in this sense. They have been read as giving men in general authority over women, and as such have been generally harmful to women. It would be better, therefore, to put more emphasis on another widely quoted Pauline sentence, which seems unequivocally clear: 'There is neither Jew nor Greek, there is neither slave nor free, there is neither male nor female; for you are all one in Christ Jesus.'[16] If all divisions of status or consideration, arising from race, social class, or sex, have been set aside in Christ, customs about the subordination of women cannot stand.

The Christian tradition as a whole has come to see that both slavery and the subordination of women are in conflict with the principle that all persons are of equal value and dignity in the sight of God. What one has to note is that this entails regarding many of the written opinions about specific moral rules in the New Testament as well as in the Old as failing to rise to the insights that the gospel of human freedom and dignity in Christ demand. The written code has always to be judged in the light of the gospel of freedom in Christ, for 'Christ is the end of the law'—not the end of moral rules, but the end of adherence to moral rules when they cannot be seen to uphold the freedom and dignity of every person in a fair and loving society.

So the Christian attitude to revealed moral law questions the whole idea of specific commands which are to be obeyed just because they are revealed. In the Torah, the reason why eating animals without hooves is forbidden is not really an early form of public health legislation, as some commentators have suggested. Anthropologists might suggest that it probably depends on some early tribal taboo about classifying kinds of living things and the proper relationships between them.[17] One is forbidden to eat animals or birds which seem to cross the boundaries between proper kinds of organism. But this taboo has come to be incorporated into the food laws of Judaism as a sign of Jewish difference, and a

---

[16] Galatians 3: 28.
[17] Cf. Mary Douglas, *Purity and Danger* (London: Routledge, 1966), 53.

reminder of the way in which God is involved in every area of life. Christians generally regard such food rules as having no moral force at all, but orthodox Jews take them to be strictly obligatory, simply because they are part of Torah (because God commanded them).

It is hard to see how such food laws are fulfilled in Christ, except in the sense that they are signs of obedience to God. In that case they are fulfilled, as is circumcision, by the inward attitude of total devotion to God, as God is revealed in Jesus Christ. This shows that it would be vain to seek to find a particular fulfilment for every command of Torah. Many such commands are simply contingent signs of obedience, which might very well have been different, and can be disregarded by Christians in their precise formulation.

Should the whole of Torah then be disregarded in its precise regulations, in favour of a more general obedience to God? That seems to me the only consistent view to take, though some Christians have tried to distinguish between ritual laws, which can be ignored, and moral laws, which remain in force.[18] Such a distinction is quite foreign to orthodox Judaism, which regards all the laws as obligatory, and disallows making lists of laws under different categories or levels of importance. Nor is it clear that all the laws that might be called 'moral' would be acceptable to Christians in any case.

Laws about capital punishment, the right of families to pursue blood-vengeance, polygamy, slavery, and levirate marriage are surely moral rather than ritual laws. But few Christians would take them to be obligatory, as they stand. In orthodox Judaism, there is a long and continuing rabbinic tradition which can reinterpret such laws and modify them for different situations. There is no such continuing legal tradition in Christianity, and it cannot be claimed that Christians spend a lot of time and effort—as Jews do—in puzzling over the intricacies of Torah, to see how it should be interpreted in modern conditions. It is more typical of Christians to regard many particular ordinances of Torah as simply superseded by Christ, and so as having no further relevance for the modern world.

One needs, I think, to be quite clear that one should aim at consistency in one's attitude to Torah. If one believes that large parts of

[18] So John Calvin, *Institutes of the Christian Religion*, trans. H. Beveridge (Grand Rapids: Eerdmans, 1989), bk. 2, chs. 7–8, where he divides 'the Law' into Moral, Ceremonial, and Judicial.

it have been superseded by Christ, one cannot then appeal to other parts of it as morally binding in themselves, without reference to the life and teaching of Jesus. One will need to ask of each part of it how it must be modified, and perhaps rejected for the Christian community, in the light of our understanding of the moral message of Jesus' life.

The difficulty of this procedure should not be ignored. Jesus gave very few specific moral teachings, and they are often phrased in the exaggerated or obscure way which is typical of his recorded words. Of course it is not hopeless: some things are unambiguously clear. Jesus absolutely opposes hypocrisy, pride, hatred, and contempt, and lack of concern for others. It is the formulation of precise moral rules which is largely lacking, and perhaps the deepest reason for this is that Christianity does not, as such, have any special competence in formulating moral rules for everyone. There is no longer a set of God-given laws which must be simply obeyed. There is just the exemplary life of Jesus, and the stunning demand of the divine love. The details have to be worked out by discussion and argument, and by asking what most makes for human flourishing, in the light of Jesus' disclosure of what human flourishing is, in relation to God.

NATURAL LAW

It is therefore not surprising that Christian moral reflection, at least in the Catholic tradition, has not in practice been founded on that sort of close study of Torah or of scriptural texts that is characteristic of orthodox Judaism. It has been founded on the general requirement of maximizing human flourishing, in the light of a general doctrine of creation, and the revelation in Jesus of what human nature truly is. So the church has developed in its moral thinking the tradition of 'Natural Law', which originated with Aristotle and continued with the philosophers of Stoicism.

In its Christian version, there is a natural moral law in three senses—it is natural and not revealed, it is a law that can be discovered by reflection on the structures of nature, and it is a moral law that should apply to all human beings, as opposed to the positive law of particular human societies.

Although it is not given by specific revelation, the existence of a natural law is dependent upon God in that it is the will of a Creator God that makes the structures of the natural order such that they give rise to a knowledge of basic human obligations. God has created the universe, and has done so for a purpose. The structures of the universe are bound to give some clue about what that purpose is. It is a natural human obligation to help to realize the divine purposes in creation, and thus to fulfil the natural structures of the created order.

One classical statement of such a view is given by Thomas Aquinas, who suggests beginning the process of moral reflection by analysing the natural inclinations of human beings. He asserts that there is first, a tendency of each substance 'to preserve its own natural being'.[19] It is thus a natural human inclination to ensure that the elementary requirements of human life are obtainable—food, clothing, shelter, and medical aid, if it exists.

Secondly, Thomas holds that there are things which 'nature teaches all animals', things to do with the procreation and rearing of young, for example. It is a natural inclination to seek a mate, to care for children, and have some form of social organization which will enable groups to live in security.

Thirdly, some things are specific to humans as rational beings. He suggests that it is a natural inclination to know truths, and to cultivate creative or artistic pursuits.

Thomas' underlying thought is that, since God has created human nature, those inclinations which are natural to it must be those which bring the proper potentialities of nature into actualization. Humans can trust their natural inclinations precisely because they are created by God, and lead to the proper realization of human good.

It is worth noting how very general Thomas's inferences from natural inclinations are. They do not suggest specific institutions for sexual relationship, but only that there should be stable forms of such relationship, which will be conducive to the rearing of children and a sense of personal security. Many more specific arguments would be needed to come to very specific moral conclusions—about the legitimacy of divorce, for example—and it is possible that these conclusions might differ from one time or culture to another, if the relevant circumstances are very different.

Appeal is sometimes made to natural law as a set of principles on which all humans can and should agree, whatever their world-views.

[19] Aquinas, *Summa Theologiae* I-II q. 94 a. 2, trans. Thomas Gilby (London: Blackfriars, 1966), 80.

But it is apparent that the view Thomas takes depends upon a purposive view of nature, and in fact upon an acceptance that there is a Creator God who has a good purpose which humans have the obligation to help to realize. In a theological perspective, the ultimate purpose of creation is that creatures should glorify God, so there is a hierarchy of inclinations, subordinating those of lower levels to those of higher levels, and relating all of them to the love and worship of God.

A very different view might be taken by an atheistic evolutionary biologist (I will call such a biologist a 'naturalist', but of course that does not imply acceptance of Thomist natural law theory), who regards natural inclinations as survival mechanisms or relics of earlier survival mechanisms which may easily become dysfunctional, or which may conflict with one another in fundamental ways.[20] So the tendency to self-preservation may naturally give rise to aggression against competitors, and one may well find that our most natural inclination is the survival of the strong—not quite what Thomas has in mind. Similarly the sexual instinct may promote promiscuous and lustful behaviour in males, and so-called 'rationality' may be seen as a natural inclination to invent more efficient ways of sustaining the dominance of one's preferred social group.

For such a naturalist view, appeal to natural inclinations would not disclose fundamental goals which humans are obligated to pursue. They might rather disclose biologically imprinted tendencies which may need to be checked if humans are to survive. Nature is simply not constituted purposefully, but is the result of many random mutations and contingencies. So there are not really any purposes in nature at all. And if there were, we would have no obligation to pursue them. We might even, as T. H. Huxley once suggested, have an obligation to oppose them, for the sake of a more rationally, not biologically, based set of moral principles.[21] The naturalist would throw doubt on the very notion of objective obligation, regarding it perhaps as a compulsion hard-wired into the brain by generations of survival-oriented behaviour. Of course, the naturalist would say that if a certain moral strategy is in fact conducive to survival, it is rationally choosable, and one should perhaps seek to

---

[20] A good example of such an approach can be found in Matt Ridley, *The Origins of Virtue* (London: Viking, 1996).

[21] T. H. Huxley, *Evolution and Ethics* (London: Pilot, 1947).

reinforce it in the species whenever one can. But some such compulsions may be both irrational and ineffective. Then, if one could get rid of them, one should do so.

It may well seem that theists and naturalists would not be able to agree at all on the basis for morality. But in fact it is still possible for them to find a common foundation for morality in the existence of basic human desires and the conditions of their rational realization, which it would be generally bad to frustrate. This could still be called a 'natural law theory', though it would make no appeal either to alleged biological purposes of nature or to the necessity of conforming to natural inclinations just as such.

For such a view, it would be rational to adopt strategies that were conducive to survival (the first level), to efficient reproduction and social cohesion (the second level), and to the discovery of truth and the pursuit of aesthetic pleasures (the third level). At least those things would be rational if one desired to survive, and if one had desires for children, rational activity, and so on.

The morally rational is, in other words, concerned with the realization of basic desires one happens to have. It may be true that most people have those desires, that they are typical of human beings. But that would be a contingent fact. Many things one felt a sense of obligation about might not be rational in that sense (some sexual rules, perhaps), and many things one could see to be rational might simply not be felt to be obligatory (treating animals with respect).

Nevertheless, given some common human desires, it would be rational to support and sanction moral rules that best enabled those desires to be realised, for most people most of the time. That might be called a psychological natural law theory, since it bases the fundamental rules of morality upon almost universally shared human desires.

There is a difference between this view and Thomas's, which can be brought out with the aid of an example. Both agree that, since most people desire to survive, it is rational to sanction social rules that are conducive to survival—to forbid murder, and to enjoin some duties of medical care, perhaps. But what of those who do not want to survive—many thousands, if not millions of people? Might one not say that there is no reason why they should not commit suicide, if they are not harming anyone else by doing so? The naturalist might well say so, and even regard it as immoral for anyone to regard assisting a suicide as a crime, since such an act would undermine all the major relevant desires.

Thomas, however, regards suicide as a sin, because God has created each human life with a natural inclination to survive, and that inclination is meant to support God's wish that each life should survive until God decrees that it should be ended. Suicide is regarded as a disobedience to God's will, a rejection of the gift of life. This is a dimension of belief the naturalist does not have, so one can see here the way in which belief in a Creator God might affect one's view of moral obligation in many particular cases, though perhaps there is no obvious difference in the majority of normal cases.

One can also see how appeal to God would give a rigour to obligation that a naturalist would not have good reason to defend. For a naturalist, moral rules are those which society sanctions as giving the best chance of realizing human desires for most people. Sometimes, however, it will be opportune to break such rules, in a way that does not destroy the whole system. In other words, there will be nothing really wrong with taking advantage of the system—although one will have to say in public that such action is wrong. There is admittedly a contradiction in this situation, whereby one privately does what one publicly says to be wrong. But such practical contradictions are commonplace in human life, and it is how society actually seems to function. The theist might point out, however, that the survival of the system really depends upon the fact that some people take moral rules with greater seriousness, a seriousness that demands belief in something like a moral order of the universe, or the will of God. In that sense, having absolute moral rules, about not taking innocent human life for example, may be essential to the survival of morality itself.

There is a further twist to this example, however. One can take moral rules as absolutely obligatory, without believing that moral rules are absolute (i.e. exceptionless). Some theists might throw doubt on the assumption that God wants every life to survive until it comes to a 'natural' end. It is true that the ending of a life is also the ending of any opportunity to do God's will on earth, to worship God, or serve God or others in any way. For these reasons, suicide at a young age, or in circumstances that will grieve others, or out of a sense of despair that sees no good in life, is contrary to the will of God. But is it absolutely clear that God wills everyone to go on existing, whatever the circumstances?

One would be thinking here of very extreme cases, when extreme suffering and incapacity exist without apparent hope of remedy, and when it is possible to end a life quickly and painlessly, under strict conditions of medical supervision and family consultation. The traditional Catholic view is that moral prohibitions are absolute, so that it would never in any circumstances be permissible to take an innocent life, even one's own (except by direct command of God).[22] But can natural law support the existence of such absolute prohibitions?

Obviously it cannot for a naturalist, whose moral decisions must always be to some extent contingent on the existence of specific human desires. But can it for a theist, who founds moral obligations on a natural human desire to survive, as an indicator of God's purposes in creation? Suppose God gives to all conscious beings a natural desire to survive, and indeed that it is the 'purpose of nature' that conscious beings should survive. If one supposes that one can discern the purposes of nature, that the survival of conscious beings is such a purpose, and that, since God implanted them, one should never impede or frustrate a purpose of nature, it will become an obligation not to frustrate the purpose of nature by committing or assisting suicide. This is a form of argument that is often found in traditional Catholic moral theology.

There are, however, two questionable aspects of the argument. The first is that it is not clear there are any purposes of nature at all, or that one can discern what they are by inspecting natural processes. The second is that it is not clear that God would will that the general purposes of nature should never be impeded or frustrated by human beings (namely, in conditions in which those general purposes seem to conflict with other rationally desirable ends or purposes).

PURPOSES OF GOD AND PURPOSES OF NATURE

The theist is committed to saying that there are purposes of *God*, which are to be realised in the natural order. But is that the same as saying that there are purposes of *nature*, and that we can discern what they are? Some Reformed Christians have thought that our insight into the purposes of nature is so corrupted that one cannot use it as a reliable moral guide. They therefore tend to reject appeal

---

[22] This point is argued in the Encyclical *Veritatis Splendor*.

to natural law as a basis for morality. But in any case evolutionary theory places large question marks on how far one can speak of purposes in nature at all. In Aristotelian science, each substance had an inner teleology. It tended to realize its essential nature, its proper good or formal cause. Modern science has dropped this notion in favour of seeing natural processes as developing in accordance with law-like regulative principles.

I have defended the view that the evolutionary process can be plausibly said to have a purpose, which is the development of complex organic self-replicating forms which can be the bearers of consciousness and value. But the mechanisms by which that purpose is realised are stochastic processes in which random mutation plays an important part, and in which the general goal is often impeded or frustrated by intrinsic parts of the natural process.

The natural inclinations that exist in humans may or may not be conducive to the attainment of the overall goal of the process. In this respect any evolutionary theorist must agree with the naturalist that one cannot simply read off moral rules from the inspection of natural processes. Such processes may be harmful or undesirable, and if so they must be opposed or modified. So it may be perfectly natural for cancer cells to form. Yet their formation must be prevented by humans, since they destroy human organisms, which we take to be more important.

The psychological naturalist assesses the acceptability of natural processes by appealing to basic human desires, which will allow exceptions, though the exceptions cannot determine the general rules. I think this is a reasonable position for a theist also to adopt. We value such things as knowledge of truth and beauty because they are both desirable in themselves and a means to many other desirable states. However, for a theist, appeal to the fact of desire is not enough—the Reformers are right, desires may be corrupt. The theist needs to appeal to what humans ought to desire, and that is the ultimate goal that God sets for creation, which is knowledge of and co-operation with the divine Being itself.

A theist may allow an appeal to nature as giving, in its overall structure, an idea of what the Creator's goal in creation may be. That is because the Creator must at least make it possible for creation's goal to be realised. Even if creation is as much corrupted as some Reformed Christians think, it must issue in the existence of beings who can eventually realize God's will, if only beyond this universe. Minimally, any theist must see the existence of human beings, with their distinctive capacities for seeking God, as part of the purpose of creation. Part of the purpose of God in creation is to generate personal beings who can relate to God in some appropriate way. It makes good sense to say that such a purpose should never be impeded or frustrated.

This does not entail, however, that there are specific biological processes or natural tendencies that should never be impeded. In fact, if one is an evolutionary theist, it rather strongly suggests that some biological processes may well need to be impeded or adapted to make them conform more nearly to the overall purpose of generating personal beings who can find their fulfilment in the knowledge and love of God. This is not because such processes have been corrupted by sin, but because they have been generated by a mutational process which, by its very nature, must contain some non-directed or 'random' elements.

So if one looks at the instinct or tendency for self-preservation which, as Thomas says, is held in common by all substances, it seems clear that one could not reasonably have a moral rule that prohibited interference with such tendencies in all cases. We have to cut down trees to make paper. We have to kill deer to preserve trees. We have to kill tigers to preserve deer. We commonly arrange beings in a hierarchy of importance, and we may hold that we should only destroy beings for the sake of an important good for some being higher in that hierarchy. We may also hold that humans are highest in the hierarchy on earth. But could we deduce from any of this that we should never in any circumstances kill innocent human beings, or take our own lives?

What requires explanation is why the absolute prohibition should apply only to humans, when the 'tendency' applies to all substances. I do not think there is anything in natural law which can explain that, unless one appeals to an additional principle that humans are worthy of unique moral respect. Unless this is part of divine revelation (and therefore not part of natural law) that will mean articulating the elements of human life that are morally distinctive. One is likely to find them in such things as the capacity for rational and moral thought, or more generally in the capacity for personal being, being which is capable of creative action, appreciative knowledge, and freely co-operative relationship.

But now one has significantly moved from a consideration of

tendencies of nature as such, to a consideration of the aspects of existence that are of special moral value. A Christian theist will find personal being of such value, because persons are created in the image of God,[23] as limited reflections of the supreme goodness of God, and as capable of conscious personal relation to the source of all created being. Natural processes have been designed by God to lead to the existence of persons, but they also have elements of randomness and dysteleology in their essential structure. Human beings, as emergent parts of the structure, have a responsibility for shaping their natural environment so that it can achieve the goal of personal being more effectively. Indeed, part of the reason why nature is not perfect in its ordering may be that, if it were, humans could play no part in its further development.

For some traditional religious thought the given orders of nature are sacrosanct. God has made them what they are, and humans are obliged to respect them. It is difficult for one who accepts evolutionary theory to accept such an argument. God may have created the process of random mutation and selection which gives rise to personal life, but it does not follow that God wishes every part of the order to be just as it is. The evolutionary process produces many deformed births, and kills many mothers in giving birth. God does not intend such things. They are parts of a process God does intend, but if they could be changed by human action, to make childbirth safer and hereditary defect less common, then it is surely God's will that they should be changed. In that case humans are not obliged to respect the processes of nature, in the sense of leaving them just as they are. They are obliged responsibly to change them, for the sake of the true goal, which is the maintenance and welfare of personal life. Natural law, understood in this way, does not forbid all interference in the process of nature. It rather recommends a responsible shaping of natural processes to enable personal lives to flourish.

Traditional Catholic moral theologians respond to this point by distinguishing the 'true purpose' of nature, which is to produce well-formed children, from pathological processes which produce harmful genetic mutations. But how is one to identify the true purpose, when it is not how nature always acts? A determined naturalist could say that the purpose of nature is to regulate the number of births by killing off a certain proportion. This can be clearly seen in animal

---

[23] Genesis 1: 26–7.

births, where many offspring must be produced if any are to survive, and it can be seen in the large number of human infant deaths in tribal societies. But this is not usually taken to be a good argument for letting handicapped infants die. It seems clear that the 'true purpose' of nature is identified with the aid of a theological point, that God wills to preserve human life wherever possible. Though it might be controversial, one might then well extend the point to argue, for instance, that a compassionate God would not will the continuance of a human life in terrible terminal pain. It might then be permitted to take an innocent human life in extreme cases where an agonizing death is inevitable and imminent, and where there is no possibility of relieving pain. In both these cases, what naturally tends to happen in nature will not be allowed to determine how one ought to act. Nor, if one could identify a purpose of nature, could it determine that it should never in any circumstances, however exceptional, be frustrated.

This is significant because it means that one must evaluate biological principles in terms of their enhancement or frustration of personal principles. No longer will one be able to say that, once it is established that a certain tendency is 'natural', one should never frustrate it. On the contrary, biological principles that frustrate the flourishing of personal life or make a worthwhile life impossible may need to be frustrated.

One may call this the personalist principle in morality. There are absolutely binding moral principles, but few absolutely exceptionless principles, and they are at a high level of generality. Principles like 'Love your neighbour as yourself'[24] probably admit of no exceptions, but it is very unspecific what such love implies. Does it imply the taking of a life in terminal agony, or the refusal ever to take innocent life? If one accepts that moral rules must always be tailored to the love of persons (to a concern for their ultimate welfare), one may be inclined to admit the possibility that rules can be adjusted to take account of particular hard cases.

Love of neighbour does imply some positive and important moral rules. It is far from being vacuous. One cannot be concerned for the welfare of a person without doing what one can to sustain their life and make it as pleasant as possible, and without doing what is in one's power to orient them to the knowledge and love of God. The hard

[24] Leviticus 19: 18.

cases occur when the duty of sustaining life comes into conflict with another duty—say, the duty to alleviate pain or the duty of saving many other lives. In such cases I do not think appeal to natural inclinations is of much use. For one has an inclination to avoid pain as well as to sustain life, to preserve the group as well as to preserve oneself. In such hard cases, the test must be, not what natural inclinations imply, but what is for the true welfare of the persons concerned.

This has important implications for the other allegedly exceptionless prohibitions which traditional Catholic moral theologians derive from an absolutist interpretation of natural law. The purpose of sexual activity, it is said, is procreation. Contraceptive practices frustrate the possibility of procreation and are therefore forbidden.[25] But if the criterion is what makes for the welfare of persons, it is clear that conception of children when it is mortally dangerous, or when it would produce economic disaster, can legitimately be frustrated. Such frustration will then only be a shaping of natural processes to further the ends of personal welfare. It would no doubt be wrong to refuse to have children out of despair at the world's future, or out of a purely selfish desire to have a good time. But it would not be wrong to exercise responsible control over procreation so as to maximize the welfare both of existing persons and also of the persons who may be born as a result.

Similar points hold true of the Roman Catholic view that every child has the right to be born of a man and a woman, as a result of a physical act expressive of love (a principle which forbids *in vitro* fertilization, for example). Apart from the fact that this would be impossible to verify (how many sexual acts express love?), what is important is that each child should be desired by people committed to care for it. If physical means exist to make this possible where the parents are infertile, there is no reason to forbid them.

Attitudes to homosexuality have also been influenced by the consideration that every sexual act should be open to the possibility of conceiving a child in love, as well as by the obvious biblical prohibitions.[26] Both biblical and natural law considerations, however, need to be assessed in the light of what is conducive to the flourishing of personal values, to human fellowship, and to love of God. There is good reason to say that all human relationships should promote, and

---

[25] The Papal Encyclical *Humanae Vitae* argues this strongly.
[26] e.g. Leviticus 20: 13.

never impede, the values of loyalty and fidelity, of respect and trust. Sexual relationships, that involve the deepest aspects of the human personality, should be expressive of such trust and fidelity, which entail long-term commitment and the acceptance of mutual responsibility. That being said, however, it does seem that homosexual acts are capable of expressing love within a faithful long-term relationship, and may positively build up such relationships for people who are perhaps genetically attracted to others of the same sex. Here is another case where appeal to what seems to be 'natural', or to be a 'purpose of nature', should not be used to forbid possibilities of positive loving relationship between persons, just because the conception of children is known to be impossible.

When it comes to duties of social obligation, it seems unduly difficult to forbid telling lies in any circumstances, even small lies to save many lives. In such dilemmas, appeal to processes of nature does not of itself clearly license an absolute prohibition, and to say that God wills such an absolute prohibition is to assume a knowledge of the divine that is not open to most people (so it is no longer based on 'natural law' at all).

In general, the moral principles of traditional Catholic theology tend to be very conservative with regard to sexual matters, where norms of what is 'natural' suggest very constrained norms of sexual behaviour. But they tend to be rather radical in matters of political life, where the 'natural' law is always a possible critical force against unjust systems of positive law, which would be seen as not laws at all.[27] Many Protestants, too, hold similar views on moral matters, though largely on the different ground that the Bible appears to recommend such views. Protestants tend to reject both the axioms that one should never frustrate a natural process, and that there are specific absolute prohibitions, as neither clear to reason nor clearly based on revelation (which, in the Bible, contains well-known cases of exceptions to laws about suicide and killing the innocent). So the apparent agreement between Catholic and Protestant traditionalists partly disguises a very different approach to deciding moral issues.

It is perhaps understandable that the churches should be conservative in morality, in reaction to the seeming collapse of moral standards in the post-Christian West. But I think that the Christian

---

[27] Aquinas says that unjust laws are 'outrages rather than laws', *Summa Theologiae*, I-II q. 96 a. 4, op. cit. 130.

gospel is actually a very radical moral force, which challenges both sexual and social preconceptions about acceptable human behaviour. If the principle of consistency is applied in interpreting particular moral injunctions to be found in the Bible, and if evolutionary theory is generally correct in its description of the natural processes of biology, then moral appeals both to the Bible and to natural law will do what Paul did—but more consistently—and reject written laws and conventions in favour of seeking ways of life which are obedient to the Spirit of love and personal fulfilment, which the church is meant to mediate to the world.

It is important to see that neither the Bible nor natural law are thereby made irrelevant to moral reflection. With regard to natural law, one can find a more general interpretation, not too far from that of Aquinas, according to which God, as Creator, with the purpose of bringing into being persons capable of responsible action, understanding, and love, will forbid those acts that frustrate such a purpose, and encourage acts that realize it. Christian morality is not based on a set of arbitrary divine commands. The Creator has a purpose for the created order, and fundamental moral principles are based on helping to realize that purpose. It cannot simply be read off from the structure of particular biological processes—that would be the moral equivalent of Paley-type design arguments, which give to every biological form a specific designed purpose. In an evolutionary universe, such specific design is not to be found, since many particular processes are due to random variation. But theists must believe that there is a more general design, an overall goal in creation to which its processes tend, which is selected in the long run. One can see, in the emergence of conscious and partly self-directed personal agents, the general outlines of the divine purpose in creation. God is concerned with the flourishing of persons, and the most fundamental moral principles are aimed at personal flourishing. This is a natural basis for morality, which may be shared by all human beings.

This interpretation implies some specific principles, such as forbidding acts that limit responsible freedom for any human agent, which restrict understanding, and which breed hatred and lack of concern for others, and commending acts that enlarge responsible freedom, understanding, and co-operation. For a theist, such principles will obligate objectively and absolutely—but if they conflict with one another, as they sometimes do, one will have to choose the principle which best realises personal welfare, assuming that is what God wills.

THE CHRISTIAN MORAL PERSPECTIVE

One would expect theists to have a more rigorous sense of obligation than atheists, but one might not expect that theists will have privileged access to knowledge of what is morally right in particular cases. They will have to work out what is obligatory from a general belief in creation and in the things that make for personal flourishing. One would expect theists and humanists to agree in general on the sorts of things that are right, though theists will think that God's purposes make certain basic human desires obligatory, and not just contingent, and give to those obligations an inescapable character that atheists might find it hard to justify. In addition, theists will usually believe that God will eventually realize the divine purposes, so that theists have ground for confidence that moral commitment and sacrifice will not be in vain, but will help in the realization of goodness, however useless their acts may seem from a human point of view.

Christians will also think the objective moral purpose involves a growing sense of relationship with God, and so the moral life may not be one of resolute effort, so much as one of growing in a co-operative relationship with God. This is where the Bible is always relevant to Christian moral reflection. A Christian theist will appeal to the discernment of the divine purpose which is found in the life of Jesus. In the light of that revelation many otherwise acceptable human desires may need to be redirected, so that they can have knowledge and love of God as their final aim. Through the sacramental life of the church the power of Christ to transform human lives into vehicles of the divine Spirit may add a new dimension to the practice of the moral life. The Christian moral life will be modelled on the life of Jesus, empowered by the Holy Spirit, and directed towards the realization of a trans-historical goal of *theopoiesis*, the rule of God made present in a community of created persons.

Christians thus have a view of personal flourishing which is not necessarily set in sharp contrast with other views, but which does express a distinctive perspective on human life and its ultimate goal. This is set out most succinctly in the Beatitudes,[28] where Jesus

---

[28] Matthew 5: 1–11.

teaches that the truly happy are those who are poor (or poor in spirit), who mourn, who are meek, who are hungry (for righteousness), merciful, and pure in heart, who are peacemakers, and who are persecuted and reviled. This is the most important moral teaching in the New Testament, and it sets out what constitutes the heart of morality for the Christian church—not a set of absolute but achievable rules, but a set of commanding and asymptotic ideals.

The Beatitudes affirm that it is important that happiness is the goal of human life. It would be odd to think that persons could flourish and be fulfilled while being completely miserable. But the paradox of happiness is that those who seek it for its own sake usually fail to find it. It comes as a gift to those who aim truly at personal fulfilment. So the basic question is what personal fulfilment consists in. Jesus' teaching is that it lies in non-attachment and non-possessiveness.

In a Christian context, this cannot mean complete renunciation of the world, for God has created the world to realize goodness, and part of being 'like God' must be a sharing in the creativity of God. The Christ of John's Gospel who began his public ministry by miraculously producing thirty gallons of wine[29] is not a wholly ascetic sage. So non-attachment lies in not using the good things of the world for one's own pleasure, but in using them in the service of others. There is no specific 'moral rule' here, but a teaching that true happiness and fulfilment will be found when one has the mental attitude of not being attached to possessions, but of wishing to share their goodness with others. This might be called the first spiritual attitude that marks the life of the disciple of Jesus.

A second spiritual attitude is contrition for the sorrow and pain one has brought to others. This does not mean getting into a mournful and agonized mental state, since the whole purpose of Jesus' ministry was to offer forgiveness for sin, not to induce a greater sense of guilt.[30] It means that one must be receptive to divine forgiveness, aware that one cannot be justified by one's own moral efforts, and filled with gratitude that one is nevertheless accepted in fellowship by God. It is an attitude which refuses to be self-justifying, and which relies wholly on the divine love for a continual reorientation of life.

A third spiritual attitude is meekness or humility. This is not an

[29] John 2: 1–11. [30] Mark 2: 1–12.

attitude by which one regards oneself as worthless or as of no account, since God has created each person for a purpose. It is an attitude that regards all talents and good attributes as gifts of God, so that honour must be given only to God, as the source of all goodness.

A fourth spiritual attitude is a relentless seeking (a hunger) for justice and goodness. Human society should make it possible for each person to co-operate with others in creative action and sensitive appreciation, but in practice every society excludes many persons from playing a full part in the productive and cultural life of the community. Every person has a duty to play an active part in trying to change society so as to make it embody the ideals of a just community more fully. This requires a commitment to principles of fairness and equal consideration. It also requires a commitment to mercy, to seeking to ensure that the sanctions of punishment should so far as possible be aimed at reform of offenders and compensation for victims, rather than at the strict imposition of retributive punishments. We should also be reconcilers rather than people who exacerbate hatred and division, seeking to build up the whole human community, and not divide it into hostile racial, cultural, or religious groups.

A fifth spiritual attitude is 'purity of heart', seeking to see all things with eyes of innocence, discerning the good and not dwelling on the evil, relating to other persons as images of God, not as objects to be used or ignored. A consistent strain of Jesus' recorded teaching is the priority of inner attitudes over public moral rules. He never says that moral rules are unimportant. In fact at the beginning of the 'sermon on the mount', Matthew has him say that every tiniest detail of Torah ought to be observed.[31] But he was in constant trouble with some of the Pharisees because of his personalist interpretation of Torah. He stressed that healing on the Sabbath was not 'work', and so was permitted.[32] Personal need overrode interpretations that insisted on rule-observance even when it was harmful to human welfare. He taught that keeping food laws was not enough to make one truly religious, because purity of heart, having a heart filled with compassion and loving-kindness, is what matters, not ritual purity of the stomach.[33] He was scornful of religious hypocrisy, which regards the observance of external rules as of more importance than helping even one's parents in practical ways.[34]

---

[31] Matthew 5: 18.   [32] Mark 3: 1–4.
[33] Ibid. 7: 18–22.   [34] Ibid. 7: 9–13.

Even though the evidence is that Jesus himself observed Torah, it is thus understandable how the early church could come to regard its observance as unnecessary for what was becoming a largely Gentile community. In the process of discarding Torah, the church came to a new understanding of what obedience to God involved. It was not henceforth to be seen as obedience to specific revealed laws. It was to be seen as co-operation in realizing the purposes of God which had been disclosed in Jesus, as entrance into a loving relationship with God as disclosed in Jesus, and as participation in the love of God, active in the world through the Holy Spirit. Christians saw themselves as moving from the status of servants of God (who had to obey the commands they were given) to the status of mature children of God (who could enter more creatively into the purposes of their parents). They could move on to become, as a community, 'the Bride of Christ', whose love for their divine spouse becomes a full sharing in a loving relationship. And finally they could move to the closest possible union, becoming the 'body of Christ', when they would be channels of the continuing action of Christ.

Christian morality transcends natural human morality, which is founded on basic human desires, by placing human life in relation to a Creator God who acts in the world to reconcile it to the divine life, and who promises the ultimate goal of the fulfilment of creation in God. That relation enables one to see human desires, not as by-products of evolutionary survival-mechanisms, but as hints and traces of the orientation of human life towards the future goal of a cosmic community filled with the supremely creative and responsive love of God. In such a perspective, moral rules become the minimum requirements of living in a society which preserves respect for the human welfare of all its members, requirements which are binding upon all, and which are knowable by all without appeal to revelation. What the Christian churches add to this are the ideals of the kingdom that Jesus places before his disciples, ideals that apply primarily to inner attitudes rather than to specific actions, and which specify that perfection towards which disciples seek to move, while being aware that in this life they will never be fully achieved.

Catholic tradition has seen a broad distinction between duties and ideals, and has formulated it as a distinction between precepts of duty and counsels of perfection. The trouble with formulating it in this way is that it can seem that the counsels apply only to special groups of people, the 'religious', who take vows of poverty, celibacy, and obedience, and who thus live on a higher religious plane than ordinary Christians. This runs counter to the insistence in Christian tradition that there is not a spiritual élite, an inner circle, who are the 'true believers', but that all equally are under the judgement and mercy of God.

Perhaps one should say that the counsels, the ideals of Christian perfection, apply to all Christians, who are indeed called to non-possessiveness, fidelity, and loyalty in personal relationships, and a commitment to live together in reconciliation and peace. The Christian way of life is not a matter of keeping moral rules—which is why it is such a misperception to think that one is a good Christian when one has done one's best to be good. It is a life of growing into an ideal, growing into the mind of Christ, a living, personal reality upon which we shape our lives, or rather which shapes itself in us. For it is not, properly speaking, we who grow. It is the Holy Spirit who grows in us, as we allow the Spirit to do so. Paul's letters speak of the 'fruits of the Spirit',[35] the dispositions of love, joy, peace, patience, kindness, goodness, faithfulness, gentleness, and self-control, which the Spirit infuses into human lives. It is God's love that reshapes our innermost attitudes and goals. As Paul says, those who live thus live beyond any written law.

The church's primary moral role is to keep that ideal, that goal, and that empowering reality of love alive in the many social and political contexts in which the churches exist. Some people like the church to have a clear moral view on every difficult moral question, so that at least 'the church knows what it thinks'. On such a view, the church is an authoritative moral teacher, to whose judgement one must submit. The church, as an influential social institution, does have a responsibility to arrange for the serious consideration of moral questions, to attempt to arrive at an informed consensus with regard to them, and to make the substance of these deliberations widely known. It will often be right for a Christian to accept the judgement of the church (which will in fact be the judgement of some committee), as a trustworthy, responsible, and prayerful authority. Yet official church decisions have been wrong often enough to make one hesitate to make such authority absolute.

Among the practices that the church has enjoined are participation in the Crusades, the rightness of burning heretics, the banning

---

[35] Galatians 5: 22.

of vaccination (seen as against 'the law of nature'), opposition to methods of artificial contraception, and the repression of religious freedom. The major moral reforms of the modern world—the promotion of democratic government, freedom of thought and enquiry, equality for women, the abolition of slavery, the prevention of cruelty to animals, and reform of the penal system in a less purely retributive direction—have not been led by the church. There is moral insight in the church, but it often seems to lie in small groups of Christians who are parts of the church, though not always supported by, and sometimes in opposition to, its official leadership.

The Christian church takes as its supreme authority a radical and startling young Jewish man, who opposed the religious authorities and called for a revision of many traditional moral attitudes. The institutional church might well consider the extent to which its very structure engenders influences that mute the radical demands of gospel morality, and sustain social conventions that reinforce prejudice and bigotry.

The church can only be saved from its tendency to authoritarian moral conservatism by the careful safeguarding of radical and marginalized voices within its community. Individual conscience, when informed and carefully considered, must be followed. While the church has the right to formulate an 'official view', and this view must be correctly disseminated and carefully considered, one must also preserve the right of Christians conscientiously to disagree. This may be an uncomfortable position for those who would like to see complete uniformity of moral belief. But it is probably inevitable in the complex and changing contemporary world of which the church is part.

So what above all the church should encourage, as a community of moral thought and practice, is free and rational discussion, attention to the ways in which the requirements of justice, love, and personal flourishing are impeded, and commitment to the goals of universal compassion and fellowship. The church will not have uniquely privileged insight into what is right and wrong, in particular cases. But it should have an absolute commitment to the goal of the flourishing of personal life, a distinctive insight given by Jesus Christ into what such flourishing truly is, and the power of the Spirit to inspire positive and creative action to order the world more fully towards the good. In this sense, the church is called to be a moral community, the instrument of God's creative and redemptive activity in the world.

PART III

THE CHURCH IN HISTORICAL PERSPECTIVE

10

Orthodox and Catholic Traditions

THE CHURCH AS A DISTINCTIVE RELIGIOUS COMMUNITY

In writing of the Christian community, the church, I have characterized it as a community of diverse and developing reflection on a basic
discernment of the nature and purpose of God as revealed in the
events surrounding the life of Jesus. It is called by God to be a
servant community of love, healing, reconciling, forgiving, and
proclaiming a life in the Spirit of joy, compassion, and renewal. It is
called to foreshadow the universal community of love which God
wills for the world, when egoism and suffering will be ended, and
when all who do not explicitly refuse will find true fulfilment and be
united in the knowledge and love of God.

This view is not context-free. It arises within a particular historical tradition of thought and prayer, and in its statement one can
trace the archeology of its leading ideas, the historical situations
which generated the insights which make up its component parts.

The idea of the church as a community in which creative reflection provides a developing contextualization, both fallible and
plural, of the apostolic witness, is a product of the Reformation tradition, epitomized in Calvin, of dissent from claims to an infallible
and uniform church teaching authority. It enshrines the Critical
Principle that every human formulation of belief must be subject to
free critical enquiry, and is probably susceptible of diverse interpretations. Its particular statement here is influenced by the Hindu
acceptance of a legitimate plurality of interpretative traditions
within a generally accepted framework of belief. In the Christian
theological tradition, the basic and unchanging basis of such a diversity of reflections is the redemptive act of God in the life of Jesus, as
perceived in the early church.

The idea of the church as a community of the Spirit, within which
the mental attitudes of compassion, wisdom, and joy are to be cultivated, is a product of the evangelical Pietist tradition which found
expression in the work of Friedrich Schleiermacher. It enshrines the

Experiential Principle that the core of living religious belief is an experience of God as a dynamic power both within the heart and throughout all finite things. Its particular statement here is influenced by the Buddhist insistence on the primary importance of the cultivation of a non-attached and liberated mind in religious practice. In the Christian experiential tradition, it is the Spirit of the risen Lord who brings the mind to such a liberated state.

The idea of the church as the vehicle or instrument of divine grace, uniting the finite world to the infinite God, is a product of the Catholic sacramental tradition so well expressed by Thomas Aquinas, and developed in an explicitly outward-looking direction by Karl Rahner. It enshrines the Sacramental Principle that the physical can be, and is meant to be, an appropriate and fitting expression of the presence and purpose of God. Its particular statement here is influenced by Jewish and Muslim emphases on the importance of conforming the whole of life to the divine will through shaping it upon the divine wisdom (Torah or Shari'a). In the Christian sacramental tradition, it is wisdom itself, the Spirit of God, who conforms reality to the archetypal form of the cosmic Christ.

The idea of the church as a community which is meant to bring persons to their proper fulfilment is a product of the sort of Christian and existential humanism of which a good example is found in the work of Paul Tillich. It enshrines the Personalist Principle that religious beliefs are to be assessed largely in terms of their ability to define personal fulfilment in an illuminating and effective way, and encourage its realization. Its particular statement here is influenced by the thought of the European Enlightenment, which was prepared to reject traditions which did not lead to human welfare and flourishing. In the Christian humanist tradition, human fulfilment is seen as lying in creative and co-operative relation with a dynamic and personal God, who wills to bring all persons to fulfilment.

These are the ideals which the various historical traditions which underlie the writing of this book can be seen to generate. But history is not a story of ideals. It is a story of ambiguous and interfused realities, in which ideals do play an important part, but often in practice lead to consequences that were unforeseen and undesired. The church is not just an ideal entity, but a historically embodied institution or set of institutions. So it is important to trace a little further the history which has generated such ideals, and which has given them such very different and more morally ambiguous historical forms.

I shall do this mainly by considering the ecclesiological writings of the four theologians who have just been mentioned—Aquinas, Calvin, Schleiermacher, and Tillich. I shall seek to locate their work in the context of Christian history, and draw some general conclusions about the relation of the Christian church and the human social order. I shall thereby seek to draw some morals for the sort of church order that might avoid the worst pitfalls and embody some of the deeper insights to which the history of the church points. And I shall conclude by locating the distinctiveness of the Christian religious community within the whole range of religious traditions, and restating a particular view of the nature and role of the church in the light of such a global vision.

If one thinks of the church as the community through which God wills to unite the whole world to the divine life and looks at the history of actual Christian communities, the first impression is bound to be one of deep disappointment. One basic problem is that every attempt to found a universal community of fellowship and love is faced with the awkward fact that huge numbers of people will not want to be members of it. This may be due to the fact of hatred and pride, but it is also due to the fact that people have very diverse interests and attitudes, and may not wish to be parts of one universal community in any positive way. For many, it is enough to be part of a local community which may rejoice in its distinctiveness. To take just one example, many Orthodox Jews do not wish to be part of a global community. They want to be part of a distinctive tradition, 'set apart' from others. They may not wish to harm or interfere with others, but do not see why they should cultivate positive relationships with others, much less with the whole world.

If there is to be a universal community in this world, it will have to be a much more diverse and pluralistic community than a group which insists on conformity to one set of beliefs and ritual practices. Even belief in a God of a specific character will have to be an option rather than a requirement, and the basis of community will be norms of human well-being and friendship which must be able to embrace differences of culture, race, and belief.

The church has always been torn between claiming to be a global community for all, and setting out to be a distinctive community for those who accept a fairly rigorous or ascetic practice. Some of the earliest disputes in the history of the church were between those who wished to retain very high standards of conduct within the church, refusing forgiveness to those who had fallen short of them, and those who wished to offer forgiveness and acceptance for all, even after grievous sin. The fourth century Donatists of North Africa, named after Donatus, Bishop of Carthage, were one such movement. But they were hardly less illiberal than their Catholic opponents, who persistently persecuted them. To the extent that the church requires rigorous standards, it will exclude a great number of people from membership.

A similar dilemma has always faced the church in matters of belief. How far could the church contain members whose beliefs differed from those reliably handed on by apostolic tradition, and how far could it accept anyone who wanted to join, whatever their beliefs? However liberal churches get, there will always be those who cannot agree with belief in God, or in a revelation in Jesus, and so there will always be those who will be excluded from the church, if only by themselves, and who will feel no compulsion to join a universal community that might require such beliefs of them.

There was a great range of beliefs in the early church, including many varieties of cosmogeny which offered mystical initiation into a secret doctrine sharply distinguishing matter from spirit, and deny-ing the truly human nature of Jesus—the so-called Gnostic move-ments. Councils of bishops not unnaturally decided that such views were incompatible with the basic proclamation that God had acted for human salvation in the human person of Jesus, and with an emphasis on the basic goodness of the material universe and the openness of the gospel. The apostles, the church insisted, had not passed on a secret doctrine, and so the apostolic church separated itself from the Gnostic churches, claiming that they were untrue to the apostolic witness.

Such separations seem inevitable. Indeed, if one has any beliefs at all, it is always possible, and given human nature it is highly likely, that some people will disagree with them, and perhaps wish to set up an organization to propagate their differing views. One has to have some way of defining the basic beliefs of a religious institution, and one has to be prepared to see competing institutions spring up through disagreement with this basis, whatever it is. Thus it seems that the church cannot realistically look forward to actually becom-ing an all-inclusive community. It will remain one religious group among a set of groups, religious and non-religious. What the church might realistically hope for is that it will contribute in a positive way to a wider global community, which wider community will have more minimal moral standards and few or no specifically religious beliefs. The church will naturally think that more demanding moral standards really do exist, and that the realization of a positive relationship to the God revealed in Jesus will be part of full human happiness and proper human perfection. But any foreseeable global community will not agree on such claims. So the church must see its role as one of setting out its own moral and religious truth-claims as persuasively as possible, while not requiring them of all, let alone trying to compel all to accept them.

UNITY AND INTOLERANCE

The church has not found it easy to accept that it is witnessing to one set of moral and religious truth-claims, along with many other competing groups and individuals. Commitment to the truth of one set of beliefs has time and again led to the practice of intolerance, by which competing sets of beliefs are repressed by the dominant institution. Unfortunately, that is in large part the way the church chose. As the church became a powerful political institution, departure from its norms was regarded as virtually treasonable, and bishops who disputed the currently accepted orthodoxy—which changed and even reversed in bewildering ways in the early centuries—were exiled, recalled, and exiled again repeatedly, only the eventual survivors finally gaining the palm of 'orthodoxy'.

There was an early development in the understanding of the nature of the church that could easily be used to support such intolerance. It is well expressed in Cyprian's *On the Unity of the Catholic Church*, which was read out by him at the Council of Carthage in 251 CE, probably in the face of a schism by Novatian, who wanted a more 'purist' church. Cyprian depicts the church as an organism which takes its life from one central stem: 'The Church, flooded with the light of the Lord, extends her rays over all the globe: yet it is one light which is diffused everywhere and the unity of the body is not broken up.'[1] The church should be one, because it is one body, deriving its life from one central source. This is an impressive argument for the unity of the church, and it may seem unanswerable.

---

[1] Cyprian, *De Catholicae Ecclesiae Unitate*, 4–7, ed. and trans. Henry Bettenson, *The Early Christian Fathers* (Oxford: Oxford University Press, 1956), 264.

But such unitivist arguments exact a price, and the price is that all must accept some centralized organization, which ensures unity. Cyprian finds unity in the whole body of bishops, of whom he says, 'He confers an equal power on all the Apostles . . . the other Apostles were, to be sure, what Peter was, endowed with an equal share in honour and power.'[2] This view fails to offer any solution to the problem of bishops who disagree, for it is plain that whole councils of bishops may disagree with other councils, each thinking the other to be radically mistaken—as happened at the Great Schism of the Eastern and Western churches. Episcopacy will not of itself ensure unity.

One can thus see the perceived necessity of the appeal to one source of unity: 'primacy is given to Peter . . . if a man deserts the throne of Peter . . . is he confident that he is in the church?'[3] The unity of an organization can certainly be assured by requiring submission of all members to one individual. The problem, however, is that many members may refuse to make such submission, and will then form a schismatic church. The response to this may well be that of Cyprian: 'He that leaves the Church of Christ attains not to Christ's rewards. He is an alien, an enemy.'[4]

Here one clearly sees the lurking intolerance of the unitivist case. To preserve unity, one has to deny any authenticity to those who refuse to unite. One has to see them not only as misguided, but as losing the possibility of salvation. One also, correlatively, has to maximize the authority of the bishops or of the Pope. As Cyprian says in one of his letters, 'If anyone is not with the bishop he is not in the Church.'[5] Here is the ultimate threat—no assured salvation unless you obey. Even if Cyprian himself did not explicitly believe in it, one can see here the beginning of a logical development towards giving the Pope infallibility in doctrine—for how else could one count on salvation by obeying him?

The idea of the church that Cyprian expresses is of one unitary organization, with all its members under the authority of the bishops (and perhaps under one chief bishop), who have exclusive control of the assured way to salvation. Such an idea wholly fails to come to terms with the problem of dealing lovingly with those who do not wish to submit to the bishops. But then, the argument might go,

---

[2] Cyprian, 264.   [3] Ibid. 263–4.   [4] Ibid. 265.
[5] Cyprian, *De Cath. Eccl. Unit.* 66, ibid. 266.

refusal to submit shows an unhealthy arrogance and hatred of God's will, so loving conduct towards them is not appropriate anyway.

May it not be, however, that one conscientiously (even if wrongly) thinks a particular bishop or pope to be mistaken? May it not even be that conscience requires one to oppose them, if they are advocating violence and repression, as they have done from time to time? Suppose, then, that one admits the possibility of conscientious dissent. Could one accept Cyprian's view of the church? I think not. The alternative view is of the church, not as a unitary, but as a plural organization, with many differing forms of belief and practice. To be the church at all, each would have to make a reasonable claim to be following the teaching of Christ, to be trying to form human lives on the pattern of his life, and to be proclaiming to all the hope of eternal life in him. But none might claim exclusive control of the means of salvation, and all might admit fallibility, partiality, and incompleteness on many points.

How does one deal lovingly with those who disagree? One respects their right to conscientiously disagree, one helps them if they are in difficulty, and one co-operates with them in works of mercy and love. One has to respect the right to be different. But does that not mean surrendering a missionary zeal to bring the whole world to Christ? It does mean giving up the desire to make everyone a member of my organization, whether it be the tennis club or the church. But it does not mean giving up the belief that Jesus Christ is the saviour of the world, and that it is better that people know and believe this than that they do not. It does not mean giving up the vocation to heal, forgive, reconcile, and serve those in need, whoever they are, throughout the whole world. And it does not mean giving up the hope that all people will eventually live together in compassion and fellowship, in the love of God. In other words, the church is still called to be a witness to the love of God in Jesus, a servant community of the love of God, and a promoter of unity, hope, and reconciliation among all people. It is not called to demand the submission of everyone to its teaching, as the only proper channel of the love of God, and as miraculously protected from error and therefore above criticism.

As one looks from this perspective at the development of the church in the first centuries, one can gain some insight into why the acrimonious doctrinal disputes that disfigure those centuries were so destructive—so destructive that the church in North Africa was virtually wiped out by Islam, and the church in Byzantium barely escaped the same fate. Islam triumphed partly because Christians were so divided into violent and mutually intolerant churches over issues abstract and hard to understand, that it was a relief to turn to a relatively simple-sounding and less hierarchical faith.

It is not that all the arguments about the *homoousios*, about Arianism, Monophysitism, Nestorianism, and Monothelitism, were based on the mistaken introduction of Hellenistic philosophy into Christianity, as an earlier generation of liberal theologians tended to say. The question for anyone concerned with the spiritual life of humanity is rather why such very abstract conceptual topics became the causes of major divisions in the church, giving rise to the basic division between 'orthodox' and 'heretical' beliefs. What, to put it bluntly, have such debates to do with liberation from hatred and entrance into a fuller life of wisdom, compassion, and participation in divine love?

One sometimes reads that without such debates the church would not have survived, as though the survival of the church depended upon success in philosophical argument, rather than upon the providence of God. It is not implausible to hold that a coherent and plausible doctrine of the person of Christ and the Trinitarian nature of God needed to be elaborated, to place Christianity in the intellectual forefront of its time. It is not implausible to hold that the 'orthodox' doctrines of the great ecumenical councils were successful in articulating subtle and creative approaches to these issues. It is the tone of the debates that is so distressing—the continual anathemas, accusations of wilful arrogance and treachery, the misrepresentation of opponents, and the burning or suppression of deviant works.

For some reason agreement on correct intellectual beliefs became more important than agreement on practices conducive to human compassion and the love of God. Anyone who has spent their lives dealing with abstruse conceptual issues is well aware of the diversity of human perspectives, the liability to error or exaggeration, and the impossibility of obtaining universal agreement. How, then, could the church have come to insist on drawing rigid lines between correct and incorrect belief, in such a way that holding the wrong beliefs would exclude one from membership of the community?

A large part of the explanation lies, I think, in the alliance of the church with political factions within the decaying Roman Empire. A unitivist, authoritarian, exclusivist, and imperialist church insists on one centralized form of organization, on a top-down model of authority, on the suppression of competing organizations, and on the expansion of its authority throughout the world. These features can be found clearly expressed in Eusebius' *Oration on the Tricennalia of Constantine*, a sycophantic celebration of the role of the Emperor Constantine in making Christianity the religion of the Empire.

The emperor becomes one 'whose character is formed after the Divine original . . . whose mind reflects, as in a mirror, the radiance of [God's] virtues'.[6] The capitulation of the church to the world is so complete that the autocratic head of an imperial military state is portrayed as the very image of the Logos, and the head, in all things temporal and political, of the church itself. The Emperor dominated the church until the time of Ambrose in the West, and the Eastern churches have always remained largely dependent on the state powers. Thus the unity of the church is bound inextricably to the unity of Empire. 'Orthodoxy' becomes the test of imperial loyalty, and so the church becomes, not the reconciler of difference in a pluralistic world, but a major cause of social division in the name of the unity of the state. As the Byzantine Empire collapsed into a number of nation states, those which remained Christian were left with a number of national churches, each one bound so closely to the national rulers that it was very difficult for Orthodoxy ever to be critical of government, and the orthodox churches tended to retreat into an elaborate and self-contained liturgical world. The idea of a Christian empire has long been defunct, but it remains a dream—which seems to others either absurd or dangerous—on the part of some churches.

Such an association with Empire naturally leads to a hierarchical conception of both church and state. The Emperor 'frames his earthly government according to the pattern of that Divine original', according to which all power flows down from one source through a series of levels of descending importance. 'Democratic equality of power, which is its opposite, may rather be described as anarchy and disorder.'[7] Such a view of institutional order is that of Plato's ideal Republic, wherein the 'Guardians', knowers of wisdom, order all

---

[6] Eusebius, *Oration on the Tricennalia of Constantine* (336 CE), trans. J. Stevenson, in *A New Eusebius* (London: SPCK, 1983), 394.

[7] Ibid. 392.

things to the good. A more democratic view of the political realm would advise that the power of the state be checked by allowing free expression to competing interest-groups, and making rulers answerable to the wishes of the majority. Such an order has proved impossible for almost all Christian churches. What seems clear historically is that the Constantinian alliance of church and state led to the development of an authoritarian church structure, in which beliefs were decided by bishops (for the Roman tradition, under the Pope) and simply accepted by the faithful.

Since these beliefs are authenticated by the Emperor, divergence from them is not politically acceptable. 'Our emperor . . . having purged his earthly dominion from every stain of impious error, invites each holy and pious worshipper within his imperial mansions.'[8] It might be more accurate to say 'compels' rather than 'invites', since all error is regarded as impious and to be purged from the state. 'Our emperor . . . aims at recalling the whole human race to the knowledge of God.' Herein lies the source of all the imperialistic expansions of Empire, from the conquest of Latin America to the Crusades and the British Raj, with which Christian faith is inextricably associated in the minds of resentful non-Christian nations throughout the modern world.

THE DEVELOPMENT OF THE IMPERIAL CHURCH

The story is not one of unrelieved gloom. The gain of political power enabled the church to implement some of its original moral insights. Infanticide and excessive cruelty to prisoners were curbed, the poor and sick were cared for, family life was nourished, and hard questions were asked about the exercise of military power. The church, as the servant community of the divine love, which tries to follow Christ's teaching, relying solely on Christ's grace and always keenly aware of its own imperfection, continued to exist, and the gates of Hell did not prevail against it. Yet it was intermingled with another church, a church that attempted to impose uniformity of belief and discipline instead of encouraging diversity and self-criticism, that developed an authoritarian and patriarchal structure instead of encouraging the full participation of all the faithful in its deliberations, that thought of itself as an earthly embodiment of the divine

---

[8] Eusebius, 391–2.

kingdom instead of accepting that it was a penitent and pilgrim community of imperfect response to divine grace, and that desired imperialistic rule throughout the world instead of accepting a vocation to spread the self-giving love of God to all people.

One of these is the church of the servant Christ, 'who did not count equality with God a thing to be grasped at, but emptied himself, taking the form of a servant.'[9] The other is the church of the imperial Christ, who insists on the submission of the whole world to his rule, because it is the rule of God, exercised through the institutional authorities of the church. The history of the Christian churches is, from this perspective, a history of the struggle of these two churches, and of both of them with another, the 'gathered community' of the pure in heart, who reject the claims of imperialism by retreating, either literally or metaphorically, into a total rejection of the world. All three models can plausibly claim to be founded on the pattern of Jesus' life. Jesus did come in the form of a servant. Jesus did teach with authority and inaugurate the kingdom on earth. Jesus sought no political power, and was rejected by the world.

Both the imperial and the gathered view, however, conflict with insights that seem fundamental to Christian belief. The imperial view seems inconsistent with the revelation of self-emptying and serving love in Jesus. The gathered view is in conflict with the proclamation that the love of God which is seen in Jesus is universal and unconditional, and seeks to include those—the poor, the outcast, and the alien—who might be regarded as outside the realms of religious purity. Moreover, there seem to be many outside the church who live profoundly moral and spiritual lives. Augustine, one of the most influential early theologians, saw that 'some particular men lived in this world and in other nations [i.e. not in Israel or in the church] that were belonging to the heavenly hierarchy'.[10] His concession is admittedly rather mealy-mouthed, since he continues that 'none did but such as foreknew the coming of the Messiah'. He could, however, have been referring to an *implicit* hope for the Messiah, which would cast the net more widely. Justin Martyr writes more charitably: 'Christ is the Word of whom every race of men were partakers; and those who lived with reason are Christians, even

---

[9] Philippians 2: 6–7.
[10] Augustine, *City of God*, bk. 18, ch. 47, trans. Sir Ernest Barker (London: Dent, 1957), ii. 222.

though they were thought atheists.'[11] The church is bearer of a promise for the whole world, not just for its own members. So it is not a community that gathers into its visible fold the only humans who can be saved.

Nor is the church a community that guarantees salvation to all its members. Augustine says, 'In these mischievous days . . . many reprobate live amongst the elect . . . Both swim at random in the sea of mortality.'[12] Every attempt to equate an earthly community with the community of the redeemed founders on the fact that none is without sin, however loudly one proclaims the rule of the Spirit in one's own life. The attempt to rely on the Spirit must always be made, but every attempt to proclaim success is, paradoxically, an announcement of failure since it overlooks shortcomings that are usually apparent to everyone but the unfortunate claimant.

So the church cannot be properly seen as a gathered community of the 'perfect'. There have been repeated attempts to form communities within the church, communities of monks and nuns, or of lay people bound by a rule of life, that would aim to live a disciplined life of prayer and asceticism. The monastic orders have been great sources of renewal and reform in the church. They have also, however, time and again lapsed into decadence and corruption. In any case, the church as a whole has not required such a communal discipline, preferring to remember that humans live by the grace of God, not by effort. The institutional church has in many ways, however, swung to the opposite extreme, adopting techniques to gain political power and social influence of which Machiavelli would have been proud.

The Eastern churches have often dreamed of re-establishing the empire of Christendom which was broken up with the end of the Byzantine Empire. They still tend to see the job of the ruler as being largely to defend the faith of the church, and establish Christian belief throughout his dominions, while all other religions must be strongly controlled or suppressed. This general attitude prevailed in the Western church also, but there a new understanding of the relation of church and state developed. This was due to a number of factors, among which the collapse of Rome as an imperial city, the establishment of a new form of Empire under Frankish or German

---

[11] Justin, *Apology*, 1. 46, in Stevenson, *A New Eusebius*, 63.
[12] Augustine, *City of God*, bk. 18, ch. 49, trans. Barker, ii. 223.

control, and the appropriation of imperial status and privilege by the Bishop of Rome as it bled from the dying Roman Empire were most important.

As the Eastern Patriarchates, which accepted a primacy of honour but no more than that for the Roman See, were increasingly deprived of power by the rise of Islam and of the Ottoman Empire, the Bishop of Rome was left virtually in sole charge of the expanding Western Church. Moreover, the new empire, epitomized by Charlemagne, was keen to establish its credentials by relation to ancient Rome. That could best be done by liaison with the Bishop of Rome, who was virtually the sole continuing focus of ancient Roman claims.

So in the West an alliance between pope and emperor was forged, in which from the beginning the Pope saw himself as having a greater right to political power than had ever occurred to Eastern Patriarchs, with their strongly Constantinian understanding of a Christian Empire. This led to a long struggle for dominance between pope and emperor that had no parallel in the East. The struggle was won in fact by the emperors, who simply deposed, imprisoned, and replaced popes whenever they had the power to do so, which they frequently did. But the struggle was won in principle by the popes, simply because of the fact that they continued to exist long after the Holy Roman Empire had crumbled to nothing, and the papal claims remained intact when there was no longer an emperor to dispute them.

The development of the Roman understanding can clearly be seen from its beginnings with Gregory I to its maximal statement by Boniface VIII. Gregory agreed with Augustine that 'the church of the elect before and after Christ is one'.[13] But like Augustine he applied this rather restrictively, explicitly including only the patriarchs and prophets and those who might plausibly be said to have longed for the Christ, however embryonically. Even at this time, Christians ignored the vast majority of the world's populations, and concentrated on the Mediterranean world as the focal point of divine attention.

One can see here the possibility of developing a doctrine of an 'implicit church', consisting of all who would have accepted Christ

---

[13] Gregory, *Homiliarum in Ezechielem Prophetam*, 2. 3, para. 16. The text is in Migne, *Patrologia Latina*, but this translated sentence is taken from F. Homes Dudden, *Gregory the Great* (London: Longmans, Green, 1905), ii. 407.

had they truly heard of him. But it cannot really be said that Gregory did so. Instead, he states that 'the holy universal church proclaims that God cannot truly be worshipped save within herself, and asserts that all they who are without her pale shall never be saved'.[14] To rub the point in, he asserts that not only the works of pagans, but even 'the works of heretics and schismatics are without merit',[15] for they lack both faith and love. Heretics obviously lack faith, since they have the wrong beliefs, and schismatics lack love, since they cut themselves off from the orthodox. Moreover, heretics lack love too. For 'they who think wrongly about God do not love God, and those who obstinately contend on behalf of their wrong opinions do not love their neighbour'.[16]

Gregory is apparently unable to conceive of the possibility of con-scientious disagreement. Whereas the orthodox strive valiantly to proclaim the faith, heretics contend obstinately to propagate false-hoods. There is a lack of objectivity and justice about this way of putting things that is glaringly apparent in an age where we are much more aware of the uncertainty of all human beliefs about the more recondite matters of faith. Gregory holds it as axiomatic that the church is one in faith and love. But by faith, he means, not trust in God, but acceptance of defined dogmas. And by love he means, not concern for and respect for all, but love for the brethren and concern that they should not be exposed to unsettling arguments.

So one sees developing a view of the church as protective of a set of defined beliefs which are necessary for salvation—and thus as concerned to suppress any beliefs that might disturb people's faith. If Gregory had held and clearly stated, instead, that it is necessary for salvation to follow one's conscience in matters of belief (even though the church does claim to say what salvation really is, and how it might most appropriately be aimed at in this life), and that the defin-ition of very complex and uncertain beliefs is always prone to in-exactness and even to error (even though the church claims that it will not finally err in beliefs concerning the nature of salvation), the history of the church in the West might have been very different.

At the second Vatican Council, the Roman Catholic Church came near to giving the alternative view. The declaration on religious lib-erty clearly asserts that '[man] must not be forced to act contrary to

---

[14] Gregory, *Moralia in Job*, 24. 5, in Dudden, *Gregory*, 408.
[15] *Moralia* 20. 16, ibid. 408.   [16] *Moralia* 20. 17, ibid. 407.

his conscience'.[17] *Gaudium et Spes* states that 'the Holy Spirit offers to all the possibility of being made partners, in a way known to God, in the paschal mystery'.[18] It is clear, then, that the possibility of salvation does not depend upon being a member of the Catholic Church. It is equally clear that people must follow their consciences, and their freedom to do so must be respected by the church.

This is a complete, and welcome, reversal of Gregory's stated view (a view officially affirmed at the Council of Florence). There is not such a clear and unmistakable statement of the view that the church can err and has erred in its pronouncements on particular matters. But the very fact that this is a reversal of previous papal pronouncements entails that popes and councils have erred on this precise matter. The Vatican 2 document *Lumen Gentium* makes the point clear by restating the Gregorian claim in a very different form: 'they could not be saved who, knowing that the Catholic Church was founded as necessary by God through Christ, would refuse to enter it'.[19] This does not say that all who are outside the church can never be saved. It makes the virtually platitudinous statement that, if anyone knows (or believes) that the church was founded as necessary (presumably, to salvation), and refuses to enter it, they cannot be saved.

It is absurd to believe that the church is necessary to human salvation, and refuse to join the church. One might, however, believe that, if the church did not exist, no one could be saved, and yet not think that everyone needs to join it. In particular, those who do not believe that the church is necessary to salvation might well be saved, even though they are mistaken, and it is the church which is in fact necessary to their salvation. This is a much weaker claim than Gregory's, and contradicts what Gregory asserted.

In Gregory's view the church has a duty to define the set of beliefs that are necessary to salvation. This duty must devolve upon some person or persons. Whereas the older and continuing Eastern tradition was that only councils of the whole church could define such beliefs, Gregory formulated what was to become a central doctrine of the Western church, saying, 'It is plain that to St. Peter, the Prince of the Apostles, our Lord committed the care of the whole church.'[20]

---

[17] *Vatican Council 2: Conciliar and Post-Conciliar Documents*, ed. Austin Flannery (Dublin: Dominican Publications, 1975), i. 801.

[18] Ibid. 924.   [19] Ibid. 366.

[20] *Moralia* 27. 37, in Dudden, *Gregory*, 411.

The extent of papal authority is not here defined, but the pope is given, as the successor of Peter, a primacy of authority over the whole church, East and West. This could be a pastoral office, as it is in the Eastern churches, and interpreted in that sense, the Eastern Patriarchates could possibly accept it, even though they would regard it as a new development in doctrine. But because of Gregory's emphasis on correct belief, papal primacy very easily develops into an authority to define or at least to ratify the definition of correct dogma.

That development reaches its peak just over 700 years later, in 1302, with the Bull *Unam Sanctam*, of Boniface VIII. In this document, which arises out of a conflict between the papacy and Philip IV of France (who in response plundered the papal palace and imprisoned Boniface, who died soon afterwards), the Pope claimed full temporal and spiritual authority over everyone on earth. He applied the Gregorian doctrine of exclusive salvation even more restrictively, apparently excluding all Eastern Christians from salvation as well as all non-Christians. 'It is altogether necessary for salvation for every human creature to be subject to the Roman pontiff.'[21] This is a subjection in things temporal as well as in things spiritual. In a novel interpretation of the gospel saying that the apostles had two swords, he takes these to be the material and the spiritual swords, and says, 'The one sword should be under the other, and temporal authority subject to spiritual.' Moreover, the material sword is to be used 'by kings and captains but at the will and by the permission of the priest'. The tradition of the Eastern churches was thereby completely reversed. An emperor is under the authority of a pope, even in the use of military and national force.

Boniface's bull is a public statement of the *Dictatus Papae* of Gregory VII, a document which Gregory wrote in 1075, possibly as a set of chapter headings for a fuller work which he never issued. According to those dictates, a pope is permitted to depose emperors, may not be judged by anyone, and may release subjects from their oaths of loyalty to rulers. Such remarkable claims were never made good in history, and shortly after *Unam Sanctam*, the papacy was removed to Avignon, split into two and even three opposing claimants, and at last lost all political territory and power, except for the rump of the Vatican state, which is now largely a tax haven and post office for tourists.

---

[21] Boniface, *Unam Sanctam*, ed. and trans. Henry Bettenson, *Documents of the Christian Church* (Oxford University Press, 1963), 115.

Such extreme claims (I think) no pope would make today. But the fact that they have been seriously made and believed by a number of popes throws doubt on the claim that any pope is owed complete obedience of will and intellect, even in things not defined *ex cathedra*. Here are claims which are actually rejected with embarrassment (one hopes) by contemporary Christians, popes and people alike. The question of papal authority is not by any means resolved in Christendom as yet.

THE DEVELOPMENT OF SACRAMENTAL THEOLOGY

The most characteristic development in Western Christianity was the growth of claims to papal authority, but along with it, and ultimately more important, was a specifically Latin view of the church as a sacramental community. At least in the early days of its contest with empire, the papacy was seen as an instrument of reform and civilization—protecting the church from corrupt political appointments, building up centres of learning in the great monastic houses, nurturing and patronizing a rich cultural life, and founding institutions of charity and social concern. In the twelfth and early thirteenth centuries, it could be said that Christendom triumphed in Western Europe, and had the chance to shape a Christian civilization. For a while, that civilization seemed to promise a flowering of the human spirit, for which human virtues and talents were pursued with the encouragement of the church, which related all things human to the supernatural presence of God in the sacraments.

One of the greatest Christian theologians, Thomas Aquinas, was born in that 'golden age', and in the *Summa Theologiae*, he presented a developed theology of the sacraments. For Thomas, the church is not a humanly devised organization which may help individuals to attain to knowledge and love of God. The church is instituted by Jesus Christ, and therefore by God in person, to convey the love of God to those who receive it. In the human person of Jesus, the love of God was displayed and mediated, and the church exists to continue this mediation of divine love: 'Christ possessed supreme fullness of grace', and 'grace overflowed from him to others, so that the son of God, made human, might make people gods'.[22] This

---

[22] Aquinas, *Compendium of Theology*, ch. 214, trans. in Brian Davies, *The Thought of Thomas Aquinas* (Oxford: Oxford University Press, 1992), 333.

'overflowing' occurs because 'Grace was in Christ . . . not simply as in an individual human being, but as in the Head of the whole church, to whom all are united as members to the head, forming a single mystical person.'[23] The church is thus in a real sense the channel of grace, a continuation of the work of the Holy Spirit as active in the person of Christ.

Because it conveys the love of God, 'God alone can institute a sacrament'.[24] No one else could set up a rite which is guaranteed to convey God's love. The rite must then be performed by duly appointed ministers: 'the apostles and their successors are the vicars of God . . . with regard to the sacraments of faith'.[25] Moreover, 'the sacraments are necessary for man's salvation',[26] since it is the grace of God alone that saves human beings, and the sacraments are the means by which grace is given to humans.

A sacrament is defined by Thomas as 'a sign of a sacred reality inasmuch as it has the property of sanctifying people'.[27] A sacrament has a material element (e.g. water) which calls forth the idea of a religious reality (cleansing from sin). It actually conveys that reality to the recipient. The matter is made into an *effectual sign* by the words or acts of the minister. And the institutor of the sacrament must be Jesus Christ.

Contemporary biblical scholars would be wary of claiming that Jesus actually instituted the seven sacraments (those later confirmed by the Council of Trent) listed by Thomas Aquinas, following Peter Lombard. The picture of Jesus consciously devising a sacramental means of grace and teaching it to the apostles is not one that is historically plausible. Baptism and the eucharist stand apart from the others, in having a clearer claim to institution by Jesus, and in purporting to convey new birth or continuing life in Christ, under the form of specific material elements.

Confirmation, penance and extreme unction formalize practices which were widespread in a number of forms and for a variety of reasons in the New Testament churches. Confirmation seems to be a formalization of the laying on of hands. Penance formalizes the forgiveness of sins, originally perhaps a communal rite of public confession and acceptance. Extreme unction formalizes prayers for

---

[23] Aquinas, *Summa Theologiae*, III q. 19 a. 4, trans. Thomas Gilby (London: Blackfriars, 1966).

[24] Ibid. III q. 64 a. 2.   [25] Ibid.   [26] Ibid. III q. 61 a. 1.

[27] Ibid. III q. 60 a. 2.

healing and exorcism which were used in many cases of illness in the early church. In these three rites, the blessing of the church is given, through a duly appointed person, to its members, with prayers that the Holy Spirit might strengthen and sustain them. They seem to be more like rites that reaffirm baptismal commitments, prepare one for eucharistic participation, or prepare one for death, than independent ritual uses of material elements to mediate the love of God.

Ordination is a setting apart for a specific function within the church. Thomas takes it to confer 'the power of consecrating in the person of Christ (*in persona Christi*)'.[28] This mysterious phrase is still the subject of debate between various churches. What Thomas has in mind is that certain persons are set apart to say the words of consecration at the eucharist, 'as in the person of Christ'. There are three main possible interpretations of the phrase. The strongest is that a person actually becomes Christ, at least temporarily. That interpretation does not seem sustainable, since, as Thomas points out, 'from the fact of being wicked he [a priest] does not cease to be Christ's minister'.[29] But a wicked priest has clearly not become Christ.

A second interpretation is that the priest is 'impersonating Christ'. It will be as if an actor played the part of Jesus at the Last Supper. He will not *be* Jesus, but will play the part, and through that role-play the risen Christ will actually act. The problem here is how much like the real Jesus an actor must be to play his part. Every actor brings his own interpretation to a part, and no one knows what Jesus looked like, or even what his exact words (assuming they were in Aramaic) were. Could there be a Black or Chinese priest? A handicapped or a disabled priest? A homosexual or a woman priest? The disadvantage of this interpretation is that it seems to make the efficacy of the sacrament depend upon how good and appropriate an actor the priest is. It seems quite inappropriate to comment on a priest's acting ability in the eucharist (though it happens quite often). And it seems irrational to make the act of Christ depend on the race, appearance, or sex of an actor who portrays him. As Thomas says in the case of baptism, 'It is Christ who principally baptises'.[30] So in the eucharist it is Christ who makes his self-offering present, and the minister is only an agent whose words realize Christ's presence sacramentally.

---

[28] Ibid. III q. 82 a. 1.   [29] Ibid. III q. 82 a. 5.   [30] Ibid. III q. 67 a. 4.

One can see how one might take a priest as an 'image' of the true agent, Christ, but this nevertheless confuses the bread and wine, which are material elements functioning as signs of the reality of Christ, with the person of the minister, who is simply the instrument by which that reality is made present. The minister must intend to do what the church does, but 'a person devoid of faith can confer a sacrament', since 'he acts not in his own power as an individual but in the power of Christ'.[31] So the character and beliefs of the actor do not invalidate the sacrament; it is simply his performance which counts. This suggests that the 'impersonation' interpretation is unsatisfactory, because it confuses signs with instruments, and makes the validity of the sacrament depend upon a likeness of performance to real agent which could never be established. An elderly Gentile celebrant of a Pontifical High Mass, in elaborate vestments, singing in Latin, surrounded by acolytes in imitations of Roman imperial court dress, must be accounted a very bad rendition of the historical Jesus at the Last Supper. But few have suggested that makes such a celebration invalid. This implies that the priestly ministry is not one of imitation or impersonation of Christ.

This leaves the third interpretation, that the minister is set apart by the church to be the instrument through which Christ in person offers the sacrifice of his own completed earthly life and death. The church could set apart anyone it chooses to perform this function. With regard to baptism, Thomas says that anyone, even a woman, can baptize (if there is no man present), because baptism is absolutely necessary to salvation—'all are obliged to baptism and without it no one can be saved'.[32] He qualifies this, however, by conceding that 'a person can attain salvation without actually being baptized, because of his desire'. Here again the possibility opens up that those who would be baptized if they truly understood what baptism is can attain salvation. They can be understood to have a potential or implicit desire for baptism, even if they have never so much as heard of it.

On this view, the necessity of baptism is thus conditional on a person understanding what baptism is. A complication is that Thomas defends infant baptism on the ground that it remits the guilt of original sin, though infants are incapable of understanding what baptism is. There is a largely unresolved tension between the view

---

[31] Aquinas, III q. 64 a. 9.   [32] Ibid. III q. 68 a. 2.

that unbaptized infants go to Hell, or at least cannot attain supernatural bliss, and the very different view that baptism is only necessary for those who understand what it implies.

This tension surfaces in the discussion of circumcision. Although in general Thomas holds that 'the sacraments of the Old Law did not contain within themselves any power by which they could actively contribute to the conferring of justifying grace',[33] he nevertheless believes that 'grace was conferred in circumcision', to the extent that it was a sign of the passion of Christ which was to come. This is a clear statement that grace is conferred other than through the sacraments instituted by Christ, though only because Christ's passion would make them effective. The Christian sacraments, Thomas holds, 'incorporate a person into Christ and bestow grace more abundantly'.[34] Since it is highly unlikely that he means that Christians are holier than Jews, the sense of this phrase is best taken as asserting that the Christian sacraments, being explicitly related to Christ, are adequate signs of what grace truly is, and therefore they enable the recipient to be consciously related to the love of God in a way more appropriate to the reality of God's love than is possible for those who have a different and relatively deficient understanding.

The same sort of point is suggested by Thomas's discussion of the celebration of sacraments by heretics, schismatics, and excommunicated priests. They can, he says, 'consecrate the eucharist',[35] having the power, though not using it rightly. Indeed, since the celebration and the reception of sacraments in such a way is a sin, this 'in itself prevents the sacrament from taking effect'[36]—'unless perhaps his behaviour is excusable on grounds of ignorance'. Though rather hesitantly expressed, this does imply that, if one is suitably and innocently ignorant of the truth, one can receive sacramental grace by means of those who are not members of the Roman Catholic Church.

These discussions point towards an acceptance that the grace of God is not confined to the sacraments of any church, and therefore that they are not absolutely necessary to salvation, but only conditionally so (conditional on right understanding). This in turn implies that the understanding and will of the recipients are important factors in the efficacy of sacraments.

So Thomas allows baptism to be performed by anyone, in extreme

---

[33] Ibid. III q. 62 a. 6.   [34] Ibid. III q. 70 a. 4.
[35] Ibid. III q. 82 a. 7.   [36] Ibid. III q. 64 a. 9.

cases at least, because of its importance for right relationship to God. It seems that he should similarly allow the eucharist to be celebrated by anyone in extreme cases, since the eucharist is necessary for sustaining life in Christ, which may have become weakened by sin or inattention. But he reserves the power of consecration to priests, on the grounds that communion is not absolutely necessary to salvation. If sacraments belong to the life of the church, and if the most necessary sacrament can, in extreme circumstances, be conferred by anyone who intends to do what the church does, it is not hard to see how this could be generalized to permit lay celebrations of the eucharist, which would be valid in cases where no priests could be present. In that case, ordination would be a commissioning by the church to preserve due order, rather than strictly speaking a sacrament in the sense of a means of conveying the grace of God in a special way.

The seventh sacrament, matrimony, is even further removed from the sacramental life of grace. Marriage, the lifelong commitment of a man and woman in loyalty and fidelity, can of course be graced by God, and may indeed be a sign of the union of Christ and the church. A couple may take marriage vows before God, and pray for divine grace. But the word 'sacrament' is in such cases being used in a very wide sense, of any rite within the church by which divine love is conveyed. That would include taking vows of many sorts, moving to a new job or home, and so on. There is no reason why such ceremonies of blessing should not be called sacraments, but in that case there will be many more of them than seven, and they will all be subordinated to the two chief sacraments, said in the gospels to have been instituted by Jesus, by which life in Christ is initiated and sustained.

The Eastern churches have not systematized a list of sacraments, though there is no doubt that both baptism and eucharist have a central importance as rites of the church. But Thomas's attempts to show why there are exactly seven sacraments seem rather strained. They reflect a rather overambitious concern to define and systematize the relations between God and humanity, and place them wholly under ecclesiastical control. God, it is suggested, gives grace to the world, but gives it in the ways and under the forms specified by papal authority.

THE CHURCH AS THE EXCLUSIVE MEDIATOR OF GRACE

For Thomas, the reality conveyed by a sacrament is grace, which is 'nothing else than a certain shared similitude to the divine nature'; sacraments 'are conferred upon us for the precise purpose of causing grace in and through them'.[37] The sacraments thus are effective in making us like God. God alone can do this, for it is appropriate that 'God alone should make godlike, by communicating a share in his divine nature by participation and assimilation'.[38]

Human beings have a nature which, if it were not for the Fall, would make it possible for them to do good and to love God as Creator. But even then, the attainment of final happiness, the beatific vision, lies beyond natural human capacities, and can only be given by a supernatural gift that infuses a certain divine likeness into human nature. This gift produces in human beings the theological virtues of faith, hope, and charity, thereby healing them from sin and conforming them to the image of the love of God that is infused into their hearts. There are, according to Thomas, five main effects of grace: 'first, the healing of the soul; secondly, willing the good; thirdly, the efficacious performance of the good willed; fourthly, perseverance in the good; fifthly, the attainment of glory'.[39]

Sacramental grace makes a real difference to human lives. It makes it possible for them to obey more readily the commands of the moral law, and to grow in the natural virtues of prudence, courage, justice, and temperance. But most importantly, it produces in humans the beginnings of supernatural life. Thus 'faith is that habit of mind whereby eternal life begins in us and which brings the mind to assent to things that appear not'.[40] It is an actual cleaving to God, produced in us by the being of God itself, which has as its consequence that we become firmly attached to God's promises, even though they cannot be matters of established knowledge. Faith leads on to hope, 'whereby we know that we can attain to eternal life',[41] and look forward to it with longing. And both lead to charity, by which 'we are said to be good with the goodness which is God',[42] and to enjoy God for his own sake.

What is given in the sacraments is the Holy Spirit, causing in us a conformity to the divine nature, as it is expressed and lived in Jesus

[37] Ibid. III q. 62 a. 1. [38] Ibid. I-II q. 112 a. 1.
[39] Ibid. I-II q. 111 a. 3. [40] Ibid. I-II q. 1 a. 4 ad. 1.
[41] Ibid. II-II q. 17 a. 7. [42] Ibid. II-II q. 23 a. 2 ad. 1.

Christ, by participation in that nature. So for Thomas the church is primarily the vehicle through which the Holy Spirit is communicated to the world, by which humans are liberated from bondage to sin, brought to share in the life of God, sanctified, and finally led to attain eternal happiness in the vision of God.

Thomas's careful analysis of the sacraments, of the life of grace, and the theological virtues is of enduring importance and value. But it does have one great danger, from which a number of other difficulties flow, and that is its tendency to uncompromising exclusivity. I have pointed out how the exclusive attitude is qualified in various ways by reference to such things as 'implicit desire for faith' or 'invincible ignorance'. But the qualifications never become enshrined in a normative teaching, and they had little effect on the life and practice of the church. It is inspiring to read of a condescending act of God by which, out of great love, God enters into human life to unite people to himself by pouring the divine love into their hearts. But it is unsettling to realize how very restricted in its outreach this divine act of love is sometimes seen to be.

Thomas is clear that with the life of Jesus something quite new happened in human history. Jesus opened the gate of eternal life, and the Holy Spirit was sent by Jesus to plant eternity in the hearts of men and women. But what happened to the ages before Jesus, and to cultures who have never heard of him? It would seem that, if the sacraments are necessary for salvation, those who are not members of the church cannot hope for salvation. Indeed, Thomas accepts the view that 'it is necessary for salvation to submit to the Roman Pope',[43] and adds that heretics 'do not confer the reality [the sacrament] signifies', so that 'anyone receiving the sacraments from them sins'.[44] The love of God seems to be confined to a very small number of human beings.

Thomas does make the Augustinian move of including the Old Testament patriarchs and prophets within the church, since their sacrifices were 'visible signs which people could use to attest their faith in the future coming of the Saviour'.[45] Since he also says that 'the body of the church is made up of people from the beginning to the end of the world',[46] this opens up the possibility that people in

---

[43] Aquinas, *Contra Errores Graecorum*, ed. P. Glorieux (Paris: Desclée, 1957), 171.
[44] Aquinas, *Summa Theologiae*, III q. 64 a. 10.   [45] Ibid. III q. 61 a. 3.
[46] Ibid. III q. 8 a. 3.

other cultures could be called 'potential' members of the church. He does not explore this possibility further (which he could have done, since he was well aware of the existence of Muslims), but it is at any rate clear that, once the church became known to such 'potential' members, it would become necessary for them to join it to attain salvation. There may be prefigurings of the sacraments in Old Testament history—and possibly, we might add, in other religions—but they are all superseded by the church, and people must renounce their errors upon encountering the Catholic Church.

Thus submission to the church becomes a condition of salvation, and for Thomas this means submission to the Pope, 'to whom it belongs by right to settle authoritatively what is of faith'.[47] The universal love of God thereby gets channelled through a hierarchical and overwhelmingly male and celibate clerical institution, which can claim the ultimate power of depriving people of salvation by excommunication, or of remitting the temporal punishments of Purgatory in return for penitential acts. The dangers of such a view may not have been apparent to a celibate monk under vows of obedience, but it seems odd to limit the grace of God to those who either approve of, or submit to, such a hierarchically organized institution. Throughout Christian history there have been repeated attempts to discern the activity of the Holy Spirit in groups existing in tension with such an institution, which groups see the Spirit as inspiring more egalitarian, democratic, and communal forms of fellowship.

If, as Thomas says, a major effect of grace is the creation of *amicitia*, of friendship or communion,[48] and if, as Jesus repeatedly taught, any who would be masters must act as servants, one might expect that grace would create communities in which no one feels excluded, in which there are no great differences of status and privilege, and in which all participate in decision-making processes. From such a viewpoint, an organization in which a group of elderly, unmarried men make all the important decisions and exercise a monopolistic power over ultimate entrance to or ejection from salvation, might look a rather odd image of the kingdom of God. And it seems odd that anyone who prefers an alternative vision of the church as a set of egalitarian and participatory communities would actually exclude themselves for ever from salvation.

Those who held such alternative visions were ruthlessly hunted

---

[47] Ibid. II-II q. 1 a. 10.   [48] Ibid. II-II q. 23 a. 1.

down by the Inquisition, headed by Thomas's own order, the Dominicans. The Waldensians were denounced as heretics at the fourth Lateran Council of 1215, and in 1252, when Thomas was about 28, Innocent IV confirmed the crusade against the Albigensians, condoning the use of torture and burning at the stake. Thus large groups of religious believers who, however odd their beliefs might have seemed, were committed to the pursuit of personal holiness and the love of God, were tortured, massacred, and burned alive by those who claimed to have sole possession of the Holy Spirit of love in person. In face of such evidence in his own day, Thomas continued to assert—despite the qualifications noted—that 'there can be no true virtue without charity',[49] and that charity is confined to the Roman Catholic Church. Thus 'the Old Law [of the Jews] did not confer the Holy Spirit, by whom charity is spread abroad in our hearts'.[50] Nor is the Holy Spirit properly conferred in any other way than through the sacraments of the church. To see the actions of those who renounce riches and preach the gospel to the poor as wholly lacking in charity, and the actions of those who burn them to death as being alone filled with charity, requires a reversal of the usual moral order of things. As far as the closest inspection reveals, common human kindness and friendship is found as often in heretical sects as it is in the church, and those who receive the sacrament daily are often as notable for their narrow-mindedness and censoriousness as they are for their conspicuous friendship to the poor and ostracized.

It looks as if the work of the Holy Spirit cannot be confined to any particular church, so far as any reasonably impartial observer can tell. And this increases the suspicion, which must exist in anyone who has ministered in a Christian church, that frequent reception of the sacraments does not of itself, or in all cases, appear to increase the sanctity of devotees. How can the sacraments convey grace *ex opere operato* when they have so little effect on so many people? This, of course, was a question the Reformers would raise in acute form. One of the answers they gave was that by grace God simply *imputes* goodness to people, and does not necessarily make them good. But on a Thomist view, grace must make an actual difference, increasing faith, hope, and love in a strictly supernatural way, producing fruits beyond the natural capacities of human nature.

---

[49] Aquinas, II-II q. 23 a. 7.   [50] Ibid. I-II q. 107 a. 1 ad. 2.

The underlying question here is of the part that human participation should play in the sacramental life of the church. It was established by Augustine, in controversy with the Novatians, that the unworthiness of the minister does not hinder the validity of a sacrament. But what part does the faith and responsiveness of the recipient play in the effectiveness of a sacrament? There was a tendency in medieval thought to allow the sacrament to confer grace without any positive response from the recipient, as long as they were not in a state of sin. Infant baptism, for instance, delivers a child from the guilt of original sin, even if the child is too young to make any response of faith. The offering of Masses for the dead could improve their situation, without their even being aware of it. A real change is effected in the recipient by the mere carrying out of the rite. Thus on the one hand the sanctifying work of the Spirit is confined to the Roman Church, and on the other hand that work takes effect without any response of faith from her members.

This, it could well be said, is a misunderstanding of sacramental theology. Thomas notes that 'the sinner . . . does not co-operate with God. Therefore it is useless to use baptism for justification' in the case of a sinner.[51] Grace will not take effect where sin is present. By extension, it will not take effect without the presence of faith (which is itself, for Thomas, the effect of grace). To the extent that the sacraments are rites of the church, they are both communal and participatory, requiring the faith and love of the community, as well as the acts and words of the priest, to make them effective.

But the misunderstanding of sacraments as purely priestly rituals which could be privately paid for, and which would automatically bring about objective changes, especially in the status of the dead, came to be widely current in the degeneration of church life after the twelfth century. The triumph of Christendom in Western Europe was in the longer perspective of history rather short-lived, and part of the reason for its collapse lies in an understanding of the sacramental life as defined and controlled by a hierarchy which was both repressive of alternative views and fiercely protective of its own privileges.

The church committed itself to a claim to exclusive spiritual and socio-political power, to the ideal of a Christian empire ruled by the vicar of Christ on earth. But Augustine had defined the Western

---

[51] Ibid. III q. 68 a. 4.

tradition by clearly seeing that the city of God and the city of the world are not one. The attempt to control the secular world by force could only be a capitulation to the powers of that world. In the end, papal rule was destroyed by the rising powers of European nationalism which it had unleashed in its own struggle for power, and its ultimate sanction, the control of sacramental grace, was to be overturned by a rising awareness of the free and personal power of divine grace, which could not be confined to any visible institution or controlled by any man.

II

The Reformed Tradition

The unity of the church has always been a main preoccupation of Christendom. Cyprian had argued for the maintenance of that unity through obedience to an apostolic succession of bishops, who were themselves to be united through regular general councils of the church. But each general council managed to produce further divisions in the church, as large bodies of bishops found themselves unable to accept the conciliar decisions. The Eastern Patriarchates allied themselves with the Byzantine emperor, and anathematized the Arian, Monophysite, and Nestorian churches. These Patriarchates lost almost all influence after the collapse of the Byzantine Empire, and the Eastern 'churches of the seven councils' developed into a number of national churches, most notably the Greek and Russian, which on the whole set their face against any innovation whatsoever.

The Eastern churches maintained a general unity with one another, though schisms continued to occur, as with the Old Believers in Russia, but they came increasingly to separate themselves from the See of Rome. Among the many reasons for such a separation was what they saw as a tendency to dogmatic innovation in the Latin church, and its use of scholastic and legalistic thought forms. Rejection of the Western addition of the 'filioque' clause to the Athanasian creed is just a symptom of the feeling that the Roman See was moving further away from the decrees of the first seven councils, and making claims for the primacy of the Patriarchate of Rome that were both novel and unacceptable. The sack of Constantinople by the Fourth Crusade in 1204 led the Greek-speaking churches to see the Latins as enemies, and attempts to unite Eastern and Western Christendom were afterwards doomed to failure.

The Western church sought unity by a different path, extending the claims of the pope to supremacy in doctrine and discipline over all the church. After a very complex set of struggles between pope and emperor in the newly created Western Roman Empire, papal supremacy was generally established in theory over both church and state. But it was severely undermined by the internal schisms of the fourteenth and early fifteenth centuries, when first two and then three rival claimants to the papacy existed. Even the attempt to subordinate the church to one supreme leader could be seen to fail, when there was disagreement about who that leader was.

The resolution of that disagreement might have led, as the Council of Constance (1414–18) decreed, to the assertion of the supremacy of councils over popes, but in fact papal authority soon reasserted itself. Sixtus IV cancelled the decrees of the Council, and was succeeded by the Borgias, who became infamous for corruption and vice. Papal supremacy was maintained by Inquisition, Crusade, and persecution—of the Franciscan spirituals, of the Lollards, of the Czech Jan Hus, and the Italian Savaranola, all of whom were concerned primarily to reform corruption in the church, eliminate superstitious practices, and restore a more biblically justifiable faith.

Suppression of dissent eventually evoked an even greater split in the church than that between Orthodoxy and Catholicism. Three important developments in Western Europe helped to produce this split. One—perhaps the most important—was the rediscovery of the great classical literature of ancient Greece and Rome. The new humanism led to a stress on textual study in the original and a critical questioning of the Aristotelian basis of much Christian theological teaching. Together with the invention of the printing press by Johann Gutenberg, in about 1445, this led to renewed study of the Bible, and to its wide dissemination throughout Europe. This in turn led to demands that the Roman church should justify its doctrines by clearer reference to the Bible.

Another development was the rise of movements of personal devotion, such as the 'Brethren of the Common Life', the popularity of mystical literature, and devotions to the Sacred Heart and the Virgin Mary. Though lived out within the church, such devotions prepared the way for a religion of direct experience of and personal faith in Jesus as Saviour, which could, and later did, lead to doubts about the necessity of a priesthood to mediate between God and the rest of the people.

A third development was the rise of nationalist sentiment and the imminent collapse of the Holy Roman Empire in the West. Martin Luther's refusal to recant his Ninety-Five Theses attacking the trafficking in indulgences at Augsburg in 1517, would have led to little if the princes of Saxony and the northern German states had not been ready to assert their relative independence from the empire of Charles V. The Swiss Reformation was closely bound up with the desire of the Swiss for national sovereignty, and England and the Scandinavian countries were waiting for a good reason to renounce allegiance to a pope who was seen as largely an Italian princeling, and an unwanted meddler in the affairs of other nations.

The Protestant Reformation, when it came, split Europe into warring elements. In fact Europe was in a state of almost perpetual war in any case, but religion added a new reason for mutual hostility. Catholics, Lutherans, and Calvinists all killed and executed their theological adversaries, and one result of the Reformation was that northern and southern Europe were divided along religious lines. The unity of the Western European church, always precariously sustained by force, was now broken by force, and the wars of religion that followed helped to lead to a general European revulsion against religion at the end of the second millennium.

Luther was the first instigator of the Reformation, but its most systematic theological mentor was Jean Calvin, who carried through his project of expounding a system of Christian doctrine based solely on the Bible, with some help from the early Fathers, with devastating consistency. Calvin saw and accepted all three developments which were shaping a new religious perception in Western Europe. He appealed to the Bible as the Word of God, which was not subject to authoritative interpretation by any council, bishop, or pope, but was open to every instructed believer, illuminated by the Holy Spirit. He insisted that every individual had a direct relationship with Christ, so that the whole sacramental system which depended upon a hierarchical and mediating priesthood was a human invention that often stood in the way of a true understanding of the gospel and the cultivation of faith in a personal Saviour. And he rejected all the imperial and hierarchical claims of the Roman church, which seemed to live easily alongside the grossest extremes of personal corruption at the highest level. Unlike Luther, who tended to separate church and government and rely on the civil magistrates to defend and support the church, Calvin aimed to set up self-governing and totally disciplined Christian civil communities, subordinating all civil life to the rule of Christ.

Calvin's major work, the *summa* of Reformed theology, is the

Institutio Christianae Religionis. Appearing first in six chapters in 1536, the last edition of 1559 consisted of no less than eighty chapters, divided into four books treating of creation, redemption, grace, and the church. It is in his doctrine of the church that Calvin makes a decisive break from allegiance to the Roman Catholicism in which he had been trained.

Treatises on the church as such had not been a feature of medieval theology. There is no *De Ecclesia* in Thomas Aquinas, for example. Controversies were limited to disputes between the Eastern and Western church, which both accepted a generally sacramental view of the church as an ideally unitary and visible institution, under episcopal authority. It was the growth of movements of attempted reform which led to reflection on the true nature of the church. Already in the first decade of the fifteenth century, Jan Hus wrote a treatise *On the Church*, arguing that no doctrine could be established which was contrary to the Bible. Luther's *On the Babylonian Captivity of the Church* (1520) drew the conclusion that only two sacraments had been biblically instituted by Christ, and that popes and councils can fall into error. Both of them had intended to reform the Catholic church, not leave it. But Calvin adopted a more logically ruthless approach. Only what was establishable from the Bible was to be acceptable, and by that test the whole church had to be reconstituted, root and branch.

THE VISIBLE CHURCH AND ITS MINISTRY

Calvin begins by making a clear distinction between the visible and the invisible church—a distinction familiar to Augustine. The invisible church is 'the church as it really is before God',[1] consisting of all those who are adopted as sons of God and sanctified by the Spirit, the elect of God. 'They are a small and despised number, concealed in an immense crowd.'[2] It is that invisible church in which each member is 'united with all the other members under Christ our head', which is truly one, holy and catholic. But it is concealed from us, and we cannot know its boundaries or extent. We may be sure, however, that the Lord calls whom he will into his true, invisible church, by his sheer willing: 'As the Lord by the efficacy of his

---

[1] Calvin, *Institutes of the Christian Religion*, bk. 4, ch. 1, para. 7, trans. Henry Beveridge (Grand Rapids: Eerdmans, 1989), ii. 288.

[2] Ibid. 4. 1. 2 (ii. 282).

calling accomplishes towards his elect the salvation to which he had by his eternal counsel destined them, so he has judgments against the reprobate, by which he executes his counsel concerning them.'[3]

There is also, however, a visible and external church, of which Calvin says, 'beyond the pale of the church no forgiveness of sins, no salvation, can be hoped for'.[4] God's redeeming love does not extend to the whole of the human race. Indeed, 'The paternal favour of God and the special evidence of spiritual life are confined to his peculiar people.'[5] Moreover, Christians must 'give due authority to the church',[6] regard her as their Mother,[7] and avoid schisms: 'revolt from the church is denial of God and Christ'.[8] This may seem astonishing from one who speaks so disparagingly of the popish church. Yet Calvin says, 'All who reject the spiritual food of the soul divinely offered to them by the hands of the church deserve to perish'.[9] It is important, therefore, to know where the true visible church is to be found. Despite his advocacy of visible unity, Calvin declines to locate the church in its communion with bishops or pope. Rather he says, 'Wherever we see the word of God sincerely preached and heard, wherever we see the sacraments administered according to the institution of Christ, there we cannot have any doubt that the church of God has some existence.'[10]

A large part of his objection to 'papism' is that the word of God is not truly proclaimed, and that a host of human observances and rituals replaces the two simple sacraments instituted by Christ. In the doctrine of sacramental penance, for example, he finds that penitential works replace a wholehearted reliance on the mercy of God, that the practice of private confession to a priest is made compulsory, though Christ nowhere suggests it, and that the early communal practice of unburdening oneself to others and praying together with them has been transformed into a rite which induces a special class of priests to exercise tyranny over others, and laity to fret over whether they have performed sufficient penance, instead of rejoicing in the promise of free forgiveness in Christ.[11]

In practice, then, Calvin supports the formation of independent congregations, which are to be tested only as to whether they preach

---

[3] Ibid. 3. 24. 12 (ii. 251).   [4] Ibid. 4. 1. 4 (ii. 283).
[5] Ibid. 4. 1. 4 (ii. 284).   [6] Ibid. 4. 1. 3 (ii. 282).
[7] Ibid. 4. 1. 4 (ii. 283).   [8] Ibid. 4. 1. 10 (ii. 290).
[9] Ibid. 4. 1. 6 (ii. 284).   [10] Ibid. 4. 1. 9 (ii. 289).
[11] Ibid. bk. 3. ch. 4 (vol. i).

the word of God and administer baptism and holy communion as ordained by Christ. If these things are present, differences of opinion on other matters are not very important: 'we are not on account of every minute difference to abandon a church'.[12] It is not clear, however, just what is meant by 'preaching the word of God'. Calvin had a very definite idea of what the word of God actually said, and this did not allow radical departures from the plain sense of the biblical text. The Reformed churches thus paradoxically tend to have much less freedom of interpretation of the text than Catholics do, who can rely on church tradition or various sorts of allegorical interpretation, or even point to the necessity of a development of doctrine in the church. It is harder to see how doctrine can develop, if one is committed to preservation of an ancient text as containing the full truth about God and salvation.

Calvin may have been right in desiring that people should really hear the gospel of forgiveness of sins and new life in Christ, instead of following a set of penitential and ritual practices, performed in a strange language, which are very far removed from early Christian practice. On the other hand, he probably vastly underestimated the difficulty of discovering what the early disciples of Jesus really had believed, and vastly overestimated the capacity of people to agree on what the Bible plainly said. He himself never managed to agree with either Zwingli or Luther on the interpretation of the eucharist. His doctrine of predestination seemed much too strict for all but his most committed followers. The biblical warrant for infant baptism is unclear and disputed, though Calvin encouraged it. And a whole host of critical problems were lying in wait for those who were prepared to read the New Testament in the original Greek.

Calvin set the precedent for leaving a church on the grounds that it did not preach the true word of God. Protestants after him have followed that precedent enthusiastically, continually splitting off and forming new congregations or groups because of some disagreement over what the word of God actually is. Perhaps it is part of the true freedom of religion to form new groups that can emphasize some particular doctrine or practice. But for Calvin himself schism is a sin (though he did not think he had committed it), and there is a 'true doctrine' of 'la doctrine principale de nostre salut'[13] upon which all true churches will agree.

---

[12] Calvin, 4. 1. 12 (ii. 291).   [13] Ibid.

This view is capable of a wider and a narrower interpretation. On the narrow interpretation, only churches that accept the inerrancy of the Bible, and which practice baptism and the Lord's supper in a particular way, 'as instituted by Christ', can be accounted Christian. And even then, the invisible church is a smaller and undetectable church within a church, of which one may only reasonably hope for membership if one's life of devotion and good works seems to show evidence of divine grace. This is a narrow doctrine indeed, and although Calvin protests that Catholic ritualism leaves people uncertain of salvation, it seems obvious that the doctrine of an invisible church, of which one is a member only if one is truly penitent and faithful, renders salvation even less certain, and for a much smaller group of people.

On a wider interpretation, a church exists wherever new life in Christ after repentance and confession of faith is preached, and where the two gospel sacraments are celebrated. This will include most Christian churches, including the Catholic. The invisible church, since it is after all invisible, could conceivably be extended to include many who are not in the churches at all, where Christ and the Spirit work truly but in unrecognised ways. Since God saves through grace, and not through works, it is even conceivable that the invisible church could eventually include all humanity. Such wide interpretations are possible, but they were not characteristic of Calvin's Geneva, whose dominant mood was the restriction of the redeemed to a small part of the visible church. While Calvin insists that all Christians should be united in love and worship, he clearly allows that there can be many diverse groups which form parts of the visible church, as long as their fundamental basis of faith is the preaching of Christ crucified and risen, and the administration of the gospel sacraments.

With regard to the ministry of the church, Calvin contests the exclusive right of priests to declare forgiveness of sins, and interprets the 'power of the keys' as the power to open the kingdom by the pure preaching of the Word. For, he says, 'all preachers of the Gospel can promise forgiveness of sins to all who are in Christ by faith, and can declare a sentence of condemnation against all, and upon all, who do not embrace Christ'.[14] So 'the privilege of binding and loosing . . . is annexed to the word',[15] and not to any special power handed down to priests from the apostles.

---

[14] Ibid. 3. 4. 20 (i. 552).   [15] Ibid. 3. 4. 14 (i. 546).

'The pretence of succession is vain, if posterity do not retain the truth of Christ.'[16] Although sin does not take away the efficacy of preaching, lack of true belief does. While for Thomas even wrong belief does not detract from the efficacy of the sacraments (though failing to have the intention to do what the church does would), with preaching it is otherwise. In this sense, Calvin places a greater emphasis on beliefs than on practices. This might seem to imply that anyone of true beliefs can claim full preaching authority, whether in the apostolic succession or not, and that is the view some Protestant churches have taken. But Calvin insists upon placing the government of the church in the hands of specially ordained ministers. Some must be ordained to preach, administer the sacraments, and oversee discipline of life in the church.[17] They must, he thinks, be elected, or at the very least approved, by the people of the local church, as well as by other pastors and elders. And they must be encouraged to live simply, without ostentation. Ordination should be by the laying on of hands, with prayer.

Since it is right that all Christians should be united in love, it would be proper for the wider church to be involved in ordinations, and in that sense one might hope to trace an apostolic succession, as such a rite might eventually be traced back to the apostles themselves. However, a literally demonstrable succession is not necessary to valid ordination, where it cannot be reliably established. And it is not sufficient to ordination, if the ministers have departed from gospel faith (as where, as Calvin says, bishops are appointed by the Pope at 10 years of age, without having any pastoral charge or responsibility). Calvin therefore does not accept episcopacy as necessary to the church, though he would find it desirable for there to be senior pastors and teachers (bishops), who could express the unity of the church by tracing a succession of faith back to the apostles. Unfortunately, his attitude to the papacy is such that he believes such a succession to have been comprehensively broken. Reformed churches accordingly do not hesitate to break with the Catholic episcopate, even though they are not necessarily opposed to some such system in a renewed form.

In establishing a non-hierarchical ministry, which must be ratified by the people, Reformed Christianity contributed to the formation of the democratic ideal in Western Europe. The model of imperial or

---

[16] Calvin, 4. 2. 2 (ii. 306).   [17] Ibid. 4. 7. 23 (ii. 383).

papal supremacy, flowing down through priests to the laity, is replaced by a model of a local ministry which does possess authority, but one which must be ratified by, and is replaceable by the people. Thus Calvin stresses that the church must act as a disciplinary body, with the power to exclude from its fellowship for scandalous conduct—an exclusion which 'assures them . . . that perpetual damnation will follow if they do not repent',[18] to admonish and to rebuke. But such powers properly belong to the church community as such, and pastors act on their behalf. With remarkable assurance, he adds that 'They cannot err nor disagree with the judgment of God, because they judge only according to the law of God.'[19] There is no liberalizing of Christian faith here. The church is inerrant in its judgements, and has the power to exclude from salvation—only its judgements must concur with Scripture, and the judgements are declared by the prayerful community, through its pastor. 'The apostles are prohibited to exercise dominion',[20] and so pastors should minister, not dominate. Nevertheless, it is not hard to see how, on such a view, individuals or small groups can come to exercise real power over others in very repressive ways, while claiming only to be servants of Scripture.

AUTHORITY AND FREEDOM

The moralizing tendency of Protestant Christianity is very apparent in Calvin's recommendation that, 'if any does not do his duty spontaneously, or behaves insolently . . . he must allow himself to be admonished; and every one must study to admonish his brother'.[21] What begins as a recommendation to Christian charity easily ends as an invitation to everyone to interfere in everyone else's life in an unceasingly censorious scrutiny. It is arguable that the perils Calvin sees in auricular confession are less dangerous than the perils of encouraging every Christian to be every other's judge and confessor.

The Orthodox and Catholic traditions, sensing these dangers, had devised communities of religious observance, under special vows of poverty, chastity, and obedience, wherein 'those who would be perfect' could pursue a life devoted to prayer and sanctification in community. Calvin objects to such a separation on a number of

---

[18] Ibid. 4. 12. 10 (ii. 459).   [19] Ibid. 4. 11. 2 (ii. 441).
[20] Ibid. 4. 11. 11 (ii. 448).   [21] Ibid. 4. 12. 2 (ii. 454).

grounds. All Christians are called to be saints, and are saved by grace, not by good works, even works of prayer. Calvin supports the idea of communities of prayer that will be an example of lives not of idleness but of true piety, but their members should neither be compelled to take vows (such as lifelong celibacy) which they may not be able to keep, nor be separated off from the church in seclusion.

The problem Calvin is wrestling with here is that any religious organization will have in it a core of devoted, perhaps fanatical, people who will order their whole lives to the practice of faith (the monks). There will be a wider number of those who take consolation, inspiration, or instruction, but who would not dream of spending all their lives in prayer or meditation (the householders). Yet others will value the presence of a religious institution, perhaps because it keeps alive ideals of virtue and some sense of transcendent significance, but will not wish to be active members of it (the hearers). And some will actively oppose any such institution, as repressive of human freedom of action and thought (the unbelievers).

Each faith must have some explanation of why such different groups exist, and of how they relate to the central truths that the faith exists to teach. Calvin adopts a ruthless attitude to the latter two groups. Those who are not members of the church cannot attain salvation, so their situation is desperate indeed. Since humans are saved by grace, any church member may be saved, but the only sign of grace is holiness of living, so it looks as though only the first group can really be assured of salvation—and some of them, who are trying to attain salvation by works, and so regrettably have got the order of motivation wrong, will not be saved.

It is not surprising that Calvin replaces monasticism with an appeal to all Christian families and individuals to encourage one another to live in holiness and faith as completely as possible. Thus he attempted to turn the whole of Geneva into a vast family monastery, under the godly discipline of the elders of the church. In doing so, he paradoxically undermined the very liberty of conscience that his revolt against Rome presupposed. The religion of the liberty of Christian conscience ends by requiring the conformity of all to the dictates of a council of sectarian religious believers. The religion of pure grace ends by putting more emphasis on good works and virtue than almost any other faith. And the religion of the universal love of God ends by limiting salvation to a small number of members of one set of religious organizations.

Perhaps the fundamental basis of these paradoxes is a confusion of 'election' with 'salvation'. Some, a few, are called to pursue a life of prayer above all things. They should indeed be, as Calvin says, an example to the church, and a spiritual help to the life of the church, and no doubt they are not confined to specific communities of monks and nuns. But to confuse them, or even some of them, with the saved, would be to encourage precisely that spiritual elitism that Calvin was so concerned to overthrow. Others are called to be members of the church, to share consciously in the life of Christ, and to mediate that life to the wider society of which they are part, as they respond to the revelation of God's love which they have been enabled to apprehend. Others receive no such calling. They may either value the church for the ideals it proclaims, or oppose it (as Calvin opposed the Roman Catholic Church) for the corruptions it displays. The only way the church can avoid the tyranny of moralism and the arrogance of spiritual elitism is if it clearly sees itself as elected, called, to serve the world in love, preach the universal love of God to all, and mediate that love non-judgementally through the sacraments to all who will receive it. Only then can the ministers of the church truly be servants of the world (not dictators of the church), and mediators of liberty and life in God (not of conformity and exclusive salvation in the church).

Calvin's theology is still authoritarian, in that he places everyone under the word of God, which they are bound to obey. But this authority is not placed in any person. Indeed, he says (as he is bound to do, given his theological views), 'I deny that every interpretation of Scripture is true and certain which has received the votes of a council.'[22] Even general councils of the church have erred, and the church can only be sure of truth when it walks under the guidance of the Holy Spirit, and in loyalty to the word. What Calvin did not wholly see was that even the guidance of the Holy Spirit is interpreted by fallible human beings, and that it is far from an easy matter to settle what, even in Scripture, is necessary to salvation— for surely not everything in it is. But he is committed to affirming that all churches, including his own, can err, and this is at least the beginning of that Critical Principle that was destined to change all traditional attitudes to religious authority.

Combine a democratic attitude with the invitation to everyone to

---

[22] Ibid. 4. 9. 13 (ii. 411).

read Scripture for themselves, add that most people, even the churches, have erred, and one has a recipe for the construction of innumerable differing personal versions of Christian faith. In face of that recipe, Calvin's pleas for the unity of the true visible church were hardly likely to be heard. Protestantism finally undermined even its own professed ideal of visible unity in the church, and placed that unity in an invisible and undetectable realm where it had few practical implications for church order.

Calvin agreed with the other Reformers in insisting on Christian liberty. 'Necessity ought not to be laid on consciences in matters in which Christ has made them free.'[23] But what he actually concedes is a fairly limited notion of liberty. It requires obedience to Paul's prohibition of women teaching, as well as any other principle set out in the New Testament. It is chiefly aimed at rules made by the Catholic Church, such as days of fasting. But again there are radical attitudes evoked here, since if Christ left every conscience free from the law, then even Paul's laws cannot bind in conscience, if there are good reasons to overthrow them. Calvin's attitude seems to be, to put it bluntly, that if church laws are few and reasonable and sober, as his are, they should be obeyed, whereas if they are many and irrational and fanciful, as the Catholic Church's are, they need not be obeyed. But it does not require much reflection to come to the further conclusion that any church or even biblical ruling might be disobeyed if the freedom Christ brings convinces the individual conscience that they are inexpedient. The ultimate influence of Calvin once more lies not so much in what he says as in the possibilities his words open up. He himself remained largely intolerant, authoritarian, and exclusive. But the implications of his words open up vistas for the future of tolerance, liberty of conscience, democracy, an acceptance of diversity, and a refusal to limit salvation to any particular human institution.

THE SOCIAL NATURE OF THE SACRAMENTS

Calvin objected to what he saw as Roman Catholic sacramentalism, but he by no means regarded the sacraments as unimportant. He defines a sacrament as 'a testimony of the divine favour toward us, confirmed by an external sign, with a corresponding attestation of

---

[23] Calvin, 4. 10. 1 (ii. 414).

our faith'.[24] He is very clear that sacraments are of no effect without faith. He is less clear about just what 'a testimony of the divine favour' is. On a minimal interpretation, it is just a ceremony that reminds one, or assures one, that God forgives sins and sustains us by the life of Christ. Since Calvin holds that sacraments exist for two reasons, to confirm faith and to be a public testimony of faith,[25] it may be thought that a sacrament is just a sign which, by God's ordinance, has become a pledge of divine favour. It is like a piece of paper saying 'I owe you ten pounds', a reminder of a debt and a promise to pay it, which exists whether or not the piece of paper exists. The sacrament just tells us or reminds us that God accepts us in faith.

But Calvin seems to mean more than this. 'God', he says, 'truly performs whatever he promises and figures by signs.'[26] He regards a sacrament as a performative utterance, like saying, 'I take you to be my husband', which effects what it states. He uses the example of a piece of metal which, by the imprint of a royal head, becomes a coin, and a pledge of the promise to pay the bearer a sum of money.[27] By a performative utterance one changes one's relationship to another. So in baptism, God regards sinners as forgiven—though innocence is only imputed, not established in them. And in Holy Communion, God positively helps faith. It is rather like saying, 'I love you', or even more like a renewal of marriage vows, whereby one reaffirms a commitment made, and (if it is met with the right response), one actually strengthens the bond of love.

This interpretation is strengthened when one sees that Calvin regards word and sacrament as two ways of doing the same thing. 'The Lord offers us his mercy, and a pledge of his grace, both in his sacred word and in the sacraments.'[28] Both show, in words or 'as in a picture', the reality of the love of Christ. And both are means by which that love is conveyed to the hearer or recipient, when they are met with obedient faith. Communion is, then, a rite by which the love of Christ is both expressed and conveyed, as in a personal transaction. It might be called a performative utterance of God, intended to establish and strengthen bonds of love, within the new covenant that God has established. God is actively present in the sacrament, the office of which is 'to hold forth and offer Christ to us'.[29]

---

[24] Ibid. 4. 14. 1 (ii. 492).   [25] Ibid. 4. 14. 19 (ii. 506).
[26] Ibid. 4. 14. 17 (ii. 504).   [27] Ibid. 4. 14. 18 (ii. 505).
[28] Ibid. 4. 14. 7 (ii. 495).   [29] Ibid. 4. 14. 17 (ii. 503).

I think that what Calvin is attempting is to stress the personal and active nature of the relation between God and humanity. It is a relation in which God is the initiating agent, and in which the response of faith (also caused by God, for Calvin) enables a personal relationship to be set up and confirmed, in baptism and eucharist respectively. He rejects any view of a sacrament as automatically causing a change in the soul, or as changing the substance of bread into the substance of Christ, which may remit sins and be a propitiatory prayer, whether or not any faithful are by the act of sharing the bread and wine confirmed in personal relationship to God. The adoration of the sacrament he would see as a form of idolatry, of gazing upon and adoring a finite substance, because it does not involve a performative utterance of God and a corresponding response of faith.

So he regards the Roman view as 'fatal and pestilential',[30] neglecting the proclamation of the word of God, and the action of the Spirit arousing faith in the recipient. Calvin never speaks of the sacrament as conveying grace which sanctifies the soul. He speaks of the sacrament as confirming faith, imputing goodness rather than creating it, and increasing the true knowledge of Christ when inspired by the Spirit and received in faith. His emphasis is on the personal, inward, and relational aspects of the divine–human relationship, whereas he represents the papist view as teaching an automatic, impersonal, and 'magical' bestowal of salvation. It may seem that there is no hope of reconciliation between Catholic and Reformed views on this matter. Yet in fact they are not so far apart as it may seem.

Calvin himself writes, 'that which God instituted continues firm, and retains its nature however men may vary'.[31] God's promises are truly made in the sacrament, even if they meet no response of faith. On the Catholic view, grace is nothing else than the active love of God, and it will fail to sanctify the soul if it is not met with faith. Thomas stresses that faith itself is a gift of the Spirit, which may be conveyed in the sacrament. And Calvin cannot disagree with that, since it is God who elects to salvation. 'In receiving [the sacrament]', Calvin writes, 'no work can be ascribed to them.'[32] It is God who gives the faith that enables the believer to respond to his gift.

So in the idea of a sacrament as a performative utterance, which to be effective requires a prior understanding of what is being done (the

---

[30] Calvin, 4. 14. 14 (ii. 501).   [31] Ibid. 4. 14. 16 (ii. 502).
[32] Ibid. 4. 14. 26 (ii. 511).

preaching of the word), and the illumination of the Spirit to implant the faith which can respond appropriately, there is the possibility of greater mutual understanding than was possible during the violent conflicts of the Reformation. There is no reason why a fully sacramental view should not insist upon the personal nature of the relationship between Christ and the disciples, while maintaining that the personal acts of God need to be expressed in particular material forms, which forms can both represent the character of the 'spiritual' act, and effectively embody that act.

Performative utterances are inherently social. That is, they require a social context of shared beliefs and conventions, within which they can take on meaning and significance. So Calvin is concerned to stress that God's performative utterances are contextualized in the church. And by that he does not mean a private ritual, performed by a hierarchical functionary, capable of bringing about some objective effect. He means a communal rite, in which Christ is present in a particular way to confirm and increase the faith, knowledge, and love of the community of disciples.

Calvin accordingly rejects any view of baptism that sees it as objectively removing original guilt—without which children are damned. 'Baptism', he writes, 'is the initiatory sign by which we are admitted to the fellowship of the church.'[33] Again, this could be interpreted in a totally non-sacramental way, so that it would become a ceremony of admission to a society, just like being installed as a member of a club. But Calvin, however ambiguously he puts it, means more than that. Baptism is a sign given by God, by which one is 'ingrafted into Christ'. So it is an act of God—'Whoever it is that baptises, Christ alone presides.'[34] Baptism promises that our sins are effaced. It does not make us sinless, but it assures us that the condemnation which we deserve 'is entirely withdrawn'.[35] Now for Calvin, it is not true that the sins of all humans are so effaced. Therefore baptism cannot be just a sign of a general truth that God disregards our guilt, with or without baptism. It is an effectual sign, which assures particular individuals that God forgives them. It is the performative utterance of God's forgiveness.

Calvin's ambiguity on this issue is well expressed in what he calls 'the surest rule in the sacraments'.[36] That is, 'that in corporeal things

---

[33] Ibid. 4. 15. 1 (ii. 513)   [34] Ibid. 4. 15. 8 (ii. 517).
[35] Ibid. 4. 15. 10 (ii. 518).   [36] Ibid. 4. 15. 14 (ii. 520).

we are to see spiritual, just as if they were actually exhibited to our eye'. The 'as if' implies that they are not really so exhibited. The material 'represents' the spiritual, 'not that such graces are . . . conferred by its efficacy, but only that by this badge the Lord declares to us that he is pleased to bestow all these things upon us'. The material itself has not the power to bring about the forgiveness of sins, as though such was an inherent power. But God consents to act through the medium of the material: 'nor does he merely feed our eyes with bare show; he effectually performs what he figures'. God's grace is free and personal; but God chooses to give it effectually by means of a physical medium.

But is it not faith which procures the forgiveness of sins? In which case baptism would be God's assurance that this is true, quite independently of baptism. Faith, however, must be response to a promise. That promise, it is true, may be given in the preaching of the gospel. But it is also given in baptism: 'God in baptism promises the remission of sins, and will undoubtedly perform what he has promised' if and when we receive the promise in faith.[37] For this reason, Calvin defends infant baptism, since God must promise before we can respond. Moreover, the promise is not just that our sins will be individually forgiven. It is the promise that we will be bound into the community of the body of Christ. The preaching or reading of the gospel may lead to individual faith in God's promises. But Christ's body has a visible aspect, and the promise that we are truly incorporated into it, a promise which effects our incorporation, is baptism.

Unexpectedly, Calvin does not hold that baptism is necessary to salvation. Arguing, against the Catholic tradition, that only ministers should baptize (and so being strangely more 'priestly' than the papists!), he defends himself against the accusation that thereby infant souls may be lost for want of a minister to baptize them. God, he says, promises salvation to the children of Christians, even before they are born.[38] The Jews, also, had the full spiritual benefits of forgiveness, though they were not baptized, but received circumcision (and then only the males). 'When we cannot receive [the sacraments] from the church, the grace of God is not so inseparably annexed to them that we cannot obtain it by faith.'[39]

The children of believers always belong to the body of Christ, and

---

[37] Calvin, 4. 15. 17 (ii. 522).   [38] Ibid. 4. 15. 20 (ii. 525).
[39] Ibid. 4. 15. 22 (ii. 527).

in their case baptism is 'afterwards added as a kind of seal . . . to confirm it'. His view entails that personal faith is not necessary to salvation (the faith of parents being sufficient, apparently). Similarly, the Jews can be saved through ceremonies such as circumcision, because of the later redemptive work of Christ, of which they explicitly know nothing. Calvin thereby admits the notion of 'vicarious faith', personal faith which is efficacious for others. It is not a great step from here to regarding the faith of Christians as being effective on behalf of all those throughout the world who turn to God in their hearts. Indeed, if our faith is effective for our children, to whom we may only be related by blood, how much more should it be effective for our friends, to whom we are related in friendship and love? And since we are bidden by Christ especially to love our enemies, perhaps no one can be excluded from the promise of salvation, because of our vicarious faith. Calvin, of course, does not take this path. But it would not be impossible for a Reformed Christian to do so, and Karl Barth did.

Calvin's view seems to be that God may forgive whomsoever he chooses, and is not limited to choosing those who are baptized. Those who say so 'unjustly and malignantly confine the power of God within limits, within which it can not be confined'.[40] But God can declare his forgiveness, and that is what baptism is. God declares it also in circumcision, which conveys the same grace as baptism, though baptism does so 'more clearly and splendidly'.[41]

Baptism is, then, a clear pronouncement of divine forgiveness, which demonstrates its nature definitively, by relating it explicitly to the ordinance of Christ, and making it a rite of incorporation into the church. Thus Calvin takes a very non-exclusive view of baptism. He seeks to move between the restrictive view that baptism is necessary to salvation, and the non-sacramental view that people are saved by a profession of personal faith, of which baptism is the outward sign and acceptance by the community. He views the sacrament of baptism as a performative utterance by God which affirms the divine promise, and gives a definitive representation of what divine forgiveness really is (incorporation into Christ). Yet it is not confined in its effects to those who physically receive it: 'We confess, indeed, that the word of the Lord is the only seed of spiritual regeneration; but we deny the inference that therefore the power of God cannot

---

[40] Ibid. 4. 16. 17 (ii. 541).   [41] Ibid. 4. 14. 26 (ii. 511).

regenerate infants.'[42] The word of God is truly expressed in baptism, but it is not confined to it, or to explicit preaching of the gospel, and may operate, as it does in infants, in ways 'wondrous and incomprehensible to us'.

Here Calvin seems to glimpse a wider vision of the universal love of God, which is not confined to any institution or rite, but which is nevertheless truly and definitively expressed in the sacrament of baptism, by which God assures humans of forgiveness and incorporation into Christ, not for themselves alone, but for all those for whom they have a concern.

Children are, indeed, baptized for 'future repentance and faith'. To realize God's promises, we must turn from the world to God. God's promises may be for all, but their intention is that all should embrace God in faith, in the way that God wills. Thus though people can be saved without hearing the gospel, the divine will is that they should know by whom and how they have been saved, and that they should, if at all possible, live by a conscious participation in the life of Christ. It is for that reason that membership of the church, and participation in the sacrament of the Lord's supper, is what God wills for all who can perceive its true significance.

DISPUTES ABOUT THE EUCHARIST

With regard to the eucharist, Calvin holds that it is not meant 'to hold forth the body of Christ to us without any higher consideration'.[43] He opposes the doctrine of transubstantiation both because it is philosophically obscure and because it conduces to regarding bread and wine as objectively divine, to be gazed on and adored. Whereas what is important, he thinks, is the performative utterance by which God daily 'offers himself to be partaken by us . . . when he seals that offer . . . and when he accomplishes inwardly what he externally designates'.[44] Christ crucified and risen is given in the sacrament, to be received in faith, that we might share his immortality. 'He enjoins us to receive the sacrament, not worship it.'[45]

It seems unduly unsympathetic to regard the adoration of the host as idolatry. As long as it retains its connection with the liturgical preaching of the word and commemoration of the passion, it may be

---

[42] Calvin, 4. 16. 18 (ii. 549).   [43] Ibid. 4. 17. 4 (ii. 559).
[44] Ibid. 4. 17. 5 (ii. 559).   [45] Ibid. 4. 17. 35 (ii. 593).

a helpful aid to devotion to adore the sacrament of the body and blood of Christ. The real object of Calvin's concern was to stress the necessity of the word of the gospel to the celebration of the eucharist, but that is compatible with a doctrine of the real presence in the consecrated host.

Calvin stresses God's act of giving the divine life, and the human act of reception in faith, together effecting the participation of humanity in the divine nature. He rejects the view that the presence of Christ in the sacrament is 'purely spiritual', but declines to define 'the mystery, which it is plain that the mind is inadequate to comprehend'.[46] He insists that the bread and wine remain material substances throughout, and that Christ is present in a way that 'neither affixes him to the element of bread, nor encloses him in bread'.[47] But there is 'a true and substantial communication of the body and blood of the Lord . . . enjoyed in reality as the food of eternal life',[48] and given under the symbol of bread and wine. Christ's body of flesh and blood remains in heaven, so it is not that physical (or glorified) body we eat. 'It is enough for us that Christ, out of the substance of his flesh . . . diffuses his own life into us, though the real flesh of Christ does not enter us.'[49]

Calvin's concern is that we do not, like cannibals, eat actual flesh, even glorified flesh. But we do receive the life of Christ within our lives by eating bread and wine, and the Spirit communicates that life to us in a wholly mysterious way. No one would claim that Calvin's view of the eucharist is completely satisfactory. He would not do so himself. The main lines of his case are clear. He wishes the sacrament to be a personal act of God, received in faith, accompanied by the proclamation of the word, mediated by the elements of bread and wine, building up the life of the people of God. In contrast to this doctrine, he sees the Roman church as maintaining that bread is changed into God, that we crush the flesh of Jesus with our teeth, that grace, forgiveness, and salvation is given with or without faith or understanding, and that each Mass is a new propitiatory sacrifice for the remission of sins. Considered in this light, he says, 'The mass . . . teems from head to foot with all kinds of impiety, blasphemy, idolatry, and sacrilege.'[50]

Calvin brings to mind the Last Supper as a simple meal at which

---

[46] Ibid. 4. 17. 7 (ii. 561). [47] Ibid. 4. 17. 19 (ii. 571). [48] Ibid.
[49] Ibid. 4. 17. 32 (ii. 588). [50] Ibid. 4. 18. 18 (ii. 619).

Christ communicated his life to the disciples. He contrasts that with the picture of a solitary priest offering a new sacrifice each day to appease the wrath of God, and to gain merit which can be applied to obtain release from punishment for the living or the dead. Since Christ offered himself for the sins of the world, Calvin denies that there can be any new sacrifice for sin. That, he thinks, would deny the efficacy of Christ's sacrifice, and also pretend to sacrifice Christ again and again. 'Priesthood has ceased among mortal men, because Christ, who is immortal, is the one perpetual priest.'[51] He is aware of the view that the mass is an application of the one efficacious sacrifice of Christ, but insists that it is by preaching and sharing in the sacred supper that the benefits of his sacrifice should be communicated to us, not by any sort of new oblation.

'As widely as giving differs from receiving, does sacrifice differ from the sacrament of the Supper.'[52] Here he thinks of sacrifice as a giving to God, whereas in the supper we only receive the benefits of Christ's passion. We commemorate the cross, but do not repeat it: 'The Lord has given us a table at which we may feast, not an altar on which a victim may be offered.'[53]

Calvin is surely correct in asserting that we do not need priests to offer sacrifices for us before our sins can be forgiven. But he recognizes that we do need some way of participating in the benefits that Christ's self-sacrifice can give. He is right in thinking that the Mass is not a sacrifice that can virtually compel God to grant us the gift of grace in return. But he accepts that Christ continues his priestly intercession before God, and in that sense continues to offer himself in sacrifice until the end of time. He is right, too, to stress the importance of the faithful hearing of God's word and the grateful reception of the life of Christ in the eucharist. But he is surely wrong to suppose that the eucharist is only a means of communicating the life of Christ to us, and not also a way in which 'you proclaim the Lord's death until he comes'.[54] In an age in which the political conflicts between Protestants and Catholics are not so severe, the Reformation quarrels between a sacrificing priesthood and a preaching ministry can be, and have largely been, dissolved, as both the Word that is preached and the sacrifice that is offered are recognized to be one

[51] Calvin, 4. 18. 2 (ii. 608).   [52] Ibid. 4. 18. 7 (ii. 612).
[53] Ibid. 4. 18. 12 (ii. 615).   [54] 1 Corinthians 11: 26.

and the same Christ, the only matter or substance of the sacraments, as Calvin puts it.[55]

For the three synoptic gospels, the Last Supper was the Passover meal. Even if it took place, as John thought, before the Passover festival, it quickly came to have associated with it many of the elements of that feast. The bread that Jesus blessed and broke was associated with the unleavened bread which was to remind the Israelites that they had fled from Egypt in haste. The wine was associated with the third cup of blessing, renewing the covenant with Israel's God. The whole feast commemorated the liberation of Israel from Egypt, and renewed the commitment of the Israelites to the God who had liberated them.

The first Christians came to see Jesus' death and resurrection as a liberation from the world of greed, pride, and hatred into life in the presence of God. They hoped to share in that liberation, receiving from Christ the gift of eternal life. So the eucharist developed partly as a reinterpretation of the Passover, referring not to the past liberation of an ethnic group from Egypt, but to the future liberation of the disciples, and perhaps of all humanity, from greed, pride, and hatred.

As they came to see it, at the Last Supper Jesus' own final liberation lay in the future. But the blessed and broken bread already signified the free and full offering of his life to God. Such an offering was a sacrifice in the fullest sense. Sacrifice is a costly offering made to God, an acknowledgement that we depend upon God for all things, and a prayer that God will take our lives and transform them into channels of divine compassion, wisdom, and love. The sacrifice of Jesus on the cross, which completed the sacrifice that his whole life had been, was the costly offering of his life, remaining obedient to God's will in the face of human hostility, expressing his total dependence upon the Father. It was a prayer that God would use this free offering to bring divine compassion, wisdom, and love to the world, that the kingdom which Jesus had proclaimed would come with power. At the Last Supper, both sacrifice and liberation were already present in the person of Jesus, though they had to complete the working-out of their historical destiny in the passion, crucifixion, and resurrection.

The mission of Jesus was not simply to accomplish his own liberation. It was to open the path of liberation to others. It is at this point that Christians have always seen the passion of Jesus, not just as the sacrifice and liberation of a man, but as an act of the eternal Word of God in the deepest unity with the personality of that man. Jesus does sacrifice, offer his life to the Father. But in his acts, the eternal Word is also sacrificing, giving up, we might say, the changeless bliss of the divine being to share in the sufferings and passions of creatures. The humanity of Jesus achieves freedom from suffering and death. But it is the eternal Word which is the liberating power, raising the humanity of Jesus from the beginning of its existence to union with the divine life. The Word of God renounces changeless bliss to unite with the humanity of Jesus, so that Jesus' humanity could be united to the divine life. But the whole point of this divine incarnation is that all humanity might be offered unity with the divine. So there has to be some way of conveying the actualized divine–human unity in Jesus to human beings in general.

This way is the way of faith, of union with the eternal Word who has taken the form of Jesus of Nazareth and who now comes to men and women in the form of the risen person of Jesus. The eucharist expresses this exactly. It is not just that blessing and taking bread and wine reminds one of some occurrence long ago in history, as with the Passover bread and wine. Just as Jesus' physical body of flesh and blood was the vehicle of the liberating act of the eternal Word, so this bread is to be a means of conveying to others the very same liberating activity of the Word that was present in Jesus. To eat it is to accept in oneself that activity, the liberating power of God.

The divine Spirit that was in Jesus, that empowered him and united him indissolubly to God, was never confined in its activity to the person of Jesus. The Spirit acts throughout the whole cosmos, from its beginning to its end and in every part, seeking to liberate from forces that separate creatures from God, and unite them to the divine. But the Spirit acts in many different ways, depending upon the acceptance or rejection of creatures, and particular contexts of beliefs and practice. For Christians, the uniqueness of Jesus lies in the fact that in him the Spirit found full and unrestricted expression, in a historical context appropriate for a definitive expression of its true nature.

In Jesus we see the divine Spirit realizing a true and definitive expression of the eternal divine Word. It may seem that the Word cannot be so expressed in an inert piece of bread. But what is important is not the bread as a physical substance. It is the context of action and awareness in which the bread has a specific function. Jesus takes the bread, breaks it and makes it a physical form of expressing and conveying the eternal Word—another form of his body. In the body, the human self of Jesus, sacrificial offering and liberating power were both fully present. What the eucharist signifies is that the same power, by the same Spirit, and in the same definitive form, is mediated whenever the actions of taking bread and wine are performed in remembrance of Jesus' life and passion, by those who intend it as an act of faith in Christ. That power, which in Jesus was fully and unrestrictedly actualized, will be truly—imperfectly and partially, but it is hoped fully in the ultimate future—realized in those who accept it in faith.

In the eucharist we do not just remember what Jesus did. We make present at this time and in this place what Jesus was doing at that time and in that place—offering his life to the Father so that the divine life could be offered through him to the whole world. We make present also what God was doing at that time and place, renouncing divine bliss in order to unite human nature to the divine.

The Christ whom we worship gave his life so that his disciples might live in humility and friendship, and those are two great gifts the eucharist might nourish in us. So reverencing a mystery that none of us can finally capture in words, we may affirm that the eucharist is a memorial, for an essential part of it is the bringing to mind of the redemptive act of God in the self-giving of Jesus on the cross. That life and that person define for us what the love of God is, how far it will go in order to unite any human life to God. But the eucharist is also a sacrifice, for in the rite the self-offering of Christ, made by him once on the cross, is made present to people in many times and places, so that through it God can convey the same divine power of love broken and yet triumphant that was so definitively and tragically expressed on a hill outside Jerusalem two thousand years ago.

Possibilities of reconciliation between Catholic and Protestant forms of Christianity do exist, but there will probably always remain differences of emphasis between those who see the church as a hierarchical, unitary, priestly, and sacramental institution, and those who see its unity as purely spiritual, and its worldly appearance as a set of more or less democratic, diverse, lay-led, and Bible-based communities. The crucial question is whether these differing views can coexist or accept the validity of their different visions of the same religious community.

In Calvin's day it was clear that they could not. The degree of hatred in Calvin's writings is extraordinary, and can only be accounted for by the fact that he really thought the Roman Church had been deceived by Satan, and that the Pope was Antichrist. One can explain this attitude by reference to the fact of the persecution of Protestants by the Catholic Church. Calvin himself had to flee from France, and wandered around Europe for many years, before being invited to Geneva. But the darker side of Christianity is revealed in the heterophobia, the deep fear and hatred of difference that is expressed both in Catholic and in Calvin's writings of the time. For Calvin, the Mass is not just a different way of doing things. It is an insult to God, a profaning of the divine. All defenders of God must attack and suppress it, wherever possible. For the Catholics, Protestants must be similarly exterminated with the utmost severity.

For such hatred to take root, one must have a pretty firm sense that one possesses a correct understanding of God, together with a belief that one is surrounded by forces that actively seek to hate and despise God. The situation is not that it is hard to discover the divine will, or be sure of one's own theological opinions, and that differences in such matters are natural and virtually inevitable. The divine will is clearly set out (for papists, through the Pope, and for Calvin, in the Bible), and disagreement is a sign of corruption and wilful obstinacy.

God speaks, and those who do not hear and obey are condemned. The history of the church shows, however, that there are many different understandings of God's message. Calvin, Luther, Zwingli, and Cardinal Bellarmine all thought they possessed the correct understanding. So we have the pathetic spectacle of Christians condemning one another for having rebelled against the clear word of God—clear, however, only to those who are doing the condemning.

What is required is rather more humility about the clarity with which each camp thinks that it has understood God's revelation. Appeal to the Bible has never resolved disputes in Christian history; it has repeatedly inflamed them. The lesson of Christian history is that the endeavour to enforce a visible unity of the church only breeds intolerance, repression, and hatred. Certainty is unobtainable. Difference is inevitable. Conscientious disagreement is to be valued, as a sign of honesty and a remedy against complacency. These lessons were only to be learned after decades of religious wars had exhausted Europe, and the eighteenth-century revolutionary movements had thrown aside the last remnants of real religio-political power, and enthroned Reason as the judge of every alleged revelation.

As the Byzantine Empire had crumbled, leaving in place a weakened set of national orthodox churches, so the Western Roman Empire crumbled, leaving a Europe divided into a set of Protestant states in the north and a set of Catholic states in the south. On every side, Christianity was fatally weakened as a political force. The age of imperial Christianity was at last coming to an end.

12

The Post-Enlightenment Tradition

THE RETREAT FROM AUTHORITY

The Protestant Reformation radically challenged the authority of the church, and focused attention on the text of the Bible, now widely available after the invention of the printing press. It questioned the division between clergy and laity, and insisted that the clarification of the biblical basis of faith was in principle open to all, and was not to be laid down by church authority. Protestant Christianity nevertheless tended to be extremely authoritarian, not permitting deviations from biblical truth. It quickly became both dogmatic and sectarian, each sect formulating its own rather restrictive confession of faith, insisting on its own interpretation of the Bible, and condemning most of the others. This, however, contributed further to the undermining of authority, since it became clear that even the most devout and scholarly people could not agree on what the Bible said.

The undesired consequence of this was eventually to put in question any appeal to authority, whether institutional or textual. Close textual study, freed from the dominance of one particular church, soon brought to light the diversity and difficulty of the biblical texts. Biblical fundamentalism is self-destructive, since the Bible simply does not allow itself to be plausibly interpreted as one consistent and literally true source of theological doctrines. This left the way open to the rejection of all traditional authority and of claims to certain knowledge of supernaturally revealed truth.

At the same time, a vast change in human knowledge of the world was being initiated by the development of the experimental sciences. The new heliocentric world-view of Copernicus and Galileo was foolishly opposed by the Catholic Church (and by many Protestants too), and so the development of science came to be seen by many (though not by many scientists) as opposed to Christian faith. Reason, which uncovered the nature of the world and convinced by demonstration, and faith, which was received on authority and often imposed by force, split apart. The seventeenth- and eighteenth-century Age of Reason was one which largely ignored the Christian churches, and sought the secure foundations of human knowledge in observation and experiment.

The rejection of traditional authority and the appeal to reason had radical political implications, as all social institutions were brought under the critical scrutiny of 'impartial reason', and found to be largely structures of privilege, patriarchy, and hierarchy, incapable of purely rational justification. In the ensuing revolutionary upheavals, various political adjustments were made, but in almost all of them the official churches were weighed in the balance and found wanting, being seen as bastions of the *ancien régime* rather than of the new currents of creative thought and action. There were radical Christian movements, such as the Levellers in England, but they were barely tolerated by the mainstream churches. The result was that Christianity, though still often possessing the trappings of power, was marginalized, moved to the edge of the new cultural configuration of Western Europe.

In the Catholic Church, the traditional authoritarian and clerical structure was reinforced, although the power of the church over the laity and over Catholic rulers was greatly weakened. Most Protestant churches tried to impose dogmatic and allegedly biblical rules of faith on their own populations, but it was apparent that the existence of many different Protestant groups, all of which denied inerrancy for themselves in principle, opened up the possibility of accepting many different ways of interpreting Christian faith.

Friedrich Schleiermacher is generally credited with having definitively formulated the basis of the new, 'liberal', approach to Christian belief. A Reformed pastor and university professor in Halle and Berlin, in Prussia, his *Glaubenslehre* sets out to reconstruct Christian faith on the basis of personal experience rather than on acceptance of authority.

'A church', he writes, 'is nothing but a communion or association relating to religion or piety.'[1] Piety is a modification of feeling, it is the feeling of absolute dependence—'or which is the same thing, of being in relation with God',[2] and the essential business of a church is to

---

[1] F. Schleiermacher, *The Christian Faith*, trans. H. R. MacKintosh and J. S. Stewart (Edinburgh: T. & T. Clark, 1989), para. 3, p. 5.
[2] Ibid. 4, p. 12.

maintain, regulate, and advance such a feeling. Schleiermacher is here using the term 'church' in a very wide sense, to designate any fellowship in which a totality of religious affections are recognized as identical. He holds that 'each individual communion is capable of a greater or lesser development'.[3] Christianity is one among many such fellowships, all of which possess some degree of truth, though it is 'exclusively superior'.[4] This is because forms which 'express the dependence of everything finite upon one Supreme and Infinite Being' are higher than others, and are destined to supersede all others.

Christianity is, in fact, 'the most perfect of the most highly developed forms of religion',[5] he says, brushing aside what he thinks to be its only real competitors, Judaism and Islam, as respectively prone to 'fetichism' and too restrictive in its limitation of divine concern to one nation, and as too strongly sensuous, fatalistic, and passionate, and so bound up with 'the sensible'. Christianity, as the purest form of monotheism, is thus destined to become the universal faith. Christ 'alone is destined gradually to quicken the whole human race into higher life'.[6] This may seem a slightly perverse judgement, in view of Christianity's own commitment to the sensuous in the doctrine of incarnation, its passionate commitment to Christ, and the wide acceptance of divine predestination within many Christian churches. It shows the sense of superiority of the Prussian Enlightenment more than a deep understanding of Judaism and Islam.

Schleiermacher does not, however, begin from an allegedly unique revelation in Christ, and regard all other faiths as false. He begins from the sense of piety, as a natural predisposition to experience relation to God, and finds it in many faiths. He does not regard the church as a divinely instituted vehicle of the divine love, but as a fellowship of people of similar religious feelings or experiences. Christianity is the highest religion, because it is the purest form of monotheism, but there can clearly be many diverse Christian churches—as many as there are associations of like-minded individuals to form them.

Religions are distinguished by their distinctive origins and the 'peculiar form which the religious emotions take'—each religion propounds 'a new and peculiar idea of God'. Christianity is purposive, ethical, and monotheistic, and it is distinctive because 'in it

---

[3] Schleiermacher, *Christian Faith*, 7, p. 32.   [4] Ibid. 7, p. 33.
[5] Ibid. 8, p. 38.   [6] Ibid. 13, p. 63.

everything is related to the redemption accomplished by Jesus'.[7] Redemption is the passage from an evil to a better condition, by the help of another person. The Christian communion exists only 'as a communication and propagation of that redeeming activity'[8] which was uniquely in Jesus. Schleiermacher argues that individuals should be able to participate in the church 'so long as they desire to maintain in themselves a living consciousness of God . . . by means of that communion',[9] even if they do not regard Jesus as the final redeemer, though his own view is that Jesus uniquely had redeeming power from the beginning of his life, and was not in need of redemption.

He thus sees the church as a fellowship to deliver people from evil and to propagate a living consciousness of God. Such redeeming power, he believes, was uniquely in Jesus and is communicated from him to others. But the important thing is the practical matter of personal redemption (consciousness of God), not the correctness of historical or metaphysical beliefs. His attempt is to espouse a Christianity without dogmas, whose heart is a sense of the presence of God which frees one from evil. There must be a teaching of what this God is, and a way of communicating God-consciousness. Jesus taught that God was love, and did communicate such a liberating consciousness. The church preserves his teaching of the divine nature, and communicates the consciousness of it which he gave 'from the common Spirit communicated by him'. That, and not the promulgation of dogmas about natures, persons, and substances, nor of sets of ethical rules, is the true business of the church.

THE VISIBLE AND THE INVISIBLE CHURCH

Schleiermacher accepts Calvin's distinction between the invisible church and the visible church, but he makes the distinction in a rather different way. He proposes that the invisible church is 'the totality of the effects of the Spirit as a connected whole',[10] while the visible church is 'a mixture of church and world'. The invisible church is, he says, infallible and one, while the visible church is subject to error and divided.

It is extremely hard to see just what Schleiermacher thinks the

---

[7] Ibid. 11, p. 52. [8] Ibid. 11, p. 57.
[9] Ibid. 11, p. 59. [10] Ibid. 148, p. 677.

invisible church consists in. It possesses infallible truth, but that truth is a matter of 'the life of Christ within us',[11] or the consciousness of living fellowship with Christ. As soon as it gets put into propositions, error enters in. It possesses unity, but that is a matter of 'the direct relationship to one another of all in whom the Spirit dwells'.[12] Wherever that united Christian fellowship actually exists, it does so in many national or particular forms, each different from the others.

With regard to unity, he holds that 'the Spirit unites, and . . . the fleshly mind disunites'.[13] So one must always actively endeavour to unite separate churches, and one may expect that separations will ultimately be overcome. Moreover, it is always unchristian to suspend fellowship between different parts of the visible church. Those who break the unity of the invisible church, he says, are those who break fellowship with other Christians, of whatever church. So the 'invisible unity' seems to be an inner agreement in the spirit of fellowship, which always works to overcome differences, and loves the special forms of its own church 'only as a transient form of the one abiding church'.[14] Unity is a sort of regulative ideal and goal, which guides attitudes and actions in an actually fragmented world.

Similarly, the 'truth of the life of Christ within' is an ideal, which moves us from our actual errors and partial understandings towards a greater grasp of truth. No part of the visible church is without error at some point, even in the definitions of General Councils of the church. As to whether the church will ever attain visible unity and truth, he is agnostic. Such propositions, he says, 'are not doctrines of faith, since their content . . . is not a description of our actual consciousness'.[15] We must certainly think of the visible church as reaching a consummation of its existence, when all the influences of the world have exhausted themselves. But 'the representation of [the church's] consummated state is directly useful only as a pattern to which we have to approximate'.[16] It would require that no other religion survives, and that the power of sin, which develops anew in each generation, would be finally broken. Such a state, he says, is 'entirely outside our ken'.[17]

Given his general views on religion, this is an oddly restrictive, even imperialistic view of the church. 'The Christian fellowship as

---

[11] Schleiermacher, *Christian Faith*, 149, p. 678.   [12] Ibid. 149, p. 680.
[13] Ibid. 150, p. 683.   [14] Ibid. 152, p. 686.   [15] Ibid. 157, p. 697.
[16] Ibid. 157, p. 696.   [17] Ibid. 157, p. 697.

being one cannot . . . actively will to have other fellowships alongside of it.'[18] The church should seek to supersede all other faiths. Indeed, he says, 'we hold that the saving love of God did not become effective till Christ appeared',[19] so that the church only began with the personal action of Christ. With Jesus, 'faith itself changed in kind'.[20] Before then, humanity lived under preparatory grace, and only at that point did men attain to salvation. 'The world can be viewed as a perfect revelation of divine wisdom only in proportion as the Holy Spirit makes itself felt through the Christian church as the ultimate world-shaping power.'[21]

Another way in which Schleiermacher distinguishes between the invisible and the visible church is to mark a difference between an 'inner fellowship' of faith and an outer. The former is 'the totality of those who live in the state of sanctification',[22] the true fellowship of Christian faith. The outer fellowship is 'the totality of those on whom preparatory grace is at work', the 'called', that is, those with whom the church has made some contact, but who are not yet full members of it, or perhaps who have only a nominal church membership. Rather surprisingly, in view of his earlier comments about a church as any religious fellowship, and about the general similarity of all 'churches' (religions), he later holds that 'salvation or blessedness is in the [Christian] church alone'.[23] The church is the actual presence of the kingdom of God in the fellowship of believers. As such, it 'will ever endure in antithesis to the world', but one may hope that the church will increasingly overpower the world, as the Christian fellowship gradually expands.

All 'are destined to pass into the Christian fellowship', at least to the outer circle of preparatory grace—what may be called the 'latent church'.[24] 'It is an essential of our faith that every nation will sooner or later become Christian'.[25] But we can say nothing definite about whether the world as such will sometime fully realize the kingdom, the 'inner circle' of the church. One might hope that it will, yet what we experience is the present antithesis of world and church, which suggests that never, as long as the human race endures, will all living people be taken up into the kingdom.[26]

His views on the consummation of the church require a doctrine

---

[18] Ibid. 149, p. 680.   [19] Ibid. 156, p. 693.   [20] Ibid. 156, p. 694.
[21] Ibid. 169, p. 737.   [22] Ibid. 113, p. 525.   [23] Ibid. 113, p. 527.
[24] Ibid. 115, p. 533.   [25] Ibid. 120, p. 559.   [26] Ibid. 117, p. 536.

of life after death, but he insists that 'we should not seek to determine our purposes by picturing to ourselves the form of our future life'.[27] He presages a view of the church as an eschatalogical reality, only fully present beyond historical time, yet casting its shadow back into time, and appearing there as a regulative ideal. Schleiermacher thus places the one holy, Catholic, and apostolic church in the invisible realm of redeemed human hearts, perhaps never to be unrestrictedly actualized. The church may be fully actualized in a new creation, but in this world as it is, it functions as a regulative ideal that is partly realized in many imperfect, geographically limited, and fallible visible forms of the church.

Schleiermacher's Calvinist heritage emerges in his view that calling and election are both matters of pure divine ordinance, and are not founded on any human merit or virtue. Yet he crucially modifies Calvin's doctrine by extending the divine predestination to salvation to all people. He proposes as at least an acceptable hypothesis, the 'universal restoration of all souls'.[28] After death (he does not explicitly say that, but how else could it apply to everyone?) 'everyone still outside this fellowship will some time or another be laid hold of by the divine operations of grace and brought within it'.[29] There is divine predestination, but it is a 'single divine foreordination to blessedness'.[30] By God's will, however, not all are called during this life. The 'time and place were chosen as the absolutely best, that is as yielding the maximum operative effect'.[31] But why are the elect chosen? We cannot discern the hidden purposes of God, but we may say, on the basis of experience, that 'The elect are elected to receive the communication of the Spirit,'[32] and to communicate it to others.

It would clearly be open to Schleiermacher, and would be more consistent with his general views on religion, to regard the 'latent church', the outer circle of preparatory grace, as present wherever the Spirit of God works in human hearts to promote awareness of God, while seeing the Christian church as a specific fellowship with an origin in Jesus and a distinctive emphasis on liberation from sin through grace. One might also wish to qualify his teaching, again meant to give a definite superiority to Christianity, and doubtless influenced by the Pietism of his youth, that the kingdom of God

---

[27] Schleiermacher, *Christian Faith*, 158, p. 703.　　　[28] Ibid. 163, p. 722.
[29] Ibid. 118, p. 540.　　　[30] Ibid. 119, p. 549.
[31] Ibid. 120, p. 553.　　　[32] Ibid. 125, p. 581.

actually resides on earth among the elect, in view of the continuing actuality of sin and failure even among the elect. The kingdom exists through the communication of the Holy Spirit, which 'is the union of the Divine Essence with human nature',[33] making the church one 'in the same way that a nation is one through the national character'.[34] Moreover, he writes that 'the Christian church . . . is in its purity and integrity the perfect image of the Redeemer'.[35]

The problem is, as he himself sees, that the churches are both divided and sinful, and not very obviously superior in fellowship to non-Christian faiths. One cannot confine the Spirit to the church, and one cannot pretend that it actually produces real unity and 'sinless perfection and untroubled beatitude'.[36] What one can say is that the Spirit as modelled on and originating with Jesus is unique to the church. But the operations of the Spirit are always only partially successful, in synergistic co-operation with divided and sinful human wills. Here Calvin was perhaps on stronger ground in insisting upon the 'imputed' nature of human righteousness, which relieves the elect of the burden of having to be more perfect than everyone else.

What Schleiermacher wants to insist upon is that the Spirit must produce some real awareness of God, as disclosed in Jesus. It must make a difference in human experience, and not be a mere speculative or legalistic but external transaction. Perhaps one could say that the Spirit communicates a vivid sense of God as disclosed in Jesus, and urges and helps towards the imitation of Jesus, and a real fellowship in union with him. 'The reminiscent apprehension of Christ must grow into a spontaneous imitation of him'.[37]

The church is an imperfect image of the kingdom, whose perfection lies in the future. In fact it might be better to say that the divided church presents many partial images of the kingdom, and that no part of it claims to *be* the kingdom, but to open the way to the kingdom, to plant the seeds of it in human hearts. Just as Jesus proclaimed that the kingdom was at hand, so the church, his body, has the vocation to continue his work by proclaiming the immanence of God's rule in the Spirit, its inwardness, its real if partial effectiveness, and its promise of ultimate fulfilment. Schleiermacher admits that 'each individual is . . . an imperfect image'.[38] But he concludes

---

[33] Ibid. 123, p. 569. [34] Ibid. 121, p. 563. [35] Ibid. 125, p. 578.
[36] Ibid. 123, p. 572. [37] Ibid. 122, p. 568. [38] Ibid. 123, p. 580.

that 'the perfect image of Christ is only to be found in the sum-total of all the forms'.

One might well think that a perfect whole cannot be comprised of imperfect parts, and that it would be better to admit that there is no perfect image of Christ on earth. Yet the task of the church is to work continually towards the actualization of such an image, towards a universal fellowship of love, creativity, and compassion. It may, however, be unduly limiting to insist that such a fellowship will only exist *within* the church, much less within some branch of the evangelical church. Just as many churches present different aspects of the image of Christ, so perhaps many religions present different ways of understanding the coming global community. The church's vocation would then consist in communicating the distinctive experience of God through the Spirit, which is patterned on Christ, but offered to the whole world, as a contribution to the building-up of a wider fellowship.

The church would not exist in order to make everyone a member of it, to include all (a model Schleiermacher still espouses). It would exist to help to promote true human flourishing, to serve all. But it could hold that its delineation of the nature of God as love, of the human goal as that of creating a universal fellowship with God, and of the way to that goal as participation in the love of God, is correct. To that extent, it would naturally think it would be good if all would freely choose to be members of it. But it might not expect this to happen, given human nature and the plurality of human cultures and temperaments.

So the church will in fact remain a distinctive community, which sees itself as the 'locus of the Spirit in the human race', and as striving to be conformed to the image of Christ.[39] It has an essential particularity. The Spirit has its form and origin in Jesus. But it is orientated to the widest human unity, a unity of love given by the power of God.

SCHLEIERMACHER'S IDEA OF A LIBERAL CHURCH

Schleiermacher, as a Protestant theologian, affirms Scripture as the sufficient norm for Christian doctrine. At the same time, he accepts that Scripture must be investigated by the same critical methods that

---

[39] F. Schleiermacher, *Christian Faith*, 126, p. 583.

apply to any ancient writings. He holds that 'the sense for the truly apostolic is a gift of the Spirit that is gradually increasing in the church'.[40] That is, even the fixation of the canon may be subject to revision, and the experience of the church thus functions as a criterion for interpreting Scripture. While he rejects tradition as an independent source of authority, he does accept that the testimony of Christian experience and the resources of critical scholarship, though they are fallible, must be used in interpreting and applying Scripture in the church. He looks for the 'gradual retirement' of the Old Testament into the background, relegating it to being an appendix to the New.

One thing he could not see was how limited his understanding of Jewish tradition was, how much life that tradition still contains, and how Christian understanding of Jesus was over a hundred years later to be transformed by recovering a stress on the Jewishness of Jesus. Perhaps here again there is a lesson, that it is positively good to preserve a plurality of interpretative traditions, precisely because of the fallibility and partiality of each. One might formulate the 'Protestant Principle'[41] by saying that it is not tradition that is to be rejected, but its claims to inerrancy, unrevisability, and completeness.

With regard to ministry and sacraments, Schleiermacher remains firmly in the Calvinist tradition, seeking a way between the *ex opere operato* view of the Catholic Church, which he regards as 'magical' because it operates automatically, and the Zwinglian view that sacraments are simply external ceremonies. Like Calvin, he stresses the need for personal, experiential regeneration by encounter with the love of God, and the essentially social nature of the sacraments, as incorporation into and maintenance of life in the body of Christ.

The evangelical spirit, he holds, 'concedes to every Christian the right of leadership',[42] and forbids any sharp distinction between ordained and lay Christians. Moreover, 'no individual or small group of individuals can represent Christ'.[43] It has often been said that Protestantism helped to give rise to a sense of individualism. But in fact it always sought to promote a strong sense of community and fellowship, while denying any essential hierarchy in

---

[40] Ibid. 130, p. 603.
[41] Cf. Paul Tillich, *Systematic Theology* (Welwyn: James Nisbet, 1968), i. 252.
[42] Schleiermacher, *Christian Faith*, 134, p. 617.
[43] Ibid. 134, p. 615.

the community. 'Both legislative action and administrative action derive ultimately from the congregation.'[44] The Protestant fellowship is much more egalitarian in principle, and is sensitive about associating any person (in a 'priestly' way) too closely with Christ. In the Lord's supper, the celebrant does not speak *in persona Christi*. The whole fellowship gathers *in persona Christi*, and the celebrant speaks on its behalf, while the only true priest is Christ, present in the fellowship.

Despite this difference from Catholic tradition about the ministry, Schleiermacher insists that Christ does act in the church (though not only there), and acts specifically (though not solely) through the sacraments. So baptism is 'the reception of an individual into the Christian fellowship and his justification or regeneration', in one and the same act.[45] God forgives all who repent and trust in him, but people need to know that they are forgiven, and by whom, and what true forgiveness is. Baptism declares, on the authority of Christ, that they are forgiven. They are forgiven by the God who was fully present in Christ, whose character is shown in him, and whose authority he had. Baptism shows that true forgiveness is not a solitary remission of punishment, but a placing within the fellowship of new life, wherein one can be sanctified by the love of Christ.

Thus the Reformed view of baptism aims to stress an actual fellowship of the church more than the Catholic view it opposes, which permitted baptism to be a private ritual that washed away original guilt with or without the faith either of a participating community or of the recipient. 'The fruit of baptism is . . . not merely the remission of sin but also living union with Christ.'[46] So in baptism there should be the participation of the whole fellowship, and a presentation of the word of God, which makes the meaning of life in the body of Christ clear.

Infant baptism is on such a view acceptable as incorporation into the church, though it requires a real connection with the fellowship of the church within which the child can grow, aimed at a later profession of faith to consummate it. He concludes by leaving infant baptism as a matter of parental choice, and hoping to achieve reconciliation between Baptists and others, if only both will accept the practice of the other as a valid option.

---

[44] Schleiermacher, *Christian Faith*, 145, p. 667.   [45] Ibid. 136, p. 619.
[46] Ibid. 136, p. 626.

As with baptism, so with the Lord's supper, he opposes only those who deny any conjunction between participation in the bread and wine and spiritual participation in Christ, on the one hand, and those who 'regard this connexion as independent of the act of participation', on the other.[47] The worshipper must share in communion with the Lord and with others in the fellowship. Outside that double participation, that is, outside the context of eucharistic action, the sacrament loses its proper context and meaning.

Like Calvin, he rejects any notion of the eucharist as a sacrifice, and on much the same grounds. The idea would render Christ's redeeming work insufficient without the sacrifice of the Mass; the priesthood of all believers would be compromised; and ideas of purchasable merit might be encouraged. We can now see how a fully Catholic view might avoid these corruptions, so that they might cease to be obstacles to fellowship between Christians. He is at pains to admit that no one has found a satisfactory account of how the body and blood of Christ can be present and communicated in bread and wine. So he hopes for a future convergence of Lutheran, Calvinist, and Zwinglian interpretations. We are now in the happy position of being able to include the Catholic and Orthodox traditions among those who confess to being unable to provide a complete account, and who are prepared to accept differences of emphasis in such difficult matters, together with a restraint from insisting on exclusive interpretations which have proved misleading to others.

Liberal faith, feeling less assured of its dogmatic formulations, and being more aware of their rootedness in particular philosophies and historical contexts, is ready to reinterpret received formulae and search for more conciliatory interpretations, or live with doctrinal diversity. That is perhaps the main point on which Schleiermacher takes the Reformed position beyond Calvin, and points forward to a truly ecumenical, that is, a pluralistic, Christian faith.

This pluralism does not extend beyond Christianity. He sees redemption (liberation into perfect God-consciousness) as beginning with Christ, as spreading throughout the whole world, and as reaching its consummation when truth is perfectly grasped by all, perfect unity of fellowship is achieved, and sin has ceased to exist. Most commentators have questioned whether a 'description of Christian consciousness' could generate so much, or could justify

---

[47] Ibid. 140, p. 644.

the limitation of redemption to the Christian church. One cannot be sure, on the ground of personal experience, that Jesus is the one and only person who is not in need of redemption, and that he is the only source of redemptive activity. If redemption is the increase of God-consciousness, it seems to exist in many faiths other than the Christian.

Schleiermacher's own earlier work, the *Speeches on Religion*, speaks much more liberally about religion being founded on 'the sensibility and taste for the Infinite',[48] and represents all religions as images of the Infinite in the finite. Certainly, these images are more or less morally and rationally adequate, but there seems little a priori reason to suppose that only one religion will be so adequate as to supersede all others. This is especially so if the Christian awareness of God is particularized as an awareness of God in the person of Jesus, who is then regarded as in some sense divine. This claim is one that may never be accepted by all. Jews and Muslims are unable to accept the divinity of any human being, and those in the Indian trad-itions are unable to accept a restriction of this divinity to just one person. So, while Christians may be correct in giving Jesus absolute uniqueness, this is not likely to be a belief which will supersede all others because of some obvious superiority it possesses.

One might even suggest that the superiority which Schleiermacher finds in Christianity is in fact the superiority of a critical and tolerant outlook which is open to scientific advances and free of repressive social pressures. One would then need to reflect that this version of Christian faith came very late in the day, and is by no means charac-teristic of all Christian churches even now. It was only tremulously possible in the Prussia of Schleiermacher's time, where there still existed very definite limits on the sorts of tolerance that were accept-able, and where the influence of post-Revolutionary France was regarded by the authorities with suspicion.

One might reflect, also, that other religious traditions are in prin-ciple open to such a liberalization, given the right social circum-stances, so that Christian superiority is in this respect contingent on socio-economic factors which may easily, and which probably will, change. Even more tellingly, it is precisely liberalization that puts all appeals to sheer authority and tradition in question, and that was

---

[48] Schleiermacher, *On Religion*, trans. Richard Crouter (Cambridge: Cambridge University Press, 1988), Second Speech, p. 103.

bound to lead to a severe critical questioning of the biblical testimonies to the fundamental claims of orthodox Christianity. Schleiermacher himself was prepared to regard all accounts of the miraculous as legendary. This would extend to the virgin birth of Jesus, his miracles, and his resurrection. Why should it not extend also to his claims to unique authority and experience of God? Before long it would, and the assertion that Jesus was uniquely God-conscious would be seen to be indefensible on the sort of grounds—of experience—Schleiermacher proposed.

One might still be able to speak of experience of God as the true basis of religion, and of 'churches' as fellowships for communicating particular traditions of such experience. But there would be less reason for supposing that the Christian fellowship, founded on communicating an experience of God through the presence of the Spirit which is patterned on the remembered life of Jesus, would supersede all others, and become 'the ultimate world-shaping power'. There would be less reason for supposing that Christian experience is intrinsically superior to all others. And there would be less reason for insisting upon the uniqueness of Jesus, as the only absolutely God-conscious man. It is not surprising that both Reformed and Catholic Christians adopted a defensive attitude to this new liberalism, and saw it as a dangerous attack upon the final and definitive truth of the revealed Christian faith.

THE BARTHIAN REACTION: THE CHURCH'S ROLE IN THE WORLD

The crucial question is whether liberal forms of faith can still be called Christian in a meaningful sense, or whether that really matters. In the hands of Kant and Hegel—also Prussians—the Christian church was seen either as the precurser of a true ethical commonwealth or of the true priesthood of philosophers, which would establish Christianity as true on purely speculative grounds. In both cases Christianity, in its Reformed or Lutheran form, is seen as the absolutely superior religion. But in both cases similar problems occur—namely, is a universal moral community or a final, all-inclusive, philosophical system what Jesus and his community of disciples was really concerned with? And can Christianity really claim intrinsic superiority when other traditions could, without too much difficulty, make similar claims?

In the twentieth century Karl Barth, standing in the same Reformed tradition as Schleiermacher, initiated a reaction to the liberal programme that is often known as 'neo-orthodoxy'. He rejected any appeal to general human experience, morality, or reason as a foundation for Christian faith, and reverted to something like Calvin's own proposal that God's revelation in Jesus Christ is the only foundation for faith. That revelation is not accepted because it is the most reasonable, judged by some neutral criterion, or because it gives the best morality or sort of religious experience. There is no neutral ground from which to make such comparative judgements. So one has to take one's stand simply on the proclaimed word, which is accepted because of the action of the Holy Spirit enabling one to recognize the proclamation as true.

This reversion to revelationalism, and the refusal to allow faith in Jesus as the Christ to be based on general humanly accepted criteria, may seem to be at the opposite pole of religious thought from that of Schleiermacher's defence of religious piety in general against its cultured despisers. In some ways it is. But Barth, like Schleiermacher, founds Christian faith on a form of personal experience—encounter with the living Christ in the power of the Spirit—and mounts a massive apologetic for Christianity which is deeply indebted to the heritage of the Prussian Enlightenment. The Hegelian triune Spirit which expresses itself in time stalks the pages of the *Church Dogmatics*, and even while protesting against 'liberal subjectivism', Barth uses concepts and insights developed from the objects of his attacks. Moreover, both Schleiermacher and Barth oppose the rationalist Enlightenment idea that there is a universal Reason upon whose deliverances true religion is founded. Instead, they find the heart of religion in the distinctive experience of religious community, an experience which is evoked, in Christianity, by encounter with the person of Jesus.

In contrast to Schleiermacher, however, Barth absolutely rejects any suggestion that the church is one religious community among others of a comparable sort. Other communities are products of human desire for fellowship, whereas the church is brought into existence by God as the body, the unique 'earthly-historical form' of the living Lord.[49]

---

[49] Karl Barth, *Church Dogmatics*, vol. iv, p. 3, 2nd half, para. 72, trans. G. W. Bromiley (Edinburgh: T. & T. Clark, 1962), 681.

This community is uniquely called by God, in a way unparalleled in human history (except in Judaism, which is a preparation for this fuller call). And it is called, in a way not paralleled even in Judaism, to be, in a sense to be carefully defined, the historical form of the living Lord. There is a clear danger in calling something a 'divine community'. Barth is very aware of it, and points out that the church has sometimes been tempted to 'understand and set up itself . . . as a direct representation of Jesus Christ, its existence as a vicariate, its action as a direct repetition and continuation of His'.[50] 'This', he says, 'is the very thing which it must not do.' The church has a ministry of witness to, but not of identity with Christ. It is what it ought to be only when it points beyond itself to its Lord, who indeed speaks through the church when it witnesses truly to him.

Like Calvin, Barth has a strong doctrine of election, which does not depend at all upon human desire or volition, but comes through the good pleasure of God alone. However, there is one major departure from Calvin's doctrine in Barth, which introduces a basic paradox into his doctrine of the church. Schleiermacher had distinguished between the called and the elect, holding that the former are in a realm of preparatory grace while the latter are in the presence of the kingdom of God, the fellowship of the Spirit. He thereby moved from an exclusivist Calvinist doctrine that the church is the company of those who are saved from damnation towards the view that the church has the function of progressively preparing the world for the reception of the Spirit. The church is not only the community that receives the Spirit, but also the community that communicates the Spirit more widely, until it will one day be known throughout the world. The problem this leaves is of all those who have never been touched by the church, and so who are not even within the realm of preparatory grace. Schleiermacher's earlier work suggests that the solution to this problem may lie partly in that other faiths are also media of preparatory grace, which can be fully and explicitly given only in a post-mortem existence. It must be said, however, that he is not wholly clear on either of these points.

Barth makes a similar move more explicitly and boldly, maintaining that the function of the church is to be 'the provisional representation of the calling of all humanity and indeed of all creatures as it has taken place in Him'.[51] God does not call a few to salvation,

---

[50] Ibid. 836.   [51] Ibid. 836.

and place them within the church. God calls all creatures to salvation, and the church is the witness to His calling, not the place in which alone they can be saved. The latter view, which has existed in the evangelical dogmatic tradition as well as in the traditional self-understanding of the Roman Catholic Church, he sees as a sort of 'holy egoism',[52] which fails to see that the church is called not simply to exist, but for a specific task. The church is sent throughout the world to make known that the world has already been reconciled to God in Christ, and to call the world to acknowledge that fact in gratitude and hope.

The paradox in Barth's way of putting it is that other religions are not, for him, channels of genuine grace. Only the church proclaims the word of God. Yet what it proclaims is that God has acted to redeem all creation. How can it do so, for those who never hear its voice? The desire to proclaim that God wills to redeem all is in tension with the desire to say that only in the church, and particularly in Jesus Christ as its origin, is salvation possible.

If the church witnesses to the universal possibility of salvation, then it seems precluded from asserting that it is the only channel of revelation and grace, for such a possibility must be present to every life. So there must be some revelation and saving grace, however hidden or disguised, everywhere. And if God acts everywhere, why not in non-Christian faiths? In which case the church could claim to be the completion or confirmation of all the ways of God, as it has often claimed to be of ancient Hebrew religion. Or at least it could claim to be the authentic witness of what that completion is to be.

Such a view of the church seems to be confirmed by Barth's assertion that there is no secular world which is excluded from the grace and providence of God. 'The community would be guilty of a lack of faith and discernment if it were seriously to see and understand world history as secular.'[53] That is, the church is not opposed to the world as a remnant free from the spiral towards destruction which characterizes a secular world, estranged from God. Rather, the whole world is under the providence of God, and the church's task is precisely to testify to that fact, and to help the world at large to acknowledge it, and thus begin to co-operate consciously with God's purpose. So Barth can speak of the church as the 'inner circle', to which it is given to discern and co-operate with God's

---

[52] Karl Barth, 767.   [53] Ibid. 687.

Spirit, and the world as a whole as the 'outer circle', which does not recognize the Spirit, which is nevertheless always at work to reconcile the world to God. 'The church . . . is the people which exists in the divinely given knowledge of the new reality of world-occurrence concealed in Jesus Christ, and in the resultant and distinctive resoluteness of its confidence.'[54]

So Barth insists that 'the community of Jesus Christ is for the world'.[55] It is not simply set over against the world, but is the agent of the whole world's redemption. This is so in three particular ways. It is, first, 'the fellowship in which it is given to men to know the world as it is'.[56] The church makes people aware of God, of estrangement from God, and of the destructive consequences of that estrangement. It is, secondly, 'the society in which it is given to men to know and practise their solidarity with the world'. The church is not set over against the world, as a saved remnant over against the damned, or as a gathered community of the morally perfect over against the sinful. Its destiny is bound up with the destiny of the world. It must never abandon its solidarity with the world by offering a purely other-worldly redemption. And it must never claim to be exempt from the sinful structures of the world, of which it is inseperably part. It is, thirdly, 'the society in which it is given to men to be under obligation to the world'.[57] The church has the obligation to bring the world to know of its redemption in Christ, and to open the possibility of consciously responding to that redemption. Just as Jesus gave his life for the world, so the church must set itself to serve the world by healing, reconciling, forgiving, and encouraging. Even if it remains one small community or set of communities, its vocation will be to serve the whole human community in love—not to preach its doom.

Barth is not so far away from Schleiermacher as he sometimes makes it sound. Both have a concern for the salvation of the whole world, not just for a chosen few. Both see the church as concerned very much with those who are not members of it, and as preparing the way for redemption for all. Both see the heart of the gospel as a calling into fellowship, which makes the church a real, locally diverse, but globally united instrument of the Holy Spirit. Both see Christ as the only saviour, the only human being who is the mediator between God and humanity, and the source of redemption. Just

---

[54] Ibid. 721.   [55] Ibid. 762.   [56] Ibid. 769.   [57] Ibid. 776.

as Schleiermacher faces a major difficulty in claiming that experience alone can show that Jesus is unique, so Barth faces a surprisingly similar difficulty in claiming that revelation alone shows that Jesus is unique. Experience of God is widely shared, and looks very similar, in many religious traditions. Claims to final revelation are also widely shared, and look very similar in different religions, thus making it implausible to insist that the Christian claim is the only genuine one, or that the Christian church is the only genuinely redemptive community.

The church, as the witness to God's universal salvific activity, can nevertheless claim distinctiveness as the only religious community which claims to be the earthly-historical form of its Lord. It receives the Holy Spirit, patterned on Christ, as the source of its life, and communicates that Spirit to the world, as mediator of Christ's redeeming presence to the world. That does not mean that it is the only genuine vehicle of divine revelation, or that it is not subject to rational or moral assessment in terms partly of extra-Christian (though undoubtedly still historically occasioned) criteria, which often bring to light internal Christian criteria which had remained unnoticed or underemphasized.

Ironically, Barth's own theology may be a good example of the way in which extra-Christian considerations bring into focus aspects of the tradition which had not previously been highlighted, or had even been widely denied. It is no coincidence that Barth's concern for the possible salvation of all, and for seeing the church as a witness to this universal possibility rather than as the only ark of salvation, comes in the German-speaking cultural context of Kant and Hegel. They insisted, respectively, on the universalizability of one's moral concerns and on religion as presenting in symbolic form truths which are rooted in basic features of the universal human situation. The widening of the Reformed tradition which Barth exemplifies can be seen in part as a Christian reaction to these influences, which incorporates much of the approach it is reacting against. In that sense, Barthian neo-orthodoxy remains dependent on the liberal tradition.

THE CHURCH: THE POST-ENLIGHTENMENT TRADITION

If the church really presents a universal possibility of salvation, and if it is the instrument, rather than the embodiment, of the Holy Spirit, it is hard to see the church as the only vehicle of God's true revelation and salvific will. Rather, it will be a witness to and a focal point of God's universal action, which is both kenotic and unitive, self-giving and life-giving. That action is universal, but in the church it is recognized and mediated in a form that has been brought to focused consciousness.

Because the church is the body of Christ primarily as the instrument of the Holy Spirit, Barth wishes to question any claims for a fuller embodiment, such that the church becomes in a sense 'another Christ', or that its historically conditioned institutional structures reflect those of the actualized kingdom. Standing in the Reformed tradition, Barth, like Schleiermacher, rejects a hierarchical view of the church, for which unity is achieved by obedience to one leader or group of leaders. Nothing must compromise the sole headship of Christ, and nothing must undermine the freedom of Christian conscience to follow only its Lord, and not any human institution, however exalted, in unconditional obedience. So there may properly be many forms of Christian fellowship, depending upon diverse historical and cultural circumstances. 'We may welcome and encourage the rise and continuation of particular fellowships of the few or the many within the general fellowship of all Christians.'[58] The unity of the community may be better expressed in a plurality of visible fellowships than in one structural form, as long as they live in fellowship with one another. The church is a unity of different particular forms of fellowship, each of which can take its part in witnessing in various ways to the universal redemptive work of Jesus Christ.

With the rejection of hierarchy goes the rejection of any interpretation of the 'power of the keys' which would be an exercise of hierarchical power to include or exclude from the kingdom. On Barth's view, no one has the power to exclude from the kingdom, or even to guarantee, by their own authority, that one has a place in the kingdom. The power 'primarily and properly is to be referred to the function of the community in and in relation to the world'.[59] All the church can do is proclaim the word of God. That is a word of forgiveness, which frees humans from their sins, while, if it is not received in faith, it 'binds' them, or leaves them under the bondage of sin. Barth even suggests that if the word is not received, that is because the work of the church is 'not done or done badly', so that

---

[58] Ibid. 856.   [59] Ibid. 861.

the church excludes instead of pointing to the 'door which is open to all'. The keys can only be used to open the door of forgiveness. By this work, 'God Himself is either glorified or compromised and shamed in His work'.[60]

For Barth, it is clear that the church is the fellowship, the whole community, and not a hierarchy set apart by ordination. Correspondingly the sacraments are the actions of the community 'by which it establishes fellowship'.[61] In baptism people are received into membership of the people of those called to be God's witnesses. In the Lord's supper this fellowship is kept in unity. 'They are significatory actions in which men . . . both come and are together'. This is not, however, simply a human action. The action of God is 'the prototype, the meaning and the power of the visible and significatory action of the community'. In these admittedly vague phrases, Barth keeps alive the thought that God is acting in and through the community, just as he acts in and through the proclamation of Jesus Christ. But whereas God in Jesus assumes the whole personality to be a perfect expression of the divine will, in the church God acts through an imperfect instrument, though one commissioned to be an authorized instrument through its connection to Jesus in faith. The sacraments are not invalidated by the imperfection of its human ministers, though the calling of this community is indeed to realize as well as it can the fellowship of love within which individuals can properly find both moral and personal fulfilment in God.

Though Barth presents himself as standing in reaction to liberal theology, what he really rejects is the transformation of Christian faith into a form of universal morality (Kant) or speculative metaphysics (Hegel). Like Schleiermacher, he wishes to argue for a distinctively religious component, which lies in the response of the individual to the calling of God, within a fellowship which is to proclaim this calling throughout the world. Both Schleiermacher and Barth are post-Enlightenment theologians, rejecting literalistic readings and institutionally authoritative interpretations of Scripture, and founding faith upon a personal response to a transforming encounter with God.

For both, God's action in Jesus is uniquely revelatory of God's nature and purpose, though that uniqueness can only be known through a personal experience of the grace of God working inwardly.

---

[60] Karl Barth, 862.   [61] Ibid. 901.

For both, the church is a non-hierarchical fellowship whose function it is to proclaim the liberating act of God in Jesus throughout the world, and thereby play a part in bringing all to the possibility of salvation. For both, the church is not an excluding community, dividing the world into saved and damned. It is a witnessing community, proclaiming God's universal will to save, and communicating that salvation to those who are attracted to it. The church is not a uniquely inerrant teaching authority, miraculously preserved from error, as a privileged exception to general human fallibility. Everyone in it makes mistakes, just as they often sin, but in so far as it preserves the witness to God's saving acts God acts through it despite all its imperfections.

This sort of post-Enlightenment Protestantism should not be confused with a secular Enlightenment commitment to the supremacy of pure reason and complete human autonomy. It is founded on an insistence on personal experience of God as the basis of living faith, and on an insistence that such experience must be shaped and contextualized within the fellowship of those whose experience of God is traced back to the person of Jesus of Nazareth. It is influenced by the Enlightenment ideals of a morality that cares for the fulfilment of every human life, and an intellectual perspective that provides a justifiable and comprehensive view of the totality of human experience and history. But it insists upon distinctive Christian commitment to an encounter with the commanding, liberating, fulfilling God known in Jesus and made present in the life of the church.

The vocation of the church is not to say that only in Jesus is salvation to be found, in the sense that nowhere else is salvation possible. It is to witness to God's saving action in Jesus, and make that action present throughout the world, and for all people. In the many forms of its historical existence, in all their ambiguity and imperfection, Christians in the post-Enlightenment tradition would see the church as, by God's grace, the 'earthly-historical form of the Lord', the continuing vehicle of God's universal and unrestricted forgiving and reconciling activity in human history.

13
The Meaning of History

THE PLURALITY OF CHRISTENDOM

One central paradox of Christianity is that it is a faith which recommends humility and compassion, but which has for most of its history been closely associated with the expansion and disintegration of proud and aggressive military empires. The Byzantine Empire collapsed into a set of insecure Orthodox national states. The Holy Roman Empire was finally dissolved by Napoleon, leaving Western Europe divided into Protestant and Catholic states. The European powers founded new empires in the Americas, Africa, India, and Australasia, which in turn split into many states of various Protestant and Catholic affiliations (India remaining, like most of Asia, largely resistant to Christian missionary efforts). Meanwhile Europe demonstrated that religion is not the only cause of war by a series of continuing national conflicts that culminated in two world wars of such savage ferocity that belief in a providential God was shaken to its roots.

In the aftermath of those wars, and of the attempted elimination of Jews in Germany, the secular liberal dream of an advance of all humanity through education to universal peace was shattered. The arena of human history was perceived to be a more brutal and irrational place, where the hungry drive of the will to power was a more potent factor than the calm voice of universal reason. This should not have been a surprise to Christians, with their doctrine of original sin. But one widespread nineteenth-century Christian revision of early apocalyptic beliefs had been to look for the coming of the kingdom of God in history, by a gradual but inevitable process. In undermining that belief, the great wars of the twentieth century led to perplexity about whether any providential plan could be seen in history at all, and to a gnawing doubt that Christian civilization, which had collapsed in such barbarity in Europe, was in fact the leading world-influence that it had once been imagined to be.

One result of this perplexity was an internal rebellion against all imperial forms of Christianity. 'Christian civilization', which even in such a liberal theologian as Schleiermacher had assumed that (Protestant) Christianity was clearly the most advanced of faiths, and was destined to take over the world, was seen in a very different light by those who found it to be a tool of European colonialist policies, and at least an implicit support of Aryan racism (Schleiermacher's belief that Judaism was a dead religion was one symptom of this).

The rebellion took different, more or less radical, forms. Within Europe, radical theologies that questioned the existence of an objective, providential God, and that tended to interpret Jesus as one mythologically symbolized and almost wholly legendary figure among many others, arose. Such theologies naturally suggest a form of what may be called alethic pluralism, which asserts that many, or even all, religious traditions are more or less equally true, since they all embody sets of mythical symbols which represent 'different ways of experiencing, conceiving and living in relation to an ultimate divine Reality which transcends all our varied visions of it'.[1]

This is an inherently unstable position, since in renouncing all objective truth-claims, it interprets each faith as an aesthetically or ethically chosen way of life, which has no greater justifiable claim to acceptance than any other. But it naturally follows that there is no particular reason to accept any specific faith, unless one finds it personally appealing. It cannot claim to give a correct, or true, account of the way things are, and so it might not be thought worth serious consideration by those who are concerned about questions of truth in religion.

While this extreme form of pluralism is unlikely to have lasting appeal, some of the main considerations that have given rise to it will remain important. Scriptural texts cannot reasonably continue to claim immunity from historical and textual criticism. Particular faith commitments can no longer ignore the apparently equally justifiable faith commitments of other traditions. The scientific world-view makes a reinterpretation of many pre-scientific religious beliefs necessary. Changing social and economic conditions generate new moral problems and perceptions that religious traditions partly rooted in ancient tribal customs and taboos are not well equipped to tackle.

---

[1] John Hick, *An Interpretation of Religion* (London: Macmillan, 1989), 235–6.

The impact of these considerations is to force a revision of religious traditions in a generally more self-critical, pluralistic, and reconstructive way. If alethic pluralism is rejected, there is good reason to accept epistemic pluralism, the recognition that people apprehend the ultimate framework of their lives in different ways. Those different ways cannot all be equally correct, but because of limited human knowledge and rationality, and because of the diversity of cultural histories and conceptual frameworks, one can no longer insist on the clear superiority of one's own view, and the irrelevance of other views to an adequate apprehension of ultimate truth.

To the extent that all religious traditions are influenced by such considerations, one might expect them to develop an acceptance of religious diversity. Perhaps, in an ideal world, all would agree on one truth. But in a world such as this, the existence of many traditions may play a positive role in helping self-criticism, overcoming myopia, and encouraging development. So one might expect the growth of a fluid and overlapping diversity of liberal interpretations of various religious traditions, as instantaneous global communications enable connections to be made between hitherto epistemically isolated traditions. The liberal religious world will be more confusing, more informed, less easily labelled, and more disposed to cooperative ventures in religious and social practice and action.

There will not be one global religion, the 'coming world religion' of older liberal dreams. But the old, allegedly definitive boundary-lines between traditions may be less rigid, and alliances once thought impossible may flourish. In such a world, where Christian faith will be part of the 'world-wide web' of faiths, the older Christian ecumenical movement may become obsolete, engulfed by wider global movements that seek fluid and changing alliances between many diverse traditions. A continual proliferation of interpretative schools may occur, as the old imperial attempts to enforce authority from one central point fade into irrelevance, and locally led groups explore, with more local commitment but more global awareness, new ways of living out the vision of God which the church has discerned in Jesus.

There is a place for the institution of the church in such a future. But its teaching authority will be more that of advice and guidance in sound scholarship, than a defensive reassertion of ancient dogmatic formulae. Its sacramental life will be more the offer of the unconditional and personal love of God to encourage human flourishing in an equitable and just world, than a hierarchical control of the exclusive means to eternal life. And its institutional form will be more one of humble service to the community than of patriarchal dignity and control.

Such a view of the Christian future is anathema to those who view the church as immutably patterned either on tradition or on the Bible. Some members of the Eastern Orthodox churches deplore any attempt to change either the theology or the liturgy of the church, and regard such attempts as destructive of faith. There are those in the Roman Catholic tradition who wish to reaffirm the absolute authority of the church, centred on the Supreme Pontiff, and there have been many movements in that tradition in recent years to dismiss theologians who are critical of the authoritative statements of the church, and to appoint bishops who will hold to traditionally defined and distinctively Roman formulations of faith.

Analogously, there is a huge and continuing expansion of Protestant Christianity throughout the world, particularly in Latin America, Africa, China, and Korea, often under the influence of American fundamentalist churches. All these forms of traditional faith remain vital and flourishing, and are unlikely to lose their appeal. They will remain important social factors in future. What is unclear is how they will relate to one another—traditional Catholics and Protestants all too often seem to hate each other, and in Russia Catholics and the Orthodox have uneasy relations at best—and how they will relate to more liberal forms of Christian belief, which will exist within their own ranks unless forcibly expelled.

There will always be intolerance, myopia, and supremicism in religion, and the important task is to control it by effective forms of socialization. Perhaps this will have to be done by secular authorities curbing the excesses of fanaticism. But the most effective controls must come from within. In that respect, most orthodox traditions do already possess a belief, at least theoretically, in the primacy of conscience, and so a commitment to a form of social pluralism—that those who follow conscience and do not harm others must be tolerated.

It is arguable that negative tendencies in orthodox forms of faith will be contained by the sheer pressure of globalization, and the necessity of accepting diversity in the modern world. More positively, however, the fundamentalist traditions, Orthodox, Catholic, and Protestant, are in principle committed by their basic documents to the promotion of reconciliation and peace. And their loyalty to tradition can be a reminder of the seriousness and self-discipline that faith requires, in the face of the sometimes endlessly pliable compromises that they would see as the chief temptation of liberals. For the foreseeable future, there will remain strictly orthodox forms of faith, concerned to preserve their traditions in faithfulness. But it is likely that their influence will be a more indirect one—they will lose the power to enforce orthodox rules of faith and practice throughout their defined territories, and so they will have to adapt positively to a greater degree of mutual acceptance and coexistence.

Moreover, it is possible that at least the major strands of traditional faith will be encouraged by their interaction with differing traditions to discover within themselves a less exclusive self-interpretation. This is most clearly seen in the work of such contemporary Roman Catholic theologians as Karl Rahner, who uncompromisingly continued to advocate the unique authority of the Roman Catholic Church and the papacy, while yet insisting that the grace of God is universal and not confined to the Roman Catholic Church. Such moves hold the promise of an increasing influence of forms of traditional orthodoxy that can relate positively to other traditions, respecting both their right to exist and their capacity to contribute, however imperfectly, to a more comprehensive theological perspective. While such a view may seem still too paternalistic and arrogant to others, it is vastly better than more exclusive interpretations that regard all other traditions as inspired by the Devil.

THE FUTURES OF CHRISTIANITY

What is likely to change old forms of orthodoxy more than anything else, however, is the expansion of Christianity into the ex-colonial worlds of the Southern Hemisphere and the Far East. As those worlds throw off their colonial past, and seek to establish economic parity with the West, it is very hard to predict what Christianity will look like when it is fully inculturated into Latin American, African, and Asian contexts. It seems likely that much of it will be of a rather uncritical and confrontational nature, locked into pre-scientific world-views and cultural conservatism. Yet the Christian faith is going to look very different when it is incorporated into different cultural histories, and Western forms of 'fundamentalism', both

Catholic and Protestant, may prove to be unacceptably literalistic and culturally limiting in a more global and less Europe-centred world.

There are some indications that the influence of both Rome and America is likely to decrease rapidly, as indigenous churches explore much looser forms of association, and exist in a wide variety of cultural traditions. The emphasis may well be on practice and experience rather than on the intellectual dogmatic tradition of both Catholics and Protestants from the West. It is noteworthy that the Pentecostal churches, with their stress on charismatic experience, have expanded very rapidly throughout the world. There are now over 30,000 Christian denominations world-wide. So it looks as though a positive acceptance of pluralism, an insistence on local, not centralized, organization, and a concentration on the primacy of experience will be the dominant features of global Christianity in the third millennium. Christian fundamentalism may, despite its apparent vitality, be a transient phenomenon, the final gasp of a dying Western tradition. The vibrant young churches of the 'Two Thirds World' may be more concerned with the experience of the Spirit, and the sheer pressure of their numbers may well force the conservative forces of the West to adjust their dogmatic stances to the realities of a truly multicultural world, in which the Spirit acts to foster creative diversity. In a paradoxical way, the sophisticated liberalism of parts of the Western churches aligns with the dynamic experientialism of the churches of South and East in finding many of the intellectual preoccupations of Western imperial Christianity simply irrelevant to the modern situation.

One of the lessons of the past is that one cannot safely predict the future. It is possible that literalistic and simplistic versions of Christianity may dominate whole cultures. But on the other hand, the growth of technology, of travel, and therefore of cross-cultural encounters at all levels, seems unstoppable. So there is reason to hope that more experiential and exploratory, less dogmatic and imperialistic, forms of Christian faith will mark the transfer of the centre of Christian gravity from the West to the Southern and Eastern hemispheres, and mark a new age of creativity for the churches.

A related, but different, anti-imperialist response of Christians as they move into their third millennium is the response of liberation theology. Generally taken as beginning in Latin America, especially with the second conference of Latin American bishops at Medellin in 1968, liberation theology focuses on the plight of the poor, and the apparent indifference of the Catholic hierarchy to it. Theologians such as Gutierrez and Sobrino stressed that the church must adopt a preferential option for the poor, and seek material liberation from poverty and oppression, not just an inner spiritual liberation that leaves unjust social structures in place.[2]

Liberation theology has been influenced by Marxism, which itself can easily be seen as a form of secularized Judaeo-Christian Messianism.[3] For Marx, society is a realm of conflicting interests (an echo of the 'two cities' of Augustine), which generate a dialectical progress towards a classless society (the 'Kingdom of God') through historical struggle. Marx focused on the way the oppressed class was destined to overthrow its oppressors in each historical epoch ('the meek [for Marx, the poor] shall inherit the earth'[4]), and held that persons are the sum of their social relations (arguably a secularized version of the idea of the Trinity as a community of 'persons' who are subsistent relations). Persons cannot be considered in isolation, but owe their beliefs and guiding ideals to their historical and economic situation (the hidden hand of 'providence').

Liberation theologians sought to recapture this terminology, modified by Marx from Hegel—who had thought of himself as the first truly Christian philosopher—for a truly Christian vision of the world. Accordingly, they too emphasized the essentially social and relational nature of personhood, pointed to the way in which persons were alienated from their true selves by the structures of oppression, whether they were oppressed or oppressors, and argued that salvation could only be achieved by a transformation of society which could bring human flourishing to all, even or especially the poorest.

The Roman Catholic Church reacted against many Marxist elements of this theology, especially against the claim that economic forces determine ideology, that progress can come about by revolutionary change, and that 'bourgeois freedom' is actually capitalist oppression.[5] Indeed, a Polish pope knew all too well that in practice

---

[2] Cf. especially G. Gutierrez, *A Theology of Liberation* (Maryknoll, NY: Orbis, 1973), and J. Sobrino, *The True Church and the Poor* (Maryknoll, NY: Orbis, 1984).
[3] Cf. J. Miranda, *Marx and the Bible* (Maryknoll, NY: Orbis, 1974).
[4] Matthew 5: 5.
[5] Thus the Vatican *Instruction on Certain Aspects of the Theology of Liberation*, often called the 'Ratzinger Letter', condemned liberation theology on these and other grounds.

Marxist regimes usually become totalitarian, and that the dictator-ship of the proletariat is unlikely ever to lead to the withering away of the state, and the ideal freedom of a classless society. The church in communist countries offered a different sort of liberation. It offered what was often the only space for freedom of speech and dissent, and it offered an inner spiritual fulfilment that could endure the most hostile material circumstances.

At the end of the twentieth century, rigid Marxist regimes have collapsed throughout most of the world, and the hope for a truly just and completely classless society, to be achieved through revolution-ary violence and dictatorship, seems both idle and dangerous. But some of the basic insights of liberation theology have changed the face of the churches irreversibly. If the church is concerned with the salvation of human persons, it must be concerned with the quest for a just and equitable society. If it is the church of Jesus, it must be concerned especially for the poor, the sick, the outcast, and the oppressed. If it is to be obedient to the will of a Creator God, it must be concerned with the material structures of the world, not just with inner spiritual growth.

So liberation theology signals a renewed concern with the trans-formation of the material world, away from what encourages pride, ambition, and greed, and towards communities of universal com-passion and co-operation, which can work to restore an estranged world to its creative source and goal. A feature of twentieth-century Christianity has been the rise of liberation theologies in many parts of the world, protesting against the injustice of colonial exploitation, against racial and sexual discrimination, and against institutional structures that impede human flourishing.

Socially radical strands of Christianity naturally come into con-flict with conservative ecclesial structures, but one may hope that out of the many ideological struggles that will ensue, one might have a church that is more concerned with universal human flourishing, less encumbered with an imperial past, and more enthusiastic about the prospect of positive social change. One thing that is almost bound to happen is a distancing of the world-wide churches from European imperial structures, which suggests a very different direc-tion for Christian faith in the future. For two thousand years Chris-tianity has been the vehicle of European imperial culture. That situation has now collapsed, and throughout the world there is likely to be a great variety of Christian religious communities, bringing greater, not less, diversity into the Christian faith. Liberal, orthodox, charismatic, and liberationist forms of Christian faith will exist alongside one another, and they will exist within and between the borders of the historic denominations, creating new forms of plurality and interaction. The Christianity of the third millennium is going to be more vibrant and less restrictive, more diverse and less exclusive, than its historical embodiments have so far allowed it to be.

THE AMBIGUITIES OF RELIGION

Religion as a human phenomenon will, however, always remain ambiguous, since it is bound to the ambiguous human nature that constructs its forms. The American theologians Reinhold Niebuhr and Paul Tillich have rightly emphasized the danger of utopian idealizations of religion and religious communities.[6] Tillich identifies two main ambiguities of religion. It tends to reduce itself to moral rules or cultural forms, losing the distinctive element of 'ultimate concern' (profanization), or it tends to elevate something conditional to unconditional validity (demonization).[7] Because these tendencies will always be present in every religious form, 'Religion is not the answer to the quest for unambiguous life, although the answer can only be received through religion.'[8] That answer lies in participation in the spiritual reality underlying every historical form of religion.

Tillich is clear that this reality is not confined to Christianity, and in this respect he extends the thought of Schleiermacher in a way that remained, at best, implicit in the nineteenth-century theologian. The Spirit breaks into all history in revelatory experiences, but in a fragmentary way.[9] In Christ, however, there is a decisive and unambiguous manifestation of the New Being. This manifestation is fragmentarily present in what he calls the 'Spiritual Community'. This is 'an unambiguous, though fragmentary, creation of the divine Spirit'.[10] The Spiritual Community is 'the community of faith and love, participating in the transcendent unity of unambiguous life'.[11] It is the invisible church, in dialectical relation to the visible churches, that both actualize and distort it.

---

[6] R. Niebuhr, *The Nature and Destiny of Man* (New York, Scribner's, 1943), and Tillich, *Systematic Theology* (Welwyn: James Nisbet, 1968), iii.

[7] Tillich, *Systematic Theology*, iii. 105.   [8] Ibid. 113.

[9] Ibid. 149.   [10] Ibid. 159.   [11] Ibid. 184.

The invisible church takes two forms, the latent, in 'an indefinite variety of expressions of faith',[12] both religious and secular, and the manifest, in the churches, though in a fragmentary way. The Spiritual Community is not the 'saved', and it is not merely an unrealized ideal. It is 'essentiality determining existence',[13] the hidden 'essential power' within the churches, the religious communities, or even the secular communities that are grasped by ultimate concern, throughout the world. In its explicit, Christian form, it aims at 'the ultimate reunion of all the estranged members of mankind',[14] and is open to all people. Membership of it should lead to increasing awareness, freedom, relatedness, and transcendence.[15]

Tillich's view of the latent church entails that the Christian church is the particular manifestation of what is universally latent in all human cultures. The latent community will include everyone who is grasped by ultimate concern, whereas the manifest community is the Christian churches. It may well seem that the former is too broad and the latter too narrow to do the jobs Tillich wants. Is it plausible to hold that a total devotion to music is a 'preparation for the full manifestation of the Spiritual Community in a church'?[16] Or that the Christian churches are the full manifestation of all that is potentially good in human nature? It might be better not to speak of 'latent' and 'manifest', as though the church was the fulfilment of every human potentiality, which it fairly obviously is not. The point can be made by insisting that the Spirit of God is at work in every human life and culture, but that the Spirit takes a particular form in the church, which reveals the character of its universal action. The Church identifies the character of the Spirit who is at work everywhere, but it is not either the only place where the Spirit acts, or the fulfilment of every aspect of the Spirit's action.

Christ, for Tillich, is the ultimate criterion of spiritual community, for he is 'the central manifestation of the divine Spirit'.[17] The manifest spiritual community actualizes the principle of resistance to profanization and demonization, and makes possible a radical self-negation and self-transformation. 'It is not Christianity as a religion that is absolute but the event by which Christianity is created and judged.'[18] That revelatory event contains the power to break the power of the demonic, for it criticizes all attempts to give any finite

[12] Ibid. 165.   [13] Ibid. 175.   [14] Ibid. 161.
[15] Ibid. 246.   [16] Ibid. 262.   [17] Ibid. 162.   [18] Ibid. 360.

reality unconditional worth. But any claim by a church 'to represent in its structure the Spiritual Community unambiguously' is demonic.[19] Religion must be overcome by the Spirit, so 'the church is not a religious community but the anticipatory representation of a new reality, the New Being as community'.[20]

This view of the church renounces Schleiermacher's vision of the triumph of the church throughout the world, and it may seem to imply that the goal of a universal and conscious relationship to God through Christ will never be realized. For Tillich, it is indeed doubtful if the 'New Being as community' will ever be actualized, since history is the realm of the fragmentary, the ambiguous, and the anticipatory, and there is no existence beyond history. Is it the case, then, that God's providential plan for human history is doomed to failure, or even that there is no such plan?

The question is fundamentally one of what meaning can be given to the events of human history, and of what part the church plays in the discovery or implementation of that meaning. If the liberal Christian dream of a finally world-conquering church is renounced, and if all history is ambiguous, how can the sort of ultimate meaning Christians claim be found within history? One might find meaning in many things, in good things to be enjoyed, worthwhile purposes to be realized, and fulfilling relationships to be established. Yet huge tracts of human life seem to have no value, even to be such as anyone would seek to avoid. For many human beings, there seems to be no achievable worthwhile purpose or possibility of change, and all personal relationships seem hostile and destructive. Even where purposes and values exist, there seems to be no underlying or larger pattern which would give sense and significance to the way things go. One of the deepest and most persistent questions of human existence is whether there exist true and enduring values, important purposes whereby we might help to realize them, and a morally comprehensible pattern which would set both our enjoyments and sufferings, our successes and failures, in a context that could give them meaning.

A crucial Christian insight is that the meaning of human life is not found in some state that exists after life is over—as though everything in history was an unnecessary preamble, without significance of its own. Yet neither is it found wholly within the process of history—as though what we do and experience in history is all there

---

[19] Tillich, 259.   [20] Ibid. 258.

is to human existence. In some way history must be essential to actualizing the sort of meaning human existence has, and yet it cannot be sufficient to actualize that meaning. In working out his view of providence, and of the role of the church within the divine providence, Tillich seeks to find the right balance between these contrasting emphases.

He stresses that historical existence is essentially concerned with the aims and goals of human persons or groups, which they choose and pursue in freedom, and in which they realize their unique individuality. It is historical existence that makes creative freedom, communal pursuit of purposes, and personal self-realization possible. Only within history can one actualize creativity, self-realizing individuality, and mutual relationality, as new values are brought into being both by building on continuing traditions and by co-operative action, and those values are then appreciated for their intrinsic worth. History, in the proper sense, only exists for personal agents and experients in community, who realize their natures by the co-operative actualization of purposes of new intrinsic value.

It may be thought that, at least for Christians, there is one goal towards which all things strive, one all-embracing purpose which subsumes all others under it. But that is not necessarily the case. There may be many goals, realized in many developing traditions, all of which have distinctive value, that resist subsumption under one inclusive purpose. History drives towards 'harmony . . . newness and fulfilment of being',[21] but there will always be ambiguities and conflicts, failures and negativities, in all historical being. Thus there may be many diverse goals, none of them realized unambiguously.

If there is to be any fulfilment without such restrictions, and any true harmony without conflict, it cannot therefore lie within history. It could, however, lie in a divine consciousness, a consciousness that is aware of all that comes into being in history, that can hold together many diverse values, and envisage the completion of the historically incomplete. In this sense 'the aim of history does not lie in history'.[22] History has an aim that can be realized in no other form of being. That aim is to realize new values in freedom and community. But the full range and depth of such a process of value-realization can only be fully appreciated by an all-embracing divine awareness that can give pattern and some sort of completion to the fragmentary processes of history.

---

[21] Ibid. 354.   [22] Ibid. 332.

From a theistic viewpoint, God co-operates in realizing historical values, and also experiences them in the wider context of the whole of history and of the infinite divine life beyond history. In this way God gives to them a wider meaning, as they creatively particularize possibilities in the divine mind. God can give meaning even to the negativities of historical existence, as they are seen to flow from free-dom in community, and to provide a basis for new forms of value in the future to which God leads all things. The negative never becomes positive in itself, but seen in the full context of divine experience and co-operative action its presence can be understood, and can be seen never to be outside the scope of the divine creative and renewing activity. In that sense it will be given meaning, though it will never be given value. It is the cosmic action and consciousness of God that gives a moral pattern to events, enabling even negative experiences to have meaning in relation to their eventual placing within the awareness of God.

The fulfilment of the aim that can only be undertaken in history lies beyond history, in that its historical actualization can only be given its full meaning and value when it is seen *sub specie aeternitatis*, in the light of the all-embracing experience and universally redemp-tive activity of God. What this means for each historical moment is that it must be seen in its context of a process of the realization or frustration of value, which will in turn be brought under the provi-dential action of God in due course. It must be seen in its full rela-tionality, its dependence upon other persons and upon a developing tradition of experience and action, and its positive or negative rela-tion to the aims and acts of God. It must be seen as contributing to the divine experience a distinctive and irreplaceable element which will be transformed by the wider context of the divine life.

Only God can see each historical event in that way, and so only God sees the full meaning and value of the events of human history. Or, to put it in the language of Tillich, there is a 'permanent eleva-tion of history into eternity',[23] which involves a return to what a thing essentially is, 'in so far as the essential has conquered existential dis-tortion'.[24] For Tillich, this is not to be thought of as a temporal event, coming after earthly existence, for 'eternity is the inner aim, the *telos* of the created finite'.[25]

Since all historical events find their essentialization in eternity,

[23] Tillich, 425.   [24] Ibid. 427.   [25] Ibid. 426.

one may expect that there will be particular historical events which are disclosive of the inner meaning and value which belongs, in principle, to all events. Such disclosive events will give creatures some share in the experience and activity of God (of 'Being-itself', for Tillich), so that they may at least glimpse how particular events are integrated into the one coherent divine experience, and how they are woven into the universally redemptive activity of God. Disclosive events will give a foretaste of that sharing in God's life that is the eternal destiny of all created persons.

In developing his view, Tillich lists six general interpretations of historical existence, which he rejects in favour of a seventh, Christian interpretation. The Greek view sees time as a cyclical process determined by fate, in the face of which the sage and hero show a doomed but resolute courage. The mystical view finds liberation in a non-historical state. It exhibits an admirable 'compassion for the universality of suffering',[26] but contains 'no impulse to transform history in the direction of universal humanity and justice'. The mechanistic view sees human life as a subsidiary accident in a purposeless process. Tillich rejects these views as allowing no place for creative and purposeful activity in history.

More positive views are the 'infinite progress' view, the utopian view of a final state of peace and justice, and a transcendental belief in a heavenly realm after death, with no hope for transforming the world at all. These views are rejected as either too optimistic or as, in the final case, disallowing all hope of a dynamic transformation of the world.

Tillich thus seeks to weave a way between the optimism of an achievable earthly perfection (utopianism) and the pessimism of the pointlessness and futility of all purposive action (despair). He wants to see the Spirit at work to transform the world, but allows 'the impossibility of an earthly fulfilment'.[27]

History remains the realm of divine creative and redemptive activity. But since its fulfilment lies beyond history, one should not conceive of the meaning of history as lying in an inevitable progress towards one supreme final state. Each moment of history must find fulfilment in God, and each individual life must find realization in trans-historical form. So one cannot think of the past as simply a preliminary to a future desirable existence, or of individuals as

[26] Ibid. 376.   [27] Ibid. 383.

simply contributors of experience to God. While historical existence is important, that does not entail any idea of linear progress towards a historical goal of perfection. Each age and each individual, one might say, is equally important to God. This is one way in which one can interpret the eschatalogical teachings of early Christianity. The goal of the completed kingdom of God is not far away in the future. It must be seen as the fulfilment of every time, and so as imminent in every present as its fulfilled future. The trans-historical future of the kingdom is the realized Form of the actualizing present. So the kingdom is at hand at every moment of time,[28] while historical time continues to provide the possibility of new actualizations of value and personal potentiality.

JESUS AND THE MEANING OF HISTORY

History continues to be the realm in which new values come into being. And there clearly has been progress of a sort in history. From the hunter-gatherer cultures of early *homo sapiens* to the instant global communications of the twentieth century there has been an obvious progress in technological ability, in knowledge, and in complex forms of artistic achievement. In morality, too, there has been progress from harsh tribal moralities of child sacrifice, slavery, and torture towards acceptance of human rights, democracy, and freedom. In religion, the cruel whims of good and evil spirits have been supplanted by a general acceptance that there is one underlying reality of wisdom, compassion, and bliss.

Yet there are qualifications to be made. Technological progress has made possible the destruction of the environment and of the planet itself. Warfare has increased in ferocity and scope, and whole regions of the world have been reduced to permanent poverty by a few wealthy nations, with millions of people starving while a few live in luxury. Religions still conflict with one another in hostility and mutual attempts at repression. The human race is closer to destroying itself now than at any time in the past. This is a strange sort of progress, which is constantly accompanied by the corruptions of community which flow from the misuse of human freedom.

Views of history, in their broadest sense, therefore tend to swing between an optimistic stress on progress and a pessimistic emphasis

---

[28] Mark 1: 15.

on the increasing destructive power which technological progress brings. I do not think that the Christian faith has special resources that can enable it to make secure predictions about the historical future. On the one hand, God is involved as a creative and co-operative power for good in every historical time. God commands that humans realize new and distinctive goods. God wills an increase in fellowship, in understanding, and in creative action. It should be quite clear that God intends that the good potentialities of creation should be realized by free communal and co-operative action.

On the other hand, God has given freedom to humans to live together in community, and to shape their own world to a large extent. The earliest Christians thought the world would end soon, after a catastrophic increase in violence and destruction, and that God would then institute a new and more perfect creation. Such an apocalyptic end of the world has been avoided, though many cultures and empires have ended in destruction, and given way to new forms of culture. It should again be quite clear that God will not let the world end in sheer destruction, without making possible a new beginning for all who will participate in it.

Taking these two elements together, the Christian is bound always to hope for and work for the realization of a just and creative society in the historical future. Yet Christian hope will ultimately be for a new creation, late or soon, in which all destructive possibilities have finally been rooted out. Christian hope is not utopian, in committing itself to the existence of a just society in the future of the earth. And it is not despairing, in thinking that all human effort is finally futile.

This is because, for Christian faith, the meaning of history is not found in the rise and fall of empires, or in progress towards a finally just world-order. It is found in lives of creativity, sensitivity, and friendship, or in lives of patient virtue lived out in situations of hardship and oppression. That meaning is found when one discerns within every part of history, not just at its end, a pattern oriented to intrinsic value through free co-operative activity. And that will only be fully discerned by coming to share in the divine perspective.

Even so, it seems obvious that for each individual there remain projects uncompleted and potentialities unrealized, which even the divine perspective cannot complete and make actual. For history to find any fulfilment of such incomplete actualizations there would have to be a time beyond history for each individual in which the unrealized possibilities of each individual history could be realized in a different way. This is a point which Tillich would perhaps regard as reflecting an improper translation of properly symbolic language into unduly literal 'history-copying' language. Yet it may well be felt that history is not fulfilled simply in an eternalized divine experience, in which creatures might share. If fulfilment is to be possible, there must be a continuation of individual experience beyond death. This must be envisaged as a real continuity with and a completion of the potentialities created in history, and it gives another sense in which history can only be properly fulfilled beyond history. The meaning of history lies not only in the completed and integrated divine experience, but also in the completion by individuals of projects impeded during their lives on earth. The beatific vision (the seeing of all things in the divine experience) and the resurrection of the body (the possibility of completing old and undertaking new creative projects, as part of realizing one's unique personhood) are both important elements of any concept of a fulfilment of historical existence.

Tillich is hampered at this point by his refusal to think unambiguously of there being a continuation of historical life beyond history, or to think of God as an objective reality, other than the universe, in which historical reality could be integrated into a distinct divine experience. It would be much clearer to say that history attains its full meaning in God, because God integrates all historical experiences into a pattern that transfigures each experience by its relation to the supreme final goodness of the whole (not, one must insist, the actual goodness of every part).

It is God's integrative and redeeming action that gives to each part of history its true meaning, by placing it in its eschatalogical context. God, according to Christian belief, enables creatures to share in that meaning by preparing them to share the divine experience, and also by enabling them where necessary to complete the frustrated meanings of their earthly lives, and then by making it possible for them to participate in the divine experience, from their own points of view.

The Christian faith is that God begins that enabling and healing action in history, and does so in some way and to some extent in every part of history. Some parts of the historical process will naturally be capable of channelling the healing acts of God more clearly or effectively than others. For Christians, the life of Jesus is a particular point in history at which the nature of God's universal action becomes recognizable, and in which it can therefore be consciously received and appropriated. For in Jesus God's love is seen as persuasive, suffering, co-operative, self-giving, unitive, and transformative. It is in that sense that 'Jesus as the Christ is the historical event in which history becomes aware of itself and its meaning'.[29] Here, one can recognize the nature of the divine action that will give full meaning to all history.

The role of the church is to witness to the meaning of history, to the fact that history is given its fullest meaning and brought to completion in God, and that all conscious creatures can share in the awareness of that meaning and completion. The church mediates that meaning in the paradigmatic form of Jesus the Christ, as that human life manifests the nature of God, is fulfilled in God, and becomes the mediator of the divine action of redemptive love.

One must also recognize, however, that the divine action has not yet reached its completion, and will never do so within historical time. What one sees in Jesus is not itself the full meaning of history, but the normative manifestation of the divine action that will give full meaning to history. That is why the church does not itself contain the meaning of history, but witnesses to the fact that such meaning will be realized. It is the action of the Spirit, placing within human hearts the active principle of divine love that the disciples saw to be fully manifest in the life of Jesus, that is the promise of meaning. The church is above all a community of hope for the whole world, for it makes recognizable and available the Christic form of the divine action that is the real basis for such hope.

THE GLOBAL PATTERN OF RELIGIONS: THE ABRAHAMIC STREAM

The church is not the only place where such hope is to be found, and it may sometimes almost—but never entirely—lose the form of hope that lies in the raising of all created things to share in the life of God. Tillich rightly insists that 'the history of salvation is not identical with the history of religion . . . or even with the history of the churches'.[30] God is active everywhere to bring history to its fulfilment. If one accepts a developmental account of human origins, it is quite natural that there should be a diversity of approaches to the spiritual, not all of which might be characterized as 'religious' in

---

[29] Tillich, *Systematic Theology*, iii. 393.   [30] Ibid. 387.

narrowly defined terms. Artistic experience can readily be seen in terms of attempts to represent or mediate the spiritual, and moral demands can be seen as encounters with spiritual powers. What religions do is to seek to relate human lives consciously and appropriately to the spiritual reality that underlies all history. They do this in many different ways. In fact religions seem to cover the whole range of possible relations to the divine, from a passive acceptance of sovereign divine power to an active self-achievement of a supreme spiritual state.

We tend to speak of religions when the spiritual powers are represented symbolically in myths or narratives, and when rituals develop which mediate those powers to human life, or which relate humans appropriately to the spiritual. There will be many diverse symbolic representations, and many rituals which differ according to culture, history, and temperament. The first stage of the religious history of humanity is one in which a huge diversity of tribal or local traditions of myths, symbols and rites exists, largely in ignorance of the existence of similar traditions elsewhere. An initial plurality of local traditions is natural to religion.

Yet there is a drive in the human mind towards constructing as coherent and adequate an account of the spiritual as possible. The riotous profusion of symbolic narratives, and the morally ambiguous character of much that they represent, needs to be simplified, integrated, and moralized. As social groups come into contact with their wider environment, they need to devise ways of reconciling the diversity of myths and rituals which characterize human pre-history. Sometimes, in the history of cultures, this proved to be virtually impossible. In ancient Greece, for example, the pantheon of gods could not be integrated satisfactorily into the philosophical systems of Plato or Aristotle. Religion remained at the level of pious tradition, while philosophy largely ignored the stories of the gods. The consequence was that Greek religion died, and philosophy largely lost its power for transforming human lives, and relating them to a greater spiritual reality. In ancient Egypt, no philosophical speculation developed at all, and the Egyptian gods disappeared in face of the rising philosophical theism of Jewish, Christian, and then Muslim Alexandria.

For a religious view to flourish, it needs to integrate an intellectual understanding of the world, a coherent moral view, and an effective set of symbols for mediating the power of the spiritual realm. In early tribal societies, such a need does not surface. But as great cultural empires grew, in South America, in Persia, Egypt, and Greece, in India and in China, earlier tribal traditions had to change to meet new circumstances. Most of them failed to do so. Three main strands of religious tradition more or less successfully generated different forms of adaptation, and gave rise to the second phase of religious history, that of the great imperial religions.

One strand begins with Judaism, which developed a form of rigorous ethical monotheism, under the guidance of a series of prophets. The development owed something to Egypt, Persia, and Greece, but it maintained a quite distinctive emphasis on one Creator God with a historical purpose for the Jewish people, and through them for the world. It remained to some extent a tribal tradition, for though it grew very sophisticated, it never threw off its basically ethnic roots. It never became an imperial faith, since the Hebrews never succeeded in founding an empire. But it spawned two great imperial faiths, Christianity and Islam, and it spread throughout the Mediterranean and Asian world as the first great diasporadic faith, a faith dispersed from its primal homeland throughout the world.

At times it has seemed as though Judaism might disappear, engulfed in some form of Enlightenment secular moralism, or eliminated by hostile political forces. But loyalty to the idea of a covenant established by God with the Jewish people has endured in the most adverse circumstances. It has given rise to the religious idea of vocation, of a calling by God to a specific role among the peoples of the world. In the modern world, the establishment of Israel as a secular state, strongly influenced internally by a group of rather small Orthodox communities, and loosely related to a world-wide diaspora of mostly liberal Jewish communities, has led to Judaism becoming a sometimes volatile but apparently indissoluble mixture of orthodox, liberal, and secular strands.

A total imposition of traditional religious law is rendered impossible by this mixture. Judaism has always accepted some form of religious pluralism, in its distinction between the sons of the covenant and the Gentiles. It now has to accept an internal pluralism of Orthodox (literalist or traditional), liberal (reform or radical), and secular (limiting religious law to family and community matters) forms of faith. Jewish Separatism remains a minority option for traditionalists, but it is clear that a perfectly just society cannot exist as an isolated community in an unjust world. Indeed, to choose such a path of isolation would itself be unjust, in view of the Creator's purpose for the world. So Judaism as a whole finds its religious vocation in seeking to be true to its distinctive covenant law, without insisting on just one interpretation of that law. More widely, its members seek to encourage global action for human justice and liberation, by commitment to local projects of humanitarian concern throughout the world. That at least is the ideal, and this view of religion as having a distinctive vocation within the wider world is the special insight of Judaism as the world moves into the third stage of its religious history, the stage of a global plurality of faiths.

Christianity sprang from Judaism as basically a universalized and internalized form of Jewish Messianic faith, which views the Messiah not as the liberator of Israel, but as the saviour of the world. It places the Messiah beyond history and yet as the culmination of history, thereby capturing the trans-historical and yet future elements which are distinctive of Christian eschatology. The church is a community that represents, or witnesses to, the supra-historical Christ who is believed to have once manifested in history, in Jesus, and who is also (no doubt in a very different form) the future fulfilment of history.

The imperial nature of the church as it developed in history has been sketched in previous chapters. It has made claims to an irreformable finality of truth, to an exclusive possession of saving grace, and to a privileged insight into absolute moral laws. But the true role of the church is to identify the character of the ultimate spiritual reality as kenotic, unitive, fulfilling divine love, for that is how it was seen in the life of Jesus, and to mediate that love to the whole world in a specific form, the form of the servant, healing, and reconciling Lord.

The church sees itself as the community of the Spirit of God, which is given form by the exemplary life of Jesus (a form which is not a set of definite rules, but the pattern of a life of kenotic love), which seeks to live by the power of divine love and make that love available to others, and which is oriented towards and seeks to encourage the future goal of a universal community in which compassion and fellowship will have unrestricted expression. In this form, the Christian church accepts for itself the vocational view of Judaism, but gives a distinctive Christic (or Messianic) form to its vision of the way in which God acts in human history. As such, it will, like Judaism, accept both an internal and an external plurality of religious interpretations, which will mutually influence one another in various ways, while seeking to remain loyal to its own distinctive vision of God in and through the person of Jesus the Christ.

Islam appears in history as a reaction against the fusion of a divine and finite created being which is the distinctive claim of Christianity. It reasserts the prophetic role of revealing a divine law for society, insists on the absolute unity of God, and denies that any finite thing can have real unity of being with God. So it adopts a position of intellectual opposition to Christianity, competing directly with it especially in Africa and Asia, and there are those who have seen the future as imperilled by a violent hostility between 'Christian' and 'Islamic' civilizations.[31]

But, like Christianity, Islam is in fact moving away from its imperial past under the Caliphs and the Mogul and Ottoman Empires. There are many ways of redrawing loyalty to Shari'a, and the rise of 'fundamentalist Islam' is in part a radical protest against traditional interpretations. There is a great variety of 'Islamic states', and it is becoming clear that one cannot both insist on having a totally Islamic state and on being a universal world faith. The price of universality in the modern world is pluralism, in the sense of the acceptance of the similar claims of others.

The frequently made contrast between 'Islam' and 'the West' can be misleading, except as an indicator of historical tensions between ex-colonialist powers and traditional ethnic cultures. Those tensions are, of course, very real, but there is reason to hope that continuing economic and technical progress will enable traditional cultures to maintain what is valuable in their own traditions within an integrated world economy that insists on an endeavour to promote universal human rights. The contrasting histories of Christianity and Islam in the twentieth century bring out the fact that the character of religion is closely intertwined with the social and historical factors that influence various human cultures. Religion is not a panacea for social ills. But in favourable social conditions, it can motivate a widening and deepening of vision. Even in unfavourable conditions, alongside all the ambiguities of its existence, it keeps alive some sense of the absolute demand of God for justice and mercy.

---

[31] This is the 'Huntington thesis', in Samuel Huntington, *The Clash of Civilisations and the Remaking of World Order* (New York: Simon & Schuster, 1996).

At present, the tensions between the richer and poorer nations of the world are so strong that even talk of 'human rights' can be seen as an imperialistic attempt to enforce Western values by some Muslims. But it is quite clear that the Qur'an calls for true human flourishing under the divine command of justice and peace. When it is also clear that human rights are precisely about the conditions under which humans may flourish, and when the vast historical diversity of Islam is fully accepted, it will be possible to proclaim the *umma* of Islam as a voluntary community of those who live under a particular revelation of divine law, a law which aims at human flourishing and at a true interior knowledge of God, and which allows for a diversity of interpretations of its basic precepts.

The Christian churches may then be seen as a diverse set of communities that have allegiance to a specific discernment of the nature of God as kenotic love in Jesus, and a hope for a unity of divine and human which is engendered by the Spirit of God. Muslims will not share that discernment, but will have their own discernment of the nature of God as just, compassionate, and merciful, as shown in the Qur'an, and a hope for resurrection to life with God by the mercy of God. What Christians may learn from Islam is a basic simplicity of faith in God, counteracting the intellectual contortions which have sometimes characterized Christian theology.

From a Christian viewpoint, obedience to moral, even divinely given, law will not suffice to bring union with God. It is the love of God, manifest in Jesus and made present in the Holy Spirit, that is needed for that. The difference between Christians and Muslims is not, however, a difference about which God to worship, and it is not a difference between those who obey and those who reject God. It is a difference about how God's mercy is effectively shown and received, and about how very imperfectly human minds understand God. There are real differences. But there is every reason for all to accept that in both traditions God commands universal justice and simplicity of life, and that in them God can be truly and inwardly known. The Muslim *umma* and the Christian church can both take their place in the global plurality of faiths as different visions of the same God, not disguising their differences of perception, yet not absolutizing them into rigid and unchangeable oppositions, to be defensively and confrontationally maintained.

THE GLOBAL PATTERN OF RELIGIONS:
THE INDIAN AND ASIAN STREAMS

Religious history developed differently in India, where a second main strand of religious tradition originated. Initial tribal traditions of sacrificial priesthood and rigidly enforced social laws led to a counter-culture of ascetic renunciation, which then managed to take over the system by imposing itself as the highest rung of the social and spiritual hierarchy. The key idea turned out to be that of an all-embracing spiritual reality from which the physical world of individuality and history emerged and to which the spiritually advanced could return, through a process of ascetic renunciation.

This has sometimes been seen as a rather negative tradition, which does not take the material world and its concerns seriously. But it is possible to see the return to the One as carrying with it the results of individualized existence, so that this world has a positive role to play in the evolution and self-expression of Brahman. This has happened in some twentieth-century restatements of the Vedantic tradition.[32] Until this century, Indian religion has not looked outside India to proselytize, remaining largely a culturally defined faith. But in the twentieth century it has in some of its forms set out to offer to the world a programme of meditation that offers inner peace, an experience of spiritual reality that does not appear to be bound up with non-recoverable historical facts and complex dogmas, and a religious faith that is not tied to traditional and inflexible moral views.

India, like Israel, is a secular state within which religious groups play an important role, and often claim cultural hegemony. There is an Indian diaspora, in which the loosening of religious belief from its cultural ties, and the experience of being a minority faith, can lead to a liberalization and revision of traditions. The Indian pluralism that consists in accepting differing authoritative interpretations of the Veda becomes a global pluralism that sees all religious views as revisable, incomplete, partly mistaken, and partial. So what is called Hinduism ranges from being a form of cultural allegiance within India to being a set of very diverse groups for cultivating meditation and various forms of Indian-inspired devotional practice throughout the world.

---

[32] So, for instance, the work of Aurobindo, considered in the second volume of this series, *Religion and Creation* (Oxford: Clarendon, 1996).

In so far as Indian views are able to accept the importance of individuality, history, and community, they can converge closely with Christian hopes for the realization of the kingdom of God. The comprehensiveness (within limits, admittedly) of Indian thought may again influence Christians to see the kingdom as a global, not an exclusively ecclesial, ideal, with the church being the proclaimer of the kingdom, rather than its embodiment. Its doctrine of nonduality may also remind Christians of the immanence of God, the fact that the Spirit of Christ is within everyone, waiting to be recognized and consciously received.

In China a third strand of religious tradition developed, in which neither prophets nor renouncers played a prominent role. Instead there were sages who claimed to discern principles of harmony and balance that made for a well-ordered society, and whose teaching was so much centred on the human world that both spirit-possession and world-renunciation seemed alien to a culture that sought above all to achieve an integrated life in harmony with its environment. There is no God who breaks into human life with imperious demands. There is no deathless realm that lies beyond this world of illusion, and gives true peace and freedom from sorrow. There is instead the possibility of a well-ordered life in society, within which human happiness can be found.

Confucianism and Taoism never, however, developed a very clear way of coping with the gap between the ideal of a harmonious society and the reality of power politics. For wholly secular thought, the ideal collapses if it is seen to be impossible. For utopian thought, both religious and secular, the reality becomes identified with the ideal, and a particular social system is divinized—and thereby ossified. In China, this happened both with the imperial system and with Marxism, in different ways.

The form of religion that eventually came to dominance in China and in Asia generally was Mahayana Buddhism, which developed a much more this-worldly interpretation than had been usual in the forest traditions of the Theravadin monks. Mahayana, in its Chinese forms, avoids both secularism and utopianism by distinguishing the world as samsara from the very same world as nirvana, and making the difference lie in the realization or non-realization of enlightenment. True perception will see the world as beyond attachment and suffering, whereas false perception will be bound to suffering and desire. Fully integrated life in community is lived out in the paradisal

Buddha-realms, but one can participate in it now either by meditative practice or by faith in a realized *boddhisattva*.

The idea of a God who acts in particular historical events is lacking in Buddhism. However, to the extent that Buddhist views of compassionate *boddhisattva*s develop, who bring humans to liberation by pure grace, there is a convergence with Christian views of a compassionate and liberating God. Indeed, many Buddhists would understand the Christian view to be too restrictive, making salvation depend on knowledge of one particular historical event (and that not too well attested by neutral observers). Part of the influence of Buddhism on Christianity has been to make Christians more aware of what universal compassion really implies, so that Jesus can be interpreted as a particular person who manifests universal compassion, and whose life is the pattern of the Holy Spirit, the ever-present compassionate agent of divine love. It also stands as a rebuke to authoritarian and over-confident dogmatism on highly speculative matters, which has sometimes led the church to pretend to authoritative knowledge of things virtually impossible for humans to know.

In the third Christian millennium there will continue to be many diverse religions, ranging from local cults to world-wide federations, from separatist traditionalism to syncretistic liberalism. Religion is not about to fade away. Yet in all this diversity, there are some dominant influences that will leave few traditions untouched, and that suggest that all traditions are about to move into a new phase of their existence.

One is the explosion of global communication and travel, which will confront each tradition with the fact of global pluralism. When each major faith exists partly in diaspora, there is a real incentive to support freedom of religion and conscience, and to co-operate in working for a wider community, refusing to demonize or caricature other traditions. There is also an incentive to work towards a better understanding of other traditions, which will affect each tradition's view of itself, as one distinctive strand in a global network of faiths.

Another major influence is increasing awareness of historical and scientific method, which will encourage critical attitudes to many traditional formulations of faith, and point up the symbolic and metaphorical nature of much religious language, thus decreasing tendencies to dogmatic certainty on abstruse conceptual issues, and to traditional oppositions which may be founded on archaic or out-dated interpretations.

A third influence is the positive legacy of the Enlightenment, which lies in a concern with equitable human fulfilment, and which evaluates religious practices largely in terms of their capacity to promote or frustrate such fulfilment. One may add to this the post-Enlightenment insight that religion also possesses its own distinctive evaluative criterion. That is its ability to bring about liberation from self and union with a reality or state of supreme intrinsic value. When a stress is placed on the practical and experiential elements of religion, it may be less likely to be captured by those forces of nationalism and triumphalism that have marked human history in the past.

The Christian church will exist as one community of critical, soterial, and global faith among others. It is not primarily a community of divine law, or of world-renouncing discipline, but a community that seeks to identify, participate in, and mediate to the world the power of the divine Spirit, the spirit of self-emptying, transforming, and reconciling love. It may not be God's plan that the church should become the one universal world-faith. But it is called to loyalty to its disclosive vision of the ultimate meaning of history, which originated with Jesus. Christians may justifiably believe that the whole world will be brought within the reach of unconditional divine love. That belief will, Christians believe, be confirmed with the realization of the trans-historical kingdom, when every tradition of faith will find its true meaning in God. Within history, the church's task is to witness to its vision, in the trust that God will call into its community those whom he wishes to foreshadow in themselves the destiny that will in so many diverse ways be offered to all, a destiny that Christians describe as a growth into the fullness of Christ, in whom the fullness of God is pleased to dwell.[33]

---

[33] Ephesians 4: 13; Colossians 1: 19.

14
Christian Theology in a Comparative Context

A COMPARATIVE THEOLOGY FROM A
PARTICULAR VIEWPOINT

Comparative theology is a co-operative enterprise. It is a way of doing theology in which scholars holding different world-views share together in the investigation of concepts of ultimate reality, the final human goal, and the way to achieve it. Naturally, each scholar will have a particular perspective. One might expect it to develop and deepen in the many conversations of comparative theology, but it will most probably remain the same in its fundamental elements, especially if the scholar is a member of a religious community.

The series of four books which this volume completes are intended to form a contribution to comparative theology. But the conversations upon which they are founded have taken place outside the text, and a proper comparative theology would need to include written responses and original contributions from members of many traditions. So one might best see these four books as a systematic Christian theology, undertaken in a comparative context.

My views undoubtedly reflect the fact that I am an ordained minister of the Church of England—though I became a member of that church only as an adult, and after much reflection, as careful as I could make it. The religious situation of our world requires an attempt, at least on the part of those committed to reflection, to interpret traditional beliefs in the light of our ever-growing knowledge of the material cosmos, and in awareness of the many differing traditions of belief that exist about the nature of human existence in the world. One needs to ask how far traditional formulations of belief in any tradition may need to be revised because of new scientific knowledge, and how much they may reflect an ignorance of other traditions of belief that may either be complementary to or be highly critical of them.

Because of the vast number of religious traditions in the world, one needs to be very selective in those one can consider with some degree of sensitivity and accuracy. I have chosen Hinduism, Buddhism, Judaism, and Islam as conversation partners with my own Christian perspective. This is partly because no one would deny their major importance in world history, and partly because there exist major written texts with translators and interpreters whom one can easily consult.

In the first volume, I tried to give a general overview of the main characteristics of each of these traditions, focusing on their attitude to the sort of authority that the basic canonical texts possess, which determines the main basis of various doctrinal positions.

In the second volume, I moved on to consider more specifically the written work of four major twentieth-century thinkers, focusing on the topic of the nature of God as Creator. Buddhism temporarily dropped out of this conversation, since it generally has no particular interest in the concept of a creator—though in some forms of Mahayana Buddhism a case could be made for at least a very similar concept of Pure Mind or the *Dharmakaya*. I did not, however, presume to make that case.

In the third volume, most of the comparative material on the topic of human destiny was derived from personal conversations with adherents of particular religious traditions, backed up with reference to largely classical textual material.

In this final volume, on the social impact of religion, I reverted to a more general analysis of the historical and social phenomena of religious communities, paying special attention to relevant writings of contemporary exponents of the chosen traditions. In the case of Christianity, I attempted to place the 'classical' writings of Aquinas, Calvin, Schleiermacher, and Tillich on the church within the historical development of Christianity.

The first result of the investigations in these volumes has been to provide an interpretation of Christian faith that remains recognizably mainstream, while being modified by its response to both critical and complementary insights from non-Christian traditions. The second result is, I hope, to provide a comparative investigation of the concepts of revelation, God, human nature and destiny, and of the nature of a religious community. It is precisely because that comparative study is undertaken from a Christian viewpoint (and all such study must be undertaken from some viewpoint, acknowledged or not) that it comes to constitute a positive Christian theology.

In each volume, the study of selected traditions has suggested a general characterization of the nature of religion, of the supreme good, of the final goal of humanity, and of the religious community respectively. Within that characterization, the distinctive features of a Christian viewpoint have then been outlined. Finally, criticisms from other religious viewpoints, and complementary perspectives that they offer, have been taken into account, in order to develop a Christian theology in a global context.

THE IDEA OF REVELATION

With regard to revelation and the general nature of religion, it is a feature of most religious views that they appeal to a person or persons with some form of privileged access to a reality or state beyond normal human cognitive capacities. One may speak of inspired states, in which words or concepts are placed in the minds of prophets or sages, giving information about realities inaccessible to normal cognitive process (most often about the future, or about God's purposes). One may speak of altered states of consciousness, in which visionary experiences or exalted mental states seem to give access to supranormal realms of reality and awareness. Or one may speak of objective historical events that seem to display the communicative activity of a spiritual being, promising or at least partly granting liberation from human ignorance and sin.

In primal religious traditions, shamans or religiously sensitive persons may speak the oracles of the gods or spirits in trance states. They may in dreams or visions ascend to the realm of the gods. They may display miraculous powers over physical forces, thereby foretelling the future or healing sickness and casting out demons. In considering examples of oracle, vision, and miracle from many such traditions, from the vantage-point of a post-scientific age, it seems clear that a large amount of imagination enters into such phenomena. The gods who 'possess' human agents, who appear to them and who act in extraordinary ways, are most naturally construed as symbolic figures, largely drawn from the tribal environment and history, for the main values and life-giving powers by which the tribe feels its life to be ordered.

It is possible to interpret such religious symbols, as Durkheim did, as solely imaginative projections of the values and aims of the society.[1] But it is also possible to see them as partly subjective ways of seeking to represent an objective spiritual reality which underlies the physical world. If that is so, then one can see religion as a set of developing attempts to apprehend spiritual reality, which will take on the forms of their particular historical and social contexts, but which are also felt to be responses, however incomplete and partial, to the presence or activity of such a reality.

The traditional Christian view was that the human race once had clear knowledge of the one true God, and fell from that state into ignorance because of sin. The diversity of religions is thus due to sin, and only one people, the Jews, retains knowledge of God, because God clearly reveals his presence to Moses and the prophets, and then becomes fully present in Jesus. A study of primal religious traditions suggests, by contrast, that religion begins in relative ignorance and diversity, as local groups seek to symbolize a very incompletely known spiritual reality in diverse ways. The diversity of religions is natural, and there is no one clear and indisputable primal revelation, from which all the rest are deviations. Rather, there are sets of developing traditions, many of which will die out, but some of which will survive. Some may survive for bad reasons (their conduciveness to racial superiority or ability to provide the illusion of deferred wish-fulfilment, for example). But others will survive because of their stimulus to and compatibility with growing factual knowledge and moral insight and an ability to meet basic psychological needs for personal and social integration.

Within such an evolutionary perspective, the major world faiths are relatively successful complexes of tradition that have established themselves in widespread habitats. They have developed from more local primal traditions, usually by a series of key reconfigurations of preceding tradition, and are spread across a wide spectrum of possible views of the relation between the supranatural realm and those who are taken to be in a privileged position to reveal its character to others.

Oracular or propositional views stress the conceptual element of revelation. It may be held that a god actively dictates concepts to a relatively passive prophet, or inspires by raising human minds to

---

[1] Émile Durkheim, *The Elementary Forms of the Religious Life*, trans. J. N. Swain (London: Allen & Unwin, 1967).

new insights by synergistic action. Or it may be held that wisdom and insight are attained by meditational or ascetic practice, which either puts one in touch with the ultimately Real, or gives access to an altered state of awareness in which normally hidden truths are revealed. The Abrahamic traditions stress one of the former two interpretations, and Calvin is perhaps the foremost exponent of a propositional view within Christianity. The Indian traditions stress one of the latter two interpretations, and have a generally less active view of the object of revelation.

Visionary or experiential views stress that revelation comes in the form of human experiences, which may not be primarily conceptual. They vary from views which think of God as appearing in visions in a personal form, or as a felt spiritual power within the heart, to views which think of the mind as attaining experiences of non-dual reality, or as achieving release from egoistic desires. In such cases, revelation consists primarily in evoking such experiences in others, usually by teaching techniques which may make one disposed to have them. The Abrahamic traditions stress the former two views, and Schleiermacher represents this emphasis within Christianity. The Indian traditions again generally take a less active view of the primary object of religious experience, and may not construe it in terms of a personal god.

Miracle or event views stress the occurrence of publicly observable events that manifest some form of spiritual presence or purpose. It may be said that God is known by mighty acts of power and liberation, or that God acts truly, though in ways which are only perceptible to people of faith. Or miraculous powers may be present in people who have a special relation to God, or who have attained exalted spiritual states, and who thereby demonstrate the reality and power of the spiritual realm. In this case, too, the Abrahamic traditions stress the aspect of objective divine action, with Rahner and Barth emphasizing encounter with an objective God who acts in history, while the Indian traditions are more apt to stress the realization of paranormal powers by spiritual discipline.

Religions are most fundamentally committed to the existence of a spiritual reality, in relation to which people can find liberation from egoism and from a sense of existential estrangement. The nature of that reality is variously described in a number of traditions, which originate with the paradigmatic teachings, acts, or experiences of individuals who are felt to have some form of privileged relationship with the spiritual realm. The Abrahamic traditions interpret the spiritual realm in terms of one personal and active God, who takes the initiative to draw human beings into a transforming cognitive relationship with the divine. Within those traditions, Christianity is founded on the claimed discernment of God's revelatory and redemptive action in Jesus, who is claimed to be the expected 'anointed one', the Christ, whose own person becomes the self-disclosure of God in human history.

Christians find in the gospel portraits of Jesus a revelation of the nature of God as forgiving, healing, reconciling, unitive love, and a revelation of the purpose of God as being to bring persons to their proper fulfilment by the renunciation of self and reception of the Spirit. The gospels record memories of the life, death, and resurrection of Jesus, as objective events which disclose God's nature. Those memories are interpreted by the imaginative use of materials, especially from the Old Testament, which bring out the significance of Jesus' life as a disclosure of God. Such interpretative accounts are said to be inspired, giving a propositional element to Christian ideas of revelation. They also arise out of communal reflection within the churches on their continuing experience of the Spirit and the occurrence of visions of the risen Lord, providing the experiential dimension of revelation.

Christian revelation thus has a distinctive content, within the general forms of revelation which are characteristic of religions in general. Building on the Hebrew belief in God's active revelation in historic events of liberation (the Exodus), and prophetic teachings of the judgement and mercy of God, Christians believe that Jesus realizes in his own person the final liberation of humanity from sin, and commissions his disciples to proclaim the universally redemptive mercy of God to all humanity.

From the Jewish tradition, it might be objected that Jesus is not the Messiah since he has not brought universal peace. The Christian response is to reinterpret the concept of Messiah so that he represents the historical expression of the cosmic liberation and rule of Christ, the eternal Word of God, who begins to effect and promises to complete the process of liberation in all who follow him. Muslims might insist that God and creatures must always remain distinct, but Christians believe that we are called to become the 'body' of God (that is, of Christ), the freely responsive vehicles of divine will and purpose, in the world, and to this end God can unite us to the divine nature, after the model of Jesus. Hindus might deplore the stress put on matters of mere history by Christians, but Christians would insist that history is the domain of real action, individuality and creativity, and is thus essential to any real claim to divine agency. Buddhists might point out that the cultivation of non-attachment and enlightenment is more important than any acceptance of 'correct' stories or doctrines. I hope that Christians would agree, but think that enlightenment is properly given by the Spirit, who is patterned on the life of Christ, which makes that life important as the matrix of the inner path to liberation.

Christianity can learn positively from Judaism what it is to be a vocational spiritual community in the world, from Islam that the rule of God is over the whole of life, from Hinduism that God is always present within the heart, and from Buddhism that there are invaluable spiritual disciplines leading to non-attachment. These are not, indeed, things that Christianity does not know. But one may need to look to those other traditions to remedy their neglect in much Christian practice.

Christians are thus committed to believing that God, the supreme spiritual reality, has shown what the divine nature and purpose is in a definitive way in Jesus. They can see religions as developing in a number of differing cultural contexts, with differing conceptual frameworks, interests, values, and histories. Beginning from primal myths and rituals for disclosing and mediating the many powers and values that control human life, religious traditions have developed differing focal concepts of one supreme good.

I considered four main concepts of the ultimate source and object of revelation in the world's religious traditions. One is that of God as a morally demanding and providential agent, calling one people to a special vocation (Judaism). Another is God as a wholly transcendent and sovereign power who reveals a moral law for all people (Islam). A third is the experience of Brahman as the one self-existent reality which emanates from itself the world of individual souls, which through non-attachment and realization of the 'self within' can obtain release from suffering and rebirth (various schools of Hinduism). The fourth is the realization of nirvana as a state of bliss and compassion, realizable by all who dissolve the illusion of a substantial self (Buddhism). What is common to these traditions is the postulation of a being or state of supreme wisdom, bliss, and compassion, which is in some sense the ultimate or truly real.

Specific differences between these concepts are nevertheless clear, and Christianity adds a further distinctive concept of the supreme good by thinking of God as a Creator who shares in the suffering of creation, in order that sentient creatures should come to share in the divine nature and mediate its actions in creation. It is the self-giving life of Jesus, in its unique historical context of Messianic expectation, which becomes the historical self-expression of the nature of God, and the matrix of a new specific form of divine redemptive activity through the church as the community of creative co-operators in the Spirit. Jesus is seen as embodying an original and indissoluble union of created nature and the divine Word. This 'incarnation' of the divine prefigures the assumption of the cosmos into the divine which will be the final realization of the divine creative purpose.

One might see all these faith traditions as exemplifying a common structure, which is that of liberation from egoism and alienation by a fulfilment which lies in the knowledge of the supreme being or state, disclosed by an authoritative revelation, issuing from a person or persons with privileged access to the object of revelation. The various elements of this faith structure are articulated in diverse ways in different traditions, which suggests that revelation is not given as absolutely certain and infallible, as though it should be intellectually compelling to all intelligent and informed agents. Religious faith involves personal commitment to a discernment of supreme value, positive relation to which becomes the supreme human goal of striving. But the articulation of a religious view involves imagination and a gradual, and always to some extent provisional, development in varying cultural contexts.

To a theist this suggests a view of revelation as a co-operative persuasion by God that spurs humans to continually greater understanding. Such persuasion may be apprehended and responded to by humans in rather different ways in different contexts, but it may be expected sooner or later to succeed in specifying a mode of relationship to the supreme good which truly reveals its nature and purpose.

In this situation it is plausible for a Christian to think that in and through Jesus God has shown what the divine nature and purpose is. But there is much scope for further developments in understanding a fully comprehensive description and many of the implications of that revelation. Close and sympathetic attention to those disclosures

which have occurred in other traditions may be needed to complement the Christian revelation, and provide a fully comprehensive
view of the divine in its relation to humanity. From a Christian viewpoint, nothing can be accepted which compromises the disclosure of
God's nature and purpose in Jesus, but history makes it clear that
there are a number of different interpretations of that disclosure
even within the Christian tradition. And if Christ is the archetype
and consummation of all human history, one might expect that further facets of the being of the cosmic Christ have been perceived in
other traditions. Thus one is encouraged or even obliged to look for
an interpretation of Christian faith that seems coherent with the
general testimony of the Bible, which is consistent with well-
established belief in science and morality, and which interacts positively with other religious claims as far as possible. Seeing the
Christian revelation in this way enables one to give a coherent
account of the diversity of religious traditions in the world, to show
how, from a Christian viewpoint, God is truly at work in them, and
to show in what sense the Christian faith may plausibly claim to constitute a normative revelation of the being of God.

The development of a Christian theology thus begins with a commitment to the belief that the supreme good, which is also the final
goal for human life, is truly disclosed in Jesus, even if it is not yet fully
or correctly understood by us. There is such a thing as divine revelation, which is the basis for Christian reflection. It is primarily found
in the apostolic witness to the life, death, and resurrection of Jesus.
But those paradigm events can only be understood by the use of
imagination and reflection, and may only adequately be understood
when they are placed within a context of global history, informed by
a growing scientific understanding of the nature of the cosmos, and
illuminated by other strands of religious insight and disclosure.

THE IDEA OF THE SUPREME GOOD

When one examines the characterization of the supreme good in various religious traditions, one finds a sometimes surprising mixture of
divergences and convergences that suggests a greater fluidity and
dynamism than is allowed for in many popular stereotypes of 'religions'. There is agreement between the main classical traditions of
Judaism, Christianity, Islam, and Hinduism that the supreme good
is a self-existent reality whose nature is that of intelligence, bliss, and

compassion. This reality is said to be incomprehensible in its essential nature, and to be characterized mostly negatively, as beyond space–time, as uniquely existing from itself alone, as the ground of all possibility, and the 'unlimited ocean of being'. Such an idea is clearly developed in the medieval thinkers Maimonides, Aquinas, Al Gazzali, and Sankara.[2] It is radically non-anthropomorphic, and encourages a view of prayer as the contemplation of eternity, rather than as a conversation between personal agents.

In volume two I pointed to the way in which twentieth-century writers—taking Abraham Heschel, Karl Barth, Mohammed Iqbal, and Aurobindo Ghose as examples from the four main theistic traditions—had developed a more dynamic, affective, creative, and relational view of God. It is possible to hold the classical and modern concepts together if one thinks of God as both transcending and including temporality and relationship in different aspects. So one may think of God as a self-existent plenitude of being, existing in immutable and blissful self-awareness. But that same God exists also in a different form, as realizing many creative potentialities in time, and as creating genuinely other beings who can relate to God in a genuine community of love.

Different theistic traditions have various ways of spelling out the form of relationship between God and creation. Christians have developed a Trinitarian notion, whereby God relates to the universe as its ultimate source and goal (the 'Father'), as the archetype of finite possibilities (the 'Word'), and as the co-operative creativity which shapes finite things in freely creative realizations of archetypal possibilities (the Spirit of Wisdom). As the divine being flows out into individuated creation, through the exemplary Word and in the power of the dynamic Spirit, so there is a return of the created manifold to the uncreated unity of the One. The Spirit unites and reconciles created things so that they may become freely responsive vehicles of divine action, united in conscious relationship with God, instruments of the self-expression of the Word or mind of God. Their acts and experiences will be integrated into the divine experience, and in that sense returned to their source as completions of one finite expression of the divine nature in its overflowing into relationship with created beings.

---

[2] I have tried to elucidate these agreements in *Concepts of God* (Oxford: Oneworld, 1998) (previously published as *Images of Eternity*).

From a Christian viewpoint, the Trinity is the depth of being, moving outwards in love to generate creatures and to respond to them in lovingkindness and judgement, through the archetypal pattern of divine wisdom that takes particular form in human history in Jesus, and in the power of the creative Spirit. Returning to itself, the Spirit gathers up and unites all creation in the completed form of the cosmic Christ, and returns it to the Father as the transfigured fulfilment and goal of the original creative purpose.

Such a notion is not wholly foreign to Judaism, being adumbrated in the writings of Philo of Alexandria. It is also reflected in Iqbal's characterization of God as the Infinite, the Cosmic Ego and the creative co-worker, and in Aurobindo's 'trinity' of *Sat-Cit-Ananda*, being, ideal truth-consciousness, and delight of becoming. This degree of agreement between the traditions is remarkable, and demonstrates that the hard oppositions between traditions which are sometimes drawn are neither necessary nor wholly accurate.

Of course there are Jews and Muslims who would reject such Trinitarian descriptions of God, and insist on a stricter stress on the divine unity and all-determining sovereignty. In the Abrahamic traditions, only Christianity affirms that the cosmos can be united to the divine, through the free creative response of creatures to the divine love. There are Hindus who would reject any personalizing concept of Brahman at all, and insist on the absolute non-duality of being. Most (though not all) Buddhists would deny the existence of any creator of this universe. Christians, by contrast, would insist that humans are created as autonomous agents in relation to God, that they have become alienated from God as free subjects of action, and that God unconditionally condemns moral evil, and is the basis of moral endeavour. It would be absurd to argue that all ideas of the supreme good somehow agree. Yet it is interesting that various ideas of the supreme good exist within as well as between traditions, and that the idea of a Trinitarian God is not as totally restricted to Christianity as some have thought. Christians have much to learn from other traditions about the demand of God for community and justice, about the unity of all things in God and about the importance of mindfulness and simplicity in the spiritual life.

Nevertheless, the distinctive Christian claim is that 'the Word became flesh', that the human person of Jesus was fully united with the divine Word, so as to be its true expression in time, and the realization of that unity of human and divine that is the destiny of all human beings. Further, the church exists as the body of Christ, called to continue on earth the expression of divine love and the salvation from egoism that was perfectly manifest in Jesus, and that is present in the church through the power of the Spirit. The Christian idea of the Trinity takes a distinctive form as it is shaped around the reality of God revealed in the person of Jesus.

The idea of a God of self-giving love, who enters into the alienated condition of creatures and unites them to the divine life, requires a modification of the classical idea of God as a self-sufficient, impassible, and immutable being. Divine omnipotence will lie more in an infinite potency for creative and responsive action than in a fully actualized and immutable determination of all things. Moreover, there may be inner necessities in the divine nature which make the partly conflictual and emergent nature of this cosmos necessary, if it is to produce free, emergent, personal beings, capable of community and relationship to the Creator. Some of the findings of modern cosmology suggest that the fundamental constants and principles of the natural order need to be just what they are if organic life is to exist. One may not say that God could have produced a better universe with beings like us in it. Perhaps the sorts of harms this universe produces are the price of personal lives like ours. On such a view, God will not be the purely actual and impassible being of much classical theology. Rather, God will unite in the divine Being both the ultimate necessities of existence and the values of free creativity, unifying the greatest possible power and value in one unitary, supreme reality.

What a Christian theist may say is that God has the greatest possible power compatible with the existence of communities of relatively autonomous emergent agents, the greatest possible knowledge compatible with the existence of an open future which allows real creative freedom, and the greatest possible will to realize states of intrinsic value compatible with the possibilities for destruction which are necessarily existent in the abyss of creative being, and which are unpreventably realizable by created beings capable of desire and egoistic attachment. God will share in every harmful and destructive experience the universe produces, and will be able to turn it creatively to good, for every suffering individual, if only beyond the confines of this physical space–time. God will act persuasively to bring the created universe into a community of love, though such a community may only fully exist in a new order of creation. The sorts of values that can only exist in this universe are indeed so great that this creation can unequivocally be affirmed as good. The evils that exist, which have been made very much worse by the free actions of creatures, are not preventable even by God, since they are necessarily involved in the creation of a world of autonomous, emergent agents in community. The creation of some such world may itself be a necessary expression of the self-diffusive, other-creating and unitively loving nature of God. In such a creation, evil and suffering are inevitable, and may be vastly increased by the free acts of creatures, but they are redeemable by God. Beyond the limits of this space–time, which alone can generate human lives, God can bring created subjects to final fulfilment in a completed consummation of being. This, in my view, constitutes a solution to the problem of how a good and maximally powerful God can consistently create a universe containing much innocent and grievous suffering.

For Christians, the revelatory historical events of crucifixion and resurrection express the fact that God is supremely affected by the world, but ensures that the world will find fulfilment in supreme beatitude. The purpose of creation is thereby disclosed as being the production of emergent creative agents, who can form communities that can be vehicles of the divine love, making this cosmos a necessary preparation for emergent physical organisms that can, after their apotheosis, enter into that fuller life that will be lived wholly and consciously in the presence of God. The revelation of that fuller life in the glorified body of Jesus is the gospel, the good news, which Christians are called to proclaim.

THE IDEA OF FINAL LIBERATION

All the religious traditions I considered in the third volume share the vision of human life as estranged and impaired by ignorance or egoistic desire, and see the way of religion as one of liberation from such estrangement into a state of release and transfiguring union with the supreme good. These traditions have all at some time been influenced by a strict retributivist notion of justice, according to which each person reaps an exact punishment proportioned to the gravity and nature of their crime. This can happen through an impersonal law of karma or through a judicial assessment on a Day of Judgement. Some versions of Christianity come out particularly badly on this sort of account. According to them, everyone is condemned to everlasting punishment because of the allegedly infinite insult to God of their remote ancestor, except for a few, chosen by simple divine fiat, for whom Jesus takes the punishment vicariously.

Each tradition, however, also contains a rather different soterial notion of justice, according to which the primary purpose of punishment is the reformation of offenders. It is thought right that they should truly feel the harm they have caused (that is the retributive element), and that they should attempt to compensate for it in some way. But the vital element is that they should be delivered from the power of lust, hatred, and greed, and gradually brought to that true health that lies in the capacity to give and receive love. For Indian traditions, this can happen either through many lives of striving or through the help of a saviour figure such as Krishna or a *boddhi-sattva*. For Semitic traditions, such purgation and deliverance happens after death in the realms of Sheol or *barzakh*.

Within Christianity, the soterial notion would suggest that Hell is a possible state of the ultimate self-destruction of souls which make themselves incapable of love. All humans are born into a world in which generations of past human sin, socially reinforced, make loving union with God unrealizable, and in which the presence of God is obscured by hatred and greed. A morally sensitive doctrine of original sin would see this estranged state as originating in a failure of humans, in prehistorical times, to respond to the moral challenges that should have shaped their primal dispositions towards a developing love and communal co-operativeness. This gives rise not so much to 'original guilt', but to an inability naturally to know and love God. One might say that the natural consequence of such an inability is the ultimate mutual destructiveness of human selves. When Jews and Muslims object to the doctrine of original sin, it is (rightly) to the idea that a person can be born guilty before having done anything. Belief in a common human estrangement from God, and therefore from the intended form of properly human life, is not so far from the Jewish and Muslim belief that Paradise is achieved only through the mercy of God, though the Christian view does stress rather more the desolation of the human condition without the grace of God.

This human world is never, however, without grace. God empowers and heals all who respond to the divine initiative in penitence and co-operation with the divine Spirit. The death of Jesus, on this view, is not a penalty which has to be paid by someone, which frees an arbitrary number of people from paying it. The cross is the historical paradigm of the divine initiative of unconditional love. The life and death of Jesus is the designated historical expression of the universal salvific love of God, and it is itself a new creative divine act in history, from which springs the church, the community of the Spirit of divine love.

This is the atonement. Jesus gives his life as a perfect prayer, a true sacrifice, for the healing of the world by the coming of the divine Spirit. In so doing, his sacrifice becomes the normative expression of the divine suffering, by which the eternal Word gives up eternal bliss to share in the suffering of creatures, a suffering that is largely caused by their sin, and that is endured in order that creatures might be drawn back to the divine life. 'He was wounded for our transgressions . . . and with his stripes we are healed.'[3]

The atonement is not just the death of Jesus. It is the raising of his life to be an enduring channel of the Spirit, whose action is patterned on his life, and who mediates divine power to unite humans progressively to God. And it is the final destruction of evil that is a mark of the 'new creation', when death and suffering are finally set aside, in a new form of space and time, which will be fully sacramental of the divine life, when everything in heaven and earth will be united in Christ.[4] The Christian gospel is not that a few will be saved from everlasting torture. It is that God freely offers forgiveness, restoration to personal fellowship, to all. The life, death, and resurrection of Jesus is, for Christians, precisely the performative utterance of the offer of that unrestricted salvific love.

Such a view of a universal cosmic hope has been more characteristic of Mahayana Buddhism than of historical Christianity, though it has always been present as an important strand in the New Testament. It avoids the Jewish/Muslim objection that one cannot be saved by some apparently arbitrary act of punishing an innocent person, but must diligently pursue one's own salvation. For it is clear that only the love of God can unite one to God, so that the initiative in salvation must come from God. And it comes by the divine patience which endures the suffering caused by sin, in order that salvation may be realized.

If this is true, it seems undeniable that there must be an afterlife,

---

[3] Isaiah 53: 5.   [4] Ephesians 1: 10.

since most people simply do not have the opportunity to realize salvation during earthly life. For Indian traditions, the afterlife is construed in terms of repeated incarnations, so that it is always in principle possible to achieve liberation sometime—though it usually takes aeons to do so. The Semitic traditions regard this earthly life as of more decisive importance, sometimes even limiting the possibility of repentance to this life. That seems unduly restrictive of the love of God. While this life has a definitive role in constituting the experiences and dispositions that will form a continuing individual person, the universal love shown in Christ compels one to posit an afterlife in which development and penitence remains an open possibility for all.

The afterlife is biblically characterized in terms of Sheol and Paradise, in which one can come to realization of the harms one has caused ('purgation'), and develop a fuller understanding of the breadth and depth of God's love shown in Christ. One might conceive of the afterlife as an 'image or dream world', in which souls are prepared for a final resurrection world, in which individual memories and dispositions will be fully restored, in which every past will be redeemed by being incorporated in the context of a community of fulfilled love, and in which the whole of history will find its completion and the disclosure of its meaning within the infinite life of God.

Christianity takes from the Jewish tradition a concern that there is an enduring hope for this world. But it also reflects a more typically Indian perspective that such hope will be fully realized only beyond this world. And it agrees with the Muslim insistence that the resurrection world will be the transfigured fulfilment of all the good things that this world has brought to be and made possible.

This suggests an account of the human person as an embodied, social, continuing subject of developing awareness and moral purpose, which is emergent from the material order (not inserted into the material from elsewhere), but which is capable of embodiment in different forms of space–time, while retaining the memories, complex consciousness, and formed dispositions that have characterized its earthly history. Such an account can contrast sharply with Indian ideas of the self (whether one or many) as essentially unembodied, though some Indian traditions do postulate different forms of 'heavenly' embodiment for human persons in the liberated state. It also contrasts with some literalist Christian views that human physical bodies will be reconstituted on the earth in future—views which do not take seriously enough what is implied in a new creation without death or conflict, in which all material things will be unimpeded sacraments of spiritual reality. Such a form of existence must be radically different from anything that can exist in this space–time, though it is not out of the question that, as Teilhard de Chardin imagined, this space–time might eventually be transformed from within to a closer unity with the divine. Christians may hope for such a progress towards what Teilhard calls 'point Omega', but they will believe that, even if this universe is wholly destroyed, the Creator will enable them to exist and act in a new creation.

The Christian faith thus makes available a coherent account of the human person, its estrangement from God, and its empowerment by participation in the divine Spirit to find fulfilment in a community of love. One can see how the metaphorical imagery of the Bible depicts realms of personal being beyond this space–time, which cannot be literally imagined by us. Faith in the love of God leads Christians to believe that in such realms each personal destiny can be worked out in relation to God, and that the process will culminate in a renewed creation, a resurrection world that will be an unimpeded expression of that love which binds Creator and creature together, and which was foreshadowed in the divine–human unity of the person of Jesus Christ.

THE IDEA OF RELIGIOUS COMMUNITY

The human person essentially exists in community, and it is therefore natural that human existence in relation to God should be lived in community. In this fourth volume I have considered the nature of religions as forms of social existence which aim to relate human lives adequately to their ultimate source and goal. I distinguished four 'ideal types' of religious life—those who seek to renounce the world, so as to attain union with a higher form of reality; those who seek to embody the laws of God within human society; those who seek a form of spiritual community that attempts to influence, but resists identity with, the general political and social organization of society; and those who take the view that religion is an essentially personal and individual matter, which requires no particular social or institutional forms.

In so far as persons are essentially beings in community, and in so far as religion has a view of what it is to live fully as a person, it seems that the religious life should be a communal form of life. In so far as God creates the world for the sake of its goodness, the world should not be wholly renounced. But in so far as humans corrupt the world by hatred, lust, and greed, the religious community should not be simply identified with a particular form of human society, whether a religious or a secular one. This suggests a pluralistic ideal of a number of world-affirming, non-exclusive religious institutions, each accepting its role as part of a wider global community of faith.

In considering some major faith communities, I suggested that Judaism enshrines the idea of a vocational community, one which functions as a focal image, but not an exclusive controller, of God's lovingkindness. Islam expresses the ideal of a global fellowship of obedience to the divine will. Buddhism is a continuing reminder of the virtues of self-giving, compassion, and simplicity of life. Hinduism shows the possibility of a plurality of paths to the divine. So all these traditions contribute positive insights into the nature of religious communities in the modern world.

The distinctive claim of the Christian community is that it is the 'body of Christ', the means by which the eternal Christ who was in Jesus is expressed and acts in the world, through human persons. This does not mean that the church can rule the world with the power and authority of Christ, though such an idea of an imperial church has tended to characterize some of Christian history. It means that it is to follow Jesus' example of serving others in humility and compassion. It has the vocation of healing, reconciling, and forgiving, as Jesus did. So it is called to follow the Personalist principle of aiming at universal human flourishing in relation to God's creative purposes, and so being a community which serves the needs of the world in love.

It is called, not to the exclusive control of the means of salvation, which it can give or withhold at will, but to disclose in the life, passion, and resurrection of Jesus the paradigmatic clue to the compassionate love and liberating activity of God throughout the whole human world. So it is called to follow the Sacramental principle of making the whole material world a vehicle of Spirit. As such, it will not restrict God's liberating love to its own community, but will aim to witness to that love and clarify its nature and purposes in its universal operation throughout the world. God's 'election' to membership of the church will be a calling to proclaim salvation to the whole world, not to keep it for oneself alone.

It is called to follow its Lord in dying to self and living for others. It is not given inerrant insight into difficult and obscure moral and metaphysical truths, as though its chief function were the issuing of correct propositional beliefs. It is not given an unchanging set of truths to defend in the face of new knowledge, but it is given a responsibility to come to new creative understandings of God's revelation in Christ in new cultural and historical contexts. It should be a community that encourages the creative exploration of new, always to some extent provisional, understandings of God's saving activity in the world. In pursuing such a task, it is called to follow the Experiential principle of relying wholly upon and mediating the personal and transforming power of the Spirit, as it was expressed in and as it is defined by the life of Jesus. Its task is to communicate the active personal presence of the divine Spirit, as it builds up a community of human fellowship and fulfilment. The true role of the church is to lead sentient beings to participate consciously in the dynamic and creatively expressive life of God.

It is called to defend human dignity and personhood, which includes respect for freedom of conscience and belief, not least because it follows a Lord who was put to death largely because of religious non-conformity. The church is made up of imperfect and fallible people, and it is liable to make errors of judgement and even of fact on abstruse and complex issues. Its structure should thus be such as to check its natural tendencies to harmful or unwise behaviour, and encourage compassion, humility, and benevolence both institutionally and individually. It has a responsibility to sponsor rational discussion and to give expert and theologically informed advice. But it is also, and equally importantly, called to follow the Critical principle of promoting free critical enquiry and the primacy of conscience, as it seeks to lead, but never to compel, men and women into fuller personal understanding of the spiritual reality that sustains their lives and promises them fulfilment.

These are noble and difficult ideals, but the history of the church, like the history of all religious communities, is a reminder of the ambiguity of religion as a human phenomenon, and its enmeshment in the socio-cultural struggles of human societies. Religions can become tools of tribalism and nationalism, of violence and intolerance. They often foster unthinking traditionalism and authoritarianism, or an astonishing indifference to considerations of ordinary human welfare. Against such tendencies, the protest of secularism, at its best, insists on freedom of conscience, the right of dissent, and the need to contribute positively to human flourishing. Yet secularism, too, is ambiguous, and has sometimes led, paradoxically, to the collapse of any moral sensibility, and to the advocacy of totalitarian views of the supremacy of the state.

In the light of these facts, and of the fallibility, partiality, and diversity of human cultures, minds, and temperaments, there is a strong argument for accepting and promoting a positively tolerant pluralism of faiths in the framework of a global secular society. In such a society, a common basis for morality can be founded on insight into basic human desires and the conditions of their common realization. But for many, and perhaps for most people, the deepest motivation and justification for moral commitment will be found in religious perceptions of an objective basis for moral obligation and for a cosmic moral order, which provide an insight, so Christians believe, into the true nature of human existence in its relation to a supreme spiritual reality.

The Christian church witnesses to its own distinctive insight into the divine nature and purpose, which it takes to be revealed in the divine action to liberate human lives from bondage to hatred, greed, and ignorance, and unite them to the divine, which was focally manifested in the life of Jesus. Though Christians have sometimes expressed the hope that the church would one day embrace all humanity in a common fellowship, that seems an unrealistic possibility. The church has so many specific controversial beliefs, and humans are so diverse and argumentative, that the inclusion of all humans within one church would be possible only by the effective suppression of dissent—at least, until the truth becomes much clearer than it now is. Thus the church must accept its role as being one religious community among others. It must accept plurality, though it will not cease to claim for itself a discernment of truths which are important for the salvation of humanity.

Not only should the church accept an external plurality of faiths as legitimate. The logic of these arguments points to an internal plurality of understandings, to a legitimate diversity of interpretations and practices within the universal church that is the body of Christ. This means that the church should aim rather at a union of fellowship and common commitment to the God revealed in Jesus, than at an institutional uniformity, which can be assured only by a hierarchical and authoritarian structure. In the modern world, a more egalitarian, participatory, and pluralistic world-wide church is not an impossible ideal, and it is arguable that only such a church would be truly catholic.

The diversity and creative development of Christian self-understandings can be seen in what Hans Kung has called the various paradigms of faith that have marked Christian history.[5] One might reconstruct from the New Testament the mission of Jesus to prepare Israel for a renewal of its priestly vocation in the world. In the New Testament itself one finds clear traces of a form of millennial expectation, as the visions of the risen Lord and the spiritual experiences of Pentecost gave rise to a belief in an imminent end of the age, and the return of Jesus in glory to bring in the kingdom of God. But one also finds a reinterpretation of the role of Messiah that renounces Torah, opens the community of the new covenant to the Gentiles, and conceives of a world-wide mission to proclaim the liberation of human lives from sin and their raising to participation in the life of God, through the self-giving redemptive act of God in Jesus. Also present in the New Testament, and developed beyond it in terms of Hellenistic philosophy, is the idea of Jesus, not as a prophet of the kingdom, or as a man in and through whom God acts for salvation, but as the divine Logos who assumes a human nature, and is the real agent of Jesus' acts. The God-man raises the whole fallen cosmos to participation in the divine being, through his assumption of the finite into Godhead.

Thus already in the earliest records of Christian faith there are at least four diverse understandings of what God was doing in the life, passion, resurrection, and ascension of Jesus, the content of the apostolic witness upon which all Christian reflection is based. Two of these became extinct, but the other two remain typical of Nestorian and Orthodox churches. Further paradigms developed through time. By the fourteenth century, a Latin paradigm dominated Western Europe, based upon a juridical model which saw the sacrifice of Jesus as a vicarious punishment for sin, and the church as an institution which had power to give or withhold merit from the 'treasury of grace', and which, through the administration of the sacraments, had the exclusive power of rescuing souls from eternal damnation.

The sixteenth-century Protestant Reformation rejected the power

---

[5] Hans Kung, *Christianity: the Religious Situation of our Time*, trans. John Bowden (London: SCM, 1995).

of the church as an institution, as an interpreter of Scripture, and as a necessary intermediary between God and humans, and interpreted faith as an inward acceptance of the person of the risen Jesus, held in common by members of the 'invisible catholic church'. It thereby laid the foundation for the ideals of liberty of conscience and dissent, and a more participatory and egalitarian ecclesial and political society. It insisted upon the importance of personal faith, communal participation, and open access to the Scriptures. At the same time, and in continuity with the medieval tradition, it stressed the necessity for salvation of submission to revealed truth, and membership of the true, if invisible, church of Christ. It also continued to accept a generally juridical view of sin and salvation, according to which salvation is only gained by the substitutionary sacrifice of Jesus on the cross, for those who explicitly acknowledge that sacrifice.

In the nineteenth century, forms of post-Enlightenment Christianity arose, which accepted critical views of both Scripture and tradition, and stressed the role of Jesus as a teacher of the Fatherhood of God and of the need for moral fellowship among all persons. There was growing acceptance of the view that the church is not the only place wherein to find salvation, but rather the proclaimer of the universal possibility of salvation, and a witness to the unconditional love of God. Though it was generally held that Christianity is the highest form of faith, destined to supersede all others, it was also clear that, since the church primarily exists to evoke distinctive experiences of God, the absolute uniqueness of Jesus among world religious teachers became increasingly difficult to defend in its traditional form.

So in the twentieth century the church is generally seen as one religious community among others, though a community which claims a distinctive vision of and calling from God. Some would speak, as Hans Kung does, of a new ecumenical or global paradigm,[6] for which the old divisions of Christendom are largely relegated to history, and there is an attempt to rethink Christian faith in the light of new scientific discoveries, and a greater acceptance of human diversity, of the need for global unity, and of the provisionality of all propositional knowledge. Within such a paradigm, the church would be more self-critical, recognizing the historical conditionality

---

[6] Hans Kung, *Global Responsibility*, trans. John Bowden (London: SCM, 1991), 120–30.

of its formulations and the primarily symbolic nature of many of its basic images. It would be more openly plural, accepting a diversity of religious insights, and seeking positive interaction between them. It would be open to continuous reinterpretation, in the light of new knowledge and understanding. And it would be committed to social structures making for liberation and fulfilment for all humans, and ideally for all sentient beings.

Such a church would no longer harbour the ambition of taking over the world, religious or secular. It would consist of those who have been grasped by a vision of the ultimate goodness of a suffering and universally loving God, of the ultimate hope for the whole world of sharing in the life of God, of liberation from an estranged world into a renewed community of persons, and of being empowered by the Spirit of God to serve the world in other-regarding love. This vision is evoked by and patterned on the biblical witness to the life, death, and resurrection of Jesus, and the continuing experience of the risen Lord in the community of the church.

It is a vision that seems to be shared by relatively small groups of odd, imperfect, and quarrelsome people. Whether and to what extent it will in future be shared more widely, and how their commitment to it will further the wider divine purpose for this planet, is in the hands of God. But those who are Christians will feel themselves compellingly called to be such, and will accept that their primary vocation is to witness to the universal salvific love of God in a world of many disputes and many destructive hatreds. They will try to mediate that love without restriction, however feebly, and by their very imperfections they will testify to the patient and forgiving lovingkindness of the God they have discerned in Jesus the Christ. Above all, they will know that the church is only truly such when it expresses in its own life as an institution that which each individual is called to express in hers or his: 'Whoever would save his life will lose it, and whoever loses his life for my sake will find it.'[7]

---

[7] Matthew 16: 25.

INDEX OF AUTHORS CITED

INDEX OF SUBJECTS